Love and Organiz

MW01590848

Organizations are not human, but they are made up of people. Examining the organization, its functioning, growing and developing, and moving together as one unit, the well-being and success of that organization depend on the well-being of people that make it up.

Love, in its various forms, is the energy that motivates and fuels creativity, care, innovation, progress, and well-being. Traditionally, organizational structures have been set up to support compliance and command and control, which often discourages love and creates policies against love at the workplace. The result has been reduced growth, productivity, and retention of businesses as well as reduced well-being for employees. This reduced connectivity between individuals has also, at a higher level, adversely affected society. Without love, people are working and performing with reduced energy, and at reduced capacity. While prior research has been focused on love at the workplace from the viewpoint of psychologists, this book explores the impact of love within organizational contexts from various viewpoints, including management, psychology, and philosophy. It explores love in the organizational context by looking at how it affects meaning, purpose, well-being, motivation, faith, care, and spiritual development, and how the identity and well-being of each person in the organization positively affect retention and the growth and success of that organization.

This book will be of interest to researchers, academics, and advanced students in the fields of organizational studies, leadership, and management.

Michael Pirson holds the Felix E. Larkin Chaired Professorship in Humanistic Management at Fordham University, and is a full Professor with a focus on Global Sustainability and Social Entrepreneurship. He is a research associate at Harvard University's Human Flourishing Program (HFP). He co-founded the Humanistic Management Network and is founder and president of the International Humanistic Management Association. He is the Editor in Chief of the Humanistic Management Journal. Pirson is a full member of the Club of Rome, leads the Humanistic Management working group at the UNPRME and advises a number of social enterprises. He has won numerous awards for his work including from the Academy of Management and the Association of Jesuit Universities.

Humanistic Management

Series Editors: Michael Pirson, Erica Steckler, David Wasieleski, Benito Teehankee, Ricardo Aguado and Ernestina Giudici

Humanistic Management draws together the concepts of social business, sustainability, social entrepreneurship, business ethics, conscious capitalism, and cooperative capitalism to present a new humanistically based research paradigm. This new paradigm challenges the prevailing neoliberal "economistic" approach that dominates twentieth-century management theory and practice, and instead emphasizes the need to protect human dignity and well-being as well as economic drivers.

Love and Organization
Lessons of Love for Human Dignity, Leadership and Motivation

Edited by
Michael Pirson

Routledge
Taylor & Francis Group

NEW YORK AND LONDON

First published 2022
by Routledge
605 Third Avenue, New York, NY 10158

and by Routledge
4 Park Square, Milton Park, Abingdon, Oxon, OX14 4RN

Routledge is an imprint of the Taylor & Francis Group, an informa business

© 2022 selection and editorial matter, Michael Pirson; individual chapters, the contributors

The right of Michael Pirson to be identified as the author of the editorial material, and of the authors for their individual chapters, has been asserted in accordance with sections 77 and 78 of the Copyright, Designs and Patents Act 1988.

All rights reserved. No part of this book may be reprinted or reproduced or utilised in any form or by any electronic, mechanical, or other means, now known or hereafter invented, including photocopying and recording, or in any information storage or retrieval system, without permission in writing from the publishers.

Trademark notice: Product or corporate names may be trademarks or registered trademarks, and are used only for identification and explanation without intent to infringe.

Library of Congress Cataloging-in-Publication Data
Names: Pirson, Michael, editor.
Title: Love and organization: lessons of love for human dignity,
leadership and motivation / edited by Michael Pirson.
Description: New York, NY: Routledge, 2022. |
Includes bibliographical references and index.
Identifiers: LCCN 2021061868 (print) | LCCN 2021061869 (ebook) |
ISBN 9781032183190 (hardback) | ISBN 9781032183206 (paperback) |
ISBN 9781003254034 (ebook)
Subjects: LCSH: Organizational sociology. | Quality of work life.
Classification: LCC HM786 .L68 2022 (print) | LCC HM786 (ebook) |
DDC 302.3/5–dc23/eng/20220104
LC record available at https://lccn.loc.gov/2021061868
LC ebook record available at https://lccn.loc.gov/2021061869

ISBN: 978-1-032-18319-0 (hbk)
ISBN: 978-1-032-18320-6 (pbk)
ISBN: 978-1-003-25403-4 (ebk)

DOI: 10.4324/9781003254034

Typeset in Sabon
by Newgen Publishing UK

Contents

Contributors

Editor

Michael Pirson holds the Felix E. Larkin Chaired Professorship in Humanistic Management at Fordham University, and is a full Professor with a focus on Global Sustainability and Social Entrepreneurship. He is a research associate at Harvard University's Human Flourishing Program (HFP). He co-founded the Humanistic Management Network and is founder and president of the International Humanistic Management Association. He is the Editor in Chief of the *Humanistic Management Journal*. Pirson is a full member of the Club of Rome, leads the Humanistic Management working group at the UNPRME and advises a number of social enterprises. He has won numerous awards for his work including from the Academy of Management and the Association of Jesuit Universities.

Authors

William A. Andrews, PhD, CFM, CMAA, is an Associate Professor of Management at Stetson University. His primary teaching and research interests are organizational behavior, strategic management, and new venture financing. He is on the editorial board of the Case Research Journal, holds a PhD in Strategic Management from University of Georgia, an MIM in International Management from Thunderbird School of Global Management, and a BBA in International Business from University of Georgia. Dr. Andrews has held professional certifications with the Institute of Management Accountants (CFM) and Alliance of Mergers and Acquisitions Advisors (CMAA).

Elena P. Antonacopoulou PhD is Professor of Organisation Behaviour and Strategy at Ivey Business School, Canada and held full-time appointments at the Universities of Liverpool, Manchester and Warwick, UK. Her principal research expertise is in The Future of Work, Organisational Learning and Strategic Resilience and Renewal, with a focus on the Leadership implications. She is published widely in international refereed journals and edited books (over 100 publications) as well as policy reports. Her practice-relevant scholarship has earned her many research grants, awards and accolades recognising the impact of the ideas developed. She has been elected and served in multiple leadership roles in the top professional bodies in the management field and has received several awards for her outstanding leadership and service contributions and teaching excellence. ORCIT: 0000-0002-0872-7883 https://www.linkedin.com/in/elena-p-antonacopoulou-a179013/.

Yannick Bammens is an Associate Professor of Management at Maastricht University School of Business and Economics. Yannick is program leader of the MSc program Entrepreneurship & Business Development, as well as a co-founder and leader of the cross-departmental research group Creativity, Innovation & Entrepreneurship. His research spans the fields of entrepreneurship, strategy and governance, and has been published in journals such as Journal of Management, Journal of Management Studies, and Harvard Business Review. Yannick holds a master's degree in Business Engineering from KU Leuven (2004) and a PhD degree in Business Economics from Hasselt University (2008). He has been affiliated with Maastricht University since 2008, first as an Assistant Professor (2008–2015) and subsequently as an Associate Professor (2016–present).

Francesco Barbera is an Associate Professor of Entrepreneurship and Strategy at the Ted Rogers School of Management at Ryerson University. His teaching and research interests encompass a wide range of topics related to family business, entrepreneurship, small business management, and family business education. In 2014, he received his PhD from Bond University while working at the Australian Centre for Family Business. Francesco is an international, award-winning author and educator and regularly presents at renowned conferences and workshops. His research has been published in journals such as the *Journal of Business Ethics, Family Business Review, Long Range Planning, Small Business Economics*, and the *Academy of Management Learning and Education* journal. A former family entrepreneur himself, Francesco's expertise in the family business includes designing and delivering various family business curricula in Australia, Canada, and the USA, directing Family Business centers at both the University of Adelaide and Stetson University.

Clive Boddy is currently an Associate Professor in Management at Anglia Ruskin University in the UK and an Adjunct Research Fellow in Leadership at Curtin University in Australia. He was previously Professor of Management at the University of Tasmania, Professor of Leadership and Professor of Marketing in London. He also held Visiting Professorships at Lincoln, Curtin and Middlesex Universities. Clive's research interests include qualitative research techniques, toxic leadership and particularly in researching the effects of corporate psychopaths on employees, the organization and society. Clive's publications on corporate psychopaths include two books, most recently: A Climate of Fear: Stone Cold Psychopaths at Work. Clive's TEDx talk: "Bullying and Corporate Psychopaths at Work" can be seen on youtube.

Louise Boulter is a Senior Lecturer in the Department of Management, Leadership and Organisations, Middlesex University Business School, London. Louise is Programme Leader for the largest undergraduate programme across the University. Her research is focussed on causes of outlier organisational performance good and bad practices. This includes sub-clinical psychopathy, positive deviance, and organisational excellence strategies. Current research includes organisational change in action which she lectures on and has a forthcoming book on the same due for publication by Bloomsbury in 2023.

Duncan Coombe is a teacher, researcher, author, and advisor. His work with executives focuses on the development of leadership, organization, culture, and teams as well as change management. The central theme of all his work is the well-being of teams, organizations, and societies. Coombe has co-authored the award-winning book *Care to Dare: Unleashing the Astonishing Power of Secure Base Leadership*. He has a Doctorate in Organizational Behavior from the Weatherhead School of Management, an MBA from International Institute for Management Development (IMD), an LLB (Dean's Merit List) and a Bachelor of Social Science (majors in Psychology and Economics). He is also on the faculty of the Gestalt Center for Organization and Systems Development.

Coralie Fiori-Khayat is a French Associate Professor of Legal Studies and Ethics at ICN Business School (Nancy, France). She studied Private Law at Paris Assas University and then completed her doctoral degree in Private International Law at Versailles University. Simultaneously, she completed a PhD in American Civilization at Paris-Sorbonne University. Her dual competence led her to specialize in the disciplinary field of international and comparative law. Coralie has shared her passion for law with students at institutions such as Paris-Dauphine, La Sorbonne, and ESCP. Her research work focuses mainly on the themes of business ethics, corporate social responsibility, and sustainable development. She is a member of several academic societies, including the Academy of Management, the European Group of Organization Studies, the Society of Business Ethics, the International Association for Business and Society, and the International Humanistic Management Association.

David A. Greenway is a doctoral candidate in Leadership/Organization Studies at the University of Massachusetts Lowell. His research explores the lived experience of moral injury in the workplace – the lasting psychological-biological-social-spiritual harm – resulting from one's own actions or those of another that violate deeply held moral beliefs.

Myk Habets, a graduate of Laidlaw, AUT University, and Otago University, has taught theology for a number of schools and universities in New Zealand and abroad and is the Head of Theology and a Senior Lecturer in Theology at Laidlaw College. Myk has a passion to teach theology – the great doctrines of the Christian faith, founded in Scripture, forged in tradition, applied to culture, and lived out in experience. Myk's teaching and research center around constructive contemporary theology and moral theology (ethics). He has a special interest in pneumatology and is a world-leading scholar of Third Article Theology, theosis, Spirit Christology, the theology of Thomas F. Torrance, Evangelical Calvinism, and the theological interpretation of Scripture. Myk is an Associate Pastor, and his wife is a Senior Pastor at Albany Baptist Church.

Bart Henssen, Assistant Professor, is the head of the Center for Sustainable Entrepreneurship (CenSE) at Odisee University of Applied Sciences (Belgium). Bart is also Affiliated Researcher at the Center for Family Entrepreneurship and Ownership (CeFEO, Jönköping, Sweden), and Visiting Professor Sustainable Business Models at Vilnius University Business School (Lithuania). Bart holds a PhD in Applied Economics from the University of Hasselt (Belgium) and a PhD in Economics and Business Administration from the University of Jyväskylä (Finland), a master's in Human Resource Management, and a master's in Social Work and Social Welfare Studies. His research interests are focused on sustainable entrepreneurship, sustainable human resources management, and psychological ownership in family businesses.

Harry Hummels is a seasoned professional in the field of corporate responsibility, responsible investing, impact investing, ethics, and social entrepreneurship. He was co-managing director of Impact Investing at ACTIAM, European liaison for the Global Impact Investing Network (GIIN), and Special Advisor on Impact Investing to the Executive Director of the United Nations Office of Project Services (UNOPS). As a social entrepreneur he initiated Le Souk d'Orient to provide job and learning opportunities to refugees. Dr. Harry Hummels is Full Professor of Ethics, Organisations, and Society at Maastricht University and a fellow of the University's European Centre for Corporate Engagement (ECCE). In addition, Harry is a Professor of Social Entrepreneurship at Utrecht University. He is also a member of the Board of Society

Impact. Harry loves cooking, traveling with his wife and daughters, reading, and workouts – but doesn't overdo the latter. His favorite pub is Frowijn in Nijmegen.

Matthew T. Lee is the Director of Empirical Research and Senior Research Scientist at the Human Flourishing Program within the Institute for Quantitative Social Science at Harvard University. He is also a Distinguished Visiting Scholar of Health, Flourishing, and Positive Psychology at Stony Brook University's Center for Medical Humanities, Compassionate Care, and Bioethics and a Visiting Scholar at the Benson-Henry Institute for Mind Body Medicine at Massachusetts General Hospital. His research explores topics such as the relationship between love and flourishing, benevolent service to others, and the integration of social science and the humanities. He is the lead editor of *Measuring Well-Being: Interdisciplinary Perspectives from the Social Sciences and the Humanities* (Oxford University Press, 2021).

Thomas G. Maridada is the President of The Center for Strategic Leadership and Organizational Coherence. Tom is the former President and CEO of BRIGHT New Leaders for Ohio Schools and the former National Director of Education Policy, Practice and Strategic Initiatives at the Children's Defense Fund (CDF) in Washington, DC. Prior to his former roles, Tom served as superintendent of several urban school districts in Michigan where was named *Michigan Superintendent of the Year*, and awarded the CBS Broadcasters *Innovators Award*, and the *Arc Benders Award for Restorative Social Justice*. Tom has also served as a member of the leadership team of two U. S. Department of Education National Blue Ribbon Schools. Tom holds a doctorate degree from the University of Pennsylvania and a Master of Divinity from Harvard Divinity School. Tom also has a Master of Education from Wayne State University and Bachelor of Arts in Education from the University of Detroit-Mercy.

Franklin Alexander Markow has been teaching and leading in Christian higher education administration for over 20 years. His passion is to help leaders and organizations become all that God has called them to be through innovative approaches to education. He teaches at the undergraduate, graduate, and doctoral levels, and loves helping students discover more about themselves, and expand their capacity to be more effective leaders. Research interests include leader vocation and calling, religious leadership, and leader identity.

Michael F. Mascolo is a Professor of Psychology at Merrimack College, where he is also the Academic Director of the Compass Program. His areas of expertise are development of self, emotion and morality, educational reform, how can we resolve conflict between individuals and groups, how does psychotherapy operate as a developmental process, intersubjectivity, and the origins of psychological knowledge. He holds a PhD in Developmental Psychology from the University at Albany and a BA (cum laude) in Psychology from Southern Connecticut State College.

Peter McGhee (Te Aupōuri) is a Senior Lecturer and Deputy Head of the Department of Management at AUT Business School. Before joining AUT in 2000, Peter worked for nearly a decade as a risk analyst and operations manager for two different multinationals in the financial services industry. His expertise and research interests lie in business ethics, workplace spirituality, sustainability, and critical management studies; his recent work focuses on ethical leadership, human flourishing at work, and education for sustainability. Peter is widely published in a range of esteemed business, ethics, and sustainability journals. He is a board member of The Leprosy Mission New Zealand (TLMNZ), a global development agency working with people affected by leprosy.

Nava Michael-Tsabari is the founder and director of the Raya Strauss Center for Family Business Research at the School of Management, Tel Aviv University. Nava received the first PhD. On family firms in Israel from the Technion, Israel Institute of Technology. Nava is a researcher and an educator on the subject of family businesses. Since 2009 she teaches the first and only course to owning families at Lahav, the School of Management, Tel Aviv University. She is an acknowledged speaker on family firms in Israel and abroad, to academic and professional audiences as well as to families. Nava is also a third generation of the industrial Strauss family. She worked in the group and served on the board of directors of its publicly traded company.

Maria Prats has a PhD and MA in Government and Organizational Culture from the University of Navarra, Spain. She earned a Law degree from Barcelona University. Her dissertation deals with altruistic motives and their repercussions on human well-being and organizations. Her research is on human motivation and its relationship to leadership, ethics, and well-being. Maria has worked in private banking, marketing consulting, retail sector, and Higher Education. She teaches leadership and business ethics courses at the undergraduate and graduate levels.

Linda Robson is a consultant, performance coach, and educator. Linda's work focuses on the languages of change and of high-performing teams and organizations. In the classroom, Linda works with executives, building their understanding of leadership dynamics, executive presence, and creating intentional impact. Linda has a PhD in Organizational Behavior from Case Western Reserve University and is the co-author of *Flourishing Enterprise: The New Spirit of Business*. Linda is a faculty member of the Gestalt Organizational Systems and

Development Center, as well as in the Executive MBA program at Kent State University. Linda lives in London.

Teresa J. Rothausen PhD, is Executive Academic Director and Leadership Professor at the Center for Leadership Formation at Seattle University and President of Wiser Wilder Leadership, LLC, which she founded to support experienced leaders using her approach based on research she published in top academic journals including *Journal of Management, Journal of Organizational Behavior, and Journal of Business Ethics,* some of which won honors. For example, her 2019 article on meaning at work was named a *Journal of Business and Psychology* top-12 contribution from over 800 articles submitted. She is writing the book *Wiser Wilder Leadership,* showing how wisdom can guide leadership and leadership can activate wisdom. She holds a Ph.D. in human resources / industrial relations from the *University of Minnesota*; B.A. from St. Olaf College; CPA; diversity, equity, and inclusion certification from *MultiCultural Institute*; graduate certificate in spiritual direction from *St. Catherine University*; and MDiv candidacy at *Harvard Divinity School.* She is a poet, hiker, and mother of three.

Renato Ruffini is a Professor of Organization and Management at the University of Milan, with a special interest in management of human resources, public administration, performance management, pay for performance, audit and integrity management. He graduated in Business and Management from the University "Luigi Bocconi" in Milan. Previously he taught at University "C. Cattaneo LIUC" and Bocconi University. Encompassing more than 181 journal articles, he is the author of 13 textbook chapters and 9 books (edited as well as monographs).

Roberta Sferrazzo is Assistant Professor of Management at Audencia Business School (France, Nantes). Her research background navigates between critical and ethical perspectives applied to the fields of Organization Studies and Management. She is also investigating the connections between business ethics and new forms of work organization. She is author of several articles published in international journals, such as British Journal of Management, Journal of Business Ethics, Journal of Management Studies and Work, Employment and Society.

Maike van Dijk (1983) is a lawyer. At Nyenrode Business University she worked at the intersection of entrepreneurship and creating positive impact from change theory and relationships. She has also contributed to setting up an international master class that brings together the worlds of private money and nature conservation. Her most recent research contribution was in the research project "Agapè in companies" of Maastricht University and the Goldschmeding Foundation. At Anders Invest, she is a Project Manager Sustainability in creating an online place for inspiration in the field of sustainability in all its facets. In addition to her work at Anders Invest, Maike is involved in the Kromkommer Foundation and the Work-with-Nature Foundation.

Annelies van Uden is an Assistant Professor at the Copernicus Institute of Sustainable Development. Annelies' key research interests include social innovation, socially sustainable organizations, agape, solidarity, innovation in lower-income countries, inequality, and ethics of economics. The overarching research question of Annelies's present research aspirations focuses precisely on how organizations organize themselves in a time in which societal meaningful contributions become more and more urgent. Annelies teaches various courses, ranging from economics to organization theory, innovation, inequality, and ethics within economics.

Introduction

Michael Pirson

"What's love got to do with it" is a famous song by Tina Turner. It is also a question we typically hear when discussing love in the context of business management. Organizations are not human, but they are made up of people; naturally then all that which is relevant to people is also relevant to organizations. And yet, this is not a common perspective.

If we look at the organization, its functioning, growing and developing, and moving together as one unit, the well-being and success of that organization depend on the well-being of people that make up the organization. Love in its various forms is the energy that motivates and fuels creativity, care, innovation, progress, and well-being. Traditionally organizational structures have been set up to support compliance and command and control, which often discourage expression of sympathy, empathy, care and love, and at its extreme creates policies against (mostly romantic) love at the workplace. Some argue that such suppression of fundamental humanity has resulted in reduced growth, productivity, and retention of businesses, as well as reduced well-being for employees. This reduced connectivity between individuals has also at a higher level adversely affected our societies. Without love, each person is working and performing with reduced energy, and at reduced capacity. The evidence of this can be witnessed in the high disengagement at work.

Previous research has been mainly focused on love at the workplace from the viewpoint of psychologists. Our book *Love and Organizing* looks at the impact of love within organizational contexts from various viewpoints, including management, psychology, philosophy, and more. We explore love in the organizational context by looking at how it affects meaning, purpose, well-being, motivation, faith, care, and spiritual development, and how the identity and well-being of each person in the organization positively affect retention, well-being, and the growth and success of that organization.

In the opening chapter, Matthew T. Lee argues that a healthy, mature conception of love is a foundational and unifying principle that might more intentionally guide the project of humanistic management (Spitzeck et al. 2010) in ways that ultimately contribute to the promotion of *flourishing*: more complete forms of healthy, life-affirming well-being

DOI: 10.4324/9781003254034-1

across multiple domains. Stated simply, the quality of our awareness of love is a crucial – and generally overlooked – factor that fundamentally shapes our individual and collective ability to thrive.

In Chapter 2, Roberta Sferrazo and Renato Ruffini develop a conceptual model for love and organizations. In their work, the authors state that there are three fundamental elements in the bonds between individuals in a specific social or organizational context: (a) personal interests, which can be interpreted in utilitarian terms; (b) affective and emotional relationships, which involve companionate love and can be interpreted in psychological terms; and (c) managerial tools, which are oriented toward the achievement of common aims. All of these elements have a fundamental role in the cohesion, functionality, and elasticity of an organization.

In Chapter 3, Linda Robson and Duncan Coombe share their perspectives of the territory of love and work, based on existing research and what they're learning about love at work from interviews with executives and teams in organizations representing a variety of sectors and industries, as well as their own lived experience in organizations as teachers and consultants. Their inquiry seeks to understand what the expressions of love are, across levels of organizational system, and how they can generate more love. Their research asks simply, "how do organizations express love?"

In Chapter 4, Harry Hummels, Yannick Bammens, Maike van Dijk, and Annelies van Uden develop an understanding of love as agape for the organizational context. They argue that agape means more than simply living up to the expectation of corporate social responsibility and creating shared value. It allows rethinking the ways in which we do business, while aiming to achieve the mission and objectives of the business. Even though for many agape has roots in the Judeo-Christian tradition, the authors argue that it is a meaningful concept and can be applied in a secular business world that aims to create (long-term) value for its stakeholders, including shareholders.

Extending this perspective, Michael F. Mascolo and David A. Greenway in Chapter 5 look at business and the role of love and morality in business, questioning "is business just business?" They argue for an updated model of organizing that supersedes the "business as usual" model which separates business from love, societal values, morality, and responsibility.

In Chapter 6, Peter McGhee and Myk Habets extend the notion of agape by drawing on the work of Emmanuel Levinas and C.S. Lewis. This chapter draws on the existing literature and examines the differing yet converging views of agapic love. McGhee argues that both perspectives challenge and extend the management literature, and ultimately provide novel and distinctive ways of thinking about love and business.

In Chapter 7, Maria Prats considers how "donal-love" can be present at work through the motivation of our actions, specifically through our altruistic or transcendent motivations. Donal-love is a selfless love that leads us to act looking for the good of others.

In Chapter 8, William A. Andrews proposes the humanistic Organizational Development Matrix as a managerial tool by which critical human development milestones can be identified, operationalized, and pursued in the organizational context. Drawing heavily from Erikson's work on psychosocial development, the author asserts that the Loving Organization is one that is committed to developing the essential humanness of its employees, which when successfully done creates a virtuous cycle of self-giving employees contributing to and benefitting from the human flourishing of others.

In Chapter 9, Elena P. Antonacopoulou examines how Putting Love First as a governing principle enables new ways of relating, working, and uniting in serving the common good as essential to the future of work. To address ways of embedding love in managing and organizing, she introduces new "love languages," extending previous references to the five love languages (Chapman, 2010) that have also been translated into the five languages of appreciation in the workplace (Chapman and White, 2012). The main thesis of previous references to love language in human affairs is the proposition that each person has the tendency to favor some over other gestures or expressions of love (e.g., gifting, appreciation, acts of service, touch, and quality time) that may be limited to a primary and a secondary language which may be developed if they seek to understand and respond to the other's needs and preferences.

In Chapter 10, Coralie Fiori-Khayat explores romantic love in the context of the organization. The chapter examines how romance carries a socio-emotional value linked to dignity, which is then confronted with explicit or implicit rules within an organization, bringing the relationship into conflict with the workplace. The author develops a theoretical background by contextualizing the wider subject of romantic relationships in the workplace and then develops an ethical framework in which they take place.

In Chapter 11, Teresa J. Rothausen and Thomas G. Maridada develop a conceptual model of love in organizational context by drawing on insights from faith and wisdom traditions. Many faith and wisdom traditions emphasize the importance of love over fear, and this (re-)orientation may be a key marker for development of wisdom, brought about in part by spiritual practices and spiritual development. The authors argue that today's organizations need wiser leadership, that is, leaders who manifest love and caring above self- and organization-specific interests.

Nava Michael-Tsabari, Francesco Barbera, and Bart Henssen in Chapter 12 explore another form of love that is "tough love." They argue that "tough love" is often practiced in family firms and examine paternalism. This chapter presents a study of paternalistic leadership in family firms.

Franklin Alexander Markow develops a Seven Desires model as a way to conceptualize practical expressions of love in the workplace. He shares the result of an exploratory study that sought to demonstrate an empirical connection between the model and the outcomes of job satisfaction and work engagement.

Finally, in Chapter 14, Clive Boddy and Louise Boulter discuss the absence of love in organizations as they discuss psychopathy. They examine what the influence of a psychopathic absence of love in organizations means for employees, organizations, and society. For employees the results of psychopathic leadership are initially experienced as being emotional in nature, with negative affect, at levels as extreme as hatred, leading to withdrawal. Organizations lose committed employees and therefore stagnate or decay. For society, as the above quote asserts, the loveless organization may bring into being events that are detrimental to future human survival. These may include environmental pollution and resource depletion beyond sustainable levels.

With this book we trust we have contributed insightful and provocative thought development as stepping stones for more conversation, research, and practice.

References

Chapman, G. D. (2010). *The 5 love languages: The secret to love that lasts.* Chicago, IL: Northfield Publishing.

Chapman, G. D., and White, P. E. (2012). *The five languages of appreciation in the workplace: Empowering organizations by encouraging people.* Chicago, IL: Northfield Publishing.

Spitzeck, H., Pirson, M., von Kimakowitz, E., and Dierksmeier, C. (2010). The humanistic management network. *Zeitschrift Fur Psychologie*, 218(4), 246–248. 10.1027/0044-3409/a000035.

1 Love as a Foundational Principle for Humanistic Management

Matthew T. Lee

Confusion about love is both widespread and enduring (Reeve 2005). This confusion continues to harm human health and well-being. It has fatal consequences whenever cultural narratives about love promote harmful emotions such as jealousy and hatred that justify violence (Borochowitz and Eisikovits 2002; Conde et al. 2018; Wood 2001). The quality of our awareness about love has extraordinary implications for how we organize, manage, and lead. Disordered notions of love represent a serious threat to group and organizational stability (Yeung 2005; Poloma and Hood 2008). Positive understandings and expressions of love are associated with desired organizational outcomes (Barsade and O'Neill 2014) and with deeper humanistic ends that cannot be quantified in narrow financial or other material terms (Keir 2017).

In this chapter, I will argue that a healthy, mature conception of love is a foundational and unifying principle that might more intentionally guide the project of humanistic management (HM) (Von Kimakowitz et al. 2010) in ways that ultimately contribute to the promotion of *flourishing:* more complete forms of healthy, life-affirming well-being across multiple domains. In general terms, these domains are manifest at the individual (VanderWeele 2017), community (VanderWeele 2019), and planetary levels (Carlisle et al. 2009; Willett et al. 2019). Well-being is also understood by many people in specifically spiritual terms (Messer 2021; VanderWeele et al. 2021). Stated simply, the quality of our awareness of love is a crucial – and generally overlooked – factor that fundamentally shapes our individual and collective ability to thrive.

I draw attention to awareness because social scientists continue to confirm a bedrock truth that philosophers and the founders of religious orders have promoted for millennia: "the control of consciousness determines the quality of life" (Csikszentmihalyi 1991, p. 20). Although perhaps not widely appreciated, there is great wisdom in the statement that the "principal form that the work of love takes is attention" (Peck 1978, p. 120). By means of thoughtful attention, we become empowered to love more effectively. A healthier and more virtuous understanding of love provides a means for focusing awareness on that which is truly life-affirming, as well as greater clarity about the criteria that might be used

DOI: 10.4324/9781003254034-2

to discern which actions to take at both the individual and organizational levels in order to promote the highest amount and quality of flourishing.

A First Glance at Love in the Context of Humanistic Management

Any discussion of love must acknowledge that the word is most frequently defined as a noun, often in terms of strong feelings or emotions that evoke desire – "I am in love!" "I love ice cream!" – in fact, as the "supreme emotion" (Fredrickson 2013, p. 10). This is not wholly inappropriate. Indeed, there is perhaps no better word in English to evoke the intense feelings of self-transcendence experienced in the giddiness of romantic infatuation, the ecstasy of spiritual communion, or the great joy of consuming a delicious dessert. These disparate experiences involve very different modulations of love (Johnson 2001; Lewis 1960). The words of the 13th century Sufi poet Rumi (1998, p. 243) still resonate: "The way of love is not a subtle argument. The door there is devastation." The devastation of unrequited romantic love immediately springs to mind, particularly in its headline-grabbing manifestations when obsessive understandings of love result in deadly violence. It is indeed difficult to distinguish love and hate when considering "possessive love" (Lomas 2018, p. 142).

But Rumi may have had a more theological understanding of love in mind: it is the selfish self that is "devastated" by a transformative experience of love – an experience that allows a more generous self to come into being. This chapter promotes management practice that is grounded in a *healthy* and *mature* understanding of love, one that is life-affirming and promotes generosity rather than possessiveness (see also Vallerand 2008, on harmonious as opposed to obsessive passions). From a mature vantage point, operating from a spirit of generous love is not a sacrifice. Instead, it involves the giving up of a lower good, such as a self-centered accumulation of power, status, or wealth, in order to seek a higher good: the flourishing of all. In this way, we discover our best possible self: "In the giving of self lies the unsought discovery of self" (Post 2003, p. 3). The characteristics and outcomes of this kind of love have been enumerated in countless classic and contemporary works: patience, kindness, truthfulness, courage, unity, respect, trust, generosity, effectiveness, empowerment, warmth, understanding, perseverance, purity, and so forth (*1 Corinthians 13:4–8*; Beck 1989; Hooks 2001; Kongtrul 2018; Post 2003; Sorokin 2002/1954).

In addition to noun-based understandings of love, prominent cultural observers and psychologists suggest that "we would all love better if we used [the word] as a verb" (Hooks 2001, p. 4; see also Chapman 2009; Peck 1978). In Western culture, the Greek concept of *agape* (see Silverman 2019; Kreeft 2004, especially chapter 3; Templeton 1999), sometimes translated as *charity* or *altruistic love*, captures this sensibility that love is much more than just a feeling or an experience (see also Sorokin 2002/ 1954). Love is a self-giving action, an intentional activity that involves nurturing the growth of others and, perhaps indirectly, the self. In some instances, "love is primarily *giving*, not receiving" (Fromm 2000/1956, p. 21). Of course, a skillful ability to receive love is also important. I will draw upon these ideas to advance a *stipulative* definition of love that has relevance for all types of relationships (friends, relatives, romantic partners, colleagues, strangers, and even enemies) and also positions the concept as a foundational principle for HM.

The core principles of HM indicate that this movement within the broader field of management represents an "interpretive commu- nity" (Fish 1980) whose members may be receptive to the cultural understandings that I use to develop my stipulative definition of love. As articulated by Von Kimakowitz et al. (2010, p. 4, emphasis added), HM is built upon three dimensions: (1) "unconditional respect for the *dignity* of every person," (2) "*ethical reflection* [as] an integrated part of all business decisions," and (3) the search for "normative *legitimacy* for corporate activities" in the context of striving to meet "corporate *respon- sibilities*." Inherent dignity, ethical reflection, and legitimacy linked to responsibility are all in alignment with the conceptualization of love that I will advance. They also work to achieve a shared outcome:

> Taken together, these three dimensions promote human flourishing through economic activities that are life-conducive and add value to society at large. Submitting business decisions to these three guiding principles is what we call humanistic management.
>
> (Von Kimakowitz et al. 2010, pp. 4–5)

The perspective on love that I will develop offers a unifying prin- ciple for humanistic managers in a pluralistic context who seek to (re-) organize, manage, and lead in life-conducive ways guided by these three dimensions. Framed in terms of the three dimensions and the primary aim of HM, I suggest that healthy love fosters an awareness of dignity, it encourages ethical reflection and responsible action, and it promotes flourishing. I am seeking convergent thinking across diverse perspectives in order to arrive at an understanding of love that will be both conceptu- ally and practically useful to the broadest possible group. This is why my exploration of the concept of love is broader than a single philosophical or religious tradition, or for that matter, a reductionistic social scientific approach.

An analogous situation confronted the founders of Alcoholics Anonymous (AA) as they encountered resistance to the particularistic features of the initial iteration of their step-based addiction recovery pro- cess. Through their own trial-and-error experiences, they broadened their spiritually based approach so that it became universally accessible in a manner that still honored the Christian inspiration from which it was born. This standpoint continues to emphasize adherence to the spiritual "absolutes" of honesty, unselfishness, purity, and love, while reaching both religious and nonreligious audiences. The entire process "boiled down," in the words of AA co-founder Dr. Bob Smith, to the two primary virtues of "love and service" (Lee et al. 2017, p. 163).

This chapter builds on the contention that a boiled-down *essence* of healthy, mature love might be used to more intentionally and skillfully guide life-conducive management and leadership practice. Or perhaps, *spirit* of love, if the word "essence" is too strong for our deconstructionist era. Regardless of word choice, the fact of the matter is that some more or less healthy forms of love already serve as foundational and unifying principles within culturally legitimated narratives that guide behavior, provide resources for making meaning, and foster collective identities. The word itself may not always figure prominently in these extant narratives, but many are at least implicitly rooted in some conceptualization of love. Unhealthy conceptions obviously contribute to domestic violence among intimate partners as well as caregivers and children (the "near and dear"). Disordered concepts of love also contribute to the *Tragedy of Tribal Altruism*: an intense love of in-group which results in an equally intense "out-group antagonism" (Sorokin 2002/ 1954, p. 459). Even the most brutal tyrants in history have waxed eloquently about love of country or family ("I can fight only for something that I love..."). This is the source of much group conflict and suffering on a global scale.

But we also find an abundance of inspiring examples of positive social transformation grounded in healthy understandings of love, as evidenced by Martin Luther King, Jr.'s creation of a "new narrative of America with his 'I Have a Dream' speech" (Wood 2001, p. 258). For King – steeped as he was in the Christian tradition of *agape* – love was a powerful force capable of remaking the world (see also Kahane 2010; Sorokin 2002/ 1954). As he famously put it:

> What is needed is a realization that power without love is reckless and abusive, and that love without power is sentimental and anemic. Power at its best is love implementing the demands of justice, and justice at its best is power correcting everything that stands against love.
>
> (King 1967, n.p.)

This kind of awareness of love is not "sentimental and anemic," it is a powerful source of motivation and energy to *lead* in the best sense of the word, in ways that promote benevolence and the empowerment of others (Lee et al. 2013). This thoughtful, mature understanding of love has beneficial effects on the motivation to persevere through difficulties and provides guidance for the shape that positive social change might take in a specific context. King's perspective was shaped by his specifically

Christian understanding that "God is love" (*1 John 7:16*), that "Love bears all things" (*1 Corinthians 13:7*), and that "the greatest [of the theological virtues] is love" (*1 Corinthians 13:13*, Roberts 2012). Other religious traditions also affirm this perspective. For example, Gandhi's (1999/1971, p. 35) Hindu perspective argued that "God is truth and love," while some versions of Buddhism emphasize the cultivation of a compassionate and loving "warm heart" as the "source of everything positive in the world" (Kongtrul 2018, p. 16). In its broadest sense, spirituality itself may be "summarily described by its embodiment in one word: *love*" (Fricchione 2011, p. 5).

Humanistic managers are well positioned to inspire positive social change through the creation narratives in the tradition of "I Have a Dream" that are based on a healthy, mature love as a unifying principle. Such narratives have a central role to play in organizing to heal the many harmful structural disconnects in the ecological, social, and spiritual-cultural realms (Laloux 2014; Scharmer and Kaufer 2013; Sisodia and Gelb 2019). For humanistic managers, organizational goals are not framed exclusively in instrumental terms, such as profit or market share, but – in the words of the co-founder of one prominent software company – in higher-order, substantive terms like "bringing delight or ending suffering" for "everyone" (Sheridan 2015, p. 9, 62), not just for customers, employees, and shareholders. Thus, the "primary challenge" facing humanistic managers is how to foster a "basic love and trust within the individuals who comprise organizations" (Keir 2017, p. 8) so that organizing around these principles becomes a real possibility. This requires a fundamental shift in collective awareness, a move from confusion about love to clarity, and the ability to consistently frame organizational action as an expression of healthy love. Such leaders might appear as "Chief Energy Officers, responsible for mobilizing, focusing, inspiring, and regularly recharging the energy of those they lead" (Harvard Business Review and The Energy Project 2014, p. 5) by skillfully attending to the physical, emotional, cognitive, and spiritual domains of human existence.

A change in consciousness and narrative is not sufficient. I emphasize *organizing* guided by the principle of love, and not only *management*, because the discrediting of harmful narratives is ultimately an institutional accomplishment and not primarily within the power of a single manager or group of executives. Leaders within this movement often emerge from the grassroots, rather than from the apex of social hierarchies. Furthermore, all types of organizations are implicated, not just businesses: "families, schools, and the workplace must confer persuasive power on new narratives and diminish the acceptability of toxic ones" (Wood 2001, p. 259). Mere talk about love is insufficient, as is "outward CSR-style agreement on lowest-common-denominator ethical principles within an otherwise amoral and underregulated global economic system"

(Keir 2017, p. 13). Love provides an expanded horizon to guide fundamental reorganization.

What Is Love?

The influential psychiatrist Harry Stack Sullivan emphasized that human
life is not understandable without reference to relationship/communion.
He famously defined love by stating,

> When the satisfaction or the security of another person becomes as
> significant to one as one's own satisfaction or security, then the state
> of love exists. So far as I know, under no other circumstances is a
> state of love present, regardless of the popular usage of the word.
> (Sullivan 1947/1940, pp. 42–43)

And yet, reviewing the psychological research on love, Shaver and Hazen
(1988, p. 475) conclude that "many books and articles begin by discussing
types of it or ways of falling into it, without saying what it is." This is
perhaps forgivable because love is such a "many-dimensional cosmos"
(Sorokin 2002/1954, p. 15) that the word has become "polysemous in the
extreme" (Berscheid 2010, p. 6). It has been used "more promiscuously
than almost any other word in the English language" (Murstein 1988).

Philosopher Eric Silverman (2019, p. 419) argues that "we should not
speak of 'Christian love' as if it is a single doctrine or view" and instead
points to the significant differences that exist across Platonic, Aristotelian,
and Kantian models of love within this single tradition. The situation
becomes even more complicated when other traditions are considered.
It is little wonder that one thoughtful philosophical treatment resorts to
a work of fiction to express this fraught situation in the exasperation of
a third-grader: "You use this word love all the time, Mother, applying
it to many different things. But could you possibly tell me, please, what
the *one* thing is that you are speaking of whenever you use that word"
(Nussbaum 1990, p. 282)? Nussbaum (1990, p. 282) concludes that this
child "won't be answered." Partially due to this disorganized state of
affairs, rigorous organizational scholarship has generally avoided direct
engagement with the term love (but see Barsade and O'Neill 2014).

Confusion about love stems from the various ways that the word has
been used to describe different kinds of feelings *and* actions. Dictionaries,
as chroniclers of the most popular uses of words, tend to define love first
and foremost as a noun – "an intense feeling of deep affection" – and sec-
ondarily as a verb, but still connected to strong emotions: to "feel a deep
affection" (Oxford English Dictionary 2020). Loftier definitions have also
been advanced. For example, the definition on Wikipedia (2020) includes
"sublime virtue or good habit." It is perhaps not possible to resolve the
problems that have resulted from the polysemous nature of the word and
this situation is likely to persist because of these past precedents with

regard to how the word has generally been used. Furthermore, many adopt the position articulated by prominent theologian Paul Tillich: "I have given no definition of love... because there is no higher principle by which it could be defined" (quoted in Sorokin 2002/1954, p. 3). Or, in the influential words of bestselling psychiatrist Peck M. S. (1978/1985, p. 81), "love is too large, too deep ever to be truly understood or measured or limited within the framework of words."

I accept the presupposition that words are not sufficient to fully encompass the heights and depths hinted at by the word "love." The implication is that all definitions of love must begin with a *stipulated* meaning that becomes more or less accepted by an interpretive community (Fish 1980). This fact provides an opportunity for organizational leaders to take on the role of "cultural entrepreneur" (Lounsbury and Glynn 2019, p. 3) by creatively deploying existing cultural resources that resonate with organizational members in order to advance a new definition of love that minimizes unhealthy aspects. Some of the definitions that are created will be more expansive than others; some are likely to have more beneficial effects than others.

For example, although keenly aware of the inadequacy of all definitions, Peck (1978/1985, pp. 81, 116) argues emphatically that "love is not a feeling" and stipulates his own definition that love is "the will to extend one's self for the purpose of nurturing one's own or another's spiritual growth." There is an echo of Aquinas in this language, as we will see. Spiritual growth involves an integration of mind, body, and spirit, a movement towards self-actualization, and an ability to "engage in communion with the world" (Hooks 2001, p. 13). As Jean Vanier (1992, p. 17) frames love within a Christian perspective, "to love someone is to reveal to them their capacities for life, the light that is shining in them. To be in communion with someone also means to walk with them." Other traditions concur: "No one can become fully aware of another human being unless [they] love [them].... by [this] love, the loving person enables the beloved person to actualize these potentialities" (Frankl 1984/1959, p. 116; see also Buber 2000/1923; Templeton 1999). The "central meaning" of love involves a process of revealing the deep value of the beloved through "communion," whereas the "opposite of love" involves an "invalidation of being, and the related objectification, mockery, disparagement, and destruction of being" (Post 2003, p. 52). We would expect humanistic managers informed by this loving sensibility to be better able to perceive human dignity, which is the precondition to ethical reflection and responsible action necessary to foster widespread flourishing (Von Kimakowitz et al. 2010). This perception of inherent dignity can be expanded through the practice of "techniques of altruistic transformation" to include all others without exception (Post 2003; Sorokin 2002/1954, p. 285; Templeton 1999).

Bestselling authors such as Fromm, Peck, and Hooks have subsequently popularized the notion of *love as action* that fosters deepest growth and builds healthy relationships, in contrast to love as an uncontrollably intense emotion or feeling. Indeed, for Peck (pp. 81, 117) love is seen as "judicious giving," implying practical wisdom and discernment in accordance with higher, spiritual principles. Sorokin (2002/1954) argued that such an elevated form of love would be both more *adequate* (effective in promoting good in the world) and *extensive* (applied to an increasingly wider circle of beneficiaries until it stretches to all without exception). There is a strong resonance here with the *effective altruism* social movement (MacAskill 2015; cf. Oakley 2011). These principles give us some initial criteria for determining the healthiness of a particular definition of love: does it promote actual benefits and do these benefits extend beyond the boundaries of an in-group?

Love > Cathexis

This discerning view of love goes well beyond mere *cathexis*: the investment of emotional "energy" in another person (see also Hooks 2001, p. 5). A romantic infatuation – the classic case of cathexis – that promotes jealousy and intimate partner violence performs poorly according to the criteria of extensity and adequacy, and certainly does not live up to the vision of love as a theological virtue (Roberts 2012). The investment of emotional energy is not incompatible with love, and indeed, love is often most powerfully experienced as "the feeling force of connection" (Fricchione 2011, p. 5). But such feelings are certainly not sufficient to qualify as highest love, which would involve a thoughtful consideration of the extent to which the effect of this cathexis is beneficial to self and others. We might therefore suggest that healthy and mature love includes volitional and reflective aspects, not just passionate desire. At the level of cultural narratives, and therefore in the lived experiences of individuals, we do tend to "confuse cathecting with loving" in ways that lead to harm, whereas connecting love to the promotion spiritual growth would seem to suggest that "love and abuse cannot coexist" (Hooks 2001, pp. 5–6). The encyclical "God is Love" (*Deus Caritas Est*) developed by Pope Benedict XVI (2005, pp. 3–6, author copy) from the foundational writings of Pope John Paul II similarly argued that love is not an undisciplined "vice," that it is attained "simply by submitting to instinct," but instead that the experience of ecstasy that is associated with involuntary experiences of love may "lead us beyond ourselves" on a "path of ascent" to a higher experience and expression of love. This notion of a lower state of love being "dethroned" and "tamed" in order to experience a higher form has roots in writings of Plato, Augustine, and other classic works of philosophy and theology (Silverman 2019, p. 413).

In other words, despite popular usage, both secular (Hooks 2001; Peck 1978; Fromm 2000/1956) and religious (Benedict XVI 2005;

Aquinas 1920/1485) writings suggest that cathexis itself is not a fully developed form of love. It may, in fact, degenerate into a "number of forms of pseudo-love which are in reality so many forms of the disintegration of love" (Fromm 2000/1956, p. 77). Unhealthy fixations on cathexis are to be opposed when they encourage the violation of the essential criteria of love (e.g., extensive honoring of human dignity). Furthermore, cathexis-induced forms of need fulfillment and population expansion are not life conducive when these activities exceed the carrying capacity, or ecological ceilings, of the local or global environment (Raworth 2017). This is why care and love are not synonymous. One may express care and affection in ways that are harmful in the short- or long term, or that mix unkindness and even abuse (Hooks 2001). Psychological definitions of love increasingly reflect "a motive to invest in each other's well-being that brings mutual care" (Fredrickson 2013, p. 15).

But cathexis experiences may also serve as a primary means of shifting our awareness in the direction of a greater, more extensive, and more adequate horizon of love. Therefore, this chapter does not necessarily seek to replace the dominant cathexis-based understanding of love that is so firmly ingrained in cultural narratives that circulate outside an organization's boundaries. Instead, I advance the more modest argument that management practice would be enhanced (i.e., more humanistic) if a specific definition of love that de-emphasizes, but does not eliminate, cathexis is stipulated and used within an organization as an important part of the foundation of individual and group morality, as well as influencing the institutional logic that guides processes of organizing. Such organizing practices, if adopted by many organizations, could eventually shift the broader awareness of a society.

The point is that a humanistic manager need not wait for broad social change and should instead work to become a catalyst for such changes. The working definition of love developed in this chapter draws on the long-standing wisdom of the social sciences and humanities – including theology, which is usually ignored in management scholarship (but see also Guillen et al. 2015; Guillen 2021) – to promote a clear awareness of the essence of all types of love, regardless of whether we are considering its romantic, parental, neighborly, or spiritual forms. Guided by this awareness, the most pernicious aspects of current organizing practice are readily identified so that they might be overcome through skillful and intentional love-based leadership. Such unhealthy aspects include widespread *objectification* in patterns of relationships, the proliferation of *externalities* and *rituals of exclusion*, and *alienation* from morally good purposes, including healthy spiritual growth. All are fundamentally incompatible with love, as I will define it, and inconsistent with integrative forms of awareness that represent the leading edge of organizing practice.

Modulations of Love versus Its Essential Features

As we progress toward a definition of love, it is helpful to consider philosopher Rolf Johnson's (2001, pp. 4–5) "three faces of love" – union-love, care-love, and appreciation-love – a classification that he describes as "more analytic than historical and springs from the wish to dig deeper than the distinctions already embedded in the language." Beyond their conceptual value, these three primary modulations have proven useful for understanding patterns that emerge from empirical research (Poloma and Hood 2008). To set the stage for this tripartite conceptualization, Johnson contends that there are some core features of love. These include (1) there is a subject (lover) and an object (the beloved); (2) there is a sense of "value or the process of valuation" in that what is loved is judged to be valuable; (3) the lover is drawn or inclined toward the love object; and (4) "love must have an affective component." While recognizing that it is possible that the affective component in which "the lover must feel something for or with the loved" may be questioned by some, Johnson (2001, p. 14) insists that it is "widely agreed upon, if not absolutely non-controversial," particularly in the modern Western world. With these "universal features of love" in place, Johnson (p. 24) then puts forth his primary thesis regarding "what kinds of relations between a subject and an object, and what kinds of inclination or action tendencies regarding it, enable us to identify a relation as love." He succinctly states:

> A central thesis of the present work is that, if we allow ourselves to be guided by ordinary English usage and also by the history of love theory… there are three distinguishable phenomena we call 'love.' The names we will use for these phenomena are 'care-love,' 'union-love,' and 'appreciation-love.' They differ from each other principally in how the lover is inclined toward the loved and, thus in their respective action tendencies. [E]ach love has a different objective, though not necessarily a different object.
>
> (p. 24)

Care-love provides one way in which we "relate to an object we love," namely, to "simply care for or about it." According to Johnson, "care-love embraces all forms of concern for the well-being of the loved. Its objective is simply the good of the love object" (p. 24). Affect or feelings associated with this modulation of love are commonly care, concern, and compassion. While care-love is about relationships that involve concern for the loved, *union-love* is about joining together the lover and the loved. Union-love tends to be more passionate than care-love, with "action tendencies hav[ing] to do with efforts to effect, preserve, or deepen the valued union" (p. 25). Mystical love and romantic love are both examples, suggesting that the lovers and the loved ones may be either divine or human persons.

Taken together, care-love and union-love express Aquinas's position that love in a "perfect sense... requires two interconnected desires: 1) the desire for the good of the beloved, and 2) the desire for union with the beloved" (Stump 2006, p. 27). Importantly, this desire for union might apply to an idealized or improved beloved, not "as that person currently is" (Stump 2006, p. 28). The desire for the good of the beloved, for Aquinas, is a desire for "that which is truly conducive to the beloved's well-being," for "those things which in fact contribute to the beloved's flourishing" (p. 28). This points to well-being in an ultimate sense, as with religious salvation (Messer 2021) or the more generic phrase "spiritual growth" (Peck 1978), not with hedonistic or materialistic forms of well-being.

The third face, *appreciation-love*, is commonly both more abstract and more passive than are the other two faces of love. Johnson (2001, p. 25) notes, "Instead of reaching out to care for or striving to unite with, these lovers merely behold what they love, appreciating it for being what it is (or is taken to be)." While appreciation for a person is usually mixed with the other two faces of love, appreciation-love embraces a wider range of phenomena (e.g., ideals, principles, visions, and a sense of calling) where simply valuing the loved entity is central.

Love, then, is expressed toward others because of a desire to care for them in a way that promotes deepest flourishing, a desire to be in relationship with them, and a desire to simply appreciate the good that they represent. This will even apply to an "enemy": a person who seeks to do us harm. In fact, the *agape* tradition, along with its more generic and secular offshoots (e.g., Peck 1978), reorients our perspective away from notions like "enemy" and toward an understanding of the other's inherent dignity and capacity to be loving toward us. As Kierkegaard put it, it is always possible to " 'love forth' or elicit the good in them" (Walsh 2018, p. 89). This kind of awareness is essential in accounts of the life of Jesus ("love your enemies," *Matthew 5:44*). Such love is extensive, not insular (Sorokin 2002/1954). It was this broad horizon of love that inspired the contemporary Christians who were active during the Civil Rights Movement and who worked for the ideal of the Beloved Community in which former enemies would prosper together.

Even prior to this social transformation and the expansion of Beloved Community, leaders of the Civil Rights Movement operated from an awareness that was grounded in what Martin Buber (2000/1923) called an "I/Thou" relation. In this kind of relationship, both parties are fully realized human beings, not mere objects to be manipulated and used, which is signified by "I/It." An I/Thou relation expresses a deep appreciation for the inherent dignity of the other. For the religiously inclined, the other is a "child of God," with just as much intrinsic worth as one's own self. Secular thinkers have argued that such dignity flows from an "indisputable human solidarity" (Camus 2008, p. 222). I/Thou relations do not harm or otherwise diminish the other, or the self. Instead, there is a deep appreciation – perhaps even an appreciation-love, in Johnson's typology – for both self and other. Regardless of the cultural context, deeply relating to others as ends in themselves – and developing a level of knowledge of them that is perhaps best signified by the term *communion* – is required by the kind of love that I envision.

It is at this point that I part ways with many of the extant definitions and typologies of love developed by social scientists, although I certainly find much of value in their conceptualizations, theorizing, and research. But I do reject defining love primarily as an emotion (Fredrickson 2013), sharply separating "love" from "altruistic love," "nurturance," "compassion," and related concepts (Peterson and Seligman 2004), or including the maximization of pleasure (Levin and Kaplan 2010) or feelings of possessiveness (Rubin 1970) as elements of love. Love includes emotions and ideally will involve pleasure at least sometimes – although love also requires sacrifice, and even heartbreak (Whyte 2015), both of which are far from pleasurable – but it involves much more, as we have already discussed. Love is also not just compassion, the desire and attempt to reduce suffering, but it is not separate from it either. In fact, attempts to define compassion often require love as the deeper principle. The theologian Oliver Davies (2001, p. 17), for example, claims that "any formal typology of love" will be "deeply unsatisfactory" and that "compassion" is the preferable term. And yet, he must describe compassion in terms of love: as "kenotic love," or the "exceptional self-giving love" that represents "a moral ideal... without which social civilization would founder" (Davies 2001, p. 21).

Similarly, there is great value in examining specific types of love, such as passionate love (Hatfield and Sprecher 1986), companionate love (Sternberg 1997), compassionate love (Fehr et al. 2009), and love based on attachment (Berscheid 2010). Such concepts recognize that love will not be expressed in exactly the same manner with friends, spouses, relatives, strangers, etc. There are four different Greek words for love: *storge* (affection), *philia* (friendship), *eros* (romance), and *agape* (charity, or divine love). In his influential book, *The Four Loves*, C. S. Lewis (1960, p. 17) further analyzes these types according to whether they derive from the experience of scarcity or abundance: "Need-love cries to God from our poverty; Gift-love longs to serve, or even to suffer for, God." Abraham Maslow (1999/1968, p. 48) made a similar distinction between "Deficiency-Love" and "Being-Love." Such frameworks help us to understand how a word like "love" has come to signify such diverse experiences as the self-centered jealousy of the jilted lover as well as the inspirational altruism associated with the anonymous donation of a kidney to a stranger whose identity will never be known. But what matters for guiding the practice of HM are the essential aspects of love, not the specific modulations of love or their types. The core features of love should be present across all types and expressions.

To make this point, it is helpful to synthesize classic and contemporary sources. Aristotle (*Rhetoric*, Chapter 1, Section 4, Book 2) argued that love involved "wishing for anyone the things which we believe to be good, for his sake but not for our own, and procuring them for him as far as lies in our power." Aquinas (1920/1485, parts 1–2, 26, 4) drew upon Aristotle when he argued, "To love is to will a good for someone." From a theological standpoint, then, "love always includes emotion, yet it is more than emotion"; it is a "praxis," drawing us "more deeply into the entire network of loving relations" (Jeanrond 2009, pp. 2, 5, 242). Understood as a caregiving system from the vantage point of psychology, "momentary surges" of joy and affection feed "enduring relational love" (Noller and Feeney 2000, p. 92). We therefore concur with philosophers who have argued that all forms of love share a common foundation of "emotional caring" for the "well-being of the beloved" (Krishek 2019, p. 252), or a "positive valuation" of the beloved that inclines action and involves "an affective component" (Johnson 2001, p. 21). Love is preferable when it produces actual, rather than merely intentional, benefits and when these benefits are extended beyond the near and dear in the creation of a Beloved Community (*Liebesgemeinschaft*) that does not exclude (Buckley 2001; Stikkers 2009; Sorokin 2002/1954). These core features of "love" illuminate the deeper motivations (Guillen et al. 2015) of humanistic managers and enliven "healing organizations" (Sisodia and Gelb 2019; Laloux 2014).

We have implied, but not fully developed, the aspects of love associated with tenderness, warmth, and joy. These aspects provide one reason why love is not reducible to beneficence, compassion, or altruism. These noble practices may or may not involve "emotional caring" (Krishek 2019), "surges of joy" (Noller and Feeney 2000), or "micro moments of warmth" … and "positively charged connections" (Fredreickson 2013, pp. 4, 10). But love, if it is to be worthy of its name, must eventually get us in touch with these vital aspects that enliven life. Helping to reveal the "light shining within" another person, as Vanier (1992) put it, should be an occasion of joy. But love is not just another system of competitive achievement within a confrontational world; it offers a refuge of tenderness. We might be wary of love that moves with "speed and aggression," that expresses the same "drive" as "other people's hatred" (Trungpa 2003/1973, p. 78). This is why feminist writers contrast "love-based technologies of change" (Maparyan 2012, p. xvi) with projects rooted in aggression that serve what they view as a masculine understanding of "greatness": "the advance of a part of the world at the expense of the whole; the overweening sense of the 'I' and the consequent forgetting of the 'Thou' " (DuBois, quoted by Bologh 1990, p. 324). It is therefore incumbent upon anyone advancing a definition of love to consider the importance of warm tenderness as an end in itself.

It is well known that adolescents who experience a warm, loving upbringing that provides them with a range of positive developmental assets (Benson et al., 1998) will manifest stronger character and higher levels of well-being later in life. Conversely, youths who experience "relationships that are cold, unsupportive, and neglectful" (Repetti, Tayler, and Seeman 2002, p. 330) will have the opposite outcomes. As an aspect of love, "parental warmth" has been shown in cross-cultural settings to enhance intimacy and sensitivity to others, as well as contributing to healthy, secure attachments (McCarthy and Casey 2008; Yun et al. 2016; Yun 2015). Warm relations set in motion a virtuous cycle whereby adequate care-love (involving both nurturing actions and warm affect) increases empathy, deepens relationships, inhibits anti-social behavior, and contributes to a flourishing life. Thus, warmth is an important part of "adequate" love and offers a variety of benefits.

The Path of Ascent: Cultivation of the Awareness of an Expanding Horizon of Love

Consistent with the emphasis on love as a verb, I conceive of love in HM as primarily a dynamic process, rather than as a static thing. Humanistic leaders need not begin with deep wisdom about love; they, and their organizations, might instead seek to grow in healthy love through a practice that becomes more skillful over time. It is helpful to have a vision of what healthy love is and what the furthest horizon might be. The source of such visions is found in cultural materials associated with secular or religious interpretive communities. Psychologists represent one such community and are often, but not always, secular in nature. They suggest that we grow into a more "mature love" (Beck 1989, p. 238) if we make the effort; and that "mature love may be best conceptualized as creating an environment in which both the lovers and those who depend on them can grow and develop" (Noller 1996, p. 97). Maslow (1999/1968, pp. 47–48) distinguished between the immature craving associated with the pathologies of "love hunger," rooted in Deficiency-Love, and compared this to the "healthy" person who is grounded in the "higher" and more mature Being-Love ("love for the Being of the other person," "unselfish love"). The latter type of person is better able to give benevolently and effectively to others. Proficiency in B-Love might rise to the level of mystic experience, which for Maslow (1999/1968, p. 48) represented the "peak experience" and highest form of awareness a human being might attain.

Viktor Frankl (1984/1959, p. 115) stressed that the "true meaning of life is to be discovered" through the "self-transcendence of human existence" (see also Maslow 1971). This involves overcoming egoistic instincts in the service of a cause that it is larger than the self, or through loving another person. Indeed, one can only truly "experience another human being" by "loving" and in the process, "the loving person enables the beloved person to actualize [their highest] potentialities" (pp. 115–116). For contemporary psychologists Aron and Tomlinson (2018, p. 2, emphasis added), "love is the desire to *expand the self* by including a desirable other in the self." Again and again, the notion of higher forms of love – mature, authentic, healthy – stresses the agency of the lover, the connection to growth and self-expansion, the intentional creation of a loving context that offers mutual benefits to lover and beloved, and above all, the decisive role of awareness. Consider this emphasis on *attitudes* and the value of the *realization* of love's deeper nature as activity in the service of authentic *becoming*:

> Authentic love is something within our capabilities, originating in our attitudes and culminating in our actions. If we think of love as a feeling, we shall be frustrated when we can't always work up that feeling. When we realize love is primarily an action, we are ready to use the tools we have to love better. Authentic love brings out our authentic selves, the people we want to become.
>
> (Chapman 2009, p. 6)

Such authentic forms of love point toward a life of enhanced virtue and well-being. But it is possible that social science disciplines, in a legitimate attempt to be precise for purposes of standardized measurement and replicability, or because of a focus on penultimate rather than ultimate – or spiritual – ends (Messer 2021), may define away some aspects of love:

> Psychologists, as scientists, try to clearly delimit words, defining them by observations. The Judeo-Christian tradition uses a different linguistic approach. It defines words in ways that *expand their meaning* beyond the merely observable. For scientists words point to things; in the Bible words point *beyond* them.
>
> (Clough 2006, p. 23, emphasis added)

Empirical approaches may adopt an implicitly reductionist stance that limits the horizon of love that serves as the object of study. As Hampson and Boyd-MacMillan (2008, p. 102) put it, "psychology is largely opaque as to its embedded ontologies," including both a methodological and a philosophical "naturalism," as well as a "tacit philosophical atheism." Given this situation, it is instructive to explore an understanding of love as a "path of ascent" (Benedict XVI 2005) in the context of a particular tradition, in this case, Christianity. My intention is not to impose this viewpoint on all practitioners of HM, but instead to offer a vision of love that invites *hospitable* (Hampson and Boyd-MacMillan 2008, p. 98) dialogue about common ground with other traditions in a pluralistic context (see Levin and Post 2010; Templeton 1999).

The philosopher Sylvia Walsh (2018, p. 16) contends that "the moral task in Christianity ultimately can be summed up in one word: love—properly understood and expressed as an unselfish, sacrificial, self-giving love for God and the neighbor." Love is therefore "a central feature of

Christian ethics" (Silverman 2019, p. 409). This is consistent with the scriptural admonition to "love as you have been loved" (*John 13:34–35*), as well as the popular phrase that we are "created by Love for love," in other words created by a God who is Love for the purpose of giving and receiving love. For Walsh (2018, p. 146), drawing on the conceptualization established by Kierkegaard, there are three classes of virtues ("initial, fundamental, and higher") that must be "pursued through habitual practice." Even higher "contemplative virtues" include love and aim to "promote union with God" (p. 146) and find resonance in earlier writings by seventh century monk Johannes Climacus. Climacus conceived of a "ladder of virtue," at the top of which was *agape* love and the attainment of salvation.

The Christian perspective developed here is that the difficult goal of practicing unconditional love, even for enemies, is aided when "out of charity, we love for God's sake" (Aquinas, quoted in Roberts 2012, p. 161) and that this form of love operates within a "unity of virtues" (p. 169). Indeed, Aquinas viewed the virtues "not as acts of reason, but as strategies of love" (Wadell 2008, p. 1). At times, a powerful religious conversion experience – or Road-to-Damascus-moment – may instantaneously shift awareness (Lee et al. 2013). But more commonly, it is necessary to cultivate a set of related virtuous dispositions through habitual practice. Such disciplined efforts enable a person experience and express love at higher levels. Conversely, a lower experience of love, such as romantic infatuation:

> ...needs to be disciplined and purified if it is to provide not just fleeting pleasure, but a certain foretaste of the pinnacle of our existence, of that beatitude for which our whole being yearns.... [T]he way to attain this goal is not simply by submitting to instinct. Purification and growth in maturity are called for; and these also pass through the path of renunciation.
>
> (Benedict XVI 2005, p. 3)

This "path of ascent" is arduous, involving purification and renunciation of instinctual sources of happiness, as it "leads us beyond ourselves" and also beyond "insecure" forms of love (Benedict XVI 2005, pp. 3–4). It involves a "liberation through self-giving" leading, like the ladder of virtue described by Climacus, to "discovery of God" (Benedict XVI 2005, p. 4). This *kenosis* is epitomized by the sacrifice of Jesus, which is the "fulfillment" and "essence" of love "and indeed of human life itself" (p. 4). Again, such a path is difficult, but it does not deny the experience of love as a form of unmerited grace. Rather, disciplined practices that cultivate virtue are helpful for sustaining healthy expressions of love over the life course.

What are the practical implications of traveling this path of ascent toward an expanded awareness of the centrality of love for the life of flourishing? One consequence is the ability to connect one's work within an organization to a deeper set of motivations than mere achievement or respect; for example, to align one's labors with religious gratitude, worship, or the "giving of spiritual good to others" (Guillen 2015, p. 811). In short, to reframe both mundane tasks and visionary leadership as expressions of agape – as highest virtue. Another outcome is the growing awareness that we have a *duty to go beyond the call of duty*, which might be understood as "an overarching mandate to transform ourselves and surpass our limitations" (Flescher 2003, p. 96). This is evident from this portion of the screenplay for the powerful film *Schindler's List* (Zaillian, 1990):

STERN: Oskar, there are twelve hundred people who are alive because of you. Look at them.
> *He can't.*
SCHINDLER: If I'd made more money …I threw away so much money, you have no idea. If I'd just …
STERN: There will be generations because of what you did.
SCHINDLER: I didn't do enough.
STERN: You did so much.
> *Schindler starts to lose it, the tears coming. Stern, too. The look on Schindler's face as his eyes sweep across the faces of the workers is one of apology, begging them to forgive him for not doing more.*
SCHINDLER: This car. Goeth would've bought this car. Why did I keep the car? Ten people, right there, ten more I could've got.
> *Looking around.*
SCHINDLER: This pin…
> *He rips the elaborate Hakenkreus, the swastika, from his lapel and holds it out to Stern pathetically.*
SCHINDLER: Two people. This is gold. Two more people. He would've given me two for it. At least one. He would've given me one. One more. One more person. A person, Stern. For this. One more. I could've gotten one more person. I didn't.
> *He completely breaks down, weeping convulsively, the emotion he's been holding in for years spilling out, the guilt consuming him.*
SCHINDLER: They killed so many people.…

The main character of the film, Oskar Schindler, laments his failure to do more for the Jews that he employed at his factory. By any normal person's standards, Schindler was an altruistic hero. His efforts, after all, helped save 1,200 Jews. Yet looking back, Schindler is consumed with guilt for not having done more. Why? His initial moral blindness contributed to preventable suffering and death. In other words, he failed to model an extensive and adequate love of neighbor. Flescher (2003, p. 6) suggests that dichotomizing saints and ordinary people fosters "moral complacency" because the duty to go beyond the call of duty is seen as applying only to a select few endowed with superhuman morality and willpower.

Without traveling a path of ascent that raises consciousness, it is easy to become comfortable with loving in the "normal" manner, at the socially sanctioned level. Consider Stern's comforting remark to Schindler reprinted above: "You did so much." What Stern is really saying is, "You did so much for an ordinary person, nobody expected you to do as even as much as you did—you are not a saint." Schindler feels guilty because his perception of duty has increased at the end of the film, while the perceptions of those of us who admire him have remained the same. A transformative vision or experience of love calls us to go beyond the minimal sense of duty we acquire through our socialization experiences. In this regard, even though Christianity is the dominant religion in the United States (US), this arduous path of ascent is counter-cultural – "narrow the road that leads to life, and only a few find it" (*Matthew 7:14*) – because it demands more of us in terms of virtue than other sectors of the culture. Mere legal or bureaucratic compliance is insufficient. There are of course many secular sources of motivation and practices to aid in climbing this virtuous path, but many people in the US will be assisted by their sense of "union with God" (recall Johnson's notion of union-love) and "the experience of God's grace," which provides "the capacity to love the neighbor as God loves him or her, and thereby to act charitably" (Flescher 2003, p. 97; see also Lee et al. 2013).

Turning from film to literature, we find that a path of ascent is the foundation of the doctrines of *active love* and *responsibility for all*, as envisioned by the character Zossima, in Dostoyevsky's great novel *The Brothers Karamazov* (Trepanier 2009). In fact, these two concepts provide the interpretive keys to the entire story. Aligned with the dimensions of love that Sorokin (2002/1954) labeled adequacy and extensity, they serve as core aspects of the definition of love that I will put forth as the North Star for HM. As Tepanier (2009, p. 200) argues, alienated individuals:

> …allow their pride and egoism to dictate their 'Karamazov baseness' toward continual sensual and material pleasure. The cure for this modern condition is *kenosis*: the negation of selfhood, by which we feel a responsibility for everyone and everything that prompts us to engage in active love to improve our individual and communal condition…. [Zossima states] that it is necessary 'to love a man even in his sin, for that is the semblance of the Divine love and is the highest love on earth . . . [and] all of God's creation, the whole and every grain of sand in it. Love every leaf, every ray of God's light, love the animals, love the plants, love everything.

The ability to engage in self-giving love, or *kenosis*, is made possible by movement toward higher, more mature experiences of love (but see Grant

2013, p. 158, for a helpful distinction between selfless and "otherish" forms of giving and the relation to burnout or effectiveness).

So, What Is Love?

In English, the word "love" encompasses what really matters in life to a great majority of people. Indeed, the "core dialectic" throughout the life course involves addressing a series of "separation challenges" (e.g., losses of job, loved one, opportunity, and one's own health) with attachment – i.e., love-based – solutions (Fricchione 2011, p. 33; Schlesinger 2014). Many scholars have begun to use the word "love" more frequently instead of more generic substitutes such as "caring" (Noller and Feeney 2000). And whereas developmental researchers have built a subspecialty around, for example, "parental warmth," the word "love" is becoming more prominent (Chen et al. 2019, p. 69; see also Lee et al., 2013). Pope Benedict XVI's *Deus Caritas Est*, along with the source rich materials that support it, enlivens this discussion of love by connecting it to a path of ascent with a broad horizon that includes the ultimate ends of life. This path requires both self-transcendence and greater extensity of beneficence (see also Sorokin 2002/1954; Maslow 1971). Many of the writers that I have discussed would disagree with each other about fundamental epistemic or ontological issues. In this regard, these writers reflect the fault lines that divide academic disciplines due to a radical pluralism in methods and theory, traceable to incommensurate underlying constructs and presuppositions (Fletcher 2021). But despite this diversity, I argue that there are important lines of contact, and even convergent thinking, about core aspects of mature, virtuous, higher forms of love.

First and foremost, such love should involve *action* that is adequate or *effective*, in Sorokin's sense, in the long run: It should express wisdom and confer virtuous benefits that foster deep *growth* for self and others. Again, in the long run, this kind of growth should contribute to *unity* rather than conflict, as Sorokin (2002/1954, p. 3, 6) explains through diverse voices ranging from pre-Socratic philosopher Empedocles to 20th century theologian Paul Tillich's argument that love encompasses the "forms and structures in which life itself overcomes [life's] self-destructive forces." For the religiously inclined, such benefits will lead to *ultimate ends*, such as union with God and the ability to love charitably. For the nonreligious, the peak experiences associated with Being-Love, as described by Maslow, may serve as ultimate ends. This love should also be *extensive*, expressing Zossima's value of responsibility for all, but also be *warm* and caring in tone. All of this is predicated on loving *awareness*: a "capacity to see" (Murdoch, quoted in Reeve 2005, p. 16) or "way of seeing" (Furtak 2013, p. 236) beyond selfish instinct to grasp the other in an *I-Thou relation* or to glimpse a wider horizon of possibility. Such awareness led Kirkegaard (quoted in Furtak 2013, p. 240) to declare that "'to love [others] is the only thing worth living for,' and without love we do not truly exist." This love is expressed in *care, union,* and/or *appreciation* for the beloved (which could, of course, include the self).

My definition of a healthy, mature love developed through a path of ascent is therefore *to effectively foster deep growth, including ultimate ends, through extensive acts of warm caring that unfold in healthy I-Thou relationships and that express a resolute awareness of the inherent value of self and all others without exception.* These essential elements of love might guide HM practice. As my literature review indicates, it is sometimes helpful to conceive of love as a noun or a verb, as something that an individual feels or does. But love more than an individual experience or act. It is also a context and a latent property of interactions, even a kind of "energy" (Sorokin 2002/1954, p. 26) or "cosmic force" (Buber 2000/1923, p. 66). According to Buber (2000/1923, p. 66), "love does not cling to an I... it is between I and You." This perception that love is *between* suggests that although love is partially comprised of constituents that promote flourishing for self and others, these elements must be arranged with practical wisdom according to a unifying grammar (Travers, 1991), in a manner that signifies a life-affirming story. This story is far larger than any individual or dyad. A healthy grammar of love tells the story of how we are each "loved into being" (Pollak, 2019) by a community over time. As Buber (2000/1923, p. 62) put it, "I require a You to become; becoming I, I say You."

My definition of love, and even my consideration of the grammar and story of love, does not encompass the full mystery of love. Nor does it engage with the fickleness of Cupid's arrow and other experiences that are perhaps better understood as cathexis rather than love. From the standpoint of neuroscience, as well as theology, philosophy, and many other scholarly disciplines, an arbitrary and instinctual passion, although it may provide a useful spark for forming a profoundly meaningful attachment, turns out to be a poor basis for lasting romantic relationships (Lewis et al. 2000). It certainly does not provide a stable platform forHM.

A much better foundation for both stable romantic love and HM is a deep knowing (intimacy) nurtured in a context of warm, beneficial, and reciprocal giving (mutuality; Lewis et al. 2000). This is why I have stressed that mature love is greater than cathexis, although warm, caring feelings are an essential component. Indeed, such feelings distinguish – and in my view, elevate – love from related concepts like compassion, altruism, and benevolence. As laudable as these other terms might be, a calculative rationality may be sufficient to motivate actions that offer positive benefits for others or reduce their suffering. Not so with love. It seems like a misuse of that term without some level of warm, perhaps even tender, "emotional caring" (Krishek 2019, p. 252). This is why a purified love, born of a renunciation of instinct (Benedict XVI 2005), is capable of restraining the drive for MORE that seems to infect so many of our individual, organizational, and societal appetites. In contrast with the emphasis on financial metrics, as measured in a reductionist manner in quantitative analyses that studiously exclude negative externalities to the full extent of the law, Goethe's "tender empiricism" (Wahl 2005, p. 74) points in the direction of more holistic – and loving – ways of knowing the world.

The modulations of love will differ across types of relationships. Extensity, for example, is not the goal of a committed, monogamous, romantic relationship. But in most contexts, including HM, the definition of love that I have stipulated should prove useful, even to those who do not identify with all the particularistic sources I have cited. My definition contains many components and therefore represents an ideal toward which an HM leader might strive. Again, a path of ascent is required; instinct is likely to be insufficient. The value of this vision of healthy, mature love will be found in the practical guidance that it provides leaders in their efforts to promote greater flourishing at the individual, community, and planetary levels.

Practical Applications of Love as a Foundational and Unifying Principle

It is necessary for conversations about love to move from abstract concepts to practical applications: "simply telling people that they must love and trust is counterproductive" (Keir 2017, p. 10). In the sections that follow, I offer specific examples of how the mature, path-of-ascent understanding of love that I have developed might guide HM practice, including upstream reorganizing in cases in which existing organizational structures are inherently unloving. Because no research has yet been conducted based on the definition of love that I have presented in this chapter, my discussion will be either conceptual or based on evidence from a partial engagement with the elements of love found in the definition. The empirical research that I briefly cite provides the interested reader with a set of resources to explore. All aspects of love are theoretically applicable, even if I may highlight only one or two in each instance. It is nevertheless important to keep the full list of elements in mind. It is also necessary to remember that the term "leader" does not primarily refer to individuals vested with decision-making authority within an organization (e.g., president and chief executive officer), although such individuals do play an important role. Rather, everyone is a potential leader and leadership itself is a "collective capacity in a system" (Scharmer and Kaufer 2013, p. 112).

This discussion is grounded in the understanding that collective, and not just individual, awareness is crucial: "The quality of results produced by any system depends on the quality of awareness from which people in the system operate" (Scharmer and Kaufer 2013, p. 18). Leaders tend to operate from an awareness of what is best for themselves, their organization, and perhaps their nation. Yet our reality is defined by "globally interdependent eco-systems" (Scharmer and Kaufer 2013, p. 111). This ecosystem is holistic, inclusive of "ecological, social, intellectual, and spiritual" contexts – the "whole house," as the Greek root of the word "ecology" suggests (Scharmer and Kaufer 2013, p. 67). What might motivate organizational leaders, regardless of their position in a particular hierarchy, to care more effectively for the whole house? The answer is "love." The central task of the humanistic manager is to connect more fully with an expanded understanding of love, develop a loving awareness that is more effective and extensive in its reach, help others do the same, and act collectively in accordance with this awareness.

Adequate, Extensive Love and Inherent Dignity as the Bedrock Criteria for Organizational Decision-Making and Reorganizing

Insufficient understanding of love and failure to act effectively on its demands have caused a range of undesirable outcomes that humanistic managers wish to avoid, including organizational death. For example, the demise of a prominent social ministry was partly caused by an over-emphasis on appreciation-love (Johnson 2001) – directed toward a lofty vision rather than people – coupled with inadequate forms of care-love that were not sufficiently extensive despite the emphasis of the vision on care-love (Poloma and Hood 2008). Similarly, communes that conflate love with charisma and narcissism are organizationally unstable, despite their emphasis on warm, loving relationships (Yeung 2005). This raises a question about which aspects of my definition of love are most essential. Ideally, all would be present. But it seems that devaluing the inherent worth of organizational members is a strong indicator that love is poorly understood or devalued.

For example, violations of inherent dignity are often the deepest root of conflicts between management and labor and, in one recent case, proved fatal to the organization as an independent entity (Hicks 2016). Dignity is of course only one element of my definition of love, but it is a nonnegotiable bedrock. Greater attention to just this single aspect of love would have profound transformative effects on how people relate to each other and how groups are organized. Reflecting on her failed attempt to encourage non-humanistic managers to overcome their "self-preservation instincts gone awry," Hicks (2016, pp. 122, 124, emphasis added) concludes that:

> ...people who lead with dignity end up with not only an internal culture where employees and management alike experience a sense of well-being and fulfillment, but with a dignified company with its face to the world. People are yearning for a *new narrative* about what humans are capable of, and dignity might just show us the way.

I began this chapter with a discussion of the need for new narratives about love, contrasting Martin Luther King, Jr.'s "I Have a Dream" speech with narratives of love that promote harm and violence. It is fitting to return to the issue of collective narratives. Whatever else the word "love" might mean, it must at minimum honor the inherent worth of all people and encourage their growth in the direction of deepest flourishing. If the full definition of love that I have offered in this chapter is too complicated, this "boiled-down" essence may suffice. HM might incorporate this understanding as a core part of the cultural narratives that it seeks to promote.

In many cases, reorganization will be required in order to implement even this partial definition because some organizational structures and cultures are actively opposed to whole-person flourishing and planetary well-being (Laloux 2014). Incorporating a process for "dignity assessment," as laudable as such a process may be, may not promote desired outcomes if it is embedded in a fundamentally unloving context (Hicks 2016). It is helpful to remember that organizations are not fixed entities; rather, they are fluid processes that must be reinforced through consistent interactions. This also means that there is much more freedom to reorganize than many people realize. An "organization" is first and foremost the reification of mental structures that reveal what members believe is possible or desirable. Here it is helpful for the dominant "downstream representational mode of thinking" to be "replaced by an upstream deconstructive modality in which fundamental concepts and categories used in the analysis of organization are themselves subjected to critical scrutiny" (Chia 2014, p. 20). This mode of awareness reveals the upstream "organizing processes" that create the appearance of a downstream "organization." This is an optimistic and liberating way of understanding organizational reality because it is prepared to see more degrees of freedom for deep structural and cultural change. It is also historically more realistic because seemingly fixed organizations have quite porous boundaries and do change dramatically over time.

A striking example is provided by an organization in the Netherlands that provides home-based skilled nursing services (Laloux 2014). In the 1980s, the Dutch government imposed a bureaucratic model on neighborhood nursing services that had existed since the 18th century. Hoping to take advantage of economies of scale and other mechanisms of efficiency, managers radically changed how the nurses organized their day and their time with patients. The effect was dehumanized and unloving interactions that both the nurses and the patients detested. One nurse was dissatisfied by these dramatic changes and created Buurtzorg as a non-bureaucratic alternative. Organized into teams of 10–12 nurses who self-manage – there is no higher management or even team leader – Buurtzorg reestablished the primacy of I-Thou relationships. Upon meeting a new patient for the first time, the nurse and patient talk casually over coffee in the patient's home. The goal is a high level of intimacy and warmth of human connection and the nurse plays a key role in expanding the patient's network of support, which includes family members and neighbors, not just paid experts. The nurse sees the same patient for years and is often present when the person takes their last breath. Buurtzorg's organizing practice is infused with many of the elements of love as I have defined it and it represents the antithesis of the depersonalized and uncompassionate "managed care" system that prevails in the US (Trzeciak and Mazzarelli 2019). A nurse led the change. Everyone at Buurtzorg is a leader.

Turning to the field of education, consider one creative approach in the Oakland Unified School District to resolving entrenched disparities in academic achievement, along with and the inequitable use of punitive disciplinary measures. Radical change began with the observation that, "society and the schools embedded within it have made love a foreign thing for Black males" (Chatmon and Givens 2019, p. 2). Building the requisite level of foundational trust between students and faculty in order to shift the extant hostile and unhealthy dynamic required the "concept of *agape*—the highest form of brotherly love—as the guide for everything we do" (Chatmon and Givens 2019, p. 83). Legal coercion in the form of a Federal Consent Decree was necessary to open space in Oakland for a different kind of teacher, and a different kind of classroom, to emerge. In this caring, open space, standard teaching credentials and practices were supplanted by an effective solution to the legal, social, and political crisis. Rules that appeared fixed and inviolable turned out to be quite malleable, once there was appropriate motivation to make deep changes rooted in love. A similar approach can be adopted in other settings without waiting for outside legal intervention, if there is a consensus about the value of adopting a pedagogy grounded in caring and aimed at whole-person flourishing (Noddings 2005).

Love Promotes a Virtuous and Caring Organizational Culture that Protects Health and Nurtures Complete Well-Being

It is no secret that many contemporary organizations are filled with disengaged and burned out members, unnecessary forms of suffering, unsatisfying relationships, and alienated styles of interaction (Hari 2018; Laloux 2014; Miller et al. 2017; Trzeciak and Mazzarelli 2019). Well-designed Gallup surveys have so routinely shown that seven out of ten employees across virtually all sectors of the economy are not "engaged" at work that it has become clear that complacency about this issue is now quite entrenched. High levels of dehumanization and disengagement (i.e., low levels of love and compassion) are taken for granted, even in the fields that are specifically charged with nurturing human well-being such as health care and education (Trzeciak and Mazzarelli 2019; Miller et al. 2017). And for the 30% of workers who are not disengaged... fully 20% of them are "engaged-exhausted" (Seppala and Moeller 2018, n.p.). The percentage of organizational members that are fully flourishing is therefore rather small indeed. Intentional and effective reorganizing guided by mature love would likely help to shift these unhealthy dynamics. In fact, a loving awareness grounded in a bedrock commitment to I-Thou relationships at a high level of extensity may be necessary before leaders are able to fully perceive the sources of the problem and muster sufficient motivation for solving it.

Fortunately, there has been significant movement in this direction. Leading-edge research and organizational change efforts led by Eileen McNeely and her team at the Sustainability and Health Initiative for NetPositive Enterprise (SHINE) at the Harvard T.H. Chan School of Public Health have conceived of the "regenerative workplace" as a platform for promoting holistic flourishing (SHINE 2020; see also the "healing organization" described by Sisodia and Gelb 2019). Consistent with the definition of love developed in this chapter, SHINE promotes the empirical measurement and skillful enhancement of a "caring culture" within an organization and its supply chain in order to foster complete well-being at a wide extensity. They specifically incorporate VanderWeele's (2017) domains of flourishing in their empirical assessments and interventions. Their integrative model considers the contributions made by such diverse organizational resources as fair wages, supportive relationships, manageable workloads, work/life integration, safe working conditions, and so forth. By seeing the interconnections among the material conditions of the work (financial security, physical safety) and caring relational conditions, the aspirations of loving leaders to promote complete well-being might attain greater effectiveness.

It is also instructive to look at the more explicit attempts to assess love in organizational contexts, or at least some aspects of love as I have defined it. For example, Barsade and O'Neill (2014) found that the degree of "companionate love" at a long-term healthcare facility was positively associated with higher employee satisfaction and teamwork and negatively related to their absenteeism and emotional exhaustion. They also found beneficial effects on clients: better mood, quality of life, and satisfaction, as well as fewer trips to the emergency room.

The research of Lilius and colleagues (2011; see also Trzeciak and Mazzarelli 2019) on organizational "compassion capability" – the everyday practices and the relational conditions that foster noticing and alleviating suffering as a component of regular organizational routines – represents another partial implementation of my definition of love. Much of the disengagement and burnout found in organizations is likely the result of unskillful expressions of love and compassion. Work groups and entire organizations can effectively and efficiently organize members to contribute to the resolution of each other's suffering, but in the absence of intentional planning and design this work invariably falls upon a few especially selfless and empathetic "toxin handlers" who are likely to suffer burnout as a result (Frost, 2003; Grant 2013). For these individuals, an excess of empathy without the ability to act compassionately in an adequate way to reduce suffering triggers the pain center in the brain, whereas compassion engages the brain's reward center (Trzeciak and Mazzarelli 2019). The overwhelming demand for emotional labor placed upon such people should raise a red flag for a manager with a loving awareness, and for an organization with a culture that embodies mature love, indicating the existence of a systemic problem. The infrequency with which this occurs is indicative of an absence of loving leadership and, again, I conceive of leadership as a distributed responsibility of all organizational members.

When it comes to worker safety, an absence of love becomes a matter of life and death. Research has found that the culture of some business organizations socializes managers to take responsibility for the prevention of fatal worker "accidents," while organizations with nonvirtuous cultures may promote the belief that worker safety is beyond their control (Haines 1997). It is simply inconceivable that a caring culture grounded in the definition of love that I have developed would routinely permit serious injury and death on the job. The empirical fact is that many of these injuries and deaths are indeed preventable. The variation we see across organizations operating in the same sector of the economy and subject to the same market and regulatory forces shows the urgent need for loving HM.

Finally, prisons are probably the last type of organization that we might call to mind when we think of healthy, mature love. And yet there is great variation across prisons in the degree to which love and flourishing are explicit organizational goals. Often, a program within a prison is the most appropriate unit of analysis, as it may represent a loving subculture within an otherwise nonloving (and nonvirtuous) setting. The Christian seminary at Angola Prison in Louisiana offers a model of a love-based approach to fostering flourishing, situated within a maximum security men's prison that has historically had one of the most violent reputations in the country. In the words of the seminary director, their program "deinstitutionalizes the dehumanization of punitive justice" within the prison (Hallett et al. 2017, p. 13). As one of their ministers put it, "Love work is the only work" and "when you demand a behavior without setting a man free to love, you will fail" (p. 14). How is a person to be set free? According to this minister:

> How we help inmates is we enter into their suffering with them and help them come to a point of freedom. The primary opportunity is to love an individual.... When someone meets me they are not meeting a program. They are meeting me; and I am meeting them.

This loving approach is grounded in the inherent dignity of all of the prisoners, builds warm I-Thou relationships, emphasizes spiritual growth, and seeks to inculcate a sense of responsibility for the well-being of all. If this can happen in a violent place like Angola, what is stopping an increase in this kind of love from infusing hospitals, schools, businesses, government agencies, and other organizations?

Love and the Shift from Negative to Positive Externalities

Business publications occasionally run features with titles such as "Leading with Love" (Cuellar 2018). This is a healthy development, although the advice given is usually framed in terms of interpersonal kindness, empathy, and compassion. At times, such articles advocate the creation of an internal organizational culture around such values. Again, this is beneficial, but the implications of mature love extend far beyond the interpersonal level. HM includes a concern with the broader world outside of the focal organization. This concern takes many forms. At a minimum, for those who seek to lead with love, the awareness that mature love encourages must be associated with an increased perception of externalities and a motivation to expand positive externalities while reducing negative ones.

An externality is "a cost or benefit that stems from the production or consumption of a good or service" (Investopedia 2019, n.p.) that is imposed on a third party. The classic example of a negative externality is a factory that generates pollution but does not include all of the costs associated with this pollution in the price of its products. These burdens fall to the population living downwind or downstream of the factory and include harms to health and well-being that must be paid in economic, human, and environmental terms. Turning a blind eye to such externalities is incompatible with healthy, mature love. Social goods like high-quality higher education and strong community organizations, on the other hand, tend to produce positive externalities by contributing to economic and cultural development within populations that do not directly subsidize the costs of these organizations.

From the standpoint of governance, "policymakers should look to subsidize markets with positive externalities and punish those with negative externalities" (Investopedia 2019, n.p.). Leadership grounded in love would seek to take greater initiative to drive the shift from negative to positive externalities without legislative or market coercion. This process need not be financially reckless. Effort could simultaneously be directed to an increase in love-based government policies to create structural conditions that are more conducive to businesses and other organizations participating in this shift. The point is that humanistic managers can help lead this process, rather than reacting to changes in government regulations and market conditions.

One specific example is the urgent need to sort out the extent to which "green" technologies for power generation are actually healthier in terms of planetary well-being – once a full accounting of costs and benefits is conducted that recognizes all externalities – than those rooted in fossil fuels. Once the greenhouse gas emissions associated with crop production and related processes are included, some biomass crops may perform no better than fossil fuels (McCalmont et al. 2017). A biomass power plant leader guided by love would not be content to allow such externalities to remain undefined and instead would work to ensure that the operation of plant is actually resulting in efficient and effective carbon dioxide mitigation once the impacts on the entire ecological and financial systems are included. Existing government regulatory policy and taxpayer subsidies may not encourage this form of leadership, but love provides a more expansive horizon of awareness and motivation than either legal or bureaucratic minimum standards. An extensive love aligns leadership and organizational practice with *system stewardship* (Well-Being in the Nation Network 2019) and economic frameworks that balance human needs with *ecological ceilings* (Raworth 2017).

One "system stewardship" approach involving the interconnections among human diet, health, food production, and a sustainable biosphere was developed by the EAT-Lancet Commission on Food, Planet, Health. This Commission estimates that reducing the production and consumption of unhealthy animal-based foods and building diets instead on a foundation of healthy, high-quality plant-based foods would save an estimated 11 million lives per year globally due to a reduction in noncommunicable disease (a roughly 20% reduction in mortality), while also promoting sustainable food production processes that work within "global biophysical limits... to ensure a stable and resilient Earth system" (Willett et al. 2019, p. 450). Well-being for the individual turns out to be congruent with well-being for the ecosystem. Because the good of the individual and the collective are not mutually exclusive, it makes little sense to assess the flourishing of individuals without also connecting their well-being to global thriving. Organizational leaders have the power to insist on changes if current practices are out of line with this system stewardship.

Conclusion

Most people consider themselves to be loving. And indeed, they are, at least as they understand the term. The real issue is what love means in terms of a healthy and mature practice. This is the point at which conflicts over incommensurable perspectives arise. I have emphasized the need to have a clear awareness of love. I have found that such awareness is enhanced by distinguishing between healthy and unhealthy forms of love and by consideration of whether there are certain core characteristics that might distinguish the former from the latter. Grounded primarily in writings from the Western social sciences and humanities, and in the spirit of hospitable dialogue with other traditions, I have put forth a definition of love that assumes progress along a morally – and, for some, spiritually – rigorous path of ascent. There is nothing particularly original in my arguments, but there is value in synthesizing and applying diverse cultural materials in the search for a common ground.

I have attempted to illustrate how this conceptualization of love relates to concrete instances of organizing practice and leadership. More development is needed, but it does seem that there is already a strong consensus that a healthy awareness of love is a source of empowerment for benevolent action and provides a blueprint for remaking the world. The perspective I have sketched aligns with the notion of "generative love" that fosters a "power-to" that overcomes oppression, as opposed to "degenerative love," or "power-over," that "destroys people" (Kahane 2010, pp. 38, 46, drawing on Tillich's classic framework). The aim is a "spiritualization of power" within a "radically noncoercive... community of love (*Liebesgemeinschaft*)," or what the leaders of the Civil Rights Movement have called the Beloved Community (Stikkers 2009, p. 53). It is my hope that humanistic managers guided by a healthy and mature awareness of love will be much more effective in inspiring others to collaborate on the project of promoting flourishing for individuals, communities, and the world.

Acknowledgments

I am grateful to Juan Xi, Manuel Guillen, Tyler VanderWeele, Katy Granville-Chapman, Eileen McNeely, Fr. Robert Gahl, Sharon Krishek, and Andrew Wylie for our conversations about how to conceptualize love or for feedback on a draft of this chapter. An early presentation of some of the material contained in this chapter was presented as part of a public lecture series hosted in the spring of 2019 by the Abagail Adams Institute. I appreciate the feedback provided by attendees and especially AAI's Director, Danilo Petranovich. All of these good people are, of course, not responsible for any errors in my thinking or writing.

References

Aquinas, T. 1920. *Summa Theologica*. Retrieved from www.newadvent.org/summa /3029.htm (Original work published in 1485).

Aron, A., and J. Tomlinson, J. 2018. Love as expansion of the self. In R. Sternberg and K. Sternberg (Eds.), *The new psychology of love* (pp. 1–24). Cambridge: Cambridge University.

Barsade, S. G., and O. A. O'Neill. 2014. What's love got to do with it? A longitudinal study of the culture of companionate love and employee and client outcomes in a long-term care setting. *Administrative Science Quarterly* 59: 551–598.

Beck, A. T. 1989. *Love is never enough*. New York, NY: HarperPerennial.

Borochowitz, D. Y., and Z. Eisikovits. 2002. To love violently: Strategies for reconciling love and violence. *Violence against Women* 8: 476–494.

Buber, Martin. 2000. *I and thou*. New York, NY: Scribner (Original work published in 1923).

Camus, A. 2008. *Resistance, rebellion, and death: Essays*. New York, NY: Vintage (Original work published in 1957).

Carlisle, S., Henderson, G., and P. W. Hanlon. 2009. 'Wellbeing': A collateral casualty of modernity? *Social Science & Medicine* 69: 1556–1560.

Chapman, G. 2009. *Love as a way of life: Seven keys to transforming every aspect of your life*. Colorado Springs, CO: Waterbrook.

Chatmon, C. P., and J. R. Givens. 2019. *We dare say love: Supporting achievement in the educational life of black boys*. New York, NY: Teachers College.

Chen, Y., L. D. Kubzansky, and T. J. VanderWeele. 2019. Parental warmth and flourishing in mid-life. *Social Science & Medicine* 220: 65–72.

Chia, R. 2014. *Organizational analysis as deconstructive practice*. New York, NY: Walter de Gruyter.

Conde, R., R. A. Gonçalves, and C. Manita. 2018. Narratives of those who "love" violently: Identity issues and construction of meaning of the batterers. *Journal of Humanistic Psychology*. doi.org/10.1177/0022167818784989

Csikszentmihalyi, M. 1991. *Flow: The psychology of optimal experience*. New York, NY: HarperPerennial.

Cueller, T. 2018. Leading with love: An unconventional approach to leadership. Retrieved from www.forbes.com/sites/forbescoachescouncil/2018/06/29/leading-with-love-an-unconventional-approach-to-leadership/#73805b851123.

Fehr, B., S. Sprecher, and L. G. Underwood. 2009. *The science of compassionate love*. Chichester: Wiley-Blackwell.

Fish, S. F. 1980. *Is there a text in this class? The authority of interpretive communities*. Cambridge, MA: Harvard University.

Flescher, A. M. 2003. *Heroes, saints, & ordinary morality*. Washington, DC: Georgetown University.

Fletcher, G. 2021. Philosophy of well-being for the social sciences: A primer. In M. T. Lee, Laura D. Kubzansky, & T.J. VanderWeele (Eds.), *Measuring well-being: Interdisciplinary perspectives from the social sciences and the humanities*. New York, NY: Oxford University.

Frankl, V. E. [1959]1984. *Man's search for meaning*. New York, NY: Simon & Schuster.

Fredrickson, B. 2013. *Love 2.0: How our supreme emotion affects everything we feel, think, do, and become*. New York, NY: Hudson Street.

Fromm, E. 2000. *The art of loving*. New York, NY: Harper and Row (Original work published in 1956).

Frost, P. J. 2003. *Toxic emotions at work: How compassionate managers handle pain and conflict*. Boston, MA: Harvard Business School.

Furtak, R. A. 2013. Love as a relation to truth: Envisioning the person in Works of Love. *Kierkegaard Studies Yearbook* 1: 217–242.

Gandhi, M. K. 1999. *The way to God*. Berkeley, CA: Berkeley Hills.

Grant, A. 2013. *Give and take: A revolutionary approach to success*. New York, NY: Viking.

Guillen, M., I. 2021. *Motivation in organisations: Searching for a meaningful work-life balance*. New York, NY: Routledge.

Guillen, M., I. Ferrero, and W.M. Hoffman. 2015. The neglected ethical and spiritual motivations in the workplace. *Journal of Business Ethics* 128: 803–816.

Haines, Fiona 1997. *Corporate regulation: Beyond 'punish or persuade.'* New York, NY: Oxford University.

Hallett, M., J. Hays, B. Johnson, S. J. Jang, and G. Duwe. 2017. "First stop dying": Angola's Christian Seminary as positive criminology. *International Journal of Offender Therapy and Comparative Criminology* 61: 445–463.

Hari, J. 2018. *Lost connections: Uncovering the real causes of depression—And the unexpected solutions.* New York, NY: Bloomsbury.

Harvard Business Review, The Energy Project. 2014. *The human era @ work.* Retrieved from https://uli.org/wp-content/uploads/ULI-Documents/The-Human-Era-at-Work.pdf.

Hicks, D. 2016. A culture of indignity and the failure of leadership. *Humanistic Management Journal* 1: 113–126.

Hooks, B. 2001. *All about love: New visions.* New York, NY: HarperPerennial.In vestopedia. 2019 (July 15). *How do externalities affect equilibrium and create market failure?* Retrieved from www.investopedia.com/ask/answers/051515/how-do-externalities-affect-equilibrium-and-create-market-failure.asp.

Kahane, A. 2010. *Power and love: A theory and practice of social change.* San Francisco, CA: Berrett-Koehler.

Keir, J. (2017). A world ethos for humanistic management: love story or dialogue platform? *Humanistic Management Journal* 2: 7–14.

King, M. L., Jr. 1967. *Where do we go from here? Address delivered at the Eleventh Annual SCLC Convention.* Retrieved from https://kinginstitute.stanford.edu/king-papers/documents/where-do-we-go-here-address-delivered-eleventh-annual-sclc-convention.

Kongtrul, D. 2018. *Training in tenderness: Buddhist teachings on tsewa, the radical openness of heart that can change the world.* Boulder, CO: Shambhala.

Kreeft, P. 2004. *The god who loves you: Love divine, all loves excelling.* San Francisco, CA: Ignatius Press.

Laloux, F. 2014. *Reinventing organizations: A guide to creating organizations inspired by the next stage of human consciousness.* Brussels: Nelson Parker.

Lee, M. T., M. E. Pagano, B. R. Johnson, S. G. Post, G. S. Leibowitz, and M. Dudash. 2017. From defiance to reliance: Spiritual virtue as a pathway towards desistence, humility, and recovery among juvenile offenders. *Spirituality in Clinical Practice* 4: 161–175.

Lee, M. T., M. M. Poloma, and S. G. Post. 2013. *The heart of religion: Spiritual empowerment, benevolence, and the experience of god's love.* New York, NY: Oxford University.

Levin, J., and B. H. Kaplan. 2010. The Sorokin multidimensional inventory of love experience (SMILE): Development, validation, and religious determinants. *Review of Religious Research* 51(4): 380–401.

Levin, J., and S. G. Post. 2010. *Divine love: Perspectives from the world's religious traditions.* Conshohocken, PA: Templeton.

Lewis, C. S. (1960). *The four loves.* New York, NY: Harcourt, Brace, Jovanovich.

Lewis, T., A. Fari, and R. Lannon. 2000. *A general theory of love.* New York, NY: Vintage.

Lilius, J. M., M. C. Worline, J. E. Dutton, J. M. Kanov, and S. Maitlis. 2011. Understanding compassion capability. *Human Relations* 64: 873–899.

Lomas, T. 2018. The flavours of love: A cross-cultural lexical analysis. *Journal for the Theory of Social Behaviour* 48(1): 134–152.

Lounsbury, M., and M. A. Glynn. 2019. *Cultural entrepreneurship.* New York, NY: Cambridge University.

MacAskill, W. 2015. *Doing good better: Effective altruism and a radical new way to make a difference.* New York, NY: Gotham.

Maparyan, L. 2012. *The womanist idea.* New York, NY: Routledge.

Maslow, A. H. 1971. *The farther reaches of human nature*. New York, NY: Viking.

Maslow, A. H. 1999. *Toward a psychology of being*. New York, NY: John Wiley & Sons (Original work published in 1968).

McCalmont, J. P., A. Hastings, N. P. McNamara, G. M. Richter, P. Robson, I. S. Donnison, and J. Clifton-Brown. 2017. Environmental costs and benefits of growing Miscanthus for bioenergy in the UK. *GCB Bioenergy* 9: 489–507.

Messer, N. 2021. Human flourishing: A Christian theological perspective. In M. T. Lee, Laura D. Kubzansky, and T. J. VanderWeele (Eds.), *Measuring well-being: Interdisciplinary perspectives from the social sciences and the humanities*. New York, NY: Oxford University.

Miller, R., B. Latham, and B. Cahill. 2017. *Humanizing the education machine: How to create schools that turn disengaged kids into inspired learners*. Hoboken, NJ: Wiley.

Noddings, N. 2005. *The challenge to care in schools: An alternative approach to education*. New York, NY: Columbia University.

Noller, P. 1996. What is this thing called love? Defining the love that supports marriage and family. *Personal Relationships* 3: 97–115.

Noller, P., and J. A. Feeney. 2000. Parent-child emotional bonds: Loving or caring? *Psychological Inquiry* 11: 91–94.

Nussbaum, M. C. 1990. *Love's knowledge: Essays on philosophy and literature*. New York, NY: Oxford University.

Oakley, B., A. Knafo, G. Madhavan, and D. S. Wilson. (Eds.). 2011. *Pathological altruism*. New York, NY: Oxford University.

Oxford English Dictionary. 2020. *Definition of love*. Retrieved from https://en.oxford dictionaries.com/definition/love.

Peck, M. S. 1978. *The road less travelled: A new psychology of love, traditional values, and spiritual growth*. New York: Simon and Schuster.

Pollak, S. M. 2019. Who has loved you into being: A guided meditation. *Psychology Today Blog*. Retrieved from www.psychologytoday.com/us/blog/the-art-now/201905/who-has-loved-you-being.

Poloma, M. M., and R. W. Hood, Jr. 2008. *Blood and fire: Godly love in a Pentecostal emerging church*. New York, NY: New York University.

Post, S. G. 2003. *Unlimited love: Altruism, compassion, and service*. Philadelphia, PA: Templeton Foundation.

Raworth, K. 2017. *Doughnut economics: Seven ways to think like a 21st-century economist*. White River Junction, VT: Chelsea Green.

Reeve, C. D. C. 2005. *Love's confusions*. Cambridge, MA: Harvard University.

Roberts, R. 2012. Unconditional love and spiritual virtues. In P. K. Moser and M. T. McFall (Eds.), *The wisdom of the Christian faith* (pp. 156–172). Cambridge: Cambridge University.

Rumi, J. 1998. *The essential Rumi*. New York, NY: HarperSanFranscisco.

Scharmer, O., and K. Kaufer. 2013. *Leading from the emerging future: From ego-system to eco-system economies*. San Francisco, CA: Berrett-Koehler.

Schlesinger, G. 2014. Attachment, relationship, and love. In M. Lionells et al. (Eds.) *Handbook of interpersonal psychoanalysis* (pp. 63–77). New York, NY: Routledge.

Seppala, E., and J. Moeller. 2018. 1 in 5 employees is highly engaged and at risk of burnout. *Harvard Business Review* (February 2). Retrieved from https://hbr.org/2018/02/1-in-5-highly-engaged-employees-is-at-risk.

Shaver, P. R., and C. Hazan. 1988. A biased overview of the study of love. *Journal of Social and Personal Relationships* 5: 473–501.

Sheridan, R. 2015. *Joy, Inc.: How we built a workplace people love*. New York, NY: Portfolio.

SHINE. 2020. Well-being through work. *Website for the Sustainability and Health Initiative for NetPositive Enterprise at the Harvard T.H. Chan School of Public Health*. Retrieved from https://sites.sph.harvard.edu/shine/research/well-being-metrics/.

Silverman, E. J. 2019. Three models of Christian love: Platonic, Aristotelian, and Kantian. In A. M. Martin (Ed.), *The Routledge handbook of love in philosophy* (pp. 409–421). New York, NY: Routledge.

Sisodia, R., and M. J. Gelb. 2019. *The healing organization: Awakening the conscience of business to help save the world*. New York, NY: HarperCollins Leadership.

Sorokin, P. A. [1954] 2002. *The ways and power of love: Types, factors, and techniques of moral transformation*. Philadelphia, PA: Templeton Press.

Stump, E. 2006. Love, by all accounts. *Proceedings and Addresses of the American Philosophical Association* 80: 25–43.

Sullivan, H. S. 1947. *Conceptions of modern psychiatry*. New York, NY: Norton (Original work published in 1940).

Templeton, J. 1999. *Agape love: A tradition in eight world religions*. Philadelphia, PA: Templeton Foundation.

Travers, J. A. 1991. A grammar of love. *Journal of Couples Therapy* 2(3): 25–27.

Trungpa, C. 2003. *Cutting through spiritual materialism*. Boston, MA: Shambhala (Original work published in 1973).

Trzeciak, S., and A. Mazzarelli. 2019. *Compassionomics: The revolutionary scientific evidence that caring makes a difference*. Pensacola, FL: Studer Group.

Vallerand, R. J. 2008. On the psychology of passion: In search of what makes people's lives most worth living. *Canadian Psychology* 49(1): 1–13.

VanderWeele, T. J. 2017. On the promotion of human flourishing. *Proceedings of the National Academy of Sciences* 31: 8148–8156.

VanderWeele, T. J. 2019. Measures of community well-being: A template. *International Journal of Community Well-Being* 2: 253–275.

VanderWeele, T. J., K. N. Long, and M. J. Balboni. 2021. Tradition-specific measures of spiritual well-being. In M. T. Lee, Laura D. Kubzansky, and T.J. VanderWeele (Eds.), *Measuring well-being: Interdisciplinary perspectives from the social sciences and the humanities*. New York, NY: Oxford University.

Vanier, J. 1992. *From brokenness to community*. New York, NY: Paulist.

Von Kimakowitz, E., M. Pirson, H. Spitzeck, C. Dierksmeier, and W. Amann. 2010. Introducing this book and humanistic management. In E. Von Kimakowitz et al. (Eds.), *Humanistic management in practice* (pp. 1–12). New York, NY: Palgrave Macmillan.

Wadell, P. 2008. *The primacy of love: An introduction to the ethics of Thomas Aquinas*. Eugene, OR: Wipf & Stock.

Wahl, D. C. 2005. "Zarte Empirie": Goethean science as a way of knowing. *Janus Head* 8: 58–76.

Well-Being in the Nation Network. 2019. *Theory of change and action plan: What does it take to secure legacies of intergenerational well-being for all?* Retrieved from https://winnetwork.org/about/win theory of change/.

Whyte, D. 2015. *Consolations: The solace, nourishment, and underlying meaning of everyday words*. Langley, WA: Many Rivers.

Wikipedia. 2020. *Love*. Retrieved from https://en.wikipedia.org/wiki/Love.

Willett, W., J. Rockström, B. Loken, M. Springmann, T. Lang, S. Vermeulen, et al. 2019. Food in the Anthropocene: the EAT–Lancet Commission on healthy diets from sustainable food systems. *The Lancet* 393: 447–492.

Wood, J. T. 2001. The normalization of violence in heterosexual romantic relationships: Women's narratives of love and violence. *Journal of Social and Personal Relationships* 18: 239–261.

Yeung, K. T. 2005. What does love mean? Exploring network culture in two network settings. *Social Forces* 84: 391–420.

Zaillian, S. 1990. *Schindler's list. Screenplay, first revision*. Retrieved from: www.un-official.com/The_Daily_Script/slist.doc.

2 Love and Organizational Models

How to Interpret Forms of Love within Companies

Roberta Sferrazzo and Renato Ruffini

Introduction

What binds people together in a social context and allows them to live in harmony within organizations? In this work, we assume that there are three fundamental bonding elements in a specific social or organizational context: (a) individual interests, which can be interpreted in utilitarian terms; (b) affective and emotional relationships, which involve companionate love and can be interpreted in psychological terms (Barsade and O'Neill, 2014); and (c) managerial tools, which are oriented toward the achievement of common aims. All of these elements play a fundamental role in the cohesion, functionality, and elasticity of organizations.

Normally, organizations are analyzed by economists, who think that their relational foundations are based on opportunistic behaviors, on individual interests understood in a utilitarian sense, on limited information, and on "conditioned reciprocity" and mistrust (Bruni, 2008). Likewise, many management studies and practices are based on applying a relational structure within organizations, such as by developing control and incentive systems. These systems are thought by managers as instruments of alignment in a logic of agency; however, in a totally instrumental and manipulative manner, they also invoke positive feelings of worker participation and empowerment (Sitkin et al., 2010).

In practice, although organizations cannot be based on suspicion and distrust, it is precisely on these latter parameters that theories, methodologies, and instrumentations for most economic and managerial analyses have been built. Consequently, this logic orients the concrete behaviors of the agents who work day after day in firms. Much more rarely, the affective and relational elements of the organizational actions between people on the basis of their love relationships are analyzed. These elements bind people together in an organizational context based on both immaterial elements and gratuitous relationships (Buscaglia, 1982).

We blend our definition of love from psychologists who have studied companionate love, defining it as feelings of affection, compassion, caring, and tenderness for others, which can be considered necessary for all human beings (Walster and Walster, 1978; Reis and Aron, 2008).

DOI: 10.4324/9781003254034-3

Companionate love is not based on passion but arises from connections developed with other people and is defined as the "affection we feel for those with whom our lives are deeply intertwined" (Berscheid and Walster, 1978, p. 177).

In our analysis, we will use the classic forms of love already addressed in managerial and organizational studies: eros, philia, and agape (Tasselli, 2018). At first glance, this topic may seem irrelevant for organizational aims. Indeed, love is considered unscientific by definition, and scientists from all disciplines are careful not to examine it. As such, there are few organizational studies focused on the subject of love; as Tasselli claimed, "love is avoided because it calls for a full expression of the self, something conflicting with the normative authority of organizations" (2018, p.1074). Even Barsade and O'Neill emphasized that "love is a word rarely found in the modern organization literature" (p. 552).

Nevertheless, we believe that it is useful to review organizations based on the three forms of love (eros, philia, and agape), examining their characteristics to see how they relate to organizational models. In fact, a different way of interpreting organizations may even lead to a critical rereading of the logic of organizational incentives. Indeed, the incentive system is unable to measure elements, such as imagination, honesty, dedication, and effort of workers, and often causes distorted and negative motivational effects (Sferrazzo, 2019).

In brief, in this chapter, we ponder what is the best logic to appreciate the real value of work within organizations, knowing well that, in production systems, the real significance of people's work risks to not be properly recognized. Moved by this puzzle, we describe organizations and their evolution from a love point of view, analyzing them according to the logic of love. Then, we try to understand how different forms of affectivity generate distinctive structural models in the organizational context. Finally, we provide some practical implications related to the recognition of different forms of love within companies and suggest some future research prospects.

Three Forms of Love: Philia, Eros, and Agape

Human collective entities, such as families or several organizations, are held together by pragmatic reasons, such as supporting each other and benefitting from various resources to better achieve a common economic, military, or social goal; this creates a critical mass for organizations' continuation and increases their symbolic power so that they can establish and sustain relationships with other entities. However, this opportunistic form of cohesion is insufficient to maintain the aggregation of the organization under pressure caused by external events, governance changes, or due to the unpredictability of individual drivers. In reference to this matter, Benedetto Gui (1987) introduced in economic literature the concept of "relational goods," to highlight the importance of relationality between people. Recalling Gui's words, relational goods are "immaterial goods, and yet not services that can be consumed individually, but connected to interpersonal relationships . . . goods that we may call 'relational'" (1987: 37). Generally speaking, a more powerful centripetal tension is needed for group survival and effectiveness, which is here presented as affective and emotional relationships, where the other person is implied beyond each employee's economic or functional role. Next, we will synthetically describe these forms of love and their implications for organizations.

The Philia Form of Love

The term "philia" derives from the Greek and refers to a primordial form of attraction – probably the first one experienced by every human being – toward those who are similar in ways, including gender, race, age, language, dress code, and fundamental decisions and opinions at the highest possible level and abstraction, such as visions of the world. This form of unifying driver is rather regressive and typical of children. For instance, boys with boys, girls with girls, is a common criterion for gathering at school to the extent that the other gender specimen can appear as a "monster."

This form of love is as reassuring as any form of shared similarity. Moreover, philia creates a sense of belonging and endogenous authorization; we are not alone in our personal characteristics, at least as far as some crucial ones are concerned. Philia is regressive because individuals seem to increasingly analyze people or the group in terms of self-references. Philia needs the exclusion or modification of the different person and can produce the well-known group think syndrome (Janis, 1982). Through this syndrome, consensus creates a sort of blindness toward the external world (and sometimes even toward the internal one). Although humankind would not continue to exist if philia was the only aggregation factor, it is a necessary growth stage focused on identity constitution.

The Eros Form of Love

The second form of love and centripetal force is eros (i.e., the tension toward diversity) (Bataille, 1986). It is a more evolved form of encountering with the other than philia, driven by the attraction for that which is not us and which cannot become ours because it would threaten our identity. It helps in our discovery of the other and is a chance to overcome our individual limits.

The erotic other, rather than enhancing the power of quantity, as philia does (by saying, e.g., that we are more than them), creates a quantum leap, shifting planes, introducing a change in performance quality, leading to a generative event. Let us consider the example of a male–female couple, which becomes able to generate when acting together. Eros does not allow integration, as philia does, as the other plays an essential and unique role in performance without mutual assimilation. After the generative act, the man and the woman remain as differentiated as they were at the start (Soble, 1998).

Erotic love is quite opportunistic. Every human family likely starts with an erotic interest; sometimes, it only lasts for the time required to fulfill the biological need of reproduction; other times, it eventually decays into fraternal philia; and, in some cases, it lasts a lifetime. Sex is not the only form of eros; being intrigued by the cultural diversity of the other or by his/her personality, story, or social origin is another expression of this aggregating force (Soble, 1998).

Eros needs the determinant contribution of emotions and implies the involvement of the body far more than philia does, even when performed in a symbolic way (Lewis, 2013). People make long and tiring journeys and overcome physical and social barriers when they move toward the erotic other. Unlike mimesis,[1] eros reinforces differences; however, like mimesis, it shifts the focus to both parts, the me and you dipole, becoming a form of couple self-reference.

The performative superiority of eros over philia originates with the maturity it implies. Indeed, children become adolescents, with the relevant impulses and social problems, but they move past their auto-referential vision, whether individual or within the group.

The Agape Form of Love

Agape is a form of love that sometimes appears in family life, where the couple, under the irresistible power of eros, generates children and decides to do whatever possible in order to give them all of their attention and resources, even leading to extreme consequences, such as sacrificing their own lives.

According to Boltanski (1990), agape is more important than philia and eros in love terms and consists of an unconditional gift that does not require any form of reciprocation. However, not all scholars share Boltanski's opinion. For example, Bruni (2008) defined agape as a form of unconditional reciprocity, claiming that its founding interest is the willingness to build fraternity. Consequently, agape includes a reciprocal factor, even if it is unconditional.

In relation to the Christian tradition, agape is the form of love that is closest to the Christian conception of charitas, as that capability of loving beyond eros and beyond philia. In the business ethics field, Melé (2012) connected agape to the love of benevolence, blending it to the Thomistic perspective. In brief, agapic behavior can be conceived of as a relationship established with another individual that is oriented toward the achievement of the common good (Sferrazzo, 2019).

Overall, it seems clear that these three forms of love can affect the organizational context in different ways. Therefore, we describe how these forms of love can contribute to shaping organizational models in further detail below.

Three Organizational Models

Blending Barsade and O'Neill's terms (2014), we have defined love as a basic emotion that is fundamental in the human experience (Reis and Aron, 2008; Walster and Walster, 1978). Going one step further, in business organizations people are influenced "not only by the aim of making profit, but also by emotions, feelings and other irrational elements (Nugent and Abolafia 2006; Simon 1955, 1957, 1987; Thaler 2016)" (Sferrazzo, 2019, p. 2). In the organizational context, the other is a colleague or group of people outside the organization (a stakeholder or a collective subject). In this sense, the organization is a place where emotions are produced, creating an emotional culture of companionate love generated through organizational routines and rituals, as well as, of course, individuals' personal features (Barsade and O'Neil, 2014).

Routines and rituals not only bring people together in their daily work but also orient their thoughts and the performance logic pursued by the organization, determining the culture of companionate love. The functions of an organization are largely determined by recognizable and repeatedly routinized behavior patterns that guide the interdependent actions of multiple actors in the organization (Feldman and Pentland, 2003; Rebora, 2017). Routines are not identified with mere written and formal rules but constitute the most direct elements that inform individuals' behaviors within the organization. As a consequence, they are managerial elements that simultaneously stabilize the organization and allow it to innovate.

Routines are made up of several elements. The first element, the concept (which Pentland and Feldman (2005) defined as ostensive), is the ideal model used by the actors to guide their behavior and evaluate the results of their actions. The second element stems from the performance, which constitutes the concrete manifestation of the action; it is both the fruit of the ideal concept pursued and its evolutionary element within an underlying continuity. The third element is based on people's emotions.

Within this conceptual framework, routines can be described through the dynamic interaction of three components (Rebora, 2017): habit, thought (cognition), and emotion. In brief, routines consist of the technical mastery of a task, which does not necessarily mean repetition but the ability to respond to the stimuli received. Each organization, under the leaders or founders' direction, develops different orientations regarding the concept of love, which influence organizational routines and, in particular, affect the performance and emotional sphere of the company.

Another factor that deeply influences the emotional culture of an organization is ritual. Rituals are able to suspend the analytical modality of conceiving reality and foster a new mood that is related to a sense of belonging to reality and to emotionality (Rappaport, 1999). For instance, rituals associated with sports, health, and work can be very emotional and reinforce a sense of community among practitioners. This clearly emerges in the organizational context, in which rituals serve as emotional anchors for social solidarity (Islam and Zyphur, 2009), engendering a flourishing environment for collective values and group stability (Durkheim, 1961; Turner, 1991).

Several authors analyzed the emotional aspect of rituals, focusing on ritual interactions (Collins, 2004; Durkheim, 1961; Goffman, 1967). In their works, they shed light on the creation of emotional energy among participants through ritual. Indeed, the physical copresence of people, mutual attention, and the synchronization of bodies help foster group solidarity and shared symbols through the sharing of emotional energy (Collins, 2004). This aspect is magnified within companies, inasmuch as the intensive management of rituals and ceremonies could become critical in relation to the rituals' emotional intensity (Islam and Zyphur, 2009).

Moved by this puzzle, we hypothesize that, if the concept of routine is oriented toward affirming the identity of the organization, people's emotional feelings – implicit in routines and reinforced by rituals – would tend to focus on reinforcing the philia logic. For instance, companies with strong historical identities, organizations with specific ideal motives or unique missions, and firms that base their strategies on specific or unique products would probably create emotional ties by emphasizing elements of equality. Meanwhile, companies that focus on performance, creativity, and competitive capacity in their production would probably use the logic of eros. The latter group is consistent with some routine company practices, according to which the mutual satisfaction of actors is sought, and collaboration is manifested through diversity and competition among workers. This may be the case, for example, in a consulting company that orients its routines toward maximum customer satisfaction, putting the workers in the position of developing some sort of competitive collaboration between them, which is manifested in providing the best services to the customer. This can even be the case in a creative company, which produces something that makes its clients feel good. Finally, if the meaning given to routines is oriented toward a dimension of excess and gratuitousness, in which the focus is on well-done work and quality performance and understood as a gift to others, the emotional elements will be oriented toward agapic love.

At first glance, these orientations depend on directions provided by the founder of the organization or by the leadership styles adopted, but instead they are always consolidated and transformed by the micro-organizational dynamics of routines and rituals. Of course, one type of orientation rather than another should be considered the prevailing trend line. A company with an eros-based culture will inevitably encounter other forms of love, for example, when it wants to highlight its identity (following the logic of philia) or improve products in a responsibility and general service logic (following the logic of agape).

On the basis of these general observations, it is possible to develop profiles of three types of companies related to the culture of companionate love that develops within them. In practical terms, orienting toward a culture of companionate love through one of the three forms of love shifts the relationships within organizations based on feelings of affection, compassion, caring, and tenderness toward others.

The Philia-Based Culture

In the case of the philia-based culture, working procedures tend to focus on the enhancement of all elements that emphasize identity and belonging. Indeed, the dominant value is placed upon belonging to the community, relationships are oriented toward a principle of full collaboration supported by hierarchical logic, and remuneration recognition is oriented toward a substantial and intense form of equality as a good approximation of equity.

The philia factor is a frequent occurrence in many organizations, typically those structured into divisions and inspired by autonomy. Within these companies, for example, Division X ignores Division Y's needs and results even though they are both part of the same company. The members of one division could even be happy for a competing division's lower performance if its internal affiliations are benefitted and reinforced. Moreover, it is possible for a member of Y to move to X through a prescribed procedure, such as an affiliation process (Kohlrieser and Forehand, 2006).

The virtuous side of philia-based organizations is that they activate a rite of passage to evolve toward more advanced forms of aggregating forces. In the organizational context, this passage happens, for instance, when a team welcomes a new member. However, the major problem, as we mentioned above, is when affiliation becomes the main and only reason for remaining in or existing as a group because creative potential and attitude of change are inhibited. Furthermore, relationships among similar people produce and enhance the *mimesis syndrome* (Girard, 1989). This means that, in becoming increasingly similar, more and more emphasis is placed on the philia relationship, and the group goals fade into the background. Perhaps, this phenomenon is the most serious consequence of the continued practice of this form of love.

In summary, we argue that philia occurs very frequently in most companies. Indeed, many managers tend to recruit their collaborators, assistants, and replacements according to a similarity criterion (Tulshyan, 2019). This intuitive attitude justifies the important role of the human resources department, which can row against the stream, adopting or suggesting evaluation criteria to managers based on factors other than similarity between candidates and their superiors.

The Eros-Based Culture

In the eros-based culture, the connotative value of routines is oriented toward performance, which is understood as individual or group satisfaction in obtaining desired results in the best way. The internal operating logic tends to be that of the market where a silent advantage is generated through forms of collaboration and competition between people, who reach the target goal together. In this context, a company culture based on eros tends to enhance its ability to be both performance-based and collaborative. Therefore, the logic of remuneration recognition will be strongly oriented toward merit and the recognition of individual performance.

In eros-based companies, external people should be welcomed and even sought. Pioneering and exploring attitudes should be fostered, the need for assimilation and inclusion should be dramatically reduced, and the spirit of diversity acceptance should be widespread. Attraction and diversity are the ideal *mélange* for generational creativity. Silicon Valley companies are probably the most evident examples – but not the only examples – of the economic fertility of eros-based companies.

Although it appears very productive and socially convenient, the erotic mechanism is a form of selfishness and finishes when the other is no longer erotic; however, when the mystery of the difference is unveiled, and the osmotic membrane among people lets the difference mix and merge, philia returns. This phenomenon could risk engendering a sort of organizational boredom, which is similar to what happens within some couples in their personal lives. The panacea seems to be a continuous search for the exotic other; therefore, people look elsewhere for diverse attractions, looking at the new and for the new. Again, this could jeopardize organizational performance. Nevertheless, this form of aggregation force is most commonly appropriated by economically motivated organizations if they want to be creative and generative.

Some unnecessary organizational changes could be ascribed to the need to recreate the original eros within companies. However, perhaps the most negative aspect of eros as an aggregating force is that, under its effect, people or groups tend to stabilize their complementary roles. This empowers some aspects of a person but weakens him/her as far as the role performed by the other is concerned, provoking the symbiosis syndrome (Stewart and Joines, 1987). A permanent symbiosis, although appearing functional, always represents an impoverishment of the overall competences of each member. For example, if a creative person works well with a very well-organized colleague (a complementary configuration), each member will be more and more what he/she is and less and less what the other is. To counterbalance this erotic effect and avoid this symbiosis, organizations often rotate personnel.

The Agape-Based Culture

Finally, in the agape-based culture, the connotations of routines are oriented toward gratuitousness in the sense that workers are guided by an autotelic logic. This means that, in carrying out work activities, people are not concerned with the advantages brought to them by what is produced but try to do their best with respect to the need to be satisfied and also think of others' well-being. From the relational point of view, an agape-based orientation consists of the overall sharing of experience with others inside and outside the organizational boundaries. In this framework, the logic of remuneration recognition also follows the logic of sharing by directing the reward system toward forms of participation in the distribution of the value produced.

Agape, or the spirit of free donation, is often performed by organizations (Grant, 2013); non-profit groups devote some of their time, money, and professional resources to help, support, and sometimes save other people or entities as acts of donation. This donation is autotelic, which means that it is an end in itself. Agape is not the well-advertised support to social causes in the people's curriculum vitae or in the companies' values chart; although quite recommendable, this is not agape but strategy or effective marketing. Conversely, agape is not strategic; the purpose is the donation itself. The less that is known, the more it is agapic. An agapic act is indifferent to any monetary or social recognition, as the result is so satisfying that the external world has no role in its compensation. A person or group who practices agapic behaviors is acting beyond any form of obligation, convenience, interest, or need for visibility (Sferrazzo, 2019).

Coming to a more pragmatic perspective, the power of agape is evident; its exercise brings energy to the person who practices it. In groups, this is magnified, contributing to the stability of the group itself, going beyond unstable or temporary internal unifying forces. Agape helps to exit self-reference, justifying the group with exogenous motivation, which does not depend on physical events. Let us consider the example of a religious fraternity, which gathers most days to pray for people with severe illnesses. This religious community will refuse any economic contribution from its spiritually treated patients, even a chocolate box, since even the slightest form of economic or symbolic recognition will very quickly undermine the group's integrity.

We summarize the three models in Table 2.1. This is obviously an initial methodological schematization that needs empirical verification. The passage from the individual experience, typical of affective relationships, to the organizational dimension is very complex to trace, but the existence of a culture of companionate love (Barsade and O'Neill, 2014) allows us to affirm that the phenomenon of affective ties in the organizational context significantly influences the organization. We claim, indeed, that cultural love codes contribute to the overall orientation toward

Table 2.1 Organizational Models Based on Love Forms

Forms of love in organizational models	Philia-based organizational model	Eros-based organizational model	Agape-based organizational model
Concepts of routine	Identity	Performance	Gratuitousness
Types of internal relationships	Collaboration	Competition and collaboration	Sharing
Company values	Community (We)	Individual (I)	Others (All)
Organizational logic	Hierarchical orientation	Market orientation	Common good orientation
Remuneration system	Emphasis on remuneration equality	Emphasis on variable remuneration, incentives, and meritocracy	Zero focus on a remuneration system and orientation toward participative logics

organizational performance among the people who are internally and externally related to the organization.

Implications of Forms of Love for Organizational Spirituality

The concept of love has been explored in detail in spirituality literature within the organizational context (Bruni, 2017; Fry, 2003; Fry et al., 2017; Laszlo, 2017). Indeed, spirituality literature has introduced concepts and practices aiming to foster people's human flourishing within companies (Melé and Cantón, 2014). Through spirituality, human behaviors can be endowed with a lens at the individual and organizational levels (Grzeda, 2019; Tombaugh, Mayfield and Durand, 2011). Indeed, spirituality – through the concept of transcendence within the work process – infuses human behaviors with feelings of compassion and joy (Laszlo, 2019; Suriyankietkaew and Kantamara, 2019). Moreover, spirituality emphasizes the sacredness of relationships and virtuous behaviors in order to support business values (Grzeda, 2019; Mahmood et al., 2018).

Business ethics and spiritual leadership go hand in hand with organizational spirituality (Balog et al., 2014; Bindlish et al., 2012; Fairholm and Gronau, 2015). Spirituality reinforces the sense of connection with others; this is consistent with most of the world's religions (Puntasen, 2007). Buddhist economic principles, for instance, are associated with pro-social values, as well as the well-being of the whole society (Konecki, 2017; Puntasen, 2007). In this sense, they are oriented toward the promotion of altruistic love (Fry, 2003; Fry et al., 2017) – through generosity or charity – and of acts of loving kindness and compassion (Payutto, 1994, 2000; Puntasen, 2007). These acts are common also to Catholic Western economic thought, especially the notion of charitas.

Given this picture, we argue that the three forms of love described above – eros, philia, and agape – offer advantages that differ in relation to the type of organization in which they operate. Indeed, all three love forms are endowed with positive features, including: (a) the fostering of creativity through eros, (b) the strengthening of fraternal and friendship relationships through philia, and (c) the increasing of spontaneous acts of gratuitousness toward others through agape.

However, we think that the agapic form of love presents some relevant elements that should be particularly promoted within the organizational context. In the next section, we explain why agapic factors deserve particular attention within companies.

The Agapic Driver

Agape is a higher form of love compared to philia and eros (Boltanski, 1990). It is reached as a third stage in personal evolution and is not affected by the self-referencing of philia or the opportunistic and temporary egoism of eros. But, how can agape really be realized within organizations, particularly those of a financial nature? Can companies perform agape with some form of advantage? This seems to be a contradiction in terms, although it is not; not aiming to get a result enables the easier achievement of those results. A well-known example is human fertility; many doctors can cite many cases of married couples obsessed with having children and frustrated by the lack of results. However, not obsessing makes the pregnancy happen. Is there a form of sterility and fertility within organizations?

Observations of companies' behaviors and performance led us to a definite "yes." Agape exists in business, some companies practice it, and the effects are visible. However, the agapic gestures promoted by agape-based organizations are rare and not evident, as agape requires. Let us consider the example of companies where a form of free donation is systematically encouraged by their culture and top management. In these companies, agape takes the form of sharing. This sharing spirit is declared in their values chart, and employees are encouraged to share their know-how, organizational power, and talents with others. Moreover, the organization shares its physical and financial resources, such as in the form of bonuses or company stocks. These practices could generate a non-ordinary sense of community in which the individual is less central compared to the group. In other words, an individually achieved success would appear less meaningful than the overall success of the group. Even a mistake made together would be more acceptable than an individual error. This extended sharing leads to a form of *virtuous reduction of individual responsibility*. Successful ideas, just like incorrect decisions, have no guilty party or hero if they arise from a sharing process; they just happen. "Don't care for results, care for people" should be the Chief Executive Officer's recommendation. This attitude would effectively drive results.

In brief, agape does not involve procedures and precise managerial techniques could paradoxically constitute a source of problems. For instance, punctual performance measurement could lead to very regressive behaviors, such as obsessive accuracy, to calculate the effort provided by the agent. In this way, the internal organizational climate could quickly deteriorate, and personnel problems could emerge, indirectly reducing customer satisfaction. Agape is more focused on intention than visible aspects. For this reason, it is easy to misunderstand its significance. Sometimes, the donation is the non-assumption of a return, while, other times, a lack of return or advantage does not imply an agapic gesture but a frustrating absence of expected reciprocation (Bruni, 2008).

We wonder, in particular, how managers and leaders can adopt an agapic attitude. Surely, a leadership style oriented toward love should shift the focus from manipulation practices to human flourishing within companies (Sferrazzo, 2020). There is also strength in a personal example, which is exercised by a charismatic person or agapic communities. However, agape is rarely introduced as an explicit company value, since this could risk generating a complying attitude, which is not agape. The main problem is that this spirit of gratuitousness has to coexist with performance constraints and process indicators, which cannot be ignored in a company with even economic ends. The magic of agape rests in this very delicate balance between the institutional side of the organization and its charismatic expressions, manifested not only by the visible acts of leaders but also by the scattered spirit of donation for donation's sake.

Final Assumptions and Conclusions

Every organization is endowed with some cultural love codes that contribute to fostering a positive organizational climate. Indeed, an organizational culture based on love emerges, for example, when employees talk about loving or caring for their coworkers (Barsade and O'Neill, 2014). These expressions of companionate love are manifested in all three forms of love – eros, philia, and agape – but become particularly relevant in the agapic one. Agapic love, indeed, includes "workers' generosity, humanity, kindness, compassion, help for others and mercy" (Sferrazzo, 2019). In an extreme synthesis, we can expect that a philia-based company will appreciate an award system, an eros-based company an incentive system, and an agape-based company a system of unconditional reciprocity (Bruni, 2008). However, if that is true, it is necessary to consider the dynamics of relationships, that is, *it is not money that directs relationships, but the type of relationship (the cultural code in place) that modifies the interpretation of money.*

Our analysis about the forms of love within the organizational context sheds light on the fact that the relational element – the affective and emotional one – cannot be undervalued within companies. However, the love factor has never been central in organizational analysis and has not received the attention it deserves in the study of organizations (Tasselli, 2018). Therefore, we think that the future of organizational studies must be oriented toward attributing a major emphasis on the concept of love in all its forms. Several studies have already followed this research path. Indeed, many scholars are trying to reconceptualize management assumptions in different ways (Ghoshal, 2005; Gladwin et al., 1995; Hahn et al., 2010). Some academics have proposed a humanistic management style (Acevedo, 2012; Dierksmeier, 2016; Melé, 2003; Melé and Schlag, 2015; Pirson, 2017; Spitzech, 2011) focused on the promotion of human dignity in management theory. Meanwhile, other scholars have argued that no organization can work exclusively based on contracts and that all organizations need motivation that goes beyond profit and material incentives (Boltanski and Chiapello, 2005; Bruni and Smerilli, 2009; Pirson, 2017).

To continue following this research direction, a further step could be to propose a shift from companies based on traditional technical managerial levers to those based on self-control, equality, liberation, and gifts. The use of an interdisciplinary approach could certainly help achieve this goal, recalling some concepts belonging to other research fields, such as philosophy, sociology, anthropology, and psychology. Moreover, a leadership and managerial revolution is necessary to create a culture of collaboration and sharing to face the challenges of our complex, volatile, and turbulent business environment.

Acknowledgments

We thank all the participants of *Prizes and virtues: An interdisciplinary workshop* (LUMSA University, Rome, April 10–11, 2017) for their useful comments on this working paper. We would especially like to thank Luciano Traquandi, Patrizia Castellucci, and Giorgia Nigri for their contributions to the paper.

Note

1 *Mimesis* is originally a Greek word, derived from the Greek verb *mimeisthai*, which means "to imitate" and which itself comes from mimos, meaning "mime." It has been used in aesthetic or artistic theory to refer to the attempt to imitate or reproduce reality since Plato and Aristotle.

References

Acevedo, A. (2012). Personalist business ethics and humanistic management: Insights from Jacques Maritain. *Journal of Business Ethics* 105(2): 197–219.

Balog, A.M., Baker, L.T. and Walker, A.G. (2014). Religiosity and spirituality in entrepreneurship: A review and research agenda. *Journal of Management, Spirituality & Religion* 11(2): 159–186.

Barsade, S.G. and O'Neill, O.A. (2014). What's love got to do with it? A longitudinal study of the culture of companionate love and employee and client outcomes in a long-term care setting. *Administrative Science Quarterly* 59(4): 551–598.

Bataille, G. (1986). *Erotism: Death and sensuality*. San Francisco, CA: City Light Books.

Berscheid, E. and Walster, E. (1978). *Interpersonal attraction* (2d ed.). Reading, MA: Addison Wesley.

Bindlish, P., Dutt, P. and Pardasani, R. (2012). From growing convergence of spirituality and leadership towards a unified leadership theory. *Journal of Spirituality, Leadership and Management* 6(1): 3–23.

Boltanski, L. (1990). *L'amour et la justice comme compétences*. Paris: Métailié.

Boltanski, L. and Chiapello, E. (2005). The new spirit of capitalism. *International Journal of Politics, Culture, and Society* 18(3–4): 161–188.

Bruni, L. (2008). *Reciprocity, altruism and the civil society. In praise of heterogeneity*. London: Routledge.

Bruni, L. (2017). *La felicità pubblica: Economia civile e political economy a confronto*. Milan: Vita e pensiero.

Bruni, L. and Smerilli, A. (2009). The value of vocation. The crucial role of intrinsically motivated people in values-based organizations. *Review of Social Economy* 67(3): 271–288.

Buscaglia, L.F. (1982). *Living, loving & learning*. Waterville, ME: Thorndike Pr.

Collins, R. (2004). *Interaction ritual chains*. Princeton, NJ: Princeton University Press.

Crisp, R. (Ed.) (2014). *Aristotle: Nicomachean ethics*. Cambridge: Cambridge University Press.

Dierksmeier, C. (2016). *Reframing economic ethics: The philosophical foundations of humanistic management*. Springer.

Durkheim, E. (1961). *The elementary forms of the religious life*. New York, NY: Collier Books.

Fairholm, M.R. and Gronau, T.W. (2015). Spiritual leadership in the work of public administrators. *Journal of Management, Spirituality & Religion* 12(4): 354–373.

Feldman, M. S. and Pentland, B. T. (2003). Reconceptualizing organizational routines as a source of flexibility and change. *Administrative Science Quarterly* 48(1): 94–118.

Fry, L.W. (2003). Toward a theory of spiritual leadership. *The Leadership Quarterly* 14(6): 693–727.

Fry, L.W., Latham, J.R., Clinebell, S.K. and Krahnke, K. (2017). Spiritual leadership as a model for performance excellence: A study of Baldrige award recipients. *Journal of Management, Spirituality & Religion* 14(1): 22–47.

Ghoshal, S. (2005). Bad management theories are destroying good management practices. *Academy of Management Learning and Education* 4(1): 75–91.

Girard, R. (1989). *The Scapegoat*. Baltimore, MD: Johns Hopkins University Press.

Gladwin, T.N., Kennelly, J.J. and Krause, T. (1995). Shifting paradigms for sustainable development: Implications for management theory and research. *Academy of Management Review* 20(4): 874–907.

Goffman, E. (1967). *Interaction ritual: Essays on face-to-face behavior*. Garden City, NY: Anchor Books.

Grant, A.M. (2013). *Give and take: A revolutionary approach to success.* London: Penguin.

Grzeda, M. (2019). Tikkun Olam: Exploring a spiritual path to sustainability. *Journal of Management, Spirituality & Religion* 16(5): 413–427.

Gui, B. (1987). Eléments pour une définition d'"économie communautaire.' *Notes et Documents* 19–20: 32–42.

Hahn, T., Kolk, A. and Winn, M. (2010). A new future for business? Rethinking management theory and business strategy. *Business & Society* 49(3): 385–401.

Islam, G. and Zyphur, M. (2009). Rituals in organizations: A review and expansion of current theory. *Group & Organization Management* 34(1): 114–139.

Janis, I. (1982). *Groupthink: Psychological studies of policy decisions and fiascoes.* Boston, MA: Cengage Learning.

Kohlrieser, G. and Forehand, J.W. (2006). Hostage at the table: How leaders can overcome conflict. *Influence others, and raise performance.* Hoboken, NJ: Jossey-Bass.

Konecki, K.T. (2017). Contemplation for economists. Towards a social economy based on empathy and compassion. *Economics & Sociology* 10(3): 11–24.

Laszlo, C. (2017). *Quantum leadership—A primer.* www.linkedin.com/pulse/quantum-leadership-primer-chris-laszlo/.

Laszlo, C. (2019). Strengthening humanistic management. *Humanistic Management Journal.* https://doi.org/10.1007/s41463-019-00055-9.

Lewis, C. S. (2013). *The allegory of love.* New York: Cambridge University Press.

Mahmood, A., Arshad, M.A., Ahmed, A., Akhtar, S. and Khan, S. (2018). Spiritual intelligence research within human resource development: A thematic review. *Management Research Review* 41(8): 987–1006.

Melé, D. (2003). The challenge of humanistic management. *Journal of Business Ethics* 44(1): 77–88.

Melé, D. (2012). "The Christian notion of Αγάπη (agápē): Towards a more complete view of business ethics." In *Leadership through the classics* (pp. 79–91). Berlin: Springer.

Melé D. and Cantón C.G. (2014). "Action, human flourishing and moral discernment." In G.P. Prastacos, F. Wang, & K. E. Soderquist (Eds.), *Human foundations of management.* IESE Business Collection. London: Palgrave Macmillan.

Melé, D. and Schlag, M. (2015). *Christian humanism in economics and business. In Humanism in economics and business* (pp. 1–10). Dordrecht: Springer.

Payutto, P.A. (1994). *Buddhist economics.* Bangkok: Buddhadhamma Foundation.

Payutto, P.A. (2000). *Buddhist solutions for the twenty first century. Dharma rain: Sources of Buddhist environmentalism* (pp. 170–178). Boston, MA: Shambala.

Pentland, B.T. and Feldman, M.S. (2005). Organizational routines as a unit of analysis. *Industrial and Corporate Change* 14(5): 793–815.

Pirson, M. (2017). *Humanistic management: Protecting dignity and promoting well-being.* Cambridge, UK: Cambridge University Press.

Puntasen, A. (2007). *Why Buddhist economics is needed as a new paradigm for a better understanding of happiness* (Wellness). International Conference on Happiness and Public Policy, Bangkok, July 18–19. Presented at the International Conference on Happiness and Public Policy, Bangkok: Public Policy Development Office under the Office of the Prime Minister of Thailand and UNESCAP.

Rappaport, R. (1999) *Ritual and religion in the making of humanity*. New York, NY: Cambridge University Press.

Rebora, G. (2017). *Scienza dell'organizzazione: il design di strutture, processi e ruoli*. Rome, Italy: Carocci.

Reis, H.R. and Aron, A. (2008). Love: What is it, why does it matter, and how does it operate? *Perspectives on Psychological Science* 3: 80–86.

Sferrazzo, R. (2019). The 'agapic behaviors': Reconciling organizational citizenship behavior with the reward system. *Humanistic Management Journal*, 6: 19–35.

Sferrazzo, R. (2020). *Why love matters for the future of leadership: From manipulation to human flourishing*. Unpublished Doctoral Thesis. LUMSA University.

Sitkin, S.B., Cardinal, L.B. and Bijlsma-Frankema, K.M. (2010). *Introduction and history. Control in organizations: New directions in theory and research*. Cambridge: Cambridge University Press.

Soble, A. (1998). The philosophy of sex and love. *Theological Studies* 59(4): 760.

Spitzeck, H. (2011). An integrated model of humanistic management. *Journal of Business Ethics* 99(1): 51–62.

Stewart, I. and Joines, V. (1987). *TA today*. Nottingham: Lifespace Publishing.

Suriyankietkaew, S. and Kantamara, P. (2019). Business ethics and spirituality for corporate sustainability: A Buddhism perspective. *Journal of Management, Spirituality & Religion* 16(3): 264–289.

Tasselli, S. (2018). Love and organization studies: Moving beyond the perspective of avoidance. *Organization Studies* 40(7): 1073–1088. doi/10.1177/0170840617747924.

Tombaugh, J.R., Mayfield, C. and Durand, R. (2011). Spiritual expression at work: Exploring the active voice of workplace spirituality. *International Journal of Organizational Analysis* 19(2): 146–170.

Tulshyan, R. (2019). How to reduce personal bias when hiring. *Harvard Business Review*, June 28.

Turner, V. (1991). *The ritual process: Structure and anti-structure* (7th ed.). New York, NY: Cornell University Press.

Walster, E. and Walster, G.W. (1978). *A new look at love*. Reading, MA: Addison-Wesley.

3 Organizational Expressions of Love

A Level of System Inquiry

Linda Robson and Duncan Coombe

Introduction

For centuries, outside the business context, we have heard about the power and virtue of love. Love is at the center of poetry, art, music, and religious and spiritual traditions. Psychologists extol love's importance for human flourishing (Fredrickson & Joiner, 2002; Fredrickson, 2013a, 2013b; Maselko et al., 2011) and philosophers explore its depths. Tolstoy asserted that "one can live magnificently in this world if one knows how to work and how to love." Freud said, "love and work… work and love, that's all there is." Tolstoy and Freud align around the need to do both, we agree but advocate taking it a step further – engaging in work and love at the same time.

One could wager that almost all of us have, at some point in time, noticed the centrality of love to their well-being, so why have we heard relatively little about love in the context of work, particularly in scholarly circles? It seems we have been collectively skeptical about the appropriateness of this universal "good" in the place and relationships in which we spend the majority of our waking hours. Others may hold a misconception that if love is allowed in the workplace, the organization will become inefficient and will no longer be able to accomplish business goals.

Over the past few years, momentum to name love as a phenomenon worthy of study has resulted in a new map of the territory of organizing and leadership. We have been part of that effort. In 2014 we submitted a proposal for a professional development workshop at the Academy of Management (AOM) annual conference. Our design invited practitioners and academics interested in exploring more about causes and effects of love in organizational life. We were thrilled that our proposal was accepted and we were equally curious.

AOM conferences have been described, by even the most stalwart members, as stoic events. The rigor, skepticism, and precision that make for good scholarship can sometimes imbue interactions at the gathering itself. Would anyone attend our session? Who would show up for love?

DOI: 10.4324/9781003254034-4

On that humid day, in Philadelphia, aptly 25 scholars and practitioners arrived, curious and eager to share their stories, offer insights, and brainstorm questions for further research about love in organizations. That afternoon was a shift for us and for the Academy – a precedent for love had been set.

In this chapter we will share our perspective of the territory of love and work, based on existing research and what we are learning about love at work from interviews with executives and teams in organizations representing a variety of sectors and industries, as well as our own lived experience in organizations as teachers and consultants.

What is not included in this chapter is apology or doubt. We do not question whether love exists in organizations. We believe that love is innate in any human system. Our inquiry seeks to understand what the expressions of love are, across levels of organizational system, and how we can generate more love. Our research asks simply "how do organizations express love?"

Background

The idea that love is expressed at work has attracted scholars and practitioners alike. We open our survey of existing love and work contributions with that which has been contributed by practitioners. These authors have generously offered insights inspired directly from lived experiences in organizations, as leaders in the midst of change, and in daily life with teams. Practitioners have been among the first to dedicate themselves to the intersection of love and work. Moreover, the authors represented here have each been willing to use the word "love" in their writing and practice, rather than a less provocative synonym. Not too long ago, this was a risky professional step. Some might say it still is.

Love is innate to human systems; therefore, it makes sense to say love is also present in the workplace. We have discovered that it is not just present, but can support organizational engagement and mission. Several notable voices in business speak about the importance of love in their operations. John Mackey of Whole Foods (Mackey & Sisodia, 2013), investor Warren Buffet, and Jean-Claude Biver, chief executive officer (CEO) of Tag Heuer (Naas, 2020) have each spoken and written about the importance of love to their organizations' thriving.

The motto of Dr. Kazua Inamori, chairman of Japan Airlines and founder of Kyocera, is "Respect the divine and love people." Herb Kelleher of Southwest Airlines, whose stock symbol is LUV, said "A company is stronger if it is bound by love rather than fear." Jack Ma, founder of Alibaba referenced the importance of possessing a strong "love quotient" (LQ) for business success at the 2018 Davos World Economic Forum. Pete Carroll, head coach of the championship NFL team the Seattle Seahawks agrees, saying the role of Seahawks organization is to take care of the whole person, and speaking about the players, he said,

"We love these guys up and figure out what they could possibly become and help them get there."

Some executives have opted to write about their experiences with love at work. Sanders (2002), Hope-Bryant (2009), Cox (2020), and Manby (2012) give examples from their experiences in leading and influencing organizations, and how they each have made the connection between love and successfully achieving organizational outcomes. Sanders (2002) advises leaders to become "lovecats," leveraging their personal "intangibles" to support the success of others, arguing for a generosity in sharing one's compassion, knowledge, and social and professional networks. The message is through supporting the success of others, one's own success and the meaning found through work are enhanced.

Hope-Bryant (2009) makes the case that much of the economy and politics are motivated by fear. Hope-Bryant argues for tapping into the power of love as an antidote and far more effective route to success. Manby (2012), CEO of Herschen Family Entertainment Corporation, cites decades of experience leading organizations like Sea World and focuses attention on servant leadership as an expression of love at work.

Most recently, Cox (2020) encourages consideration of our organizational culture and behavior, and a quality check of customer relationships as entry points for increasing love-based engagement that wins over customer experience and allegiance to a brand. Cox differentiates his message from Roberts' (2005) ideas of love-marks and creating a love-affair with a brand because Cox challenges firms not only to get their customers in love with the brand, but that the organization must also feel love for the customer. Without the latter, it is a love-washed ad campaign.

Turning to academia, more scholarship is focused on love as the central concept, although research on synonyms of love is still more commonplace. Let's begin with the contributions who have specifically named love. Kouzes and Posner were among the first management scholars (1992: 2007) to connect excellence in leadership with those managers who are able and willing to connect their hearts to their work and teams, not just connecting via logic. They name love as the secret to life and the answer to great leadership.

Fry (2003) and Fry and Kriger (2009) include altruistic love in their dimensions of spiritual leadership. These authors define love as a sense of wholeness, harmony, and well-being produced through care, concern, and appreciation for both self and others (Fry, 2003, p. 712).

Coombe (2011) and Robson (2015) proposed that corporate social responsibility and organizational sustainability programs are two examples of how love is expressed by organizations. Both scholars point to the parallels between sustainability definitions and definitions of love, noting that both come about only after shifts from limited self-interest to a recognition of connectedness, mutuality, and interest in the well-being of others. Both sustainability, particularly when defined as flourishing (Laszlo & Brown, 2014), and love are reflections of a consciousness of interdependence and connectedness. As such, corporate social responsibility and sustainability may be some of the clearest expressions of love coming from the organizational level of system (Robson, 2015).

Coombe (2010) in a quantitative study showed a positive relationship between companionate love (Sprecher & Regan,1998) and the outcomes of follower job satisfaction and follower psychological safety. Barsade and O'Neill (2014) found a culture of companionate love in a hospital-care setting, positively related to employee satisfaction and teamwork, and negatively related to employee absenteeism and emotional exhaustion. Exploring the language of teams, Robson (2015) found high-performing work teams not only had higher ratios of positive to negative language compared to moderate and lower performing teams, but that love was one of the themes of their language.

Over the span of Fredrickson's contributions to the field of positive psychology, her work has converged on love. An early study (1998) found the power of positive emotion and positive affect fostered higher performance among individuals and teams. Shared positive emotion and affect was associated with team members and individuals who engage in "broaden and build thinking."

Fredrickson (2002) went on to produce an entire book on the topic of love, describing how ubiquitous love is, in organizational contexts and beyond. Fredrickson refers to love as *the* supreme emotion. Rather than being a synonym for care, connectedness, joy, or gratitude, it overarches these because each can be turned into an instance of love if experienced in close connection with another.

Love is supreme in an additional way. Referencing her own earlier research (2001) on positive emotions, Fredrickson writes, while all positive emotions provide benefits, like broadening your mindset and building your resourcefulness, the benefits of love run far deeper. As the supreme emotion, love makes us come most fully alive and feel most fully human. It is, she asserts, perhaps the most essential emotional experience for thriving and health (2013b).

Turning our attention to studies using synonyms for love, we have been specifically motivated by work coming from the domain of positive psychology and positive organizational development. Love is easily associated with the domains of high-quality connections (Dutton & Heaphy, 2003) and positive relationships at work (Dutton & Ragins, 2007). Glavas and Piderit (2009) found a positive relationship between corporate citizenship and high-quality connections and therefore there should be a positive association between love and corporate citizenship.

Cooperrider and Fry (2013) offer the concept of mirror flourishing – a positive, echo-effect between individuals and their organizations, when either is engaged in pro-social or pro-environmental initiatives. They describe mirror flourishing as a blurring of boundaries between "in here" and "out there," which brings positive valuing to scale, adding color and increased awareness to interactions and circumstances, resulting in a generative, two-way ripple effect.

Definitions of Love

Some may not be comfortable advocating for love in the workplace. The word "love" evokes many different meanings and images. The evocative and provocative nature of love means that defining it, especially for organizational contexts, is critical as an entry point for shifts in awareness and behavior. As we survey literature on love and organizations, we see themes exist in the variety of existing definitions.

May's oft quoted remark, the opposite of love is not hate, but apathy (1969) frames what love is, by way of what it is not. He argued for the importance of engagement with regard to love, encouraging one to think about love not only in the abstract, but also to think of love as an action, what he called will. He asserts that will makes love active in the world and is necessary to complete, or actualize love.

Maturana, a biologist who extended his writings to organizational contexts, and Maturana and Bunnell (2009) define love as the collection of relational behaviors through which another person, being, or thing arises as a legitimate other in coexistence with oneself.

Post, an altruistic love scholar, focuses on the positive, unintended consequences of loving action, describing how when we do good for others, we thrive as a result, with improved well-being, physical health, social connections, and longevity (Post, 2005). Post and colleagues (2002) describe altruism as one of the purest acts of brotherly love, predicated on "the realization that another person means as much or more to me than myself" (Post, 2003, p. 3).

Taking the above definitions together, themes emerge, about holding another as worthy or as legitimate as oneself and about the centrality of action in bringing love to life. Beyond these definitions, when we are working with executives, we find ourselves utilizing three further definitions, which are particularly useful in organizational settings.

The first definition is Sorokin's (1954) description of dimensions of love, which works particularly well when coaching leaders and teams, because the five dimensions Sorokin presents offer opportunities for experimentation and developing self-awareness. Sorokin, a social psychologist, conceived of love as multi-dimensional, including five qualities: intensity, extensity, duration, purity, and adequacy (1954).

Intensity is the depth to which love is experienced and felt. Extensity is about how far-reaching one feels love, for example, "do I love one person at work or does my love extend to several colleagues in my department?" Duration speaks about the frequency love is experienced and expressed, for example, "is it a one-time expression or occurring consistently over time?" Purity is the quality of love expressed and adequacy is about the efficacy of my expression of love, for example, "does it impact the other person as I have intended?"

The second definition comes from the phenomenological perspective of Gestalt organizational and systems development, where love is described as the most powerful force (Carter, 2019). Love, as a behavior, is the acceptance of the whole, meaning past, present, and future, as well as the accepting of all of the parts of the whole (Hopper-Carter, 2004; Carter, 2019). Tolstoy captures this intent when he wrote, "When you love someone, you love the person as they are, and not as you'd like them to be." The implication of full acceptance does not equate with agreement, rather it is the complete "seeing" of what is, and accepting all the parts (preferred or otherwise), which make up the whole of the system.

The third definition we turn to comes from Fredrickson (2013b). She provides a broadly accessible meaning, which everyone has probably experienced at some point: love is the micro-moment of warmth and connection shared with another living being.

Our Inquiry

The work cited above, and that of others, has generated momentum to name love as a phenomenon worthy of study. Collectively we are identifying the terrain of love in organizations. What has been less explored is love's presence and form at multiple levels of system in organizational contexts. The remainder of this chapter will describe our findings from interviews across sectors and industries, about how love is expressed, across levels of organizational systems.

The purpose of our work has been about collecting and amplifying examples of love occurring across a variety of levels of organizational system. We have interviewed leaders and tracked stories in the media in organizations across a wide swath of industries in the US, the UK, Europe, and South Africa, including professional sports, manufacturing, retail, financial services, and information technology (IT).

In the following sections, we present narratives of love at work, based on our research, organized by the level of system at which the phenomenon occurs. When we refer to levels of system in an organization, we begin at the largest scale with the external environment level of system, which includes the larger context of the organization, such as the community a firm is located in, their industry, society, or the planet more generally. We narrow our scope to the organizational level of system and further focus on teams within the organization. From teams, the next level of system is interpersonal, meaning any interactions between two people, and finally, the intrapsychic level of system, made up of the thoughts, feelings, and interior life of an individual (Carter, 2019). We provide at least one illustrative story for each level of system.

We begin with the external environment level of system. Organizations, like Patagonia and Tom's Shoes, come to mind easily when we think of businesses that are working for the greater good. Another noteworthy story comes from Seattle-based retailer glassybaby.

External Environment Level of System: glassybaby

Lee Rhodes, founder of manufacturer and retailer glassybaby, had been undergoing radiation and chemotherapy for cancer. The intensity of these treatment modalities represents great levelers and produces friendships among those experiencing it. Rhodes noticed gaps in treatment cycle attendance by fellow patients she had gotten to know. She learned some didn't come to a treatment session because they couldn't afford parking in the medical center garage, others had difficulty finding child care from a friend or family member and could not afford to pay for a babysitter. She noticed others sat through their lengthy treatments and did not bring food in with them. Rhodes recognized a gap between what health insurance covers and what support families provide. She observed many people were unable to cover the basics of life while they were sick and this inhibited their ability to heal (Stone, 2014; Adams, 2017).

In 1998, she founded glassybaby in her garage, producing handblown glass votives with the intent of addressing the unmet need for support for daily practicalities built into the sale of each votive. Ten percent of every sale of a glassybaby is donated, resulting in over $2 million of support so far. This story stands out to us because this is not a case of bolt-on corporate philanthropy, but rather an act of love baked in to the founding purpose and mission of the company (Stone, 2014; Adams, 2017).

Organizational Level of System: Schuberg Philis

One case of love expressed at the organizational level is a story of love being revealed and how this influenced changes in organizational design and strategy. Dutch IT solutions developer, Schuberg Philis, discovered how love drives their success during a company Appreciative Inquiry (AI) summit. "The feeling I remember most from our summit is the absolute feeling of connectedness," said employee Pim Berger (McQuaid, 2019). What emerged from the AI summit process went beyond good citizenship and supporting the organization's flourishing.

Children of the company's employees also participated in the event, and were asked to describe what their parents did for the firm, and why they were proud of their parents. From this powerful intervention, the summit tone shifted, and a new clarity emerged: Schuberg Philis is a company "based on love." Letting love permeate from the core to the strategy and daily tactics of the organization meant making some changes. Employee recruitment added dimensions, lunch at Schuberg Philis includes employees and their children, and perhaps most radically for an IT solutions developer, the firm adopted a radical, 100% open-source policy (McQuaid, 2019).

Becoming a company based on love creates cultural shifts and, in Schuberg Philis' case, also has implications for organizational strategy and design. Instead of putting structure or policies into place, one question guides action and strategy: Is this the right thing to do for the children who depend on me? Schuberg Philis is a no-manager organization, giving employees the freedom to assemble teams based on chemistry and strengths, and initiate projects based on their passions. Being a company based on love means that Schuberg Philis has the "desire for each person to flourish. We are all equal and unique. We see the whole human being- as a colleague, as a parent, and as a friend. When we connect at a deeper level, wonderful things become possible" (McQuaid, 2019).

Team Level of System: Campus Sustainability

At the team level in this scenario, love shows up through the language teams use to describe their work, and how they talk to and about each other (Robson, 2015). We studied campus sustainability teams across ten institutions of higher education. The sustainability programs had been rated by a third-party environmental report card, which gave each college and university a letter grade for the success of their campus and community efforts.

Our engagement with these programs began with a desire to study the language of sustainability and how language would differ from higher to lower rated programs. Based on the work of Gottman (1994; 1999) and Fredrickson (2013b), we hypothesized that more positive and hopeful language would be associated with the more successful teams in the study. Through analysis of team rhetoric, we indeed discovered that the high-performing sustainability programs had a 4:1 ratio of positive to negative language, which was four times what was found for the lower ranked teams in our sample. What we had not anticipated was finding clear themes of love in interviews and team meetings. These themes were most prevalent among the high-performing teams.

Sustainability leaders described how their work became an experience of a greater calling and "a gesture of love." They referred to taking care of the "whole," be that the whole institutional system, the community, or the planet and work that is greater than just their campus (Robson, 2015). One sustainability leader said, "Sustainability goes both deep and wide, I love the wide, I love seeing interconnections and supporting where they could be. [Our work] is all about being interconnected."

Individuals also described experiences in which the boundaries between self and other blurred and self-interest became less meaningful and less motivating than acting for the greater good. Diminished boundaries were reported between colleagues, between the sustainability team and the rest of campus, between the campus and the surrounding community, and between one's own campus and other colleges and universities also on a sustainability journey. "There's no more us and them," explained one participant (Robson, 2015).

Throughout the stories about their work, participants in the study shared references to shared micro-moments of positivity (Fredrickson, 2013b) and agape or a sense of brotherly love for fellow team members and others. "I think some… aspects of sustainability actually strike senti-mental cords with people. They go, 'yeah, yeah I can do that, doing good for the people around here just feels good" (Robson, 2015).

Interpersonal Level of System: Secure Base Leadership

In a mixed method study, Coombe (2010) showed that love is posi-tively correlated to desired leader-follower outcomes of follower psycho-logical safety and follower job satisfaction. The concept of Secure Base Leadership that embodies elements of love such as acceptance, affirm-ation, care and support was shown to produce positive outcomes for followers. Secure Base Leadership posits that for sustainable growth and development, an individual first needs to feel safe and supported before they can confidently take on risk and challenge. This safety and support is well understood as love in childhood development and this research showed that the same mechanism applies in adult leadership. The core process of a leader providing safety, support, and acceptance – essential for risk taking activities such as innovation – is akin to love.

Intrapsychic Level of System: Jean Claude Biver, CEO of Tag Heuer

In an interview with Forbes, Jean Claude Biver, CEO of Tag Heuer said,

> My guiding light is called love. The Beatles said 'All you need is love.' Love is not just about two people; love is 360 degrees. If you have passion, you have love. And if you have love, you have respect because that is an expression of love. This means I respect myself, I respect my people, and I respect my competition and my suppliers. [To] forgive is an act of love. You need to be able to forgive mistakes, because we all make mistakes and they are a learning process.
>
> (Naas, 2020)

Themes and Reflections

Several themes from our inquiry are worth noting, representing oppor-tunities for practitioners and further research. First, not everyone we interviewed used the word "love" in their organizations. Some interviewees described themselves as being driven by love, yet opted not to use the word in the workplace. Instead, they let their actions, policies, products, and services communicate for them. In the early stages of our interviews we concluded that it was not worth the angst to get caught up in definitional issues around love. We found moving stories of love from people who used other words. One CEO only uses words like "compassion" rather than "love," although he deeply resonates with the underlying idea.

A second observation is about love's natural habitat. While love may seem more associated with some professional roles than others, the opportunity to express love is not based just on what you do for work, it is more about how you do it. In our inquiry, we have noticed love is more easily spoken about in founder-led organizations, family businesses, or clan-like organizations such as sports teams and the military. Why is this? Our understanding is that love requires high levels of personalization – it is the opposite of the detached corporate automaton. Does that mean love cannot be expressed in large organizations? Not all, but it may be worth experimenting in spheres of influence like your team, and work on Sorokin's notion of extensivity (1954) from there.

A third takeaway has been about the clear message we have heard time and again – love does not mean one must always "be nice." Our work has revealed that leaders who operate with a love mindset, or teams who express love, are willing to be challenging and have difficult conversations around difference and decision-making. A university director shared, "I wouldn't go toe to toe and have that kind of [challenging] conversation if I didn't give a damn about [the person], or what we're doing together. I have to be willing to get uncomfortable." A CEO of an outdoor clothing company whom we interviewed described her company's journey as being riddled with stubbornness, frustration, fierce commitment, and difficult conversations – "We must do better!"

When the goal is love, nothing else will do. Love requires us to give honest feedback, to speak up when something is not right or behavior is out of alignment. Martin Luther King, Jr. summarized this well: "Power without love is reckless and abusive. Love without power is sentimental and anaemic." Leaders quite often use the phrase "tough love" to describe how they think about these aspects of work life. Love can be expressed in the drive to perform to one's fullest potential, with the expectation others will do the same. In the NFL Seattle Seahawks organization, this is expressed through Coach Carroll's motto "Always compete." Love is not found in compliance, insincere commitments to harmony, or confluence. Love goes after commitments and goals with fervor. Love has efficacy.

A fourth theme is about the heliotropic (Cooperrider, 1997) and emotionally contagious (Shoenewolf, 1990; Barsade et al., 2018) effects of love at work. When we experience micro-moments of love at work, or witness love in our teams, these interactions foster a positive expectancy (Cooperrider, 1997; Robson, 2015) and result in heliotropism –people's interest "leaning" toward experiencing and expressing love at work. Emotional contagion means that an individual or team experiencing or expressing love influences the emotions or behavior of others, consciously and non-consciously, by inducing positive emotional states, attitudes, and behaviors. As love behaviors and interactions continue to occur consistently, the initial positive expectations and images are enhanced by additional behaviors and responses that were not included previously. Simply put, love at work has a knock-on effect. The system is able to broaden and build what love is at work based on lived experience. Thus, love raises the bar for the quality of engagement in an organization.

Love expands what we are capable of seeing as possibilities. The perceptions, memories, and learning of human systems are cued and shaped by behaviors of love, as well as through the positive expectancies for more love. Through this process, human systems fall into a cycle of affirmative and prophetic expectancies, seeing "proof" of our images through, which further endows our positive prospects of the future.

Putting Love into Action, with Intention

From existing definitions of love and stories from our interviews about expressions of organizational love, we find love is often expressed in ordinary circumstances and occurs without a lot of fanfare. This suggests that daily events and interactions offer ample opportunity to operate from a love mindset. How would your experience in the security line at an airport, in a crowded grocery store, or in a difficult team meeting change if you were driven by love? Our research has led us to a model of organizational expressions and occurrences of love, which is best conveyed as an iterative cycle including phases of choice, interest, appreciation, action, exchange, and ending in a new awareness (see Figure 3.1).

The Cycle of Love Expression parallels other cycles of natural, human behavior like the Gestalt Cycle of Experience (Perls, 1947), not only meaning a process can be tracked, but interruptions to the completion of the process as well. The significance of the presented model is that it

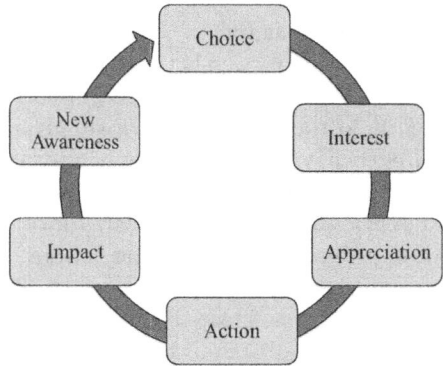

Figure 3.1 Cycle of love expression.

suggests organizational actors can become agents of love with awareness, guiding them to intentionally develop expressions of love through concrete steps.

The cycle begins with choice, an intention to express love for another, no matter at what level of system. From choice, the actor moves to interest, a stance of curiosity for the target of love, be that a person, team, or other entity. Resulting from the interest, appreciation arises, a positive affect about something observed or experienced in the target.

The actor moves to acting on the appreciation. Love needs expression or action to be realized (May, 1969) and we recommend taking an experimental stance, trying on micro-behaviors and seeing what shifts as a result. The three definitions of love we highlighted earlier from Sorokin (1954), Gestalt for organizational and systems development (Hopper-Carter, 2004; Carter 2019), and Fredrickson (2013b) each offer inspiration for what form an action might take.

Sorokin's (1954) five dimensions of love are practical for application in organizations because they are nonbinary and a manager can put love into small actions, along any of Sorokin's dimensions: intensity, extensity, duration, purity, and adequacy. The Gestalt approach (Hopper-Carter, 2004; Carter 2019), that love means fully accepting what is, can be acted upon, by the actor experimenting with their mindset and positive regard, applying to past, present, and future states of the target, or all the parts comprising the whole of the target (such as all the aspects of a person or all the strengths and weaknesses of a team). Fredrickson's frame of love as a micro-moment of warmth and connection shared with another living being (2013b) is another avenue for action, such as tracking how often one experiences micro-moments throughout the day at work, or by being more intentional about fostering more warmth and connection with members of the organization.

Once the action has occurred and love has been expressed or demonstrated, the cycle moves to the impact of the expression, an opportunity for one to scan for herself or the target, to observe what has changed as a result of the expression of love. The cycle ends with a new awareness. From here, the cycle can begin again.

Implications for practice relate to the distinction between the cognitions of love and the behaviors of love. Practitioners need to support both intention and action. With regard to the behaviors of love, given that there is not a prescribed list of love behaviors, we suggest an approach to increasing the behaviors rooted in curiosity and inquiry. An inquiry such as "what behaviors would best express our concern and care for others?" would provide guidance on the appropriate behaviors and actions.

An additional implication centers around love as an innate human capacity, which means it does not need to be created or "manufactured" in organizations. Rather, members of the organization, scholars, and practitioners should aim to support and elevate the expressions of love.

One final note to practitioners is that doubt and ambivalence is totally normal. One thing we know for sure from years of studying this subject is that it will raise a few eyebrows. Talking about love is not the norm. We know that. We have two insights to offer. First, if you are interested in this subject, know that it bumps up against the general narrative around business. For that reason, it takes great courage to lead from love. It is an act of leadership, no matter what your formal position in an organization.

Second, we have learned that speaking about love evokes deeper reflections within the listener about their own personal relationship to the subject of love and their history of work and sometimes even personal relationships. It is therefore possible that a person objecting to the idea of love has had a bad experience in the past. This is totally understandable and should be respected. Preaching about love or trying to convert people in organizations does not work in our experience.

Conclusion

Love gets expressed between colleagues, to suppliers, to the planet, and occurs at multiple levels of the business system. Our strongest message to you as a reader is that love is neither alien nor misplaced in our organizations. If you consider love to be a worthwhile pursuit in any aspect of your life, then you have the opportunity to express love throughout your life, including at work.

When we name and aim for love, we are setting the bar high. Love is extraordinary. The word "love" carries power and meaning – it calls for something more. Love invites participation in a different way. Love demands our best, our most authentic, our A-game. Love sets expectations of growth, honesty, transparency, and learning. Love at work includes difficult conversations, it includes being accessible to our teams. When we commit to love, we commit to fully showing up. If one commits to love, there is no holding back.

We can "drive past" words like "compassion" and "respect," nod approvingly, and carry on. But not with love. Love gets our attention. It is generative and evocative; it comes from the depths of the human beings living a fully lived life. It is our great hope to provide you with the courage to love. To love widely and to love unconditionally, even at work. In fact, especially at work.

References

Adams, S. (2017, October 19). With help from Jeff Bezos and Martha Stewart, a cancer survivor turns glassybaby into A $20m company. Retrieved June 27, 2020, from www.forbes.com/sites/forbestreptalks/2016/12/06/with-help-from-jeff-bezos-and-msartha-stewart-a-cancer-survivor-turns-glassybaby-into-a-20m-company/.

Barsade, S. G., Coutifaris, C. G. V., & Pillemer, J. (2018). Emotional contagion in organizational life. *Research in Organizational Behavior* 38: 137–151.

Barsade, S. G., & O'Neill, O. A. (2014). What's love got to do with it? A longitudinal study of the culture of companionate love and employee and client outcomes in the long-term care setting. *Administrative Science Quarterly* 59(4): 551–598.

Carter, J. D. (2019). *Making a difference with your presence: Use of self and self mastery.* Detroit, MI: River Place Press.

Coombe, D. (2010). *Secure base leadership: A positive theory of leadership incorporating safety, exploration and positive action* (Electronic Thesis or Dissertation). Retrieved from https://etd.ohiolink.edu/.

Coombe, D. (2011). Corporate citizenship: An expression of love. *The Journal of Corporate Citizenship* 42: 93–102.

Cooperrider, D. L. (1997). Resources for getting appreciative inquiry started. *OD Practitioner* 28(1): 28–33.

Cooperrider, D. L., & Fry, R. E. (2013). Mirror flourishing and the positive psychology of sustainability. *Journal of Corporate Citizenship* 46: 3–12.

Cox, M. (2020). *The business case for love: How companies get bragged about today.* Palgrave Macmillan.

Dutton, J. E., & Heaphy, D. H. (2003). The power of high quality connections. In K. S. Cameron, J. E. Dutton & R.E. Quinn (Eds.), *Positive organizational scholarship.* San Francisco, CA: Berrett-Koehler.

Dutton, J. E., & Ragins, B. (Eds.) (2007). *Exploring positive relationships at work: Building a theoretical and research foundation.* Mahwah, NJ: Lawrence Erlbaum Associates.

Fredrickson, B. L. (1998). What good are positive emotions? *Review of General Psychology* 2: 300–319.

Fredrickson, B. L. (2001). The role of positive emotions in positive psychology: The broaden-and-build theory of positive emotions. *American Psychologist* 56: 218–226.

Fredrickson, B. L. (2013a). Positive emotions broaden and build. In E. Ashby Plant & P.G. Devine (Eds.), *Advances in experimental social psychology*, 47, 1–53. BurlingtonVT: Academic Press.

Fredrickson, B.L. (2013b). *Love 2.0: Creating happiness and health in moments of connection.* New York: Plume.

Fredrickson, B. L., & Joiner, T. (2002). Positive emotions trigger upwards spirals toward emotional well-being. *Psychological Science* 12: 172–175.

Fredrickson, B. L., Tugade, M., Waugh, C. E., & Larkin, G. R. (2002). What good are positive emotions in crises? A prospective study of resilience and emotions following the terrorist attacks on the United States on September 11th, 2001. *Journal of Personality and Social Psychology* 84: 365–376.

Fry, L. (2003). Toward a theory of spiritual leadership. *Leadership Quarterly* 14: 693–727.

Fry, L., & Krieger, M. (2009). Towards a theory of being-centered leadership: Multiple levels of being as context for effective leadership. *Human Relations* 62(11): 1667–1696.

Glavas, A., & Piderit, S.K. (2009) How Does Doing Good Matter? Effects of Corporate Citizenship on Employees. *Journal of Corporate Citizenship* 2009: 51–70.

Gottman, J.M. (1994). *Why marriages succeed or fail.* New York: Simon & Schuster.

Gottman, J.M. (1999). *The marriage clinic: A scientifically-based marital therapy.* New York, NY: W.W. Norton & Company.

Hope-Bryant, J. (2009). *Love leadership: The new way to lead in a fear-based world*. New York, NY: John Wiley & Sons.

Hopper-Carter, V. (2004). Gestalt OSD and systems theory: A perspective on levels of system and intervention choices. *OD Practitioner* 36: 41–48.

Kouzes, J., & Posner, B. (1992). Ethical leaders: An essay about being in love. *Journal of Business Ethics* 11(5–6): 479.

Kouzes, J., & Posner, B. (2007). *The leadership challenge: How to make extraordinary things happen in organizations* (4th ed.). San Francisco, CA: Jossey-Bass.

Laszlo, C., & Brown, J. (2014). *The flourishing enterprise: The new spirit of business*. Palo Alto, CA: Stanford Business Books.

Mackey, J., & Sisodia, R. (2013). *Conscious capitalism: Liberating the heroic spirit of business*. Boston, MA: Harvard Business Review Press.

Manby, J. (2012). *Love works: Seven timeless principles for effective leaders*. New York, NY: Zondervan.

Maselko, J., Kubzansky, L., Lipsitt, L., & Buka, S. (2011). Mother's affection at 8 months predicts emotional distress in adulthood. *Journal of Epidemiology and Community Health* 65: 621–625.

Maturana, H., & Bunnell, P. (2009). The biology of business: Love expands Intelligence. *Reflections: The Sol Journal* 1: 58–66.

May, R. (1969). *Love and will*. New York, NY: W.W. Norton.

McQuaid, M. (2019). *How do appreciative inquiry summits help organizational systems to flourish?* (Published doctoral dissertation). University of Twente.

Naas, R. (n.d.). [Editorial]. *Forbes*. Retrieved March 30, 2020, from www.forbes.com/sites/robertanaas/2020/01/18/watchmaking-legend-jean-claude-biver-awarded--french-legion-of-honor/#d9ecbdb23fe6.

Perls, Frederick S. (1947). *Ego, hunger and aggression: A revision of Freud's theory and method*. Gouldsboro, ME: The Gestalt Journal Press, Inc.

Post, S. G. (2003). *Unlimited love: Altruism, compassion and service*. Philadelphia, PA: Templeton Foundation Press.

Post, S. G. (2005). Altruism, happiness, and health: It's good to be good. *International Journal of Behavioral Medicine* 12(2): 66–77.

Post, S. G., Underwood, L. G., Schloss, J. P., & Hurlbut, W. B. (2002). *Altruism and altruistic love: Science, philosophy, and religion in dialogue*.Oxfordshire: Oxford University Press.

Roberts, K. (2005). *Love marks: The future beyond brands*. New York: Powerhouse Books.

Robson, L. (2015). *Language of life-giving connection: The emotional tone of language that fosters flourishing campus sustainability programs* (Published doctoral dissertation). Case Western Reserve University.

Sanders, T., & Stone, G. (2002). *Love is the killer app: How to win business and influence friends*. New York, NY: Crown Publishing.

Schoenewolf, G. (1990). Emotional contagion: Behavioral induction in individuals and groups. *Modern Psychoanalysis* 15(1): 49–61.

Sorokin, P. (1954) *The ways and power of love: Types, factors, and techniques of moral transformation*. West Conshohocken, PA: Templeton Foundation Press.

Sprecher, S., & P. Regan. (1998). Passionate and companionate love in courting and young married couples. *Sociological Inquiry* 68: 163–185.

Stone, A. (2014, August 07). CEO: Giving money away helps company grow. Retrieved May 27, 2020 from https://cbsnews.com/new/ceo-giving-money-away-helps-comapny-grow/.

4 Agape in Business
Policies and Actions beyond Caritas

*Harry Hummels, Yannick Bammens,
Maike van Dijk and Annelies van Uden*

4.1 Introduction

On September 11, 2001, at 09.45 Eastern Daylight Time (EDT), US airspace closed for all commercial aviation. Numerous aircraft that were on their way to the United States at that time were ordered to land at the nearest airport, of which 38 resorted to Gander Airport on Newfoundland. Gander is a friendly provincial town with 10,000 inhabitants, which was suddenly confronted with 7,000 people looking for a place to stay. In *The Day the World Came to Gander*, Jim DeFede (2003) describes the hospitality and humanity with which the Gander people spontaneously overloaded the passengers. Within 24 hours the Newfoundlanders managed to arrange bed, bath, and food for them on a collective basis. Take George and Edna Neal, who offered shelter to four Continental 5 passengers in their home. The kindness with which the guests were received ultimately resulted in personal friendships. Or take Lisa Zale and Sara Wood. They had planned to go camping and were totally surprised when they wanted to buy air mattresses. Canadian Tires, which sells outdoor items next to car tires, not only gave them air mattresses and a tent for free, an employee also took them to a campsite and assisted in setting up the tent. These actions of the residents of Newfoundland are a form of public love or agape.

Now does this concept of public love also apply in a business world where economic interests dominate? In the theory of business, companies are often presented as a coherence or node of contracts, with self-interest as their guiding principle (cf. Jensen and Meckling, 1976; Fama and Jensen, 1983, Argandona, 2011). Owners, managers, employees, and business or social partners are supposed to act rationally in order to maximize their benefit. Therefore, skepticism is immediately lurking when love is mentioned in a business environment. This is all the more true in a Friedmanian (1970) context where serving the interests of the owners of the company is the hallmark of managerial responsibility. Increasingly, however, companies focus on the well-being of employees, customers, financiers, partners, or society in their policies, activities, and

DOI: 10.4324/9781003254034-5

behaviors. Take, for example, the public–private partnership between Dutch multinational DSM and the Government of Rwanda, leading to Africa Improved Foods (AIF). AIF manufactures Nootri food products with crops from local food cooperatives like soy, corn, and sorghum. DSM adds its nutrients to strengthen the health of women and children in their first 1,000 days. Or take Philips, another Dutch multinational, setting up community life centers in Africa in order to improve better access to high-quality healthcare. Interesting about the health facilities is that each clinic offers clean water and Internet access to its clients. As a result, various business activities arise in the immediate vicinity of the health center, which in turn contribute to the clinic's financial sustainability. DSM and Philips are just two of the many examples of large and small companies committed to the well-being of others. Whether it is international aid, the development of employees, the support of local sports clubs, or the introduction of a product line to support, for example, the elderly, companies are increasingly concerned about the welfare of others and demonstrate signs of other-oriented behavior.

Now the question arises if these examples are merely expressions of corporate social responsibility (CSR) or creating shared value (CSV). Or do they point in a direction beyond the meaning of these familiar and widely practiced notions? Introducing a new concept only makes sense if it provides a different take on and additional insights into the theory and practice of business beyond already existing conceptual frameworks. As we will argue in this chapter, agape means more than simply living up to the expectation of CSR and CSV. It allows us to rethink the ways in which we do business, while aiming to achieve the mission and objectives of the business. Even though for many agape has roots in the Judeo-Christian tradition, it is a meaningful concept and can be applied in a secular business world that aims to create (long-term) value for its stakeholders, including shareholders.

4.2 The Meaning of Love

Agape is one of the four forms of love distinguished in ancient Greece next to eros, philia, and storge (Lewis, 1960; Melé, 2012). The concept stands for genuine attention to (the needs and well-being of) others and the actions leading to this well-being and fulfilling these needs. Agape transcends the love for one's partner, family, or close friends. As already Augustine indicated, love begins close to home and focuses – by the coincidence of time, place or circumstances – on those who are usually most dear to us. This form of love is referred to as storge and is the first and most natural form of love (Lewis, 1960). Storge concerns the affection between a parent and a child. But the love for second- or third-line relatives can also have characteristics of storge. In fact, the affection can extend to others we are fond of, without there being any family ties.

Storge is characterized by familiarity and security as a solid basis for a relationship (Protasi, 2008). Or, as Lewis puts it, it is a comfortable, calm feeling of appreciation and affection for the other.

The Greek term "agape" is often associated with and considered to be a translation of the Hebrew *ahava* (Buijs, 2012), which refers to the love of God for mankind, and of man for his or her neighbor.[1] Where love is a matter of course for God and the essence of his being, mankind faces quite a challenge in relation to other people and to the natural world (McCloskey, 2006: 109). In her book *The Bourgeois Virtues*, McCloskey refers to the philosopher Michael Stoker:

> For it is essential to the very concept of love to care for the beloved. … To the extent that I act … towards you with the final goal of getting pleasure … I do not act for your sake. What is lacking in these theories is simply … the person. For love, friendship, affection, fellow feeling, and community all require that the other person be an essential part of what is valued.

Fromm (2007) emphasizes the complete lack of exclusivity when referring to the love for myself and all beings. If I have developed the capacity for love within myself, I must love all my neighbors as brothers and sisters. In charity we experience the unity with all people, we experience human solidarity and humanity as unity. All differences in giftedness, in intelligence, in knowledge can be neglected; what remains is our core of being human, which we all have in common (Fromm, 2007). Often, as Pope (2013) observes, this means that the love of others "chooses the side of the vulnerable, the marginalized, the least among us." This choice manifests itself in the commandment of charity, which in the Old Testament puts the poor, the stranger, and the orphan at the center as the object of love – and we often respond to the call. Just think of the image of a physically and emotionally exhausted mother carrying a starving child that we so often see in humanitarian crises. The image almost immediately evokes compassion, causing us, for instance, to transfer money to humanitarian relief organizations.[2] The love for others is, however, broader and also refers to, for instance, a neighbor who needs a helping hand because he is in quarantine. We often provide help with no other motivation than caring for the well-being of the other (Dees, 2012: 324).

In this chapter we argue that agape transcends the often restricted focus on those who are deprived of essential goods to "ever-widening circles of connectedness" (Buijs, 2012). Agape expresses our interest in and focus on the well-being of others, no matter whether they are poor or otherwise in need. Agape contributes to human flourishing of the other and of myself as a person and to the development of our human relationships – including those that take shape within a business context (Melé, 2012). Companies and their owners, managers, and employees often feel compelled to reach out to others like colleagues, clients, suppliers, partners, or the communities that they operate in. Take, for example, Rijk Zwaan, one of the world's largest vegetable breeding companies, where the chairman of the board of directors advocates caring for the company's coworkers when he says:

> Go and visit your sick colleague and leave the work for a while. The value of one employee is greater than all assets combined.

It is precisely this love and care for the other that Benedictus XVI (2009) sees as "a special force" that encourages people to engage courageously and selflessly in activities contributing to peace and justice. In confessional circles *Caritas in Veritate* forms an important source of inspiration (Argandona, 2011; Sison and Fontrodona, 2012; Mele and Naughton, 2011; McCann, 2011; Faldetta, 2011) for an economy that combines profit-seeking with a certain selflessness and contributes to "a civilization of the economy" (Benedict XVI, 2009). More recently, Pope Francis's latest encyclical *Fratelli Tutti* conveys a comparable message. It is in our action that we express our love of God through the love for our fellow beings (Francis, 2020, paragraph 4)[3]. In this context, agape is not (only) special because of the gift or the transfer of a good, but because of the process of giving. Christian tradition emphasizes the intention with which we care for others. Those who give find joy not only in what they give but in the heart with which they give. In his Confessions, Augustine (1961) refers to St. Paul, who was particularly joyful about the flourishing of the Philippians after paying attention to his needs. That joy, Augustine continues, is not limited to the recipient, in this case St. Paul, but is reciprocal and also extends to the giver(s).

4.3 More than Just a Focus on the Well-being of Others

Although the term "agape" is seldomly used in a commercial setting, there are signs of other-oriented behavior in the daily practice of business. We rejoice about the success of a business partner, we support a colleague who faces a burnout, and we empathize with a client when she is affected by personal grief. These forms of caring about the well-being of others are quite normal, while not being part of any standard operating procedure. They occur more or less spontaneously, as the following example shows:

> A customer of a hotel reservation service calls the service center to cancel her reservation. Because the free cancellation period had already expired, the employee kindly asks why the customer still calls. She indicated that they had booked the hotel room because of its proximity to a neighboring veterinary clinic where her dog was scheduled for surgery. Unfortunately, her dog passed away before the surgery. She, therefore, no longer needed the room and wanted to timely inform the hotel. The room might be let to someone else instead. The employee thanked her for her attentive call and told

the customer that he would inform the hotel. Half an hour later the customer received an email in which the employee expressed his sympathy with the passing away of her dog. He also wrote her that the hotel had indicated not to charge any costs for her late cancellation.

The employee reacted both spontaneously and compassionately that was truly appreciated by the client, but – unintendedly – also resulted in a clear and positive result for the service center: a customer who is forever committed to the company (Worline and Dutton, 2017: 21). This expression of other-oriented behavior transcends the domain of rational management, in which employees are carefully instructed how to respond to customers. In this example, the employee shows a genuine interest in the well-being of the client. He expresses his condolences, thereby making an assessment of the emotions of the customer (cf. Lewis, 1960). In addition, he acts concretely in the sense that the customer no longer has to pay for the hotel room, despite the fact that her cancellation was too late. In almost every daily context we come across people sympathizing with others, rejoicing in their happiness, comforting them when they feel grief or paying attention to their concerns. Already Adam Smith in his *Theory of Moral Sentiments* (1759/2010) and David Hume in *A Treatise of Human Nature* (1738) or *An Inquiry Concerning the Principles of Morals* (1751) indicated that no one is indifferent to the happiness or misery of another. According to Smith, even the greatest misanthrope can rejoice in the well-being of others:

> No matter how selfish you think man is, it's obvious that there are some principles in his nature that give him an interest in the welfare of others, and make their happiness necessary to him, even if he gets nothing from it but the pleasure of seeing it.

It is nice to rejoice in the happiness or well-being of others – or to sympathize if the other is confronted with adversity. In line with Pope Francis, it is through action that compassion for others becomes truly meaningful. One of the best-known and most cited examples of active interventions to relieve grief is obviously that of the Good Samaritan. The Samaritan noticed the victim by the side of the road, something a priest and a Levite prior to him deliberately failed to do. More importantly, however, the Samaritan took care of his wounds, brought him to the nearest inn, and paid for his recovery. Yet the incident raises the question on what grounds the Samaritan intervened when he lovingly approached and cared for the victim. Almost instantly, we assume that the Samaritan acts in the interest of the assaulted man. In many cases this assumption appears to be adequate – ex post. But how do we know ex ante the needs of someone else? How sure are we about his or her needs when we help someone without asking, because we think he or she needs our assistance? Often we do not know, Michael Ignatieff (1984) argues in his book *The Needs of Strangers*. Writing about the elderly people in his neighborhood, he clearly witnesses that they are poor and needy. Like everyone else, they need food, clothes, shelter, etc. But maybe their greatest need is just having a chat, a pat on the back, or a little help with their groceries? Cautiousness and restraint are required to determine what is good for others. In human relationships few assumptions are more dangerous than the idea that one knows best what the other person needs, Ignatieff claims. The writer issues a warning (Ignatieff, 1984):

> In politics this presumption is a warrant to ignore democratic preferences and to trample on freedom. In other realms too, the arrogation of the right by doctors to define the needs of their patients, of social workers to administer the needs of their clients, and finally, of parents to decide the needs of their children is in each case a warrant for abuse.

American pragmatist philosopher John Dewey is equally cautious when he points out that a person or an organization may be moved "to labor for the good of others, but because of lack of deliberation and thoughtfulness, be quite ignorant of what their good really is, and do a great deal of harm" (Dewey quoted in Dees, 2012). We contend that it not possible to be sure of what the good for others is, what their needs really are, if we do not actively allow them to express their thoughts. The other person is not merely a passive object of our good intentions. He or she is a human being with the right to express what contributes to or detracts from his or her well-being, and to be listened to and heard (Ignatieff, 1984):

> It is the manner of the giving that counts and the moral basis on which it is given: whether strangers at my door get their stories listened to by the social worker, whether the ambulance man takes care not to jostle them when they are taken down the steep stairs of their apartment building, whether a nurse sits with them in the hospital when they are frightened and alone. Respect and dignity are conferred by gestures such as these.

It is only by listening to, hearing what is being said and acting upon this information coming from the other person, that we prevent ending up in a situation of "totalization" (Levinas, 1980, 2003) or "egology" (Kaulingfreks and Ten Bos, 2007). By "totalization" Levinas means that we cannot know the world outside ourselves independent of our own senses and thoughts. Humans are always at the center of their own totalizing: they make the world to their own personal world through observing, acting, and giving meaning. Totalization is not an act that is subject to our will. We cannot simply choose to do it or leave it behind. My totalizing is inevitable, and nothing falls outside of this totalizing grasp (Duyndam and Poorthuis, 2003). The other person is a radically different person, an alterity, which positions itself opposite of me. I cannot know that person through my own perception. It is only through the other speaking to me and making an appeal on me – and I listening to the other and hearing what the other says – that a relationship develops. In other words, it is not my perception of the other's needs, interests, and flourishing that is relevant to constitute a relationship, but opening up to the other who appeals to me, thereby enabling mutual communication.[4] Levinas (1980) describes this perspective as the other person's face looking at me – not as a passive activity, but as an active address. The fact that the other looks at me – and I become aware of its address, its appeal to me – may have significant consequences. In looking and speaking, we become aware of the fundamental "differentness" or alterity of the other. The appeal may provoke a reaction in us – even though I have the freedom to ignore it.

Like Levinas, Outka (1972) places a great deal of emphasis on listening to the other hearing what he or she says as a basis for the development of human relationships. Unlike Levinas, Outka assumes a normative position when he sees love as "equal regard". Others have the right to be heard. The love for others is seen an ethical imperative that starts from a universal love for man as a unique and worthy being that in itself deserves respect. In his operationalization of love, Outka gives a Kantian twist to the concept. The bottom line is that we always have to consider the other as an end in itself and never just as a means to achieve our own objectives. Love may not be consumed purely out of the self-interest of the love giver, thereby reducing the receiver – the other – to an instrument. It means, Outka continues, that the other should have an opportunity to be heard. Because how else can we know that we respect the other and look after his or her welfare? In doing so, we may experience the benefit or joy resulting from other-regarding behavior (cf. Buijs, 2012; Fromm, 2007). It means that in our view selflessness is not a necessary condition or characteristic of agape, although self-interest cannot be the motive for agapeic behavior in the first place, Outka argues.

4.4 Other-Oriented Behavior in the Business and Management Literature

The theme of love in business, although not widely propagated and picked up, emerged three decades ago in business and management in the United States (Autry, 1991; Sanders, 2002; Roberts, 2005; Sheth et al., 2007; Sisodia et al., 2014). Despite these initial contributions, the idea of love for others plays virtually no role in the business and management literature. Only a few authors have addressed the role and relevance of agape[5] in the context of business (Hill, 2002; Argandona, 2011; Mèle, 2012; Barsada et al., 2014; Cavanaugh et al., 2015), or the role of benevolence and caring in business (Karakas and Sarigollu, 2013; André and Pache, 2016; Mercier and Deslandes, 2019).

An important contribution to the understanding and management of different types of other-oriented behavior in business is made by Dees

(2012), who distinguished two organizational cultures. Dees took the idea of the two cultures from a lecture by C.P. Snow, in which he distinguished the culture of the humanities and that of the sciences. Each has its own strengths and weaknesses, but they do not seem to interact. Likewise, Dees introduces two clusters of values, described as two different organizational cultures. The first culture is an age-old culture "that is tied to the heart and steeped in moral traditions around the world." This culture is found across the globe and not dependent on any world or business view. It is based on the Humean assumption that charity and benevolence is a basic element of human nature (Hume, 1960, 1961). It is a disposition, a character trait, a virtue (Kekes, 1987; Frankena, 1987). When addressing hardship, many businesses approach the challenge by offering those in need some kind of charity – or allow their employees to show their humanity. Examples of charitable or benevolent behavior in this context are, *inter alia*, taking over tasks of a colleague who is on the brink of a burnout, visiting a colleague who has fallen ill, giving someone a ride home, running the marathon with colleagues to collect money for cancer research, etc. Ignatieff (2017) speaks of "ordinary virtues" to denote these activities. Quoting Muhammad Yunus, Dees (2012:321) argues, however, that charity avoids recognizing the problem: "charity becomes a way to shrug off our responsibility," while appeasing our consciences. It only perpetuates the problem, as it does not address its root causes. Why is the colleague susceptible for a burnout? Did management ever pay attention to the person's workload and the organization of his or her work?

Clearly charitable behavior has its benefits, even though most of these benefits befall the charitable actor or the community (Dees, 2012). Generally speaking, an ethical climate that focuses on the well-being of others has a positive effect on the individual's commitment to a group or an organization (Cullen et al., 2003), while also contributing to the emergence of trust throughout the organization (Mèle, 2012). As such, a culture of charity that elicits spontaneous responses to a perceived need, a grief or a desire, is beneficial to the organization (cf. Cullen et al., 2003; Karakas and Sarigollu, 2013; Mercier and Deslandes, 2019). The benefits even extend to society, reinforcing social bonds and making it more resilient and cohesive (cf. Victor and Cullen, 1988; Cullen et al., 2003; Dees, 2012).[6] While the prospected utility may be a driving force for an individual or group to act in the best interest of others, virtuous behavior will often be inspired by an ethical orientation towards the well-being of others (Mèle, 2012; Karakas and Sarigollu, 2013; Mercier and Deslandes, 2019). Nevertheless, a culture of charity does not fundamentally address the needs of others, it merely mitigates negative outcomes for an individual or a group.

Acts of heartfelt caritas, as beautiful as they might be, will not do the job to relieve others or to promote health, happiness, and well-being if the challenges are more structural (Dees, 2012). A more systematic and rational problem-solving culture is needed to overcome the pitfalls of mere charity. According to Dees (2012), this culture emerged from the scientific, industrial, and entrepreneurial age and comprises a strategy toward solving complex issues and creating economic, financial, social, and environmental values. Reinforcing this culture aimed at the well-being of others calls for a systemic approach to decision-making and policy-making, including the resulting behavior and actions, and the evaluation of the outputs and outcomes potentially leading to adjustments.

4.5 Defining Agape

Based on the views of Ignatieff, Levinas, Dewey, and Dees, we come to the conclusion that agape is more than charity, compassion, empathy, sympathy, benevolence, or comparable concepts. As such, a definition and operationalization of agape is required that takes the concept beyond charity, compassion or sympathy. Against the background of the explor-ation of other-oriented behavior above, it seems justified to describe agape with the use of three key elements: flourishing of others, consensus or consent, and effort and results. We propose the following definition of agape:

> A commitment to the flourishing of someone or something[7] else that the other explicitly agrees with or consents to and expresses itself in concrete actions and realizations.

In more practical terms that allow us to study agape in business, three dimensions are relevant in determining the nature, extent, and forms of expression of agape in a business environment:

- The *dimension of connectivity* that refers to the relationship between ourselves and the other and that respects the other as an end in him-self or herself,
- The *dimension of the alterity* that refers to the uniqueness of the other as a person and that is expressed in the other speaking to us – and us listening to what is being said,[8]
- The *dimension of the activity* that refers to the activities intended to improve the well-being of the other.

It is, in particular, the dimension of alterity that sets agape apart as it does not start with my view of the other, but with the other's view of himself or herself and his or her needs. In a purposeful business context, where behavior is to a large extent guided by processes and procedures, agape calls for a "from the outside looking inwards" approach – listening to what the other has to say about one's actions and behavior – instead of a "from the inside looking outwards" approach. It is here that agape differs from corporate responsibility, CSV, stakeholder management or endear-ment, as these concepts generally put the interests of the company first while taking some precautions not to cause too much harm to others.[9] It also differentiates agape from those conceptions of other-oriented behavior that refer to selfless behavior, which is so often associated with love (Kierkegaard, 1962; Nygren, 1953). If agape is to play a bigger role in the development of other-oriented business organizations, we have to take the logic of business into account while not succumbing to a shareholder orientation only. As Argandona (2011) rightfully observes, "the theory of the firm does not take love into account. Given its assumptions, it does not seem to need it." It is our contention that businesses might be mistaken and that the concept of agape, in principle, is applicable to business organizations that are dedicated to the creation of financial and economic value[10].

By putting emphasis on a culture of systemic problem-solving, we place agape in a wider context of organizational decision- and policy-making regarding interpersonal behavior and the values that should guide these processes. Based on our definition and operationalization of agape, in which we put the needs and wants of others first, the love for others starts by listening to them and hearing what they have to say. This is followed by actions containing a response to what the other has said – at least implicitly.[11] Ultimately, the actions that emerge from the interaction must demonstrate results that address the needs and wants of others. Finally, agape calls for an evaluation of the actions (and eventually of policies, processes, and practices addressing the other-oriented interactions and their outcomes), eventually leading to adjustments in the processes. We call this the *agapeic turn* of business, referring to the process of continuously improving the engagement and dialogue with employees, customers, business partners, suppliers, financiers, and the community in which the business organization operates.

4.6 The Agapeic Turn in Business

What does an agapeic turn mean that goes beyond CSR, CSV, and even charity or endearment? What does it mean that agape is distinct from the kindness to others and the focus on their well-being that fortunately characterizes many businesses? In an empirical study[12] we dissected the ways in which companies operationalized and implemented the dimensions of connectivity, alterity, and action in a systematic way – based on the culture of problem-solving and value creation. The eight companies participating in our case study research ranged from small family businesses to listed multinational companies. In this section, we provide examples of company expressions of their respect for humans as means in themselves and for nonhuman nature, the engagement with others – and more in particular the ways in which the companies listened to relevant others – and finally the actions that they took based on listening to their employees, suppliers, and customers and hearing what they were saying.

Connectivity

Without exception the eight companies disposed of clear policies focusing on the well-being of others. They differed in the extent to which the policies were formalized. The smaller (family) businesses displayed more of an informal culture of listening to others and systematically promoting their well-being, while the larger corporations worked along formal lines. Asito Cleaning Services is one of the largest in the country, with over 10,000 employees and 100 nationalities. Respecting workers with a multi-ethnic and cultural background has become one of the strongholds of the company's culture. To stimulate the integration of the large variety of nationalities and cultures, and to learn from each other, the company organized the so-called diversity dinners of all its employees. They were invited to bring food and snacks from their home countries and share them with colleagues. It led the company to initiate the National Integration Dinner with 25,000 people attending, gathering in 300 locations across the country. A second result was the launch of the Diversity Advisory Board, representing employees from different branches and layers of the organization to start a dialogue and to enhance the respect for each and every individual – no matter whatever their origination is.

Interface, on the other hand, exhibited policies respecting both human and nonhuman nature. The listed company produces and sells modular carpet tiles, luxury vinyl tile, and rubber flooring. Ray Anderson, the company's founder, got inspired in 1993 by Paul Hawken's book *The Ecology of Commerce* (1993). The author argues for an 80 percent reduction of our consumption of energy and natural resources before 2040, and for restoring degraded ecosystems to their fullest biological capacity. Both objectives inspired Anderson in 1994 to adopt *Mission Zero*. It challenged Interface to eliminate waste, reduce molecular and toxic waste emissions to zero, switch to renewable energy, redesign processes and products, use resource-efficient transportation, and sensitize stakeholders by 2020. To achieve these objectives, Interface started collaborating with The Natural Step[13] and Biomimicry 3.8.[14] With the support of both organizations it developed an approach that, over time, resulted in replacing latex with recycled PVB[15] in precoats, or in using discarded fishing nets for its fibers through its Net-Works® program. In 2018 the company announced that all products were carbon neutral across the entire product lifecycle.

A third example that we like to mention comes from Schijvens Corporate Fashion. The company is a precursor in circularly produced garments for employees of retail and service chains. Apart from the focus on circularity, Schijvens respects its own employees and those of its suppliers. As a token of that respect, managing director Shirley Schijvens and two of her Dutch employees even learn to speak and read Turkish, in order to improve communication with local employees. As one of the first companies in the garment sector Schijvens expresses its respect for employees in the value chain by paying living wages – starting in Turkey and Pakistan. The decision to pay living wages was made top-down, its implementation was left to local managers and employees in dialogue with company management. Local needlewomen, their managers and local NGOs assisted in compiling a full list of the cost of living. The decision made by management has, to some extent, charitable implications. Many, but not all, customers are willing to pay the premium price allowing the company to pay living wages to Turkish and Pakistani employees. When they opt out and pay the basic price for the yarn and the garments, Schijvens pays for the difference out of its own pocket: "It cannot be the case that we, for example, in Pakistan will not pay a living wage due to the choice of our customers not paying the premium price", the managing director explains.

Alterity

Hutten Catering is a caterer employing over 2,000 coworkers. The company has grown rapidly over the last few years but continues to emphasize the importance of each and every individual in its organization. Every coworker joining the company receives a suitcase – indicating the journey that the individual and the company jointly commence. The suitcase contains information about the company, a labor contract, and, most importantly, a vitality agreement. This means that both company and team worker agree on what the company, according to the coworker, can do to promote his or her well-being. In addition, the coworker agrees to taking the necessary measures to stay healthy and happy. Twice a year, the coworker and manager will have a "vitality talk," to discuss the coworker's general state of well-being. Also they discuss whether the catering company needs to take additional measures to improve the worker's well-being. In addition to the start of this collective journey, Hutten invites newly joining coworkers to paint what happiness means in five years time. If personal health is what you aspire, then the company will support you in becoming more healthy during the upcoming years. If, on the other hand, you are more into engaging customers, then the caterer will provide you with opportunities and training to improve your skills and knowledge in customer relations. More important is that coworkers are invited to share and explain their "happiness painting" with a wider audience. The idea is that others may be able and willing to support you in making your dream come true. With this playful but systematic approach, Hutten Catering has found ways to listen to its team workers and to structure the dialogue aimed at promoting the interests and needs of the coworkers. In the end, the company hopes to benefit from this other-oriented approach to conducting its business.

A second example is provided by Pluryn, which is one of the largest care organizations for the disabled in The Netherlands. Its service offering ranges from care provisions for the mildly disabled to those suffering from very severe disorders. A cornerstone of its policies and practices is what people with disabilities can do – instead of what they cannot do. This philosophy led to the start of the first of many social enterprises in 1997. BliXem is a restaurant run by people with disabilities, mostly but not exclusively people with Down's syndrome. One of Pluryn's clients was a young woman suffering from severe spasms. She communicates via a screen that she operates with her eyes. Very motivated and talented, she wanted a job in Pluryn's communications department – preferably working for BliXem. After making some adjustments to her working conditions and schedule, it was possible to put her in charge of social media communications.

Activity

Randstad is the largest human resources provider and temporary staffing firm in the world.[16] Being a listed company Randstad has to deal with varying needs and desires of stakeholders as diverse as clients – both companies and individuals looking for work – own employees and shareholders. Despite the size of its global operations the company remains focused on adding value to clients. Therefore, listening is seen as a core competence. Through its Customer Delight program, Randstad aims to optimize the balance between the interests of companies looking for temporary hires and job seekers looking for work that meets their material and immaterial needs. A second example of a client-oriented program is Work as a Service (WaaS). Even though it is still in its infancy, WaaS offers a promise for those perpetually looking for temporary employment. Through the program Randstad guarantees job seekers suitable and challenging work and additional education and training. They have become Randstad employees that the company is able to deploy and place at clients looking for talented and motivated workers.

Interface's biophilic design approach[17] also provides an interesting example of agapeic activity aimed at improving the well-being of others. Together with UK architect Oliver Heath the company created a "positive space" in a school for children with autism in Hackney (London), based on a child's innate attraction to nature.[18] An unused space in the school was turned into a safe and recuperative area, well away from the usual noise and bustle of a playground. Depending on their mood, the space allows children to reach out and play with others, but also to hide away from others in one of the many alcoves and cubes it is filled with. The children are in control about their activities and the (avoidance of) interactions with other children.

Our final example comes from Schijvens. The management runs the business as if all partners are family members. "We are here to help each other and by taking care of each other's concerns - and celebrating both individual and collective successes, the best business results are achieved," managing director Shirley Schijvens comments. To strengthen the relationship with its partners, the organization introduced a WhatsApp group to facilitate the communication between all members. News about the business as well as personal information is shared. In addition, Schijvens invites and pays the partners to attend the annual Suppliers Day, hosted by one of the members of this "extended family." It results in "a feeling of belonging."

4.7 Analysis

When Randstad founder Frits Goldschmeding introduced the concept of agape in what is now the largest temporary staffing firm in the world, his idea was that agape would permeate and inspire the behavior and actions of his company and its employees – and contribute to the transformation of the economy. More than 50 years later, management is still inspired by the philosophy of its founder. The same counts for all companies that took part in our research. The inspiration of the founders and the role of senior management in keeping the values associated with agape alive appear to be crucial factors in the way these businesses operate and the extent to which they are other-oriented. All companies are explicit in their focus on the well-being of others – even though the attention for the well-being of some stakeholders takes priority over that of others. Companies like Hutten, Randstad, and Asito emphasize the importance of putting employees first. Their well-being, personal growth, recognition of who they are and where they come from, and the fit between job and personality are put center stage. For Schijvens, MAAS Coffee, and Peeze Coffee the relationship with their suppliers and their employees or farmers comes first, while Pluryn prioritizes the well-being of its clients. Interface takes a more holistic approach in its love for nature and – as a result – focuses on the well-being of employees, clients, business partners, and others as ends in themselves and as agents to create value for society and nature. The fact that in their agapeic focus some stakeholders are more important than others does not mean that we are dealing with exclusivity. On the contrary. A company like Schijvens put an incredible amount of effort in making sure that its business is one hundred percent circular in 2021, while caterer Hutten sees organic food and the reduction of food waste as top priorities next to its focus on the well-being of its coworkers. It leads to the conclusion that some companies take a more integral approach to agape, while other focus more on aspects or specific stakeholder interests. In rating the companies, their commitment to a more integral approach is also dependent on the extent to which they see humans and nonhumans as ends in themselves, listen to others and hear what they say, and translate this into their actions and policies.

Even though all companies had a clear purpose that exceeds making money, we found significant differences in the ways in which (financial) incentives and motivations were aligned with the focus on agape. Here we see differences between listed companies and non-listed companies – and more in particular between family businesses and nonfamily businesses. In listed companies – or those controlled by private equity – there is clearly more focus on meeting financial targets than in non-listed companies, including family businesses. Defining characteristic of the decision-making and policy-making in family businesses is their focus on sustaining the business for the next generations and preparing the next generations to take the helm. This often means that family businesses with strong values and a focus on agape see growth and financial return as a necessary condition for survival. These are not ends in themselves. Obviously, the companies expect financial benefits from their agapeic business operations. But it is more like an investment in the way that (Mauss, 2006) describes a gift: in the end you expect the gift to be reciprocated. More importantly, the family businesses were geared toward the flourishing of the business, the legacy they leave behind, and the contribution they make to human (and nonhuman) progress. This brought us to the conclusion that companies differ in the resources they are able and willing to commit to the implementation of agape. For some a commitment to agape is unconditional, while for others it is conditional, for instance, of the success of an agapeic way of doing business in terms of financial return, operational success, innovation, or employee satisfaction.

Using the abovementioned distinctions, we can compile an overview with four quadrants of agapeic profiling (Figure 4.1). On the X-axis companies can be profiled on the basis of their (un)conditional commitment to agape. The Y-axis indicates whether companies take an integral approach versus those that focus on one aspect or stakeholder group only.

Although agape is often described as extended love toward all human beings (Outka, 1972; Fromm, 2007; Francis, 2020), businesses appear to

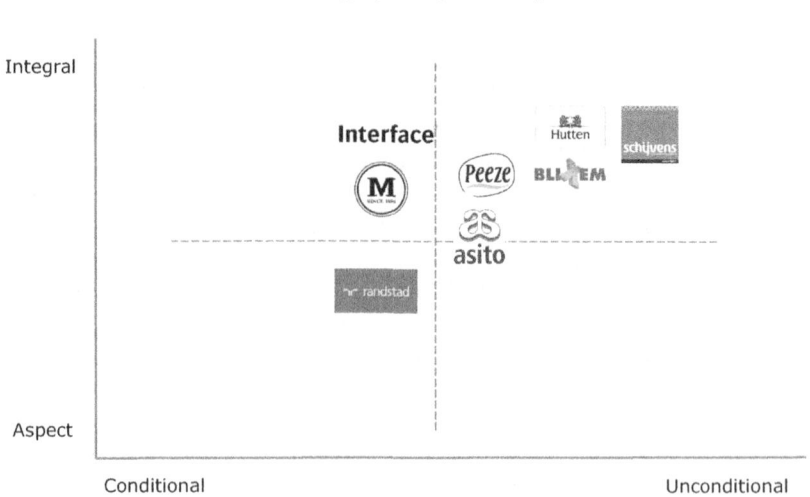

Figure 4.1 Agapeic profiling of companies

be more selective in the commitment to the well-being of others and their flourishing.[19] Drawing an analogy with Michael Walzer's (1983) concept of "spheres of justice" we could characterize the other-oriented priorities and efforts of businesses as "spheres of love." A company like Randstad displays a more "transactional" approach towards agape, while Schijvens, Hutten, BliXem, and Peeze appear to be more "transcendent." The focus of Interface and MAAS we consider as being cooperative, whereas Asito finds itself somewhere between transcendent and, what we would like to call, "considerate."

4.8 Conclusion

According to Adam Smith and David Hume, sympathy and benevolence are considered to be basic human dispositions. In the opening words of his *Theory of Moral Sentiments* Smith argues that no matter how selfish you think man is,

> it's obvious that there are some principles in his nature that give him an interest in the welfare of others, and make *their* happiness necessary to *him*, even if he gets nothing from it but the pleasure of seeing it.

Managers and employees working in business organizations are no different in this respect than any other human being. The employee of the hotel reservation service company provided an example of a spontaneous "agapeic moment," or an ordinary virtue, as Ignatieff (2017) has denoted this type of behavior. Studying eight, rather diverse, value-driven companies in The Netherlands, we come to the conclusion that it is not only individuals within businesses that are open to the needs of others, but that businesses themselves have varying ways of committing to human and nonhuman flourishing.

Agape is an expression of a value-based approach to business and management. Following Dees (2012) we distinguished between a culture of charity and an agapeic culture of problem-solving. Agape, we argue, is more than charity, compassion, empathy, sympathy, benevolence, or comparable concepts and belongs to the domain of the culture of problem-solving and value creation. At the core of the concept are three key elements: flourishing of others, consensus or consent, and effort and results. It resulted in the following definition of agape:

> A commitment to the flourishing of someone or something else that the other explicitly agrees with or consents to, and expresses itself in concrete actions and realizations.

This definition makes clear that agape is more than just another expression of CSR and CSV. It even goes beyond benevolence and sympathy that both seem to address the dimensions of *connectivity* – engaging in a relationship with others and sensing their needs, wants and opportunities – and *activity* – actions following these perceived needs or opportunities – but not the dimension of *alterity*. It is, in particular, the dimension of alterity that sets agape apart. Listening to others and hearing what they say may not necessarily be the forte of business organizations. It is here that management effort has to materialize and result in a culture that:

- Engages with others,
- Listens to them and hears what they say,
- Demonstrates that it uses this information in decision-making and the development of policies,
- Evaluates the actions, policies, processes, practices, and outcomes of other-oriented interactions,
- Makes adjustments based on what it has learned.

We have called this the *agapeic turn*, going from an "inside looking outwards" approach of doing business to an "outside looking inwards" approach. Our research has shown that this concept of agape is, in principle, applicable to all business organizations – even to those dedicated to the creation of financial and economic value. The ways in which they are committed to the flourishing of someone or something else will, however, differ from one company to another.

Further research is needed to highlight the importance of agape as a new concept in the context of business and the additionality of this concept, compared to notions ranging from CSR and CSV to humanistic management, corporate philanthropy, or social entrepreneurship. First, comparative, international research is required to better understand potential differences between companies and the context in which they operate with regard to connectivity, activity, and alterity. Second, additional research is needed to improve our understanding of how companies can best stimulate, enlarge, and improve their agapeic policies, processes, and actions. Third, more insight is needed in the agapeic capabilities (cf. Sen, 1989, 1993, 2003; Nussbaum, 2011) of C-level and senior managers and of board members to create and maintain thriving business environments which respect and support the needs, interests, and opportunities of others and, as a consequence, those of their.

Acknowledgments

The authors like to thank the Goldschmeding Foundation for its generous support of this work as part of a larger project.

Notes

1 Abstained from its religious meaning, in ancient Greek the term referred to the concept of protection.
2 Dees (2012) refers to the public response to the Tsunami in 2005, when relief organizations received more funds than they could actually deploy. Doctors without Borders even turned donors away.

3 In his encyclical *Laudato Si*, Pope Francis (2015) already called on us to respect nature and our natural environment.

4 Obviously, what counts for me also counts for the other if the objective is to establish mutual communication and a relationship that acknowledges the other as a person.

5 The authors speak of agape in the sense of charity and not in the stricter way as we have described agape in section 4.

6 The economist Joel Waldfogel (2009) argues that charity increases society's net social (and economic) satisfaction. In general, goods and services are worth more to persons having fewer of them than to those having plenty. Giving to the deprived can therefore ease the burden on the state.

7 Although agape is a concept that is mainly used in the relationship and interaction between humans, theoretically there is no reason to exclude the concept of agape from a relationship between humans and the earth system of which we are just a part. We can feel love and affection for animals, for nature that surrounds us and even for Gaia. However, to meet the requirement of alterity (see hereafter), the needs, interests and flourishing of nature is always mediated by humans.

8 Ultimately, it is not about hearing what the other has to say, instead of just listening. Whether the other has been heard depends on the extent to which his or her message is translated into concrete activities by the listener.

9 It is not the benefits for the company that justify the actions or the behavior, but the orientation on the other as an end in herself or himself. That does imply that the business cannot benefit from other-directed or oriented behavior. On the contrary. What is crucial, however, is the other as an end in her- or himself as perceived by the other.

10 Where Mèle (2012) particularly focuses on agape in an attempt to create a more complete view of business ethics, it is our intention to create a more complete view on agape in the economic, financial, production, human relations, customer relations and societal practice of business.

11 With this reference to an implicit response we refer to actions that may not necessarily give the other what she or he needs or wants, but that the actions are informed by what has been said.

12 The empirical research consisted of a survey with approx. 500 respondents and case-study research among eight companies.

13 https://thenaturalstep.org/

14 https://biomimicry.net/

15 Polyvinyl butyral (PVB) is a resin with a strong cohesiveness, optical clarity, adhering easily to many surfaces.

16 www.statista.com/statistics/257876/staffing-companies-worldwide-by-revenue/

17 The term refers to E.O. Wilson's Biophilia (1984) which is "innate tendency to focus on life and lifelike processes". Elsewhere Wilson (1984) describes biophilia as "inborn affinity human beings have for other forms of life, an affiliation evoked, according to circumstances, by pleasure, or a sense of security, or awe, or even fascination blended with revulsion"

18 https://www.interface.com/EU/en-GB/campaign/positive-spaces/hackney-garden-school-en_GB

19 Obviously, this case-study research comprised only eight companies. Conclusions can, therefore, not be generalized. The current study does, however, provide interesting insights that can tested in more comprehensive empirical research.

References

Argandona, A. (2011). Beyond contracts: Love in firms. *Journal of Business Ethics*, 99: 77–85.

Augustine. (1961). *Confessions*. London: Penguin.

Autry, J. (1991). *Love and profit: The art of caring leadership*. New York, NY: William Morrow and Co.

Benedictus XVI. (2009). *Caritas in Veritate*. Encyclical Letter, Vatican City, 29 June.

Buijs, G. (2012). *Publieke liefde*. [Public love], Inaugural address. Amsterdam: Free University.

Cavanaugh, L., Bettman, J., and Luce, M. F. (2015, October). Feeling love and doing more for distant others. *Journal of Marketing Research*, 52(5): 657–673.

Cullen, J., Praveen Parboteeah, K., and Victor, B. (2003). The effects of ethical climates on organizational commitment. *Journal of Business Ethics*, 46: 127–141.

Dees, J. G. (2012). A tale of two cultures. *Journal of Business Ethics*, 111: 321–334.

DeFede, J. (2003). *The day the world came to Gander*. New York, NY: HarperCollins Publishers.

Duyndam, J., and Poorthuis, M. (2003). *Levinas*. Rotterdam: Lemniscaat

Faldetta, G. (2011). The logic of gift and gratuitousness in business relationships. *Journal of Business Ethics*, 100(1): 67–77.

Fama, E. F., and Jensen, M. C. (1983). The separation of ownership and control. *Journal of Law and Economics*, 26: 301–325.

Francis. (2015). *Laudato Si*, Encyclical letter, Vatican City, 24 May.

Francis. (2020). *Fratelli Tutti*, Encyclical letter, Vatican City, 3 October.

Frankena. (1987). Beneficence/benevolence. *Social Philosophy & Policy*, 4(2): 1–20.

Friedman, M. (1970). The social responsibility of business is to increase its profits. *New York Times Magazine*, September 13: 32–33.

Fromm, E. (2007). *The art of loving*. New York, NY: HarperCollins Publishers.

Hawken, P. (1993). *The ecology of commerce. A declaration of sustainability*. New York, NY: HarperCollins Publishers.

Hill, R. P. (2002, June). Compassionate love, agape and altruism. *Journal of Macromarketing*, 22(1): 19–31

Hume, D. (1960). *A treatise of human nature* (originally published in 1738). Oxford: Clarendon.

Hume, D. (1961). *An enquiry concerning the principles of morals* (originally published in 1751). Oxford: Clarendon.

Ignatieff, M. (1984). *The needs of strangers*. New York, NY: Viking.

Ignatieff, M. (2017). *The ordinary virtues*. Cambridge, MA: Harvard University Press.

Jensen, M. C., and Meckling, W. H. (1976). Theory of the firm: Managerial behavior, agency costs and ownership structure. *Journal of Financial Economics*, 3(4): 305–360.

Karakas, F., & Sarigollu, E. (2013). The role of leadership in creating virtuous and compassionate organizations: Narratives of benevolent leadership in an Anatolian tiger. *Journal of Business Ethics*, 113(4), 663–678.

Kaulingfreks, R., and Ten Bos, R. (2007). On faces and defacement. *Business Ethics: A European Review*, 16(3), July.

Kekes, J. (1987). Benevolence: A minor virtue. *Social Philosophy & Policy*, 4(2): 21–36.

Kierkegaard, S. (1962). *Works of love*. New York, NY: Harper Row.

Levinas, E. (1980). *Totality and infinity*. Dordrecht: Kluwer.

Levinas, E. (2003). *Het menselijk gelaat* [*The human face*]. Amsterdam: Ambo.

Lewis, C. S. (1960). *The four loves*. New York, NY: Harcourt, Brace, Jovanovich.

Mauss, M. (2006). *The gift*. London: Taylor & Francis Ltd.

McCann, D. (2011). The principle of gratuitousness. *Journal of Business Ethics*, 100: 55–66.

McCloskey, D. (2006). *Bourgeois virtues. Ethics for an age of commerce*. Chicago, IL: University of Chicago Press.

Melé, D. (2012). The Christian notion of Αγάπη (agápē): Towards a more complete view of business ethics. In Prastacos, G., Wang, F., and Soderquist, K. (Eds.), *Leadership through the classics*. New York, NY: Springer, 79–91.

Melé, D., and Naughton, M. (2011). The encyclical-letter "Caritas in Veritate." *Journal of Business Ethics*, 100: 1–7.

Mercier, G., and Deslandes, G. (2019). Formal and informal benevolence in a profit-oriented context. *Journal of Business Ethics*, 165, 125–143 https://doi.org/10.1007/s10551-019-04108-9

Nussbaum, M. (2011). *Creating capabilities*. Cambridge, MA: Belknap Press of Harvard University Press.

Nygren, A. (1953). *Agape and eros*. London: S.P.C.K.

Outka, G. (1972). *Agape: An ethical analysis*. New Haven, CT: Yale University Press.

Pope, A. (2013). Agape. In LaFollette, H. (Ed.), *The international encyclopedia of ethics* (pp. 138–144). Oxford: Blackwell Publishing Ltd.

Protasi, S. (2008). A necessary conflict: Eros and philia in a love relationship. *Nordic-Mediterraneum*, 3(1): 68–97.

Roberts, K. (2005). *Lovemarks: The future beyond brands*, New York: Power House Books.

Sanders, T. (2002). *Love is a killer app*, New York, Random House

Sen, A. (1989). Development as capability expansion. *Journal of Development Planning*, 19, 41–58

Sen, A. (1993). Capability and well-being. In Nussbaum M., and Sen, A. (Eds.), *The quality of life*. Oxford: Clarendon Press, 30–53.

Sen, A. (2003). Development as capability expansion. In Fukuda-Parr S. et al. (Eds.), *Readings in human development*. New Delhi and New York, NY: Oxford University Press.

Sheth, J., Sisodia, R., Sheth, J. N., Wolfe, D. B., & Wolfe, D. (2007). *Firms of endearment: How world-class companies profit from passion and purpose*. Pearson.

Sisodia, R. et al. (2014). *Firms of endearment*. New York, NY: Pearson Education.

Sison, A., and Fontrodona, J. (2012). The common good of the firm in the Aristotelian-Thomistic tradition. *Business Ethics Quarterly*, 22(2): 211–246.

Smith, A. (2010). *The theory of moral sentiments* (originally published in 1759). London: Penguin.

Victor, B., and Cullen, J. (1988). The organizational basis of ethical work climates. *Administrative Science Quarterly*, 33: 101–125.

Waldfogel, J. (2009). *Scroogenomics: Why you shouldn't buy presents for the holidays*. Princeton, NJ: Princeton University Press.

Walzer, M. (1983). *Spheres of justice: A defense of pluralism and equality*. New York, NY: Basic Books.

Wilson, E. O. (1984). *Biophilia*. Harvard University Press.

Worline, M., and Dutton, J. (2017). *Awakening compassion at work*. Oakland, CA: Berrett-Koehler.

5 Love and the Moral Structure of Business

Toward a Tripartite Ethos of Human Enterprise

Michael F. Mascolo and David A. Greenway

Is Business Just Business?

We tend to think of business and love as occupying separate spheres of life. Business operates in the impersonal public sphere, whereas love occurs in the private or interpersonal sphere. Business practices are largely separate and distinct from individual morals, societal values, and responsibility – what Freeman describes as the "separation thesis" (1994). There is, however, nothing natural or inevitable about this bifurcation. Indeed, the common belief that love properly belongs to the private sphere functions to protect business from its moral force. However, love is not something that is encased in the private sphere. It already exists within the practice of business. To the extent that self-interest is a form of self-love, it already exists, sotto voce, in the public sphere of business. If this is so, in business as in other forms of life, love of self will necessarily come into conflict with love for the other (Macmurray, 1961). When this happens, love functions as a moral emotion (Velleman, 1999). Our love for the other is self-arresting: it calls on us to include the other within the sphere of our own interests. In this way, in business as in everyday life, a moral identity is born.

Theologian John Macmurray (1961) suggested that human action is organized around two primary emotions: fear for the self and love for the other. We understand love as "care," while fear for the self consists of the human tendency to avoid vulnerability in favor of emotional self-protection from others. Depending on the context and particular sphere of action (e.g., public or private), we may find ourselves vacillating between these poles of experience. One might suggest that it is in the very tension between self-interest and love for the other that moral selfhood emerges and takes form (Cima & Schubeck, 2001; Macmurray, 1961). Evolutionary biologist David Sloan Wilson remarked that "self-interest is the greatest impediment to love" (Wilson & Barsade, 2020). From this perspective, it is by intentionally reconciling the contradiction between self-interest and concern for others that we come to create a moral identity. We do this when we acknowledge the experience and suffering of

DOI: 10.4324/9781003254034-6

others and define our self-interest to include the value and well-being of others. Therefore, we adopt a view of love as the felt state of bestowing value onto some beloved object (Singer, 1984).

In this chapter we propose a tripartite ethos of organizations and human organization and enterprise. Current business practices are defined primarily in terms of *rights and freedom* – e.g., self-interest, the free market, the rights of owners (versus the rights of employees and consumers, etc.) – and *virtue* (doing what's good) – e.g. corporate responsibility. We suggest that *love* – i.e., acting out of concern and care for the other – is the critical and missing component of the moral framework that guides contemporary business practices. In offering this tripartite ethos, we draw on a relational approach to morality and moral development (Frimer & Walker, 2009; Mascolo et al., under review; Mascolo & DiBianca Fasoli, 2020). To better understand love within human enterprise, we first examine what it means to speak about love as an emotion and follow with a discussion of the structure and forms of love. We then outline our model of a tripartite ethos of human enterprise. We illustrate the role of love within this tripartite model, with an analysis of the philosophy and practices of the Market Basket corporation, a popular grocery chain located in Massachusetts that earned high levels of employee and customer loyalty through a commitment to a "people first, groceries second" ethos.

What It Means to Love

To what does the word *love* refer? Love is broadly considered to be a form of emotion. To understand what we mean by love, it is helpful to first situate love within a broader understanding of the nature of emotional experience. Drawing on a relational conception of emotion (Mascolo, 2009, 2020; Fogel, 1993; Lazarus, 1991), emotional experiences consist of felt modes of engaging the world. As such, emotions are not simply inner states encased within the private interior of individuals; instead, they are relational processes that arise between the person and the world. It is helpful to understand emotional states in terms of at least three broad categories of interacting systems. These include (a) motive-event relations (sometimes referred to as appraisals), (b) phenomenal experience, and (c) motive-action tendencies (Frijda, 2009; Frijda et al., 1989; Mascolo, 2020; Young & Zhu, 2019).

Appraisals (i.e., motive-event relations) consist of ongoing assessments of changes between one's circumstances and one's goals, motives, desires, and concerns (Frijda, 1986). In any given situation, appraisals typically operate outside of consciousness (Mascolo & Kallio, 2019). Different forms of appraisal produce bodily changes and different forms of phenomenal experience (Schwarz & Clore, 2007) which correspond to the felt aspects of the person's mode of engaging the world. Motive-action tendencies, as the focus of our exploration, consist of what a person is motivated to do in the context of the ongoing appraisal (Frijda, 2004). They consist of patterns of expressive (Ekman, 1993) and instrumental action (Frijda, 2004) that function in the service of operate goals, motives, and concerns. Unless regulated, expressive and bodily aspects of emotional states communicate a person's emotional state to others. Instrumental actions function to bring events in line with the goals, motives, and concerns involved in a person's appraisal of a given event (Scherer, 1982).

Felt experience plays a central role in organizing representations of personally significant circumstances in consciousness. At any given point in time, nonconscious appraisal processes monitor the full range of events for their adaptive significance – i.e., functioning in the service of operate goals, motives, and concerns (Moors et al., 2013). Appraisals that have implications for the fate of one's motives evoke affective changes (Roseman, 2004). Those affective changes thereupon select, from the full range of unconsciously appraised events, those events that are most significant to the person's goals, motives, and concerns (Lazarus, 1991; Lewis, 1986). They amplify their importance and organize representations of those events into consciousness for more deliberate action (Tomkins, 1981). In this way, emotions play a central role in the organization of conscious life (W. J. Freeman, 2000).

The Structure of Love

Love is the felt state of bestowing value onto an object (Rempel & Burris, 2005; Singer, 1984). Table 5.1 provides a generalized description of the structure of love as it is understood in Western-European cultures. The "appraisal" involved in love is better understood as a kind of bestowal. To make this point, Singer (1984) distinguishes the concept of bestowal from the everyday concept of appraisal. While an appraisal reflects the impartial, impersonal, or "market value" of the object, a bestowal is an expression of personal valuing; it is not conditioned by the "objective"

Table 5.1 The Omnibus Structure of Love

Motive-event relation (appraisal)	Phenomenal experience	Motive-action tendency (Expressive and instrumental action)
Bestowal of value on a known person	Feeling of being moved toward the other; holistic sense of communion, completion or harmony with the other.	Making the interests of the other my own; acting on the basis of the interests of the other; to take care of, nurture or protect the object; to commune or give of oneself to the other; to form a joint identity with the other; possess the object or have it as one's own.

features of the object in question. For example, when purchasing a home, a house may be appraised at some market value – an estimate of what buyers are willing to pay for the house. Because love is a bestowal rather than an appraisal, a person can thus love a house regardless of its appraised market value.

Like other emotions, love is directed toward an object (or other); it is *about* something, real or imagined. Unless we are speaking of self-love, love is not typically about the self. This stipulation is important in distinguishing mature from immature forms of love. For example, the child does not love the caregiver out of a sense of valuing him or her as a person who is known to have particular qualities; instead, the child's love consists of the embodied appreciation what the mother does *for the child* – for the care and affection she bestows onto the child. This does not render the child's love less valid – only less fully developed. In contrast to such early forms of love, mature love is born of *knowledge* (Fromm, 1961) – an appreciation of the other person as person, and not simply an appreciation for what the other does for the self. By bestowing value onto different types of objects, individuals can love their job, colleagues, or organizations.

In love, because the other has value to us, its motive-action tendency involves the desire to care for, nurture, and protect the loved object. Further, when we bestow value onto an object, we want to *possess* it – that is, to have it for ourselves. If the object of love is another person, we may seek a joint identity with the other – an "us" rather than simply "you" and "me" (Nozick, 1991). We seek to make the interests of the other part of our own. In so doing, we are motivated to give of ourselves to the other. Giving of our self is different from sacrificing the self for the other (Fromm, 1961). When we give of ourselves, we not only retain our integrity, our selves are also enhanced: we feel our own vitality, our power in being to contribute to the well-being of the beloved.

The phenomenal experience of love consists of the felt aspects of acting on the basis of one's bestowal of value onto the object or person. When we care for, nurture, or act on the basis of the interests of the other, we experience a sense of vitality – the power that comes from contributing to the well-being of the other or the loved object. We feel an increased sense of communion with the other, completion, or harmony with the other (Davitz, 2016). The experience is not something that is separate from the bestowal or motive-action tendency; instead, it is felt state of the bestowal and pattern of action readiness toward the other.

How Love Transforms Self-Interest

At this point, we return to Macmurray's (1961) distinction between fear for the self and love for the other. Viewed as an expression of self-interest, and to the extent that business activity is typically understood as an expression of self-interest, love for the other is typically seen as secondary or even irrelevant (George, 2014). But this assertion depends heavily on what it means to speak of self-interest. Self-interest is not necessarily to be equated with selfishness (Duska, 2014; Rocha & Ghoshal, 2006)—that is to act in the service of one's self. However, self-interest need not be narrowly focused on the self. In love, the well-being of the other becomes part of the interests of the self. As a result, the self becomes enhanced as one incorporates the other into one's own sense of self (Deepak et al., 2019; Fromm, 1961).

Therefore, love transforms self-interest by bringing us outside of ourselves. When this happens, love becomes a moral emotion (Velleman, 1999). Drawing on the Kantian notion of reverence for the other, Velleman (1999) suggests that when we love, our awareness of the value of the other "arrests" self-love. That is, love for the other "arrests our tendencies toward emotional self-protection from another person, tendencies to draw ourselves in and close ourselves off from being affected by him. Love disarms our emotional defenses; it makes us vulnerable to the other" (p. 361). In this way, when we act out of a genuine appreciation of the value and dignity of the other, we are motivated to treat the other as an end unto themselves, and not merely as a means toward one's own end.

Frimer and Walker (2009) advance a similar thesis in their reconciliation model of the development of moral identity. They suggest that moral identity develops through the constructive integration of self-interest and concern for others. Contrary to the idea that humans are primarily self-interested beings, it is possible to identify expressions of both self-interest and concern for others early in life. Self-interest, of course, is easily identifiable in the young infant's emotional reactions to failures to meet her biological and physical needs. However, infants also show signs of concern for others early in life. Neonates cry in response to hearing another infant cry, a reaction that is broadly understood to indicate an early form of empathy (Stern & Cassidy, 2018). Empathy develops over the course of infancy (Uzefovsky et al., 2020). Infants as young as 8 months of age have been observed in proactive attempts to help others in simple situations (e.g., retrieving an object unknowingly dropped by an adult (Schuhmacher et al., 2019). Over the course of development, children increasingly express concern for others who are in physical and emotional pain (Stern & Cassidy, 2018; Zahn-Waxler et al., 1983).

Over the course of early childhood, self-interest and concern for other develop along separate pathways. In any given context, children tend to exhibit either self-interest or concern for others – but not both simultaneously. With further development, however, children become aware of circumstances in which self-interest and concern for others come into conflict (Hoffmann et al., 2015; Killen & Nucci, 1995). A child may wish to keep a toy for the self, but simultaneously be concerned about her friend's exclusion. In such circumstances, children have difficulty resolving the conflict. They tend to vacillate between acting out of self-interest and concern for the other. As children develop into adolescents, they gain skills for addressing this conflict. In so doing, they can adopt at least three broad strategies for resolving the tension. They can (a) marginalize concern for the other and develop an identity around self-interest, (b) marginalize self-interest and move toward a self-less identity organized around concern for others, or (c) reconcile self-interest and concern for others. In so doing, the developing individual consolidates a moral identity in which concern for the other becomes part of the interests and values that define the self.

Over the course of development, the process of reconciling self-interest and concern for self produces a moral self that is increasingly defined in terms of systems of virtue – images of the good – that include but extend beyond the individual concern for self. The virtues that define our moral selves become the values we live by. Self-interest becomes transformed. It is in our interest to act out of virtue, care, and love for the other because those values constitute our sense of who we are. To fail to honor them is to do damage to both self and other.

The process of forging a moral identity is restricted neither to childhood nor to individual persons. In individuals, the construction of moral identity is a life-long process. While a business is not a person, businesses and other organizations have cultures, missions, values, and identities. Their practices are organized by their sense of purpose, as well as a shared sense – however centralized or diffuse – of what it means to be a company. The life of a business – like that of an individual – is enhanced through the process of forging an acting upon a moral identity – by making virtue and care part of the actual business enterprise itself (André & Pache, 2016; Bejou, 2011). This view, of course, is consistent with that articulated by Adam Smith (1776), who argued that self-interest must be subordinated a broader moral agenda (Bevan & Werhane, 2015).

Love within a Tripartite Ethos of Human Enterprise

It is easy to make the case that caring for the needs of employees and customers is good for business (Adhariani & Siregar, 2018; Bejou, 2011; Bowie, 1991). If a business wants to make a profit, it is necessary to offer a product or service of value to the customer. Leaders who act out of care for their employees and customers tend to generate loyalty, productivity, and profit (Francis & Keegan, 2020; Hill & Watkins, 2009). Despite the validity and lure of these statements, this is not the argument we wish to make.

Instead, we want to call into question common suppositions that locate moral concerns as somehow external to the activities of businesses. We seek to call into question common distinctions such as business versus ethics, public versus private, self-interest versus love for the other. All forms of social action necessarily occur against the backdrop of inescapable moral frameworks (Taylor, 1989). As forms of social activity, businesses are always embedded in socio-moral frameworks. In what follows, we argue that socio-moral issues are not external to business activity, but instead are foundational components of business activity itself. Indeed, the very assertion that self-interest and the pursuit of profit are proper motives for business activity is itself as moral judgment. We suggest that moral concerns are not merely constraints that put limitations on business activity; they are also positive forces that function to enhance businesses that transform them into self-sustaining vehicles for promoting human flourishing, including the flourishing of the business itself.

The most common moral justification for business activity is based on an ethos of individual rights. This includes, of course, the right to pursue one's own business agenda by seeking profits. The focus on the inviolate rights of individuals is the bedrock of a democratic society. However, while it provides dominant economic ethos in Western culture, it is by no means the only possible one. Haidt and Kesebir (2010) have commented on what they call the "great narrowing" of moral frameworks in Western society and moral psychology. Traditionally, what constitutes the domain of moral concerns was quite broad. Moral life was variously organized around concerns of rights, freedom, harm, virtue, character, care, loyalty, honor, duty, purity, hierarchy, divinity, taste, and other standards of strong evaluation. We suggest that the range of moral concerns that are applicable to business and organizations should be extended beyond the narrow confines of economic self-interest. As shown in Figure 5.1, at the very least, it is possible to envision business ethos – a core moral identity – embraces a triad of moral concerns, including considerations of rights, virtue, and care.

Love plays an important role in a tripartite economic ethos. It does so in three basic ways. First, as discussed above, love for the other plays a role in "arresting" self-interest. The clash between fear for the self and love for the other fosters the development of a moral self, one that transforms self-interest to include a concern for the welfare of the other. Second, love plays a direct role in mediating the ethos of care. Love implies care. To say that love is the feeling of bestowing value on the other implies that one cares about the valued other or object. In turn, the activity of extending care to another is a core expression of love. Thus, any moral code that embraces the ethos of care implies the desirability of acting out of love.

The third role of love is both more fundamental and obscure. As stated throughout, love is a form of valuing; it is the felt state of bestowing of value onto some object. Moral concerns are forms of strong evaluation (Taylor, 1989). At base, moral concerns involve judgments of what ought or ought not to exist. As forms of strong evaluation, any moral norm is defined in terms of some form of good. To the extent that we love that which is good, love plays a role in each ethos described in Figure 5.1. We love what is good in ourselves; we love our rights to pursue the good of happiness; we love virtue. And, of course, to act out of care is to act out

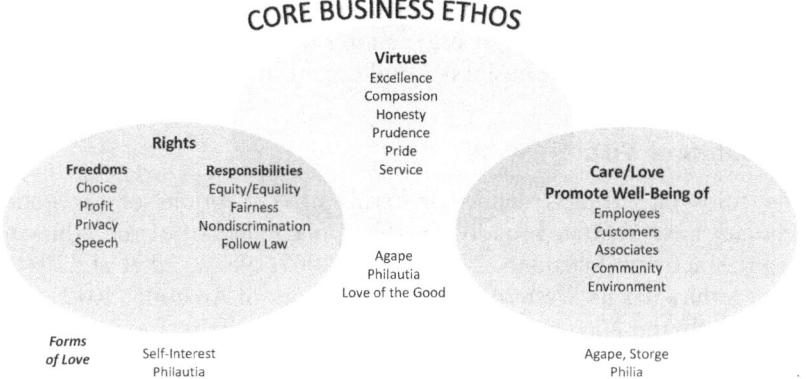

Figure 5.1 A tripartite economic ethos.

of love. To the extent that love is the felt sense of valuing something, to act on the basis of moral values is to act on the basis of some form of love.

The Ethos of Rights

An ethos of rights provides the freedom to pursue self-interest and profit (Machan, 1995, 2015; Robinson, 1978). People have the right to pursue their own agendas, free from arbitrary intrusion by government or another social agent. The concept of rights is founded upon the idea of the primacy of the inviolate and bounded individual. Individuals are free to exercise their right to pursue their own self-interest (e.g., profit), but in so doing must respect the rights and boundaries of others. Although it is not always acknowledged, within the ethos of rights, rights have traditionally been understood as implying a set of responsibilities. From this framework, moral and legal rules are necessary primarily to ensure that businesses honor those responsibilities. These include stipulations that guard against abuse (e.g., that people are paid a fair wage; to protect the environment) to ensure that businesses do not infringe upon the rights of others (e.g., ensuring safety, fair prices); that businesses operate on principles of equality and fairness (e.g., nondiscrimination and sexual harassment); and to assure that businesses contribute broadly to the common good (i.e., through tax policy).

Beyond the concept of rights, it is also possible to justify the moral status of self-interest based upon beliefs about its contribution to the common good. For example, the profit motive is often justified with reference to the good that free markets can achieve – that free markets are successful in producing goods and services, increase the general wealth of the population; and so forth (Machan, 1995, 2015). Some approaches to self-interest suggest that self-interest – even selfishness – needs no moral justification (Gauthier, 1982), that it is both right and good for people to pursue self-interest simply for the sake of self-interest (Rand, 1964). However, Rand's analysis not only ignores but also devalues the role of "love" in the context of businesses and organizations.

The Ethos of Virtue

The ethos of virtue is defined in terms of conceptions of the good. Scholars have written broadly on the applicability of virtue ethics to business activity (Hartman, 2008; Klein, 2002; Newstead et al., 2019). Virtue ethics has its Western origins in the work of Aristotle (2012), and particularly the *Nicomachean Ethics*. Virtues consist of forms of moral goodness. While virtues are often understood in terms of the cultivation of virtuous "traits," we prefer to think of virtues as representations of goodness. From this point of view, representations of goodness come into play in the formation of a company's moral identity.

To create a moral identity is to identify a company in terms of a set of moral virtues or values. Beyond self-interest, the moral identity asks, "what type of organization do we want to be? What is the good thing to do or be?" (Melé, 2009). Virtually all businesses and organizations embrace some series of values, however implicit or loosely defined. Within a tripartite economic ethos, the task becomes one of creating ways to identify the values that define a company and foster a sense of emotional investment in those values among employers and employees alike. While many companies have missions and value statements, it is both the emotional investment in moral values in the business enterprise itself that mobilizes action toward a genuine sense of purpose (André & Pache, 2016; Grandy & Sliwa, 2017; Ready & Truelove, 2011).

The Ethos of Care

An ethos of care is organized around promoting the well-being of others (Gilligan, 1982; Held, 2000; Simola, 2007; Wada, 2014), whether those others are employees, vendors, consumers, social groups, or the nation or world as a whole (Mercier & Deslandes, 2020; Solomon, 1998; Wada, 2014). An ethos of care is organized around a suite of interconnected practices as they are related to a company's sphere of relations (Nicholson & Kurucz, 2019; Pavlovich & Krahnke, 2012). These include engaging others with genuine concern, promoting human flourishing, respecting the inherent dignity of employees and customers, responding to individual and collective need, and building trusting and collaborative relationships (Formentin & Bortree, 2019). An ethos of care asks, "what is the caring, compassionate and even loving thing to do?" (Karakas & Sarigollu, 2013; Munro & Thanem, 2018). Within a business context, care and compassion mediates the relation between a business's economic purpose and the needs of the communities it serves.

Three Bottom Lines

Within this triad of values, instead of embracing the right to pursue profit as a singular "bottom line," a tripartite economic ethos holds out the promise of fostering a more moral marketplace without compromising self-interest as a core moral concern (Lin-Hi & Blumberg, 2012). By embracing three categories of "bottom lines" rather than merely one, no single moral concern need be primary, although each would be necessary. As a result, in organizational decision-making, each moral concern would exert a constraining influence on the other – retaining both shape and integrity of the tripartite ethos.

The tripartite ethos honors the triple bottom line of "people, profit, and planet." While "people, profit, and planet" addresses the categories of valued resources, the stakeholder approach allows business leaders and decision-makers to value these resources according to their own sensibilities and needs. Resources of The Commons (Ostrom, 1999) are valued through economic analysis return on investment (ROI) rather than through the tripartite ethos. For example, a chief executive officer (CEO) could meet the comparative standard of valuing people with a $15.00 wage. One on the surface, such an act would seem responsible – nudging a family of three over the federal poverty level. An organization that pursues such an act may be viewed quite favorably. However, in terms of caring of the other, it is difficult to imagine what type of existence or lifestyle $30k buys. The third element of love would demand a holistic look at the quality of life and the ability to meet healthcare costs, and advance economically, if only modestly.

The Market Basket Phenomenon

We explore the story of Market Basket as an example of how the three elements of the tripartite ethos – right, virtues, and care – play a structuring role in the life of an existing and vibrant organization. In so doing, we focus especially on the role of love as a virtue that structures the social organization and moral identity of an organization. Market Basket began a small family grocer in Lowell, Massachusetts. It was founded by Greek immigrants Athanasios and Efrosine Demoulas. In the latter part of the 19th century, Lowell was a booming manufacturing town located in an industrial era. However, in the early years of the 20th century, Lowell struggled economically as manufacturing migrated to other areas. During this time, Lowell remained home to a large and diverse community of immigrants. The first Demoulas business opened in 1917 – a neighborhood grocerette specializing in meats familiar to the diverse immigrant communities (Korschun & Welker, 2015). By 2014, the neighborhood market had grown to a regional chain of some 75+ stores and 25,000 employees across Massachusetts, New Hampshire, and Maine (*Company History & Timeline*, n.d.). The current and admired CEO

Arthur T. Demoulas ("Arthur T.") demonstrated an uncommon vision and work ethic. Like most of his senior leadership, Arthur T. started from the bottom – beginning with bagging groceries and working in almost every area of store operation. Arthur T. never fully shed his humble roots. Even as CEO, he could often be found behind the counter helping customers during his many visits to the stores under his oversight.

According to Korschun and Welker (2015), the organization's core values consist of the cultivation of a feeling of family, service to community, empowerment, and originality. Care for the other is thus "baked-in" to the culture. Decisions are informed by how any operational decisions and policy changes affect people. As employees are empowered to "do what is right" – a leadership philosophy championed by Arthur T. and what Greenleaf (1977) describes as "servant leadership." According to Greenleaf (1977), servant leadership is composed of both leaders who serve and servants who lead. The clarity and integrity of Market Basket's care for the other may be considered Market Basket's single greatest strength. In the summer of 2014, it would function as the spark that launched the largest non-unionized labor strike in US history. This strike brought employees, managers, suppliers, customers, and the communities together to save the culture Market Basket that each had built, while also and preserving the position of their beloved CEO Arthur T. Demoulas.

"The People Business First, The Grocery Business Second"

The grocery business is known for its paper-thin margins and heavy competition. Like most industries, the pressure to adopt new technologies, adapt to changing consumer habits, and experiment with marketing gambits would seem irresistible. At a minimum, one might expect a family business to lose strength in competition with international chains. However, Market Basket would not only resist these competitive forces, it would often perform better in some of the most difficult areas of performance. Since assuming leadership, Arthur T. has led Market Basket through significant growth and profitability – increasing the number of locations and outpacing competitors such as Stop and Shop, Shaw's, and Hannaford – each owned by large multinationals (Korschun & Welker, 2015). Customers were happy as well: Market Basket earned the number seven spot in *Consumer Reports* among the nation's largest competitors (2012, p. 2) – and continues to hold onto top national rankings (Stanger, n.d.). It offers items at much lower prices than its competitors. While an average grocery store averages 15,746 customer transactions per week, Market Basket averages 26,000 per store – countering lower margins with the earned loyalty of their customers (Korschun & Welker, 2015). In 2018, Market Basket and Trader Joes ranked in the top six nationally for competitive pricing. Importantly, Market Basket differs on another important element of any business – its people. Lower labor costs are one way in which businesses can protect their profits. However, Market Basket defied convention with payroll at 10.5% of gross sales compared to an industry average of 9.8% (Korschun & Welker, 2015). Burt Flickinger, Managing Director of a leading industry consulting group summed up this different operating philosophy as: "store staffing and service as in investment, where all their competitors look at store labor as being an expense" (Korschun & Welker, 2015, p. 24).

The distinctiveness of Market Basket can always be traced back to Arthur T.'s operating philosophy of "people business first, the grocery business second" (Korschun & Welker, 2015, p. 46). Market Basket's commitment to "people" extended far beyond the claim that "employees are our most important asset." Joe Schmidt, an operations supervisor, was quoted:

> The difference with this company is that it's a family company ... And the people aren't only co-workers; they're also family members ... so, to be able to duplicate this in the modern business world, I think it would be very difficult to find people as dedicated and loyal to a particular company as the people in this company, and I think that's the point.
>
> (Nickisch, 2014)

Thus, for Market Basket, family and community were synonymous – customers, employees, management, suppliers, and their communities were bound together by a shared belief that they were part of something both worthwhile and more important than any single person. Arthur T. understood that "Market Basket has a moral obligation to the communities we serve" (Korschun & Welker, 2015, p. 45). Whether manager, employee, or supplier, they were united by a shared mission to help people lead better lives and improve community well-being – and each internal constituency of them was empowered to make that happen.

A Display of Loyalty

The character, values, strategies, and management styles of a company's leaders are tested at crucible moments. A crucible moment is a "a transformative experience through which an individual comes to a new or an altered sense of identity" (Bennis & Thomas, 2002). The summer of 2014 was Market Basket's crucible moment – one that would test the entire Market Basket community. The strike that occurred during the summer of 2014 was the culmination of a long-running feud between the two branches of the Demoulas family.

In 2014, ownership of Market Basket was divided between two branches of the Demoulas family. The two third-generation cousins viewed the "value" of Market Basket in diametrically different ways. Arthur T. was CEO. He had learned the business from the ground up – starting part-time as a bag boy. Arthur T. held the work experience and principles of an industrious immigrant family – that he vowed never to forget. Arthur D. too had an early job at the company. Reportedly, he never accepted the idea of the family business (Korschun & Welker, 2015). Arthur T. championed the family ethos, intervened when employees faced difficult life events, and sought to remain close to customers. In contrast, Arthur D. represented the "non-laboring" side of the family. Arthur D.'s side had been awarded 50.5% of stock in a lengthy and contentious legal battle. Arthur D. viewed the organization as an asset to be leveraged and maximized. Through his influence, Market Basket provided generous distributions to the family owners. Arthur T. made significant contributions to the employee pension, supported employees in crisis, while simultaneously provided support to local civic and religious organizations.

For months, Arthur D. and his representatives on the board have been making overtures toward a takeover. In July 2014, Rafaela Evens, a minority owner who was far removed from the management of the business, changed her stance on the takeover (Korschun & Welker, 2015). As a result, the long-running feud came to a head. Supported by the majority of the Board of Directors, Arthur D fired Arthur T. Shortly after, 18 senior managers were either fired or resigned. Notably, each of these individuals had an average of almost 40 years of service with the company (Korschun & Welker, 2015). When the employees learned of the firings, their reaction became immediate. A strike emerged which quickly developed grass-roots support throughout the entire community. A "Save Market Basket" Facebook page launched after a few days gained over 10,000 "likes" overnight. Throughout the 6-week strike, "workers and managers walked the picket line and carriedsigns reading 'End Corporate Greed' and 'Honk for Artie T'" (Rhodes, 2019). The rallies grew and brought support from both the broader community and the media. The protesters seemed to intuitively understand the value of Market Basket to their lives and their communities (Rhodes, 2019).

Once the transfer was complete, the presumption was that Arthur D., and the new majority ownership, would sell Market Basket to a multinational chain bringing "modern" management techniques and new technology to the chain. Under the protection of armed escorts, Arthur D. appointed two new co-CEOs. As the strike intensified, Arthur D. and his team would find themselves at a disadvantage: *they had taken over a company with a culture and ethos they did not fully comprehend* (Korschun & Welker, 2015).

Labor disputes in the United States have had a history of violence and have seldom been settled effectively. As a result, early expectations of the strike were not optimistic. Typical management versus labor conflicts about higher wages, job security, and retirement benefits were not at issue in the Market Basket dispute. Instead, the strike was about protecting a valued organization – one that managers, workers, supplies, and community members had built together (Rhodes, 2019). Surprisingly, there was no union and thus no "safety net" to support the worker's actions. The strikers understood that their customers depended upon Market Basket – their grocery bills were 10–15% lower. However, as the strike unfolded, the shelves soon emptied. Customers refused to shop at the stores, and the ones that did, did so "almost apologetically" (Korschun & Welker, 2015, p. 131). Their solidarity was to have the desired effect – business dropped by more than 90%, costing Market Basket over $400,000,000 (Vaccaro, 2015), and the strike pressured the new owners to reconsider their position.

For striking workers, the only "reward" for having Arthur T. returned to his position was to save the job they already had. There was no pay increase or other benefit on the table. In taking this risk, the managers and employees were acutely aware what was at stake for across all Market Basket community. Steve Paulenka, with 40 years of history behind him, stated: "We're a crazy bunch… If this was a poker game, we just went all in" (Ailworth, 2014). Even with a takeover, they would likely still have jobs; however, they would have lost something much more valuable. Nonetheless, they understood that a new sign on the door would result in a decline in the quality of their working life and the values that structured it. It thus makes sense that the unofficial mascot of the Market Basket strikers was the Giraffe – a symbol of the willingness of many members of the community to stick their neck out and take risks – on behalf of both themselves and others (Korschun & Welker, 2015).

Is This Love?

Readers can be forgiven if they find the question of whether the operations of a supermarket chain may be understood as motivated by love. When we think of love, the first image that comes to our mind tends to involve the varieties of ethos and romantic love. Further, images of love tend to bring forth connotations of weakness, vulnerability, or even treacliness. These are hardly the images that are traditionally associated with the operations of business. Their invocation suggests a degree of soft headedness on the part of the person who suggests their relevance.

However, the meaning of love extends beyond its romantic connotations. The Market Basket ethos involves a *valuing of people and relationships* as if the organization was a type of *family*. Words like "family," "love," and "respect" are commonly invoked in descriptions of Market Basket culture. According to William Poulios, a life-long family friend and president of a local church that had benefitted over the years from Arthur T.'s philanthropy many times, Market Basket is characterized by a guiding attitude of "love and respect first" (Korschun & Welker, 2015, p.19). In this way, the "people first, groceries second" orientation extends toward customers, employees, and vendors alike.

The fact that many Market Basket employees began their careers and remained with the company may seem odd to outsiders. Many employees did not anticipate that they would spend their entire career working at a grocery store. One reason why this may be so has to do with the Market Basket's approach to career development. At Market Basket, employees who enter the company at the entry level work their way up not by excelling merely in one department, but instead by mastering how the store operates. Management adopts an "apprenticeship" model of career development (Rogoff, 1990) founded on what Arthur T. calls "distributed leadership." Guided slowly by management, employees develop competence and respect over time. Hard work and skill are rewarded with a "two-way lifetime commitment" (Korschun & Welker, 2015, p. 93). Employees become capable and knowledgeable members of the working community (family) who are able to function in multiple spaces and at multiple levels. While employees become highly sought-after by competitors, luring Market Basket employees away with increased compensation or career opportunities away has proven difficult (Korschun & Welker, 2015).

Within the Market Basket "family," work interactions are founded upon a friendly sense of care, responsibility, and respect for individual persons. Market Basket rejected self-service checkouts which would impede the goal of building long-term relationships with customers. Further, while many grocers moved to overnight stocking for efficiency and cost-saving motives, Market Basket continued to stock during the day. As a result, employees are granted the opportunity to "get in the way" of their customers – which, for customers, means that assistance is never far away. A particularly illustrative example of the ethos of care for individual persons involves an exchange involving a customer suffering from dementia (Tymn & Fortier, 2020). A customer realized after shopping that he had forgotten his wallet and could not pay for his weekly groceries. The store manager, who knew the man as a long-time customer, stepped forward and paid for the groceries – allowing the man to avoid embarrassment and an inconvenient second trip. The receipt was the man's "I.O.U." After learning about the incident, the gentleman's granddaughter went to the store to cover the bill and posted on social media: "in a world that is dark and broken and ugly, Charlie (the store manager) represents the light and beauty and love … So, this is not just a grocery store receipt. This is what compassion looks like" (Tymn & Fortier, 2020).

Market Basket's decision-making is also informed by a sense of *agape* – love for humanity. This is demonstrated as the search for solutions begins by asking how any action will affect people – and not just customers, but employees, suppliers, and their home communities (Korschun & Welker, 2015). Many locations are located within or serve large populations of low- and fixed-income customers. These include areas contained by elderly and immigrant communities – districts that most major chains often avoid. With prices well below their competitors, Market Basket could have easily increased prices to improve their profit margin. The decision to keep prices low is not merely a strategy for economic self-interest.

Instead, the practice "improves low income people's standard of living" (Korschun & Welker, 2015, p. 23).

Finally, the owners and employees of Market Basket can also be understood as operating out of a sense of self-love. However, this is not merely self-love defined as self-interest, but instead a version of self-love founded on a sense of virtue – a sense of cultivating and appreciating excellence in oneself. Telemachus, Arthur T's father, once stated, "Money is not what drives me. I want to be a good merchant" (Korschun & Welker, 2015, p. 33). In making this assertion, Telemachus expresses a particular from of love—a love for the excellence in performing one's craft – the virtue that Aristotle called technê.

Tripartite Ethos and the Transformation of Self-Interest

The current capitalist system in the United States is firmly grounded in a doctrine of rights. However, the exercise of rights and freedom typically eclipses commensurate moral concerns. We suggest that the case of Market Basket illustrates a business model that is based on a tripartite economic ethos – one that brings together rights, virtue, and care. The culture of Market Basket is founded in part on the principle of rights – the freedom to operate a business and to be rewarded for its industry. In this regard, the Demoulas family has achieved great wealth from their efforts and enterprise. However, one can observe an equally fervent attention to the virtue and care components of their moral charter.

A basic application of the "law" of supply and demand would suggest that Market Basket could raise their prices to levels comparable to their competitors – and enjoy the financial rewards from having done so. One might ask why they have not done so? What forces can counter these basic economic principles? The answer seems to lie in Market Basket's ability to be original – to resist the perennial lure of higher profits and aggressive growth. Korschun and Welker offer an important lesson: "Rather than trying to become more like Market Basket or some other prototype, companies need to be better at being themselves." (2015, p. 198). Their intentional commitment to the communities in which these individuals live is not a mere "business strategy"; it reflects a conscious identification with an ethos of virtue and care to ensure customer loyalty and commitment. The morality of rights and freedom does not stand in any fundamental tension with these values. To the contrary, we suggest that any conception of rights and freedom that is not defined in relation to some conception of the good is an empty one. In the pursuit of self-interest, the type of self that one seeks to pursue matters. Thus, to pursue self-interest requires reflecting upon and identifying oneself with some conception of the good – of what it means to be a good company.

A consistent theme across all the media depictions of Market Basket is their commitment to the question "What type of organization do we want to be?" Consistent with media depictions, Market Basket seeks to answer this question in terms of what is "good" for all members of their community. In this way, Market Basket builds upon the synergy that arises from the ways in which rights, virtue, and care are embodied in everyday decision-making. Many organizations seek to do good by doing well, that is, by acquiring great wealth so that they can later make an impact. Such a process separates "business" and "self-interest" from "morality" and "doing good." In this way, lower wages, use of natural resources, and the acceptance of other "externalities" can be justified. In contrast, moral concerns are a part of the very identity that organizes Market Basket's operations and initiatives.

Evolutionary biologist David Sloan Wilson argues that self-interest is the greatest impediment to love (Wilson & Barsade, 2020). Returning to MacMurray (1961), Sloan's comments echo MacMurray's (1961) contention that humans exist within a perennial tension between fear for self and love for the other. Given that the current system of business typically seeks to honor one pole of this distinction at the expense of the other, the next step is to imagine how an organization or business would operate differently by acting upon a tripartite ethos. Businesses are having difficulty escaping the gravitational pull of profits and self-interest. Perhaps part of the answer is to reflect upon what it means to be a person or a business, that is, to identify the type of self worthy of pursuing, that it is one interests to be.

Conclusion

We suggest that an ethos of rights and/or virtue is insufficient to ensure the dignity and well-being of all. In our current climate, the ethos of rights and freedom operates primarily in context of the pursuit of self-interest. Large corporate organizations augment their reputation through the practices of sponsorship and philanthropy and related practices (Lii & Lee, 2012). As such practices become the face of corporate responsibility, corporations seek rewards in improved reputation (Weber, 2008). However, as individuals experience ongoing declines in real income, and more struggle paycheck to paycheck, we question whether the majority of organizations have truly fulfilled their obligations of responsibility and the good. In some cases, many of the organization's employees and customers may very well be the benefactors of the very community organizations their employers funded. Even the most best-intentioned business practices have only made incremental progress on "grand problems," such as wage inequality, environmental exploitation, and the reliance "free" operating externalities to maintain growth and profit (Adler, 2019).

Reflecting on the fifth anniversary of the historic Market Basket strike, Grant Welker, a journalist from the Lowell Sun observed: "Market Basket wouldn't be taken away from those who loved it" (Welker, 2019) – and now six years on, the organization continues to flourish – opening new stores and serving its customers and community by keeping its commitments (along with low prices) (Welker, 2019). Market Basket (still) "provides an honorable and a dignified place in which to work" (Lepiarz, 2004).

Our argument for the tripartite ethos is grounded in the concept of love as the bestowal of value onto some person, collective, object, concept, idea, or practice. Through this bestowal, love – as a moral emotion – calls us to act in a way that cares for the other and limits self-interested behaviors. What we observe in the Market Basket strike is a spontaneous and near-complete support for what Market Basket represented to its employees and customers. In this way, concern for the other became not simply a counter to unbridled self-interest, rather it results in the transformation of self-interest. Concern for the other becomes an integrative and defining part of one's self-interest. As Arthur T. remarked when addressing his employees and customers at the termination of the Market Basket strike: "You have demonstrated to the world that it is a person's moral obligation and social responsibility to protect a culture" (Welker, 2019). Let us seek to move toward the development of such a culture.

References

Adhariani, D., & Siregar, S. V. (2018). How deep is your care? Analysis of corporations' "caring level" and impact on earnings volatility from the ethics of care perspective. *Australasian Accounting, Business and Finance Journal*, 12(4), 43–59.

Ailworth, E. (2014, July 16). *Workers demand reinstatement of ousted Market Basket leader—The Boston Globe.* www.bostonglobe.com/business/2014/07/15/allegiance-ousted-leader-market-basket-carries-risk/QCgCy4QiuueWF2zxGIciWO/story.html.

André, K., & Pache, A.-C. (2016). From caring entrepreneur to caring enterprise: Addressing the ethical challenges of scaling up social enterprises. *Journal of Business Ethics*, 133(4), 659–675.

Aristotle. (2012). *Nicomachean ethics* (R. C. Bartlett & S. D. Collins, Eds.). University of Chicago Press.

Bejou, D. (2011). Compassion as the new philosophy of business. *Journal of Relationship Marketing*, 10(1), 1–6.

Bennis, W., & Thomas, R. J. (2002, September 1). Crucibles of leadership. *Harvard Business Review*, September 2002. https://hbr.org/2002/09/crucibles-of-leadership

Bevan, D., & Werhane, P. (2015). The inexorable sociality of commerce: The individual and others in Adam Smith. *Journal of Business Ethics*, 127(2), 327–335.

Bowie, N. (1991). New directions in corporate social responsibility. *Business Horizons*, 34(4), 56–66.

Chen, L. Y., Mori, K., & Kim, S. (2019). Entertaining clients in hostess bars is still a thing in Asia. *Bloomberg*. www.bloomberg.com/news/articles/2019-01-16/dealmaking in escort bars thrives in pockets of corporate asia

Cima, L. R., & Schubeck, T. L. (2001). Self-interest, love, and economic justice: A dialogue between classical economic liberalism and catholic social teaching. *Journal of Business Ethics*, 30(3), 213–231.

Company History & Timeline. (n.d.). Market Basket. Retrieved October 15, 2020, from www.shopmarketbasket.com/timeline.

Davitz, J. R. (2016). *The language of emotion*. Academic Press.

Deepak, S., Bhatia, H., & Chadha, N. K. (2019). A psychological study on the positive impacts of experiencing love. *IAHRW International Journal of Social Sciences Review*, 7(3), 513–518.

Duska, R. (2014). Corporate responsibility: The American experience. *Business Ethics Quarterly*, 24(3), 478–482.

Ekman, P. (1993). Facial expression and emotion. *American Psychologist*, 48(4), 384.

Fogel, A. (1993). *Developing through relationships*. University of Chicago Press.

Formentin, M., & Bortree, D. (2019). Giving from the heart: Exploring how ethics of care emerges in corporate social responsibility. *Journal of Communication Management*, 23(1), 2–17.

Francis, H., & Keegan, A. (2020). The ethics of engagement in an age of austerity: A paradox perspective. *Journal of Business Ethics*, 162(3), 593–607.

Freeman, R. E. (1994). The politics of stakeholder theory: Some future directions. *Business Ethics Quarterly*, 4(4), 409–421. https://doi.org/10.1016/0007-6813(58)90078-8

Freeman, W. J. (2000). Emotion is essential to all intentional behaviors. In M. D. Lewis & I. Granic (Eds.), *Emotion, development, and self-organization: Dynamic systems approaches to emotional development*, 209–235. Cambridge University Press.

Frijda, N. H. (1986). *The emotions*. Cambridge University Press.

Frijda, N. H. (2004, April). Emotions and action. In *Feelings and emotions: The Amsterdam Symposium*, 158–173.

Frijda, N. H. (2009). Emotion experience and its varieties. *Emotion Review*, 1(3), 264–271.

Frijda, N. H., Kuipers, P., & Ter Schure, E. (1989). Relations among emotion, appraisal, and emotional action readiness. *Journal of Personality and Social Psychology*, 57(2), 212.

Frimer, J. A., & Walker, L. J. (2009). Reconciling the self and morality: An empirical model of moral centrality development. *Developmental Psychology*, 45(6), 1669–1681. https://doi.org/10.1037/a0017418

Fromm, E. (1961). *The art of loving*. Harper-Collins.

Gauthier, D. (1982). No need for morality: The case of the competitive market. *Philosophic Exchange*, 13(1), 2.

George, J. M. (2014). Compassion and capitalism: Implications for organizational studies. *Journal of Management*, 40(1), 5–15.

Gilligan, C. (1982). New maps of development: New visions of maturity. *American Journal of Orthopsychiatry*, 52(2), 199.

Grandy, G., & Sliwa, M. (2017). Contemplative leadership: The possibilities for the ethics of leadership theory and practice. *Journal of Business Ethics*, 143(3), 423–440.

Greenleaf, R. K. (1977). Servant leadership in business. In G. R. Hickman's (Ed.), *Leading organizations: Perspectives for a new era* (2nd ed.), 87–95. SAGE.

Haidt, J., & Kesebir, S. (2010). Morality. In *Handbook of social psychology* (5th ed., pp. 797–832). Wiley.

Hartman, E. M. (2008). Socratic questions and Aristotelian answers: A virtue-based approach to business ethics. In G. Flynn (Ed.), *Leadership and business ethics* (pp. 81–101). Springer.

Held, D. (2000). Regulating globalization? The reinvention of politics. *International Sociology, 15*(2), 394–408.

Hill, R. P., & Watkins, A. (2009). The profit implications of altruistic versus egoistic orientations for business-to-business exchanges. *International Journal of Research in Marketing, 26*(1), 52–59.

Hoffmann, F., Singer, T., & Steinbeis, N. (2015). Children's increased emotional egocentricity compared to adults is mediated by age-related differences in conflict processing. *Child Development, 86*(3), 765–780.

Karakas, F., & Sarigollu, E. (2013). The role of leadership in creating virtuous and compassionate organizations: Narratives of benevolent leadership in an Anatolian tiger. *Journal of Business Ethics, 113*(4), 663–678.

Killen, M., & Nucci, L. P. (1995). Morality, autonomy, and social conflict. In D. Hart (Ed.), *Developmental perspectives* (pp. 52–86). Cambridge University Press.

Klein, S. (2002). The head, the heart, and business virtues. *Journal of Business Ethics, 39*(4), 347–359.

Korschun, D., & Welker, G. (2015). *We are market basket: The story of the unlikely grassroots movement that saved a beloved business.* Amacom.

Lazarus, R. S. (1991). Progress on a cognitive-motivational-relational theory of emotion. *American Psychologist, 46*(8), 819.

Lepiarz, J. (2004, July 23). Shelves empty as market basket employees bring dispute to stores. *WBUR.org.* NRP. www.wbur.org/news/2014/07/23/market-basket-dispute

Lewis, D. (1986). *Philosophical papers II.* Oxford: Oxford University Press.

Lii, Y.-S., & Lee, M. (2012). Doing right leads to doing well: When the type of CSR and reputation interact to affect consumer evaluations of the firm. *Journal of Business Ethics, 105*(1), 69–81.

Lin-Hi, N., & Blumberg, I. (2012). The link between self-and societal interests in theory and practice. *European Management Review, 9*(1), 19–30.

Machan, T. R. (1995). *Private rights and public illusions.* Transaction Publishers.

Machan, T. R. (2015). Morality and the free market economy. *Journal of Self-Governance and Management Economics, 3*(3), 30–51.

Macmurray, J. (1961). *Persons in relations.* www.giffordlectures.org/books/persons-relation

Mascolo, M. F. (2009). Wittgenstein and the discursive analysis of emotion. *New Ideas in Psychology, 27*(2), 258–274.

Mascolo, M. F. (2020). Bridging partisan divides: dialectical engagement and deep sociality. *Journal of Constructivist Psychology*, 1–27.

Mascolo, M. F., & DiBianca Fasoli, A. (2020). The relational origins of morality and its development. In M. F. Mascolo & T. R. Bidell (Eds.), *Handbook of integrative developmental science: Essays in honor of Kurt W. Fischer* (pp. 392–421). Routledge.

Mascolo, M. F., DiBianca Fasoli, A., & Greenway, D. A. (under review). A relational approach to moral development in societies, organizations and individuals. *Integral Review.*

Mascolo, M. F., & Kallio, E. (2019). Beyond free will: The embodied emergence of conscious agency. *Philosophical Psychology*, *32*(4), 437–462.

Melé, D. (2009). Integrating personalism into virtue-based business ethics: The personalist and the common good principles. *Journal of Business Ethics*, *88*(1), 227–244. https://doi.org/10.1007/s10551-009-0108-y

Mercier, G., & Deslandes, G. (2020). Formal and informal benevolence in a profit-oriented context. *Journal of Business Ethics*, *165*(1), 125–143.

Moors, A., Ellsworth, P. C., Scherer, K. R., & Frijda, N. H. (2013). Appraisal theories of emotion: State of the art and future development. *Emotion Review*, *5*(2), 119–124.

Munro, I., & Thanem, T. (2018). The ethics of affective leadership: Organizing good encounters without leaders. *Business Ethics Quarterly*, *28*(1), 51–69.

Newstead, T., Dawkins, S., Macklin, R., & Martin, A. (2019). The Virtues Project: An approach to developing good leaders. *Journal of Business Ethics*, *15*, 1–18.

Nicholson, J., & Kurucz, E. (2019). Relational leadership for sustainability: Building an ethical framework from the moral theory of 'ethics of care.' *Journal of Business Ethics*, *156*(1), 25–43.

Nickisch, C. (2014, September 3). Market Basket shows power of organized labor without unions. In *WBUR News*. NPR. www.wbur.org/news/2014/09/03/market-basket-labor

Nozick, R. (1991). Decisions of principle, principles of decision. *Tanner Lecture on Human Values*, 117–202. Lecture delivered at Princeton University November 13 and 15, 1991.

Ostrom, E. (1999). Coping with tragedies of the commons. *Annual Review of Political Science*, *2*(1), 493–535. https://doi.org/10.1146/annurev.polisci.2.1.493

Pavlovich, K., & Krahnke, K. (2012). Empathy, connectedness and organisation. *Journal of Business Ethics*, *105*(1), 131–137.

Rand, A. (1964). *The virtue of selfishness*. Penguin.

Ready, D. A., & Truelove, E. (2011). *The power of collective ambition*. Harvard *Business Review*, *89*, 94–102, 145.

Rempel, J. K., & Burris, C. T. (2005). Let me count the ways: An integrative theory of love and hate. *Personal Relationships*, *12*(2), 297–313.

Rhodes, G. W. (2019, April 26). Stop & Shop and Market Basket: A tale of two strikes nearly 5 years apart. *The Sun Chronicle*. www.thesunchronicle.com/news/local_news/stop-shop-and-market-basket-a-tale-of-two-strikes-nearly-5-years-apart/article_ed985ed8-267d-537b-9a2f-1cf7478865dc.html

Robinson, J. (1978). The organic composition of capital. *Kyklos*, *31*(1), 5–20.

Rocha, H. O., & Ghoshal, S. (2006). Beyond self-interest revisited. *Journal of Management Studies*, *43*(3), 585–619.

Rogoff, B. (1990). *Apprenticeship in thinking: Cognitive development in social context*. New York: Oxford University Press.

Roseman, I. J. (2004). Appraisals, rather than unpleasantness or muscle movements, are the primary determinants of specific emotions. *Emotion*, *4*(2), 145–150. https://doi.org/10.1037/1528-3542.4.2.145

Scherer, K. R. (1982). *Emotion as a process: Function, origin and regulation*. Sage Publications.

Schuhmacher, N., Köster, M., & Kärtner, J. (2019). Modeling prosocial behavior increases helping in 16-month-olds. *Child Development*, *90*(5), 1789–1801.

Schwarz, N., & Clore, G. L. (2007). *Feelings and phenomenal experiences.* In A. W. Kruglanski & E. T. Higgins (Eds.), *Social psychology: Handbook of basic principles* (pp. 385–407). The Guilford Press.

Simola, S. K. (2007). The pragmatics of care in sustainable global enterprise. *Journal of Business Ethics,* 74(2), 131–147.

Singer, I. (1984). *The nature of love. 3 vols.* (Vol. 89). MIT Press.

Smith, A. (1776). *An inquiry into the nature and causes of the wealth of nations.* London: W. Strahan and T. Cadell.

Solomon, R. C. (1998). The moral psychology of business: Care and compassion in the corporation. *Business Ethics Quarterly,* 8(3), 515–533.

Stanger, T. (n.d.). Best grocery stores and supermarkets. *Consumer Reports.* Retrieved October 15, 2020, from www.consumerreports.org/grocery-stores-supermarkets/best-grocery-stores-and-supermarkets/.

Stern, J. A., & Cassidy, J. (2018). Empathy from infancy to adolescence: An attachment perspective on the development of individual differences. *Developmental Review,* 47, 1–22.

Taylor, C. (1989). *Sources of the self: The making of modern identity.* Harvard University Press.

Tomkins, S. S. (1981). The role of facial response in the experience of emotion: A reply to Tourangeau and Ellsworth, others. *Journal of Personality and Social Psychology,* 47(4), 909–917. https://doi.org/10.1037/0022-3514.47.4.909

Tymn, M., & Fortier, M. (2020). 'What compassion looks like': Market Basket manager pays for man's groceries. *NBC News Boston.* www.nbcboston.com/news/local/this-is-what-compassion-looks-like-market-basket-manager-pays-for-mans-groceries/2175137/

Uzefovsky, F., Paz, Y., & Davidov, M. (2020). Young infants are pro-victims, but it depends on the context. *British Journal of Psychology,* 111(2), 322–334.

Vaccaro, A. (2015, August 22). A year later, things are going pretty well for Market Basket. *Boston.Com.* www.boston.com/news/business/2015/08/22/a-year-later-things-are-going-pretty-well-for-market-basket

Velleman, J. D. (1999). Love as a moral emotion. *Ethics,* 109(2), 338–374.

Wada, Y. (2014). Relational care ethics from a comparative perspective: The ethics of care and Confucian ethics. *Ethics and Social Welfare,* 8(4), 350–363.

Weber, M. (2008). The business case for corporate social responsibility: A company-level measurement approach for CSR. *European Management Journal,* 26(4), 247–261.

Welker, G. (2019, August 24). Five years ago this month, Market Basket showed the unprecedented was possible. *Lowell Sun.* www.lowellsun.com/five-years-ago-this-month-market-basket-showed-the-unprecedented-was-possible

Wilson, D. S., & Barsade, S. (2020, July 27). *What's love got to do with it?* International Humanistic Management Association.

Young, M., & Zhu, Y. L. (2019). How emotions move us: An integrative framework for emotions and decision making. *Academy of Management Proceedings,* 2019(1), 14223.

Zahn-Waxler, C., Friedman, S. L., & Cummings, E. M. (1983). Children's emotions and behaviors in response to infants' cries. *Child Development,* 54(6), 1522–1528. https://doi.org/10.2307/1129815

6 Levinas and Lewis on Loving the Other in Organizations

Peter McGhee and Myk Habets

Introduction

As the song goes, "what's love got to do with it?"[1] If this question is for business, then the answer is quite a lot. Recently, a corpus of management literature has emerged that advocates for the importance of love within organizations. This literature covers the spectrum from how love might augment traditional theories of the firm (Argandoña, 2011), through human resource practices that inspire workers to be committed emotionally and impassioned about their work (Andersen & Born, 2007), to caring and empathy forming the basis of leadership (Grant, 2008). From this level of interest alone, one might conclude that love and business are made for each other. This newfound romance, however, is fraught with significant challenges. This chapter contributes to the existing literature on love in organizations using the works of Emmanuel Levinas and C. S. Lewis. Both authors offer a view of *agapē* love, albeit from slightly differing perspectives, that not only challenges and builds on the management literature, but also provides novel and distinctive ways of thinking about love and business.

What Is Love in an Organizational Context?

Life, Shakespeare (1606) tells us, "is a tale told by an idiot, full of sound and fury, signifying nothing" (*Macbeth*, Act 5, Scene 5). We suspect many have felt the same way about love through the ages. C. S. Lewis (2012a) tells us "that William Morris wrote a poem called *Love is Enough* and someone is said to have reviewed it briefly with the words 'It isn't'" (p. 141). Perhaps no other word has generated as much discussion, ambiguity, misuse, and dare we say anger, than love. If we look at a dictionary, it tells us that love is "to have a great attachment to and affection for a person or a thing" (Hanks, 1986, p. 672). Expanding on this definition, Argandoña (2011) writes that love can be an affection we feel for others and/or the desire to act in ways that benefit them, and Caldwell and Dixon (2010) define love as emotional caring and commitment to the well-being of others. For some, love is a learned "orientation of character

DOI: 10.4324/9781003254034-7

which determines the relatedness of a person to the world as a whole, not toward one 'object' of love" (Fromm, 1963, p. 38), and for others love is an ingrained moral habit that contributes to the flourishing of both the agent and others (Harris, 2002). We might characterize these conceptions as forms of *gift-love* (McIntyre, 1986), a love that is benevolent toward others (Argandoña, 2011), or as *compassionate love*, a love that is typified by consistent emotional investment, feelings of affection, and active caring toward others for their good (Underwood, 2008).

Historically, love and organizations have been oxymoronic. The emphasis in managerial discourse has been on rational (e.g., scientific management) or normative conceptions (e.g., strong organizational cultures) of control (Barley & Kunda, 1992). However, of late words like "love," "compassion," and "empathy" have woven their way into organization theory and discourse (Dutton & Workman, 2011; Rynes, Bartunek, Dutton, & Margolis, 2012; Tasselli, 2019). While this discussion takes various forms, the phrase that increasingly appears in the literature is *compassionate love* (Andersen & Born, 2008; Barsade & O'Neill, 2014; Cunha et al., 2017; Patterson, 2010). This type of love typically involves organizations caring for and respecting their employees, helping them to achieve their best, and facilitating meaning and self-actualization through their work (see, e.g., Barsade & O'Neill, 2014; Blanchard & Barrett, 2011; Dierendonck & Patterson, 2015; Kouzes & Posner, 1992).

Prima facie, this relationship seems like love at first sight. What organization would not want to foster an emotional attitude that is positively related to self-esteem, caregiving self-efficacy, forgiveness, empathy, and altruism (Oman, 2011), wisdom and self-transcendence (Le & Levenson, 2005), selflessness (Underwood, 2008), virtue (Argandoña, 2011), and sustainable leadership (Boyatzis, Smith, & Blaize, 2006)? Moreover, when applied within an organizational context, constructs such as the above have been shown to improve secondary outcomes like job satisfaction, organizational commitment, and citizenship behavior among others (see, e.g., Albrecht & Marty, 2020; Boiral, Talbot, & Paillé, 2015; Crossan, Mazutis, & Seijts, 2013; Ma, Qu, Wei, & Hsiao, 2018; Satuf et al., 2018). Simply put, compassionate love seems good for business.

Despite this lovefest, there are challenges in every new relationship. Indeed, one of the first things we consider when falling in love is whether the person (or in this case the organization) loves us for who we are rather than for what they can get out the relationship. Unfortunately, there may be reasons to distrust our organizational partners. Alvesson and Willmott (2002) in a well-cited paper argue that organizations often regulate employee identity to cultivate self-understandings and work alignments compatible with management purposes. As opposed to "objective" forms of control (e.g., structure, procedures, and measures), they argue, "control is exercised through the 'manufacture' of subjectivity ... the focus is on the employee's 'insides' – their self-image, their feelings, and identifications" (p. 622). An illustration of this might be transformational leadership models that seek devotion from employees and encourage them to love the firm and its goals (Tourish & Pinnington, 2002).

Alvesson and Willmott (2002) describe several means by which organizations regulate employee identity. Of these, some are applicable here. For instance, providing a specific vocabulary of love motivations (i.e., "we care for you," "we want what is best for you," "we want to help you flourish") invites employees to construct themselves as dependent on the organization for their well-being. By expounding morals and values associated with compassionate love, organizations also generate strong consensus about what love is, which encourages close identification with that created value system. Moreover, because compassionate love can engender feelings of belonging and community, being "a member of the wider corporate family may then become a significant source of one's self-understanding, self-monitoring and presentation to others" (p. 630). Finally, by describing conditions by which management operates as compassionately loving, employee identity is shaped or re-interpreted. For example, if behaving compassionately is said to lead to improved worker performance, then employees are invited to accept this "loving" behavior to "become enterprising persons" (p. 632).

Alvesson and Willmott (2002) are not alone in recognizing that organizations control identity. For instance, Bell and Taylor (2003) argue that managerial discourse is frequently used to integrate the separate domains of work and personal life. While focused on workplace spirituality, their ideas can be applied to the concept of love. Specifically, they highlight the use of pastoral power (taken from Foucault, 1981, 1983), which is concerned "with cultivating the welfare of an entire population of citizens" as well as looking "after each individual in particular, through his or her entire life" (p. 340). From this perspective, "compassion is hinged around relations of power conjured up in the idea of the manager 'shepherding' the flock'" (Simpson, Clegg, & Pitsis, 2014, p. 355). Therefore, when managers exercise compassionate love to facilitate employee meaning and purpose, they practice a form of individualized pastoral power. Moreover, if promoting that inner quest for meaning is yet another avenue to commercial success, then managers also practice a form of totalizing pastoral power. Either way, compassion becomes a mode of power that controls employees "through disciplinary technologies that focus on the scientific governing of the soul using primarily psychological techniques" (Bell & Taylor, 2003, p. 345).

If the above was insufficient to question this new relationship, then notions that love can transform work in the 21st century are also problematic. After all, this view implies that organizations are neutral contexts in which love simply exists (Bell & Taylor, 2003). This is not the case though, and love risks becoming another tool that resonates powerfully with the neoliberal ideal of the entrepreneurial worker (Legge, 2005), or as Tokumitsu (2015) argues, the use of which results in "a labor force that embraces its own exploitation" (p. 8). The question then is, "how do organizations genuinely love their employees as subjects (or as ends), and not simply as objects (or as means)?" Several authors have highlighted this tension (Gregg, 2011; Hochschild, 1983). However, few offer solutions either arguing the two partners (love and organizations) may be unsuited for each other (Spicer & Cederström, 2010; Weeks, 2017) or that this could be a match made in heaven (Tasselli, 2019).

Argandoña's (2011) understanding of love in organizations as not merely a "taste for benevolence" (p. 81) or simply having a positive emotional response to others, but rather as "a virtue which has rational content and motives," (p. 81) is a move in the right direction. Such love acts out of a transcendent motivation that "seeks the other's good for the other's sake" (p. 81). In a work context, this means acting benevolently for employees and the organization in ways that meet their need for internal goods (e.g., job satisfaction, technical and moral learning, and survival and development), and not just for external goods alone (e.g., wages, efficiency, and financial return) (Moore, 2005). The limitation of this approach lies with the agents themselves, who must use their judgment to decide what these internal goods are. Not only are such goods often contested and vague (Hager, 2011), but starting with the rational self invariably risks selecting them through an egocentric lens (Blok, 2017).

Despite the criticisms above, we argue there is a vital role for love in organizations. However, it needs to be the kind of love that starts with the *Infinite Other*, not with the corporatized self (Casey, 1995), or even the rational, virtuous agent (Argandoña, 2011). With that premise in mind, we turn to the philosophical work of Emmanuel Levinas and the theological work of C. S. Lewis for different lenses by which to explore this challenge.

Levinas on Love

Emmanuel Levinas (1906–1995) was a Lithuanian-born French Philosopher and Talmudic commentator who studied under Edmund Husserl and Martin Heidegger. After the Nazi invasion of France, he became a prisoner of war, during which many of his family were among the six million Jews who perished. After the war, Levinas returned to France and committed to reworking phenomenology and ethics (Jones, 2014). In his groundbreaking book *Totality and Infinity* (*TI*), Levinas (1969) argued that "the good" precedes "Being," by which he meant that ethical relationships and experiences exist before the ontological basis for "ethics in the sense of philosophically established principles, rules or codes" (Davis, 1996, p. 48). This is what Derrida (1978) referred to as "an ethics of ethics" (p. 138).

Levinas (1969) comes to this conclusion by first noting the existence of something that goes beyond human understanding and that resists assimilation by our solipsistic ego. He refers to this something as the *Infinite*

Other. Historically, for much of Western philosophy this idea has been God (e.g., Descartes, Kant, and Kierkegaard) or something similar (e.g., Aristotle's Prime Mover or Hegel's Absolute Spirit), but for Levinas, the transcendental phenomenologist, the *Infinite Other* is that which is not the conscious self or "I." Simply put, it is other persons in the world that I encounter and experience via their faces (*le visage*). As Morgan (2011) explains, these others are people like me, but because their "perspective and their experiences are inaccessible to me, they are radically separate and different from me." This exteriority demands, before anything else, that I "let them live," "let them be here too," "feed them," and "allow them to share the world and be nourished by it too" (p. 40).

This is not a cognitive experience *per se*; instead, this is an originary and primordial meeting with the transcendent, which manifests in everyday life via the domain of love for the Other (Morgan, 2011). Understanding this encounter is important for several reasons. First, it means I am not alone in the world and I do not have sovereign power over the world – there are others who must be considered. Second, these others condition my subjectivity because if they did not exist then I would be part of a whole bereft of any uniqueness (i.e., I would be all there is). Finally, these others enable my escape from self-centeredness and aloneness to develop into an authentic moral being. In summary, my individuality and my humanity are functions of my relationship with these others. Levinas considers "this encounter with the Other as the most basic subject for philosophical reflection because nothing precedes it or has priority over it" (Davis, 1996, p. 48).

When discussing ethics, Levinas (1969) starts with the Other and not the self (or the Same as he calls it), which is where ethical thinking usually begins (e.g., Aristotle's virtuous agent who aims at *eudaimonia*, Kant's rational person who applies universal categorical imperatives, Mill's sentient being who calculates utility, and so on). Unfortunately, notes Levinas, when starting with the self, we tend to reduce "the Other to the Same by interposition of a middle and neutral term that ensures the comprehension of being" (p. 43). What Levinas implies here is that we often put people into ethical boxes or collapse them to our moral worldview, and in the process compromise their individuality and their situatedness (Blok, 2017). We all have this narcissistic inclination such that when we strive to be ethical, we often perceive and comprehend others as we do ourselves (Roberts, 2001), as opposed to letting others be Other and then forming a genuinely loving perspective.

In *TI*, Levinas (1969) claims love is ambiguous. It can relate to the Other as infinite (*agapē* love), or it can reduce the Other as Same (*eros* love): "Love as a relation with the Other can be reduced to this fundamental immanence, be divested of all transcendence, seek but a connatural being, a sister soul, present itself as incest" (p. 254). *Agapē* is love for a neighbor or a stranger, not in the communal sense, but in a way that respects their transcendence and preserves their alterity. As Levinas

(1998a) writes later in *Entre Nous,* "It is precisely in this call to my responsibility by the face that summons me, that demands me, that claims me – it is in this questioning that the Other is my neighbor" (p. 146). To encounter the Other as infinite is to take responsibility for their welfare without any expectation of reciprocity. That, according to Levinas, is an authentic manifestation of *agapē* for one's fellow human being (Arman & Rehnsfeldt, 2006).

If an organization started with *agapē* love, in the sense that Levinas describes, what would this mean? Broadly speaking, organizations would be open to the innate worth and good of human beings beyond (not along with) egocentric interests. They would "leave room for differences, undecidability, absurdity, and play" (Bojesen & Muhr, 2008, p. 88). Since *agapē* love defines the Other by my desire for *their* future; "that is what is not grasped, what befalls us, and lays hold of us" (Levinas, 1987 cited in Bojesen & Muhr, 2008, p. 88), then organizations would desire stakeholder alterity, avoid reducing them to organizational needs, and allow them to transform the organization, not the other way round. Genuine love cannot be an act of assimilation (i.e., *eros* love), an act that wants to subject and consume a person for its own desires (Katz, 2007). Unfortunately, much of what is espoused in the management literature is precisely that (Bojesen & Muhr, 2008).

Lewis on Love

Levinas (1969) rightly argued for the non-instrumental use of other people, and that in loving others accordingly, we come face-to-face with God who is infinitely close but absolutely distant. By this, Levinas is not arguing for God's existence; rather God is "the moral force encountered in the Other's face as the subject's obligation to and responsibility for that other person" (Cohen, 1994 cited in Morgan, 2011, p. 144). When Levinas' ideas are brought into dialogue with a distinctively theological voice, that of C. S. Lewis, we argue that reflection upon love is deepened and the applications to business are amplified. Both Levinas and Lewis articulate the importance of *agapē* love for the Other as Other so that self and society flourish.

C. S. Lewis was an Oxford lecturer in English literature, but he is most well known as the author of a host of books on theology written for the thoughtful person, and he also penned the popular children's fiction series, *The Chronicles of Narnia.* Central to Lewis' thought is an idea he gleans from the Christian Bible that God has created creatures to approximate himself and his relation to the world. This is exemplified in love for the Other (God and creatures). In his 1960 work *The Four Loves,* he clarifies the distinction between "gift-love" and "need-love" (Lewis, 2012a, pp. 1–11). Gift-love is love motivated by altruism; need-love is motivated by, well, need. In what he narrates as a surprise to himself, need-love is just as important and legitimate as gift-love for the simple fact that need does not have to be selfish, it can and often is, simply a fact of creaturely existence. As Lewis notes, "It would be a bold and silly creature that came before its Creator with the boast 'I am no beggar. I love you disinterestedly'" (p. 4). Therefore, while relating to the *Infinite Other* is not narcissistic, self-interest does not have to be entirely removed for the Other to be rightly loved. To clarify how this can be the case, Lewis shows that underlying both loves is a third, "Appreciative-love" (*agapē*):

> Need-love says of a woman 'I cannot live without her'; Gift-love longs to give her happiness, comfort, protection – if possible, wealth; Appreciative-love gazes and holds its breath and is silent, rejoices that such wonder should exist even if not for him.
>
> (p. 21)

Appreciative-love or *agapē* is not simply the attribute of being unselfish. Unselfishness suggests that our self-denial and not Others' well-being is the essential point. Unselfishness has more to do with Kant and the Stoics than with love. Underlying Lewis' (1965) concept of the self, Others, and appreciative-love is desire. Lewis' many works illustrate the principle that the more we relate to Others and lose ourselves, the more we find ourselves remade. Desire, joy, or fulfillment can never be the objects of our love but, rather, the ones we desire and enjoy. Moreover, in a seeming paradox when we focus on Others, we find our joy complete. Lewis speculated on this in his allegory *The Great Divorce* (Lewis, 2012b), he reflected upon it in his spiritual autobiography *Surprised by Joy* (Lewis, 2012e), and he meditated upon it in his heart wrenching *A Grief Observed* (Lewis 1966). In each instance, we find ourselves and our joy is complete, only when we give ourselves in love to the Other.

When Levinas' concept of the Other is coupled with Lewis' concept of appreciative-love, we find resources for an application of love to business. Lewis (2012a) argues, "To love at all is to be vulnerable" (p. 147). If love is to enter the discussion of business, then organizations must face squarely that this will be uncomfortable and unsafe: at least from the vantage point of profit margins. As Lewis notes, "The only place outside of Heaven where you can be perfectly safe from all the dangers and perturbations of love is Hell" (p. 147). Frankly, business can be hellish if some of its interaction with individuals, society, and the environment is anything to go by (Bakan, 2004; Chomsky & McChesney, 2011; Darley, 1994). There is wantonness about true love, a sacrificial yet beautiful and satisfying uncertainty about it. When love is defined in these distinctively theological terms, it relativizes the natural loves (affections), and prioritizes love for the Other. "A man, said Jesus, who tries to serve two masters, will 'hate' the one and 'love' the other" (Lewis, 2012a, p. 149). Such reprioritization will have a direct effect upon commercial enterprise and business more generally.

The works of Levinas and Lewis are complex and fecund with applications to business. We have barely scratched the surface of their thoughts. What has been highlighted by both authors is the orientation toward Others that is needed if true love, *agapē* love, is brought to bear upon organizational behavior. Both thinkers emphasize our ethical (i.e., loving) relationship with Others, and via that encounter, with God the Wholly Other. Both thinkers also challenge modern Western assumptions about egocentrism, individuality, and what living and working within civil society means (Lewis, 2005). What follows is an application of their ideas to business.

Managerial Implications

While there are differences in their thinking, both Levinas and Lewis have an understanding of love that emphasizes others as radically different, that requires vulnerability, and that conditions true moral self-hood (i.e., it enables one to become fully human). Taking these ideas and relating them to organizations infer management reinterpreting and applying love along these lines. Usefully, Jones (2014) provides a framework that was adapted for this purpose (see Table 6.1), and while she relates this

Table 6.1 Reinterpreting Love from Levinas and Lewis for Management

	Levinas and Lewis on love	*Managerial implications*
Ethical attitude	• The Other cannot be reduced or defined. • The Other maintains their transcendence.	• Loving the Other means understanding they have a uniqueness and should not be instrumentalized by managers. • Managers need to maintain distance when loving the Other.
Encounter	• The face of the Other requires a response. • The Other teaches from a height.	• An appropriate loving response emerges in unique human encounters between managers and employees. • Loving the Other provides understanding for managers they could not achieve otherwise.
Response	• Responding to the Other is a moral obligation.	• Loving the Other means managers focus on positive social change.
Identity	• Identity is derived from loving the Other.	• Loving the Other opens a manager's consciousness and identity formation.

Source: Adapted from Jones (2014, p. 17).

to Levinas only, it is easy enough to link this with Lewis as we have done here.

Ethical Attitude

Realizing love in organizations entails managers reject anything that diminishes individual uniqueness, and that reduces human beings to figures in a financial plan or to key performance indicators (Aasland, 2007). When it comes to rules and processes, Mansell (2008) suggests applying these flexibly to account for the uniqueness of the Other while also requiring managers to continuously reflect on how applicable such rules are in a given situation. Any form of love enacted for the purpose of managing subjectivity (Alvesson & Willmott, 2002) should be avoided. Even though employees, for example, conduct certain tasks, they are not a product of their roles. Do not try to manage what is good for individuals. Instead, allow them to decide this for themselves through a process of dialogue.

Typically, dialogic models that aim at the common ground (i.e., what is best for the organization and its stakeholders) inherently favor the already-dominant position of institutional privilege (Maak & Pless, 2009) and as such inhibit, rather than support, the radical disruption of self that is central to loving the Other. Authentic dialogue means having a loving attitude of listening and learning from the Other that is paramount (Jones, 2014). This is not just about communication, but rather, involves managers "de-centering the self in order to truly experience the needs of the Other" (p. 54), which prevents assimilating the Other into their perspective, even if they have good intentions. Guidance for managers on how they can ensure this comes from Lipari (2004) who writes,

> in my dialogic encounter with you, I will not only listen for your radical alterity but I will open and make a place for it. It means that I do not resort only to what is easy — what I already know, or what we have in common. It means that I listen for and make space for the difficult, the different, the radically strange.
>
> (p. 138)

Encounter

According to Levinas (1969), the "Other has a face, and its gaze is precisely the epiphany of the face as a face" (p. 75), plus "I cannot evade by silence the discourse which the epiphany that occurs as a face opens" (p. 201). Similarly, Lewis (1966) writing in *A Grief Observed* argues that all of reality, but especially our encounters with other people (Levinas' *face-to-face*), are iconoclastic in that they shatter the images or ideas to which we try to reduce them. The face-to-face is not simply an interpretative encounter by which we try to decipher what the other person is thinking and then act accordingly. That would be totalizing; rather, it is a meeting with transcendence, or the aspect of the Other which is always beyond our comprehension, and that compels us to act responsibly toward them. In practice, this involves being open to others in a loving way that goes beyond our self-absorption to recognize their inherent worth. Moreover, because this occurs at the point of encounter with the face of the other, it is always an ethics of proximity.

Unfortunately, modern organizations leave little room for such face-to-face experiences; instead, they often foster objectification of the self and alienation from others (Jackall, 1988; Kanungo, 1992; O'Donohue & Nelson, 2014). Even attempts to codify ethics and social responsibility in organizations often become tools that serve the firm's interests (Aasland, 2004). Shifting this flawed approach, and lessening moral distance (Bauman, 1989), requires organizations ensure the Other is more proximate (Mansell, 2008). Physical immediacy is the best way to achieve this. Therefore, managers should, wherever possible, come face-to-face with organizational stakeholders. Even methods as simple as management by walking around (MBWA) can reduce moral distance (Serrat, 2017). If a physical meeting is not possible, then bringing the face of the Other before managers may also suffice. For instance, in Pajo and McGhee's (2003) study of how organizations institutionalize ethics, one firm arranged for pictures to be taken of the communities they served. These were then blown up and placed throughout the head office. Seeing these had the transformative effect of reducing moral distance between management and these stakeholders. Not surprisingly, research shows that enhancing proximity can minimize fear between groups as well as reduce biases (Pettigrew & Tropp, 2006; Stephan & Stephan, 2001).

Developing an organizational culture of inclusiveness may also enhance an ethic of love (Pless & Maak, 2004). However, this approach must embrace "diverse cultures and subjectivities as claimants to mutual recognition" and not be enacted "as part of a rather cynical signifying system aimed less at the extension of organizational responsibility and more at the penetration of potentially diverse markets and the appeasement of significant interest groups" (Hancock, 2008, p. 1370). Using the idea of embodied generosity, Hancock contends that an inclusive culture pursues openness toward others without expectation of reward. It also acknowledges that individuals "are always in process, as it were, but that such processes of becoming require a level of recognition that not only tolerates but rather embraces difference as an integral ontological precondition" (p. 1371). In an organization such as this, people affected by disability, for example, might be recognized as opposed to simply tolerated, not only for overcoming the daily challenges of working but also for how their actions change society. In doing this, managers may come to learn something of what it means to walk in the shoes of the vulnerable and marginalized in society, and how this translates into organizational practices that fulfill such people's real needs.

Response

When applied, the works of Levinas and Lewis challenge managers to consider the infinite in their stakeholders, to see each unique individual. When managers do this, their accountability to the Other becomes necessary; they become their brother's and sister's keeper (Arnett, 2008). Achieving this means embedding managerial thought processes with Levinasian ideas of vulnerability, service, and compassion.

As noted earlier, Lewis (2012a) observes "to love at all is to be vulnerable" (p. 147) because in loving others, managers must reject utilitarian notions that focus on outcomes for an ethic that requires being held hostage by the Other; what Levinas (1998b) refers to as substitution. Notably, Lewis (1966) argues that forms of self-love (e.g., self-serving or self-protective love) ultimately lead to a condition he identifies with damnation. A good example of this comes from Lewis' (1998) allegorical work *Till We Have Faces*. In this story, Lewis critiqued the so-called natural loves (*eros, storge,* and *philia*), while illustrating the triumph of the self-less or appreciative-love (*agapē*) that Orual finds in overcoming her original possessive nature. Although we do not wish to condemn organizations to perdition, there is evidence that management egocentricity can lead to hellish outcomes. For instance, Duchon and Drake's (2009) analysis of Enron's collapse found that narcissistic management was a major contributor to the company's bankruptcy. More recently, Rhodes' (2016) study of the Volkswagen Emission Scandal uncovered "rampant pursuit of business self-interest through well-orchestrated and large-scale conspiracies involving lying, cheating, fraud and lawlessness" (p. 1501).

Levinasian notion of service means subjugating organizational goals and focusing on stakeholder's needs and desires without anticipation of reward. This differs from servant leadership, which is about "being first among equals," as well as "being a steward who holds the organization in trust" (Van Dierendonck, 2011, p. 1231). Levinasian service is a moral duty, not in the Kantian sense of increasing stakeholder autonomy or responsibility (Bowie, 2000), but in a manner that upholds their alterity and affirms their humanity through positive social and environmental action. Sadly, much of what passes for such action by organizations is self-serving and marketed to influence public perception (Gatti, Seele, & Rademacher, 2019). In his analysis of corporate governance, Roberts (2001) provides a good example of this, which he labels an "ethics of narcissus" (p. 111). He quotes from a social responsibility report that announces, "We care about what you think about us" (p. 123), writing that the expressed concern for stakeholders is conditional on such concern benefiting the organization. Phrases like this are not about loving others; rather they are about giving the appearance of ethicality with little understanding of what true responsibility entails (Knights & O'Leary, 2006). Sadly, research shows that such "greenwashing" can have the contrary desired outcome and may even harm the organization (Berrone, Fosfuri, & Gelabert, 2017; Delmas & Burbano, 2011).

Compassion is a way of being that regards the flourishing of others. As Williams (2008) notes,

> It informs and, in fact, makes possible our awareness of suffering as an impediment to sentient well-being and flourishing and is thus crucial to a moral psychology of non-harm and benevolence – one by which we refuse to add suffering to the world and, positively, are inclined to remedy existing suffering wherever possible.
>
> (p. 7)

There is no doubt that compassion expands the self (Nussbaum, 2001) and is an important driver of justice. However, for both Lewis (2012d) and Levinas (1998a), compassion goes further still. Lewis, for instance, states that "Love is something more stern and splendid than simple kindness" (p. 32), while Levinas argues that compassion is "the very nexus of human subjectivity, to the point of being raised to the level of a supreme ethical principle" (p. 94). For when we experience, and act upon, the suffering of others, we are at our most moral, and therefore our most human. Unfortunately, the nature of business makes such experiences improbable (Shearer, 2002), especially if people are just a name on a list or a community on a map. Having said that, one means of engaging with stakeholders is via moral imagination (Werhane, 1998), which involves substituting oneself mentally with those that suffer (i.e., imagining yourself in their shoes or imagining their needs from their perspective).

As a case in point, over the first few months of 2020, Covid-19 has rendered many industries extraneous. This has led to hundreds of thousands of jobs being restructured or downsized, even in organizations where profit is future proofed. This creates significant distress and anguish for those who experience it (Vickers, 2009), as well as those left behind (Amundson, Borgen, Jordan, & Erlebach, 2004), and in fact, such actions often fail to achieve desired ends (Carriger, 2016; Schenkel & Teigland, 2017). When confronted with the suffering caused by downsizing, a manager might use their moral imagination to substitute themselves with the individuals involved, especially with those who are distant. In organizations fighting for survival due to Covid-19, using such thinking ought to result in managers actively supporting employees through downsizing in ways that affirm their authentic humanity. On the other hand, in organizations that are profitable, such substitutionary discernment by managers ought to lead to the abandonment of any downsizing given the amount of harm it causes.

Identity

The self is not secure in its righteousness called as it is into question by the "presence of the Other" (Levinas, 1969, p. 43) or as Arnett (2008) puts it, "phenomenologically ethics as responsibility for the Other is an act that makes possible human life — without the *Other* there is no *I*" (p. 57). Responding to others ensures managers understand "there is a sense of goodness and a realization that there is more at stake in my life than myself and my own fulfillment" (p. 58). In *Mere Christianity*, Lewis (2012c) similarly writes that "to become new [persons] means losing what we now call 'ourselves'. ... the principle runs through all life from top to bottom. Give up yourself, and you will find your real self" (pp. 224 and 226). Concurrently, Lewis' focus on the self (or the Same as Levinas would call it) is critical. Such a focus, he argues, leads to a diminishment of humanity, a shriveling up of the self – a kind of narcissistic love. Instead, when managers love along the lines of Levinas and Lewis they practice an authentic humanity that takes "up a position in being such that the other counts more than myself" (Levinas, 1969, p. 47) and that ultimately conditions their ethical self.

An illustration of such behavior comes from Seeger and Ulmer's (2001) analysis of organizational crisis at *Malden Mills* and *Cole Hardwoods*. In both cases, where fire destroyed sizeable capacity, the owners acted quickly "reducing the uncertainty of the crisis and its potential harm to stakeholders" (p. 373). Specifically, they manifested three sets of interrelated actions: (1) a commitment to keep paying workers and rebuild immediately; (2) an expressed view of stakeholders as the principal victims of the crisis and, thus, the importance of putting their needs first; and (3) and ability to see beyond the crisis to a better future for all stakeholders. Another exemplar is Anita Roddick, who started *The Bodyshop*, and who throughout her life embodied an orientation for others (Pless, 2007). As Roddick states, "the twin ideals of love and care touch everything we do: how we view our responsibilities, how we treat our staff, how we educate and communicate, how we relate to the community and the environment" (cited in Pless, 2007, p. 447). This other-orientation was not an espoused theory (Argyris, 1999) nor was it an "ethics of narcissus" (Roberts, 2001, p. 111); it was how Roddick behaved. She was "highly consistent and the identity script she constructed fits together as a coherent, virtuous whole" (Pless, 2007, p. 451). In caring about others, Roddick's moral self was conditioned, her moral values became habitual, and she consistently strove for the flourishing of others.

Conclusion

Lewis (1994) once stated definitively, "You can't get second things by putting them first; you can get second things only by putting the first things first" (p. 280). We argue that much of the literature on love in organizations is not putting love first; rather, it is putting things like efficiency and productivity, job satisfaction and organizational commitment, and financial returns first, and using a flaccid view of love as a means to achieve these. The works of Levinas and Lewis encourage us to reject this strategy outright. Organizations, and their managers, need to put *agapē* love first, which means being open to the Other, and then these secondary outcomes may follow.

Business operates in a world of reductive egocentric ontologies – a world where a materialistic value system distorts the reality of daily life (Giacalone, 2004) and where a neoliberal ideology "configures all aspects of existence in economic terms" (Brown, 2015, p. 17). In such a place, it is natural to serve the self and/or the organization's interests before the interests of others. To change this paradigm, managers ought to discern between objects they manage for organizational ends and infinite subjects irreducible to these ends. Individuals do not simply fulfill roles; they are neighbors that call "*Me voici* - yes, here I am" (Levinas, 1998b, p. 146) and, therefore, are an essential aspect of the social relations required to condition one's ethical self (Jones, 2014).

Devoid of *agapē* love, managers will struggle to be fully ethical since for both Levinas and Lewis, moral identity, and therefore action, is a product of how I respond to the call of the Other before I consider my own desires or needs. Unfortunately, most theories of positive leadership in the management literature (e.g., ethical (Brown & Trevino, 2006), servant (Van Dierendonck, 2011), and authentic (George, Sims, McLean, & Mayer, 2007)) start with the "I" who then works toward the ethics of the Other. Consequently, these styles become another form of totalizing – a collapsing of the Other's interests into that of the organization's domain. For real ethical transformation, managers must take heed of, dialog with, and be taught by, the Other. This requires a decentering of management in organizations to be replaced with that of all stakeholders (Lipari, 2004), which ultimately means letting stakeholders decide what is best for themselves. Such decentering will be difficult without the proximity of the face, which entails making the Other as real as possible for the organization. If this happens, the moral obligation to treat the Other as an end, as opposed to a means of increasing profit, may become the norm.

Both Levinas and Lewis were concerned for the Other and understood that genuine love – *agapē* love, appreciative-love – is love for the sake of and value of the Other. Both described the Other in relational terms with the profound language of *face*: Others have faces. Until we see them as such, we will treat people as commodities; we will instrumentalize them, or sentimentalize them. According to Levinas (1969), "the foreign face calls to my fraternity of the human race, my position as brother" (p. 214). This call of the Other means managers have choice – if they react as neighbors, if they alleviate the Other's suffering, then they demonstrate true ethical leadership. But it is only when they put *agapē* love first that they will be able to see the Other face-to-face. *Agapē* love demands from business organizations that they see the Other and appreciate the Other for who they are and not merely for what they can offer. But this will not happen "till we have faces" (Lewis, 1998).

Note

1 Tina Turner on the album *Private Dancer* (Capital Records, 1994).

References

Aasland, D. G. (2004). On the ethics behind "Business Ethics". *Journal of Business Ethics, 53*, 3–8.

Aasland, D. G. (2007). The exteriority of ethics in management and its transition into justice: A Levinasian approach to ethics in business. *Business Ethics: A European Review, 16*(3), 220–226.

Albrecht, S. L., & Marty, A. (2020). Personality, self-efficacy and job resources and their associations with employee engagement, affective commitment and turnover intentions. *The International Journal of Human Resource Management, 31*(5), 657–681. doi:10.1080/09585192.2017.1362660

Alvesson, M., & Willmott, H. (2002). Identity regulation as organizational control: Producing the appropriate individual. *Journal of Management Studies, 39*(5), 619–644. doi:10.1111/1467-6486.00305

Amundson, N. E., Borgen, W. A., Jordan, S., & Erlebach, A. C. (2004). Survivors of downsizing: Helpful and hindering experiences. *Career Development Quarterly, 52*(3), 256–271. doi:10.1002/j.2161-0045.2004.tb00647.x

Andersen, N., & Born, A. W. (2007). Emotional identity feelings as communicative artefacts in organisations. *International Journal of Work Organisation and Emotion, 2*(1), 35–48.

Andersen, N., & Born, A. W. (2008). The employee in the sign of love. *Culture & Organization, 14*(4), 325–343. doi:10.1080/14759550802489664

Argandoña, A. (2011). Beyond contracts: Love in firms. *Journal of Business Ethics, 99*(1), 77–85. doi:10.1007/s10551-011-0750-z

Argyris, C. (1999). *On organizational learning*. Malden, MA: Blackwell.

Arman, M., & Rehnsfeldt, A. (2006). The presence of love in ethical caring. *Nursing Forum, 41*(1), 4–12. doi:10.1111/j.1744-6198.2006.00031.x

Arnett, R. C. (2008). Provinciality and the face of the Other. In K. G. Robert & R. C. Arnett (Eds.), *Communication ethics: Between cosmopolitanism and provinciality* (pp. 69–88). New York, NY: Peter Lang.

Bakan, J. (2004). *The corporation: The pathological pursuit of profit and power*. New York, NY: Free Press.

Barley, S. R., & Kunda, G. (1992). Design and devotion: Surges of rational and normative ideologies of control in managerial discourse. *Administrative Science Quarterly, 37*(3), 363–399.

Barsade, S., & O'Neill, O. (2014). What's love got to do with it? A longitudinal study of the culture of companionate love and employee and client outcomes in the long-term care setting. *Administrative Science Quarterly, 59*(4), 551–598. doi:10.1177/0001839214538636

Bauman, Z. (1989). *Modernity and the holocaust*. Cambridge, MA: Polity Press.

Bell, E., & Taylor, S. (2003). The elevation of work: Pastoral power and the New Age work ethic. *Organization, 10*(2), 329–349. doi:10.1177/1350508403010002009

Berrone, P., Fosfuri, A., & Gelabert, L. (2017). Does greenwashing pay off? Understanding the relationship between environmental actions and environmental legitimacy. *Journal of Business Ethics, 144*(2), 363–379. doi:10.1007/s10551-015-2816-9

Blanchard, K., & Barrett, C. (2011). *Lead with LUV*. Upper Saddle River, NJ: FT Press.

Blok, V. (2017). Levinasian ethics in business. In D. C. Poff & A. C. Michalos (Eds.), *Encyclopedia of business and professional ethics* (pp. 1–5). Cham: Springer International Publishing.

Boiral, O., Talbot, D., & Paillé, P. (2015). Leading by example: A model of organizational citizenship behavior for the environment. *Business Strategy & the Environment, 24*(6), 532–550. doi:10.1002/bse.1835

Bojesen, A., & Muhr, S. L. (2008). In the name of love: Let's remember desire. *Ephemera: Theory & Politics in Organization, 8*(1), 79–93.

Bowie, N. E. (2000). A Kantian theory of leadership. *Leadership and Organization Development Journal, 21*, 185–193.

Boyatzis, R. E., Smith, M. L., & Blaize, N. (2006). Developing sustainable leaders through coaching and compassion. *Academy of Management Learning & Education, 5*(1), 8–24. doi:10.5465/AMLE.2006.20388381

Brown, M. E., & Treviño, L. K. (2006). Ethical leadership: A review and future directions. *The Leadership Quarterly, 17*(6), 595–616. doi:https://doi.org/10.1016/j.leaqua.2006.10.004

Brown, W. (2015). *Undoing the demos: Neoliberalism's stealth revolution.* New York, NY: Zone Books.

Caldwell, C., & Dixon, R. (2010). Love, forgiveness, and trust: Critical values of the modern leader. *Journal of Business Ethics, 93*(1), 91–101. doi:10.1007/s10551-009-0184-z

Carriger, M. (2016). To downsize or not to downsize – What does the empirical evidence suggest? *Journal of Strategy and Management, 9*(4), 449–473. doi:10.1108/JSMA-10-2015-0085

Casey, C. (1995). *Work, self and society*. London: Routledge.

Chomsky, N., & McChesney, R. W. (2011). *Profit over people: Neoliberalism and global order*. New York, NY: Seven Stories Press.

Crossan, M., Mazutis, D., & Seijts, G. (2013). In search of virtue: The role of virtues, values and character strengths in ethical decision making. *Journal of Business Ethics, 113*(4), 567–581. doi:10.1007/s10551-013-1680-8

Cunha, M. P. e., Clegg, S. R., Costa, C., Leite, A. P., Rego, A., Simpson, A. V., . . . Sousa, M. (2017). Gemeinschaft in the midst of Gesellschaft? Love as an organizational virtue. *Journal of Management, Spirituality & Religion, 14*(1), 3–21. doi:10.1080/14766086.2016.1184100

Darley, J. M. (1994). Organizations as a source of immoral behavior. *Global Bioethics, 7*(2), 53–63. doi:10.1080/11287462.1994.10800904

Davis, C. (1996). *Levinas*. Notre Dame, IN: University of Notre Dame Press.

Delmas, M. A., & Burbano, V. C. (2011). The drivers of greenwashing. *California Management Review, 54*(1), 64–87. doi:10.1525/cmr.2011.54.1.64

Derrida, J. (1978). Violence and metaphysics: An essay on the thought of Emmanuel Levinas. In A. Bass (Trans.), *Writing & difference* (pp. 79–153). Chicago, IL: University of Chicago Press.

Dierendonck, D., & Patterson, K. (2015). Compassionate love as a cornerstone of servant leadership: An integration of previous theorizing and research. *Journal of Business Ethics, 128*(1), 119–131. doi:10.1007/s10551-014-2085-z

Duchon, D., & Drake, B. (2009). Organizational narcissism and virtuous behavior. *Journal of Business Ethics, 85*(3), 301–308. doi:10.1007/s10551-008-9771-7

Dutton, J. E., & Workman, K. M. (2011). Commentary on 'why compassion counts!': Compassion as a generative force. *Journal of Management Inquiry, 20*(4), 402–406. doi:10.1177/1056492611421077 http://jmi.sagepub.com

Foucault, M. (1981). Omnes et singulatum: Towards a criticism of political reason. *Tanner Lectures on Human Values, 2*, 223–254.

Foucault, M. (1983). Afterward: The subject and power. In H. L. Dreyfus & P. Rabinow (Eds.), *Michel Foucault: Beyond structuralism and hermeneutics* (2nd ed., pp. 208–226). Chicago, IL: University of Chicago Press.

Fromm, E. (1963). *The art of loving.* New York, NY: Bantam.

Gatti, L., Seele, P., & Rademacher, L. (2019). Grey zone in – Greenwash out. A review of greenwashing research and implications for the voluntary-mandatory transition of CSR. *International Journal of Corporate Social Responsibility, 4*(1), 6. doi:10.1186/s40991-019-0044-9

George, B., Sims, P., McLean, A. N., & Mayer, D. (2007). Discovering your authentic leadership. *Harvard Business Review, February*, 1–8.

Giacalone, R. A. (2004). A transcendent business education for the 21st century. *Academy of Management Learning & Education, 3*(4), 415–420. doi:10.5465/AMLE.2004.15112547

Grant, K. (2008). Who are the lepers in our organizations? A case for compassionate leadership. *Business Renaissance Quarterly, 3*(2), 75–91.

Gregg, M. (2011). *Work's intimacy.* Cambridge: Polity Press.

Hager, P. (2011). Refurbishing MacIntyre's account of practice. *Journal of Philosophy of Education, 45*(3), 545–561. doi:10.1111/j.1467-9752.2011.00810.x

Hancock, P. (2008). Embodied generosity and an ethics of organization. *Organization Studies, 29*(10), 1357–1373. doi:10.1177/0170840608093545

Hanks, P. (Ed.) (1986). *Collins dictionary of the English language* (2nd ed.). London: Collins.

Harris, H. (2002). Is love a management virtue? *Business and Professional Ethics Journal, 21*(3/4), 173–184. doi:10.5840/bpej2002213/421

Hochschild, A. (1983). *The managed heart: Commercialization of human feeling.* Berkeley, CA: University of California Press.

Jackall, R. (1988). *Moral mazes: The world of corporate managers.* New York, NY: Oxford University Press.

Jones, J. (2014). Leadership lessons from Levinas: Revisiting responsible leadership. *Leadership and the Humanities, 2*(1), 44–63.

Kanungo, R. N. (1992). Alienation and empowerment: Some ethical imperatives in business. *Journal of Business Ethics, 11*(5/6), 413–422. doi:10.1007/BF00870553

Katz, C. (2007). Levinas between Agapē and Eros. *Symposium, 11*(2), 333–350.

Knights, D., & O'Leary, M. (2006). Leadership, ethics and responsibility to the other. *Journal of Business Ethics, 67*, 125–137. doi:10.1007/s10551-006-9008-6

Kouzes, J. M., & Posner, B. Z. (1992). Ethical leaders: An essay about being in love. *Journal of Business Ethics, 11*(5/6), 479–484. doi:10.1007/BF00870559

Le, T. N., & Levenson, M. R. (2005). Wisdom as self-transcendence: What's love (& individualism) got to do with it? *Journal of Research in Personality*, 39(4), 443–457. doi:10.1016/ j.jrp.2004.05.003

Legge, K. (2005). *Human resource management: Rhetorics and realities.* Basingstoke: Palgrave Macmillan.

Levinas, E. (1969). *Totality and infinity: An essay on exteriority* (A. Lingis, Trans.). Pittsburgh, PA: Duquesne University Press.

Levinas, E. (1998a). *Entres Nous* (M. B. Smith & B. Harshav, Trans.). New York, NY: Columbia University Press.

Levinas, E. (1998b). *Otherwise than being* (A. Lingis, Trans.). Pittsburgh, PA: Duquesne University Press.

Lewis, C. S. (1965). The weight of glory. In *Screwtape Proposes a Toast and Other Pieces.* (pp. 94–110). London: Fontana.

Lewis, C. S. (1966). *A grief observed.* London, UK: Faber and Faber.

Lewis, C. S. (1994). *God in the dock: Essays on theology and ethics.* Grand Rapids, MI: Eerdmans.

Lewis, C. S. (1998). *Till we have faces.* London: Fount.

Lewis, C. S. (2005). *That hideous strength.* London: Harper Collins.

Lewis, C. S. (2012a). *The four loves.* London: Collins.

Lewis, C. S. (2012b). *The great divorce: A dream.* London: Collins.

Lewis, C. S. (2012c). *Mere Christianity.* London: Collins.

Lewis, C. S. (2012d). *The problem of pain.* London: Collins.

Lewis, C. S. (2012e). *Surprised by joy: The shape of my life.* London: Collins.

Lipari, L. (2004). Listening for the other: Ethical implications of the Buber-Levinas encounter. *Communication Theory*, 14(2), 122–141.

Ma, E., Qu, F., Wei, X., & Hsiao, A. (2018). Conceptualization and operationalization of an altruistic and egoistic continuum of organizational citizenship behavior motivations. *Journal of Hospitality & Tourism Research*, 42(5), 740–771. doi:10.1177/1096348015619412

Maak, T., & Pless, N. (2009). Business leaders as citizens of the world: Advancing humanism on a global scale. *Journal of Business Ethics*, 88(3), 537–550. doi:10.1007/s10551-009-0122-0

Mansell, S. (2008). Proximity and rationalisation: The limits of a Levinasian ethics in the context of corporate governance and regulation. *Journal of Business Ethics*, 83(3), 565–577. doi:10.1007/s10551-007-9639-2

McIntyre, A. (1986). *After virtue* (2nd ed.). Notre dame, IN: Notre Dame University Press.

Moore, G. (2005). Humanizing business: A modern virtue ethics approach. *Business Ethics Quarterly*, 15(2), 237–255.

Morgan, M. L. (2011). *The Cambridge introduction to Levinas.* New York, NY: Cambridge University Press.

Nussbaum, M. (2001). *Upheavals of thought: The intelligence of emotions.* New York, NY: Cambridge University Press.

O'Donohue, W., & Nelson, L. (2014). Alienation: An old concept with contemporary relevance for human resource management. *International Journal of Organizational Analysis*, 22(3), 301–316. doi:10.1108/IJOA-01-2012-0541

Oman, D. (2011). Compassionate love: Accomplishments and challenges in an emerging scientific/spiritual research field. *Mental Health, Religion & Culture*, 14(9), 945–981. doi:10.1080/13674676.2010.541430

Pajo, K., & McGhee, P. (2003). The institutionalisation of business ethics: Are New Zealand organisations doing enough? *Journal of Management & Organization, 9*(1), 52–65. doi:10.1017/S1833367200004922

Patterson, K. (2010). Servant leadership and love. In D. van Dierendonck & K. Patterson (Eds.), *Servant leadership, developments in theory and research* (pp. 67–76). Hampshire: Palgrave Macmillan.

Pettigrew, T. F., & Tropp, L. R. (2006). A meta-analytic test of intergroup contact theory. *Journal of Personality & Social Psychology, 90*(5), 751–783.

Pless, N. (2007). Understanding responsible leadership: Role identity and motivational drivers. *Journal of Business Ethics, 74*(4), 437–456. doi:10.1007/s10551-007-9518-x

Pless, N., & Maak, T. (2004). Building an inclusive diversity culture: Principles, processes and practice. *Journal of Business Ethics, 54*(2), 129–147. doi:10.1007/s10551-004-9465-8

Rhodes, C. (2016). Democratic business ethics: Volkswagen's emissions scandal and the disruption of corporate sovereignty. *Organization Studies, 37*(10), 1501–1518. doi:10.1177/0170840616641984

Roberts, J. (2001). Corporate governance and the ethics of Narcissus. *Business Ethics Quarterly, 11*(1), 109–127. doi:10.2307/3857872

Rynes, S. L., Bartunek, J. M., Dutton, J. E., & Margolis, J. D. (2012). Care and compassion through an organizational lens: Opening up new possibilities. *Academy of Management Review, 37*(4), 503–523. doi:10.5465/amj.2012.0124

Satuf, C., Monteiro, S., Pereira, H., Esgalhado, G., Marina Afonso, R., & Loureiro, M. (2018). The protective effect of job satisfaction in health, happiness, well-being and self-esteem. *International Journal of Occupational Safety and Ergonomics, 24*(2), 181–189. doi:10.1080/10803548.2016.1216365

Schenkel, A., & Teigland, R. (2017). Why doesn't downsizing deliver? A multi-level model integrating downsizing, social capital, dynamic capabilities, and firm performance. *The International Journal of Human Resource Management, 28*(7), 1065–1107. doi:10.1080/09585192.2015.1130734

Seeger, M. W., & Ulmer, R. R. (2001). Virtuous responses to organizational crisis: Aaron Feuerstein and Milt Colt. *Journal of Business Ethics, 31*, 369–376.

Serrat, O. (2017). Managing by walking around. In *Knowledge solutions: Tools, methods, and approaches to drive organizational performance* (pp. 321–324). Singapore: Springer Singapore.

Shakespeare, W. (1606). Macbeth. In P. Alexander (Ed.), *The Tudor Edition of William Shakespeare: The complete works* (pp. 999–1027). London: Collins.

Shearer, T. (2002). Ethics and accountability: From the for-itself to the for-the-other. *Accounting, Organizations and Society, 27*, 541–573.

Simpson, A. V., Clegg, S., & Pitsis, T. (2014). "I used to care but things have changed": A genealogy of compassion in organizational theory. *Journal of Management Inquiry, 23*(4), 347–359. doi:10.1177/1056492614521895jmi.sagepub.com

Spicer, A., & Cederström, C. (2010). For the love of the organization. In C. Cederström & C. Hoedemaekers (Eds.), *Lacan and organization* (pp. 133–168). London: Mayfly.

Stephan, W. G., & Stephan, C. W. (2001). *Improving intergroup relations.* Thousand Oaks, CA: Sage.

Tasselli, S. (2019). Love and organization studies: Moving beyond the perspective of avoidance. *Organization Studies, 40*(7), 1073–1088. doi:10.1177/0170840617747924

Tokumitsu, M. (2015). *Do what you love: And other lies about success and happiness.* New York, NY: Regan Arts.

Tourish, D., & Pinnington, A. (2002). Transformational leadership, corporate cultism and the spirituality paradigm: An unholy trinity in the workplace? *Human Relations, 55*(2), 147–172.

Underwood, L. (2008). Compassionate love: A framework for research. In B. Fehr, S. Sprecher, & L. G. Underwood (Eds.), *The science of compassionate love: Theory, research, and applications* (pp. 3–25). Malden, MA: Wiley-Blackwell.

Van Dierendonck, D. (2011). Servant leadership: A review & synthesis. *Journal of Management, 37*(4), 1228–1261. doi:10.1177/0149206310380462

Vickers, M. (2009). Journeys into grief: Exploring redundancy for a new understanding of workplace grief. *Journal of Loss & Trauma, 14*(5), 401–419. doi:10.1080/15325020902724198

Weeks, K. (2017). Down with love: Feminist critique and the new ideologies of work. *Women's Studies Quarterly, 45*(3/4), 37–58.

Werhane, P. H. (1998). Moral imagination and the search for ethical decision-making in management. *Business Ethics Quarterly, 1*, 75–98.

Williams, C. R. (2008). Compassion, suffering and the self: A moral psychology of social justice. *Current Sociology, 56*(1), 5–24. doi:10.1177/0011392107084376

7 The Power of Love in People's Motivation at Work

Maria Prats

Introduction: A Conceptualization of Love

What are we talking about when talking about love? The concept of love is a multifold reality of experiences and manifestations. The distinctions among types of love in human relationships are crucial to better understand the motivations involved and their effects.

The most ancient concepts of love are *eros*, *philia*, and *agape*. According to Plato, *eros* is a common desire to seek transcendental beauty. However, the aspect of transcendence has been forgotten, and the concept is now understood as "romantic love" or acquisitive love. *Philia*, developed by Aristotle in the Nicomachean Ethics, entails a fondness and appreciation of the other. For the ancient Greeks, the term *philia* incorporated not only friendship but also loyalty to family and one's polis (political community), job, or discipline. The name of *agape* was first described in the Old Testament in the Judeo-Christian tradition. Originally, *agape* referred to the paternal love of God for man and of man for God, which is extended to include a brotherly love for all humanity. It is an unconditional love that transcends and persists regardless of circumstances. It involves going beyond the self in seeking the good for others.

Two contrasting approaches toward love have prevailed through the centuries: the first centered in the self (eros) and the second centered in the other (philia and agape). Augustine of Hippo (354–430 AD) described them as *cupiditas*, the carnal will, and *caritas*, the spiritual will (Bellusci, 2013). Caritas is the Latin translation of the Christian term *agape*, meaning selfless love. Thomas Aquinas (1235–1274 AD) commenting on the distinctions between "*amor concupiscentiae*," or concupiscent love, and "*amor benevolentia*" or "*amor amiticiae*," as benevolent love, considers them reconcilable. Explaining Aquinas' approach, Caldera (1999:50) reflects: "In no case are concupiscentiæ love and amicitiæ love on the same plane as two opposing realities or in conflict; they are coordinated moments in a single movement of love."

More recently, C.S. Lewis (1960) made a more subtle distinction between need-love and gift-love. An example of gift-love is that which motivates parents to work and save money for the future well-being of

DOI: 10.4324/9781003254034-8

their families, dying without enjoying the money directly, and preserving it for the future of the children. Need-love is, for example, that of a lonely or frightened child reaching for his mother's arms. Need-love should be identified not as selfishness but as a human need. Gift-love is not a biological need. It could be considered as a "fulfillment need" at a personal, ontological level. Gift-love involves people giving of themselves to others or being altruistic. In a relationship, when need-love is present, love is received, and when gift-love is present, love is given. Frequently, the two types of love coexist on both sides of a relationship.

Beyond making a distinction between need-love and gift-love, C.S. Lewis famously distinguished four levels of love depending on the type of relationship: affection, eros, friendship, and charity (Lewis, 1960). *Affection* is addressed to something or someone familiar, such that when it begins it may scarcely be perceived. It is the humblest love, and it includes both need-love (craving for the affection of others) and gift-love. For Lewis, affection love is not only a mere feeling; it also requires three elements: common sense, justice, and decency, described as goodness. *Eros* is the state of being in love after falling in love. Eros includes other aspects besides sexual activity (sexual experience can also occur without eros); it is not identified with sexual desire. Frequently, just an attraction comes first, provoking a delighted "pre-occupation" with the beloved – a general and unspecified pre-occupation with the beloved in his or her totality. Eros makes someone want not a person but a particular person. Affection and eros are more connected to biological tendencies than the other two types of love, friendship and charity. *Friendship* is a relationship freely chosen. Nevertheless, erotic love and friendship can concur in the same person, being different manifestations of love: "Lovers are normally 'face to face,' absorbed in each other; friends, side by side, absorbed in some common interest" (Lewis, 1960:91). True friendship is the least jealous of loves. Two friends welcome new friends as far as they are qualified to become real friends. Friendship arises out of mere companionship when common interests or insights are discovered. For Aristotle (2000), friendship seemed to be the happiest and most fully human of all loves. Finally, *charity* is the highest manifestation of love. It epitomizes gift-love, and its concept is rooted in Christian spirituality. Lewis defines charity as the love of God, who communicates to men a portion of his own gift-love. Charity implies giving of oneself to others, or contemplating others as another "I" with the same human dignity based on being an image and likeness of God. Charity is a vulnerable love because it can be unrequited. It includes manifestations such as compassion, forgiveness, and empathy, not because of a simple emotion but as a response to knowledge about a common being shared by the actor and the receiver of the act of charity.[1]

Another category of love has been analyzed by other authors: the love for humanity (Kristen R. Monroe, 1996) as fellow members of the world. This concept is close to that of companionship but has a broader sense: a relationship for sharing the same human nature.

In modern times, love has been defined by many authors as just an emotional state rather than an intention, action, or moral judgment (Singer, 1984; Wilson & Sober, 2002). Some authors believe that human love cannot be reduced to emotion because it involves seeing value in another, and bestowing worth is very much a conceptual endeavor (Post & Underwood, 2002). In addition, concepts such as freedom, moral awareness, and rational thought have been considered essential to a meaningful understanding of love (Hurlbut, 2002). Spaemann (2000) considers that love is an awakening to the reality of both the other and the self at once.

As we observe, there are many manifestations and types of love, as well as approaches to understanding its dynamics. In this chapter, I consider how "gift-love"[2] can be present at work through the motivation of our actions, specifically through our altruistic or transcendent motivations.

The construction of the chapter is as follows: first, we center our attention on the conceptualization of altruistic motives and their contextualization in the prosocial motives and the human motivational structure, respectively. Second, we consider the relationship between love and meaning at work. Third, we analyze how altruistic motives affect organizations in their leadership and organizational citizenship behaviors.

Altruistic Motives and Love

Psychologists have studied altruism as a motivation when someone is acting while seeking the well-being of others. From a behavioral economics perspective, some authors have identified altruism as charity love (Khalil, 2004). But why act altruistically? Altruistic acts inevitably seem to have ulterior motives, as some authors have noted (Schindler, 2018). We are altruistic for a reason. I consider that gift-love, in different intensities or degrees (from a close friendship to a love for humanity or universalism, rooted in a shared human being), is the ultimate reason for altruistic motives. Monroe's studies have revealed that altruists' particular perceptions of themselves in relation to others are critical to understanding the cause of altruism (2002:109):

> All the altruists I interviewed saw themselves as individuals strongly linked to others through shared humanity. Their cognitive-perceptual frameworks differed consistently and significantly from those of traditional rational actors in this one regard.

To better understand the relationship between altruistic motives and gift-love, I use an interdisciplinary approach combining studies of empirical psychology with metaphysics of psychology and philosophical anthropology. The application of only strictly empirical methods, considering just valid what can be verified through sensory observation or measured in a quantified or statistical manner, generates a circularity, excluding on *a priori* grounds intentions as causal. It is denied as a premise the possibility of any aspect of our human behavior to transcend the physical and measurable (Reichmann, 1985). Authors have adopted other approaches than empirical science in motivational theory, to study the implications of intentions and motives in human decision-making. For example, Nagel suggests (2016:5–6):

> Psychological investigation leading to ethical conclusions may require the reintroduction of metaphysics (…). Motivation theory is automatically regarded as an empirical science; it is assumed that at best we may hope to discover the influences to which men are subject and the patterns into which their behavior falls -perhaps even certain patterns and influences which are universal. But the suggestion that there must be motivational requirements on which to base ethical requirements (or perhaps that the two are identical) seems to demand a priori reasoning in motivation theory—something rather unexpected.
>
> This is the possibility which I propose to explore. Human motivation possesses features which are susceptible to metaphysical investigation and which carry some kind of necessity (though this last requires elaborate qualification).

Darley and Latane (1970) have affirmed that the question of the identity of the underlying force leading mankind toward altruism, although of enormous social interest and importance, is semi-philosophical in nature and will probably never be completely answered by reference to data. The experience when we recognize the other as *another* "*I*," the value we ascribe to a person as a "who" instead of a "what," and our self-awareness and the other-awareness as being persons, are key aspects to understanding the nature of altruistic love and altruistic motives.

Altruistic Motives: A Proposal of Definition

Altruistic motives can be described as intentional motives of an actor looking for the good of others, ultimately out of gift-love, without considering possible rewards. The behavior of altruistic motives is not necessarily prosocial and is compatible with the coexistence of other motives in the same action. According to the definition suggested, which includes some of the points in Monroe's definition (2002), let us specify each characteristic for considering a motive altruistic:

1. Intentional
2. Looking for the good of others
3. Ultimately out of gift-love for others
4. Thought without considering possible rewards.

1. Intentional

Intentionality includes a voluntary decision with a specific direction or purpose. The intentional element in the motivation of prosocial behavior has been considered by many scholars (Aronfreed, 1980; Bar-Tal, 1986; Berkowitz, 1972; Brief & Motowidlo, 1986; Eisenberg & Spinrad, 2014; Krebs & Hesteren, 1994; Leeds, 1963; Staub, 1978). Distinct intentions are what make a difference in the consequences for the acting persons given the same manifestation of prosocial behavior. A common human experience is how different we feel after a prosocial action depending on our intentions. The intention would be conditioned by the combination of many factors – biological, psychological, sociological, and circumstantial – but it is ultimately the self who decides to be or not to be altruistically motivated.[3] To have an altruistic intention changes not only the efficiency of the activity itself but also the impact on the acting person in terms of well-being, health, and psychological state (Clary et al., 1998).

To talk about intentions implies previous cognitive and volitional processes (Binswanger, 1991). Motivational theories that only consider physiological reflexes and psychological reactions responding to stimuli see the human being as a closed system, adhered to the homeostatic principle. But in humans, it seems that a second system is present when deciding our actions (Bazerman, Tenbrunsel, & Wade-Benzoni, 1998; Binswanger, 1991; Epstein, 1998; Kehr, 2004; Loewenstein, 1996; Metcalfe & Mischel, 1999; Read & Van Leeuwen, 1998) that involves rationality and volition.

Human being existence has broken with the barriers of automatisms and the environment (López Moratalla, 2021). Nonhuman vertebrates, instead of being open to the world, are bound to an environment. The consideration of intentions – which can be recognized and self-reported by the acting person – in altruistic motivational processes does not deny physiological reflexes and psychological reactions to stimuli. It implies the consideration of them as triggers, conditioning factors, in the motivational processes, but not determinant ones, and also not the unique source, as we will see in the human motivational structure.

Altruistic intentions are pointing to someone else other than the person itself. This opens the door to see ourselves as an open system capable of self-transcendence (Frankl, 2014; Guillén, Ferrero, & Hoffman, 2015; Pérez López, 2014). The man's openness to the world has also been evidenced by biologists and sociologists like Portmann and Gehlen, respectively. Gehlen states that the notion of instinct is not a sufficient anthropological explanation (Gehlen, 1988).

2. Looking for the good of others

Without an intention for seeking the good of others, there would be no altruistic motives, even though the action *per se* could be altruistic. For example, when someone is helping, but is mainly seeking praise and not the good of others, the action is prosocial, but the intention is not.

Intending to seek the good of others is specific to humans: it requires self-awareness, other-awareness, and identification of the other as a fellow person. Besides, it reflects a concern about others because they matter to us.

When seeking the good of others, action does not necessarily have to be altruistic. Batson (1998) emphasizes that altruism refers to the motivation, not to the nature of the act itself. Non-prosocial actions can be altruistically motivated. In psychology, the study of altruistic motives started through the observation of prosocial behaviors, when people act in helping others. But we seem to experience the possibility of altruistic motives in actions that are not necessarily prosocial. We can consider the situation of someone who is working as a 'big data consultant' for a company. This employee seeks to earn some money (probably a lot) but, at the same time, is seeking to improve the skills required for the position, to financially help family, and also to truly serve clients and team members. The consultant simultaneously is having *extrinsic motives* (earning money), *internal-achievement motives* (improving abilities), and *altruistic motives* (helping family, serving the team, and helping clients). This simultaneity of motives, or of some of them, is a self-evident experience. If there is an intention of seeking the good of others, there is an altruistic motive present in the action, independently of the type of the action. Another example of altruistic motives in a non-prosocial action is the case of someone declining a job offer with better conditions in another state because of the needs of other family members; for example, living in the same city might enable better care of the job applicant's grandparents. In this situation, the applicant would decide, out of love, to stay in the same state and would decline the job offer in order to help the grandparents.

3. Ultimately out of gift-love for others

Gift-love includes different love intensities and a range of possible manifestations: for example, from small favors to colleagues from another department or bringing donuts for the ones in the office, to the ones originated from long team relationships, such as make time to listen to a member of our team who has had a personal setback in a day full of work, or facilitate some information we consider interesting for a colleague, beyond our professional role. Sorokin (1954) conceptualized altruistic conduct as "love in action." The philosopher Leonardo Polo describes the proper love of the human being as "an ability to transcend oneself and, therefore, does not allow us to prescind from the other" (2012:83). He names human beings "*personal* beings" because they are capable of giving, and they are not only individuals but more: persons, a different type of being than other vertebrate beings. Human beings are capable of transcendence, going consciously beyond themselves. Schindler (2018) also considers how in altruism the acting subject looks for the good or the well-being of others ultimately out of a giving love.

An altruistic act can be initially done because of a sense of duty, as a norm (Eisenberg, VanSchyndel, & Spinrad, 2016; Schroeder & Graziano, 2015), but the duty or norm should be internalized, and the meaning of the value of the act by itself should be known. As Ryan and Deci state: "To fully internalize a regulation, and thus to become autonomous with respect to it, people must inwardly grasp its meaning and worth" (2000:64). An internalized principle or norm in this context is different from just do it because "it is the norm." To be altruistic, the internalized principle or norm should ultimately be done out of love, even if the initial learning occurred according to a norm or principle. Consequently, in a given moment, we understand the "why" of the principle or norm in its essence, not just the formality of doing it. An example of an internalized norm that is done out of love could be the learning process involved in helping elderly people: we learned at home or/and at school to take care of our elders, and sooner or later, we understand the "*why*," the importance and the meaning of it. What started as an obligation evolves into something done by love for others, appreciating them, and not doing the action because of external imposition. The action then is done out of gift-love to others who matter to us, and whom we love by themselves because they are another "I," other human beings. In the previous example, some people will always see helping the elderly as a duty or norm, and others would begin, in a given moment, to do it out of love, motivated by altruistic motives, because they have changed their intention. Even when a behavior continues to be a social norm, if the main intention is out of love, the motive is altruistic.

4. Thought without considering possible rewards
Researchers have taken different sides in defending the necessity of avoiding the expectation of rewards or allowing the option of anticipating rewards (Batson, 2011; Dovidio, Piliavin, Schroeder, & Penner, 2006; Kristen Renwick Monroe, 2002). Batson does not deny that egoistic motives may play a role and accepts that both altruistic and egoistic motives are present simultaneously. He emphasizes the importance of considering the helping motives as predominant motives to consider the action done by altruistic motives. Monroe explicitly conceptualizes altruism with no anticipation or expectation of reward for the altruist. I suggest that the critical aspect is to consider if the dominant intention is acting out of gift-love for others, regardless of the consciousness that possible rewards will be received later. What matters is not considering the rewards during the formulation of the intention, not that they do not exist; in some cases, they will exist, and they will be obvious to the decision-maker.[4]

Altruistic Motives in the Context of Helping Behaviors

Altruistic motives are considered a type of motive in prosocial behaviors. Initial studies in psychology considered altruism as a behavior of helping others without specifying the motivational aspects. Krebs describes some challenges in his literature review in reference to the conceptualization of altruism (Krebs, 1970:262):

> The question of the definition of altruism, and the related question of whether altruism exists, have [sic] posed difficult problems. Behavioral researchers have generally avoided the definitional issue, which involves establishing the intention behind apparently self-sacrificial other-oriented acts, by employing operational definitions.

Posteriorly, the denomination "prosocial" was introduced and became more predominant than "altruism." One example of this evolution is in the studies of Nancy Eisenberg, who initially addressed the same phenomenon in her research by using the term "altruism" (Eisenberg, 1986) and posteriorly by using the term "prosocial behavior" (Eisenberg, 2000). Prosocial behaviors have been defined as positive social acts carried out to produce and maintain the well-being and integrity of others (Brief & Motowidlo, 1986), or as a broad range of actions intended to benefit one or more people other than oneself, such as helping, comforting, sharing, and cooperating (Batson & Powell, 2003; Eisenberg, Fabes, & Spinrad, 2006).

Prosocial behavior can be a manifestation of altruistic motives, done for the sake of others, or can be an expression of self-interest, or a combination of both: a prosocial action motivated by the benefit to others and oneself. An example of prosocial behavior with egoistic motives is helping someone at work only to receive praise from the boss, who values these types of acts. A recent analysis of the conceptualization of prosocial motives, including altruistic motives, is the *heuristic model* of prosocial motivations from Eisenberg and colleagues (2016), which encompasses a continuum from other-oriented to egoistic motives, in prosocial actions. In the continuum model of other-oriented motives, the following nine categories are included, from more altruistic to more egoistic types of prosocial motivation: (1) sympathy/altruism, (2) adherence to internalized principles related to others' well-being, such as equality, (3) adherence to more general internalized principles, such as justice, (4) adherence to internalized norms, (5) social relatedness, (6) goal completion or increased feelings of competence/self-esteem, (7) decreased aversive arousal or emotion, (8) obtaining approval, and (9) avoiding punishment or obtaining rewards. In the *heuristic model* of prosocial motivations, altruistic motivations are classified based on Batson's definition of altruistic motivation (2011), but in contrast to Batson, who distinguishes between moral and altruistic motives, the model considers altruistic motivation – based on empathic concern or sympathy – as usually being moral.

Considering the categories of the continuum model of other-oriented motives by Eisenberg, VanSchyndel, and Spinrad (2016) and the approach

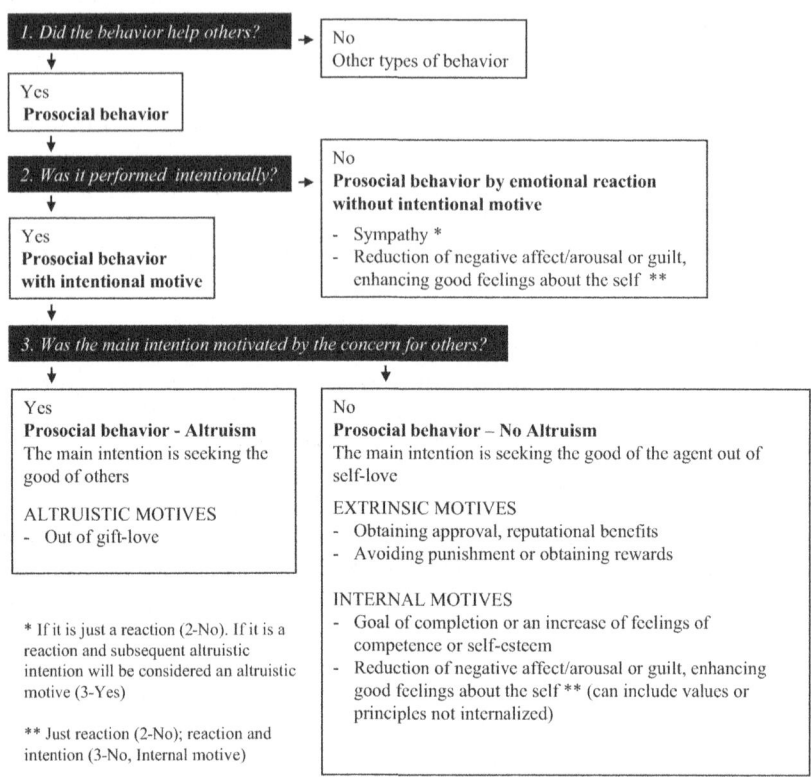

Figure 7.1 Altruistic motives vs other motives in prosocial behaviors.
Source: Own elaboration (Prats, 2020).

in the structure of Hawley's figure "behavior that benefits another proximate level" (2014), we can analyze, from a motivational perspective, the
difference between altruistic motives and other motives in a given prosocial behavior. Figure 7.1 illustrates the different possible alternatives
through three questions.

In identifying the motives in a prosocial behavior, one must consider
(1) whether the action benefits others, (2) whether it was intentional, and
(3) whether the intention was mainly seeking the good of others or oneself. In the relationship between altruistic motives and other motives in
a given prosocial behavior, we distinguish the different intentions of the
actor. We do not include the category of social relatedness observed by
Eisenberg and colleagues (2016), because, given its ambiguity, it cannot
be classified *a priori* as a proximal motive.

Altruistic motives in prosocial behavior. If the intention is mainly
seeking the good of others, it is an altruistic motive. Three possible
triggers or origins of altruistic motives have been studied by scholars:

rational thought (Nagel, 2016); adherence to internalized values or principles related to others' well-being, such as equality, or morals, such as justice (Eisenberg, Miller, Shell, McNalley, & Shea, 1991; Hawley, 2014); and sympathy (Batson & Shaw, 1991; Eisenberg, 1991; Hawley, 2014). I consider emotional reactions as altruistic motives only when they are followed by the intentional purpose of the actor.

Other motives than altruistic in prosocial behavior. If the intention is mainly seeking the good of oneself, many motives for prosocial behavior except altruistic motives may exist. The motives can be extrinsic or internal (e.g., to achieve a specific standard or sense of duty). Extrinsic motives involve seeking an external result for oneself, such as obtaining approval from others, reputational benefits, avoiding punishment, or obtaining rewards. The internal motives involve seeking results within oneself, and may involve goal completion, increased feelings of competence or self-esteem, a reduction in negative affect or feeling guilty, or an enhancement in good feelings about oneself. This is not a complete list, but it comprises the most common cases of prosocial behavior addressed by scholars. These other types of motives in prosocial behaviors, the extrinsic and internal motives, can be originated by a reaction of the actor to inputs or through rational thought. Some categories can be classified differently depending on the intention of the actor (asterisks in the figure).

I suggest identifying the term "altruistic motives" with "prosocial motives." In the case of a prosocial behavior where the principal motive is not altruistic, we can address them by the other types of motives: extrinsic or internal, as shown in Figure 7.1.

The following subsection analyzes altruistic motives in the context of human motivational structure in general.

Altruistic Motives within the Human Motivational Structure

Throughout the 20th century, psychologists developed multiple theories of human motivation. The framework of my study of human motives in general, and altruistic motives in particular, involves *activation theories* and *content theories*. *Activation theories* emphasize free will and goal anticipation in motivation versus *reactive models*, which are grounded in a more mechanistic system approach (Barberá Heredia, 2002; Garrido Gutierrez, 2002; Latham & Pinder, 2005). The preference for active versus reactive theories in the approach is derived from the relevance of purposes and intentions in humans' motivational structure, specifically in altruistic motives. The selection of content theories versus process theories is necessary in the case of altruistic motives given their "content nature": seeking the well-being of others. The theories I have analyzed in more detail are the self-determination theory (SDT) (Deci, La Guardia, Moller, Scheiner, & Ryan, 2006; Deci & Ryan, 2000) and motivational approaches (Perez Lopez, 1991, 2014; Hawley, 2014), among others.

SDT considers that we have innate psychological needs for competence, autonomy, and relatedness. Prosocial behavior has been studied by SDT according to the level of autonomy (Weinstein & Ryan, 2010). When considering how to integrate altruistic motives within SDT, two obstacles have been encountered. The first obstacle is the mismatch between altruistic motives and the innate need for relatedness. Altruism has a broader, transcendent purpose (beyond the acting subject) that has not been considered to date in descriptions of relatedness need. In altruism, there is a purpose to seek the good of others; relatedness need is considered to be a source of motivation but not a purposed goal. The second obstacle is the lack of structure in SDT to differentiate the actor's purposes from motivational sources. The Perez Lopez and Hawley theories are complementary and enriching approaches that help to elaborate on human motivational structures differentiating sources and purposes ("motivations" and "motives" in Perez Lopez; "motivations" and "intentions" in Hawley). I believe that adding these perspectives enables the integration of extrinsic, internal, and altruistic motives within the same human motivational structure. Inspired by these authors, I propose a human motivational model with two systems of sources (rational-volitional and tendential) and two types of motivational purposes (objective and subjective).

Human motivational sources. We can distinguish two main sources in the origins of human action: the tendential system and the rational-volitional system. These two systems have been named differently among the scholars: hot and cold, emotional and cognitive, and experiential and rational systems (Bazerman et al., 1998; Binswanger, 1991; Epstein, 1998; Kehr, 2004; Loewenstein, 1996; Metcalfe & Mischel, 1999; Read & Van Leeuwen, 1998). The two systems constitute different sources of human motivation, and together with the purposes or motives form the motivational structure. Figure 7.2 shows a simplified version of the relationships between these two sources.

The tendential or spontaneous system involves seeking different types of self-satisfaction. The rational-volitional system involves seeking self-satisfaction as well as other satisfactions, looking beyond personal needs to attending to others' needs. In some cases, the two systems enter in conflict because they have different principles, tendential or rational. For example, when we see a piece of chocolate cake, the tendential system arouses a desire to eat it, but the rational-volitional system might result in a decision not to eat it, for example, to maintain a diet, for health reasons, or to give it to a friend who loves chocolate cake. In these last cases, the rational-volitional system regulates spontaneous impulse and decides not to eat the cake. The impulse would be restrained not only by the decision but also by the presence of the will and its nurture habits (strength of will) to implement the decision. Similarly, one person can regulate natural impulses to act in favor of other people first. The tendential system can be understood as a closed system that follows the rules of

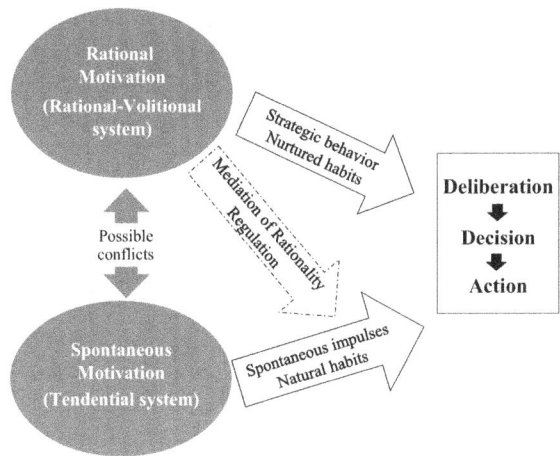

Figure 7.2 The human motivational sources.
Source: Own elaboration (Prats, 2020).

psychological homeostasis, similar to the physiological homeostasis in terms of dynamics, proper of human nature. The rational-volitional system can be considered as an open system, which, properly speaking, does not follow rules, and it is led by our freedom, that is conditioned but not determined. The rational-volitional system is specific to the human person. It is not present in the rest of the beings. Frankl addressing the relationship between the tendential and rational-volitional systems asserts that between stimulus and response there is always a space (2006). In that space is our power to choose our response.

The spontaneous system generates spontaneous impulses and natural habits. It reacts to perceptional changes. The rational-volitional system generates strategic behavior and can nurture positive habits, which becomes a kind of second nature for the person, acting with the facility and readiness of the spontaneous system. It also can generate negative habits with damaging consequences, such as becoming an alcoholic or other type of addictions. Rational-volitional system not only reacts to stimuli, and receives the perceptional knowledge, but also can proactively initiate action.

Human motivational purposes. The purposes or motives are the intentions of the actor, as noted by some authors (Ferreiro & Alcázar García, 2002; Hawley, 2014; Pérez López, 1991b, 2014). Slade describes purposes as "motives, 'motors' propelling actions of various sorts. The words *motive* and *purpose* denote something possessing and exclusively 'mental existence,' whose being is in consciousness" (Slade, 2000). When we experience tendential reactions, we do not have a specific purpose or intention. We follow biological laws, reacting when we receive inputs;

these laws can be moderated and guided by the rational-volitional system, but not changed. The rational-volitional system is a higher-level system that permits the selection of a goal, intention, or purpose because it is not predetermined but is a free system that is conditioned but not determined. If we denied a conditioned but not determined intention in humans, we would be denying real freedom or morality. Human actions are intentional, that is, they have a purpose or goal (motives). The tendential system generates activity that "happen" to us, instinct reactions such as digestive processes, reaction to danger, etc., as compared with the rational-volitional system that generates activity – actions with purposes or motives.

The purposes of human actions can be analyzed according to the goals of the action itself – the doing of the action the actor wants – which can be called "objective goals," and according to the results sought as a consequence of the action performed, or "subjective goals." Both goals are intentional, but the "objective goals" refer to the intention of the *what* of the action, and the "subjective goals" refer to the intention of the *why* of the action. The sense of the action is conferred by the subjective intentions of the actor. These two types of intention enable a distinction in a prosocial behavior between the objective goal of the action (e.g., helping someone) and the different subjective goals that the actor can consider in helping someone (e.g. prestige, enjoyment of the activity itself, or doing it for the good of others). Within the subjective goals, three subtypes of motives can be differentiated: external, internal, and altruistic:

- *Extrinsic motives*: when actors seek results from others for themselves (social or material rewards) – for example, money, prestige, or obtaining material goods.
- *Internal motives*: when actors seek results from and for themselves. It refers to any result of the execution of the action for the person who performs it and that depends only on the fact of performing it (Pérez López, 1991a). Three sub-types are included: *intrinsic motives* (in which actors seek enjoyment or pleasure during the activity itself), *achievement motives* (in which actors seek to improve abilities, competencies, or skills), as Locke and Schattke suggest (2019), and moral motives (in which actors seek to live moral values).
- *Altruistic motives*[5]: when actors seek results beyond themselves, for the good or well-being of others out of love. Altruistic motives can also be called "transcendent motives" to emphasize the purpose of going beyond oneself (Pérez López, 2014).

As mentioned above, altruistic motives can be originated in many ways: the triggers can be sympathy reactions (Batson & Shaw, 1991), adherence to internalized principles or norms (Eisenberg et al., 1991, 2016), or being initiated rationally (Nagel, 2016). I posit that these triggers will be altruistic motives only if they are followed by the intention to do good to another person; otherwise, there would be a prosocial behavior but not a proper altruistic motive. Furthermore, once a person has generated a nurture habit of altruistic actions (e.g., helping an elderly person cross the street), altruism can become a spontaneous action with an implicit rather than an explicit intention.

Figure 7.3 shows the human motivational structure, including the sources and the purposes or motives.

Having defined and contextualized altruistic motives within prosocial behaviors and the human motivational structure, the following section addresses altruistic motives and meaning at work.

Love and Meaning at Work

What are the more powerful motivations at work? Michael Douglas, in his role as Gordon Gekko in "Wall Street" movie, provided a straight-forward answer in his famous speech: "Greed is good." However, many studies reflect a different reality: making a difference, doing work that matters, and having a challenging job are very powerful motivators. Qualitative and quantitative researches have revealed that many employees describe the purpose of their work in terms of making a positive difference in others' lives (Bolino & Grant, 2016; Colby, Sippola, & Phelps, 2001; Hackman & Oldham, 1976, 1980; Rosso, Dekas, & Wrzesniewski, 2010). Also, research in diverse bodies of the literature suggests that the motivation to make a prosocial difference is prevalent in a variety of work contexts (Grant, 2007).

In his book *Man's Search for Meaning*, Frankl affirms, "Man's main concern is not to gain pleasure or to avoid pain but rather to see a meaning in his life" (2006:115). He considers that everyone has an individual vocation or mission in life to carry out a concrete assignment that demands fulfillment; everyone's task is unique, as are the specific opportunities to implement it. Meaning in our lives is to understand for what, to what, or to whom to be responsible and dedicate our lives. In addition, Frankl stresses that the true meaning of life is to be discovered in the world, outside us, rather than within us or our own psyche. He calls this constitutive human character "the self-transcendence of human existence," because humans always orient toward and are directed to something or someone other than themselves. It is meaningful to fulfill something or another human being. From Frankl's perspective, a paradox occurs in which the more one forgets oneself, the more one actualizes oneself: self-actualization occurs as a side effect of self-transcendence. Nietzsche's aphorism "He who has a *why* to live can bear almost any *how*" has been applied by Viktor Frankl, after his experiences in Nazi concentration camps, to three main sources of meaning. One is directly related to love: the experience of encountering someone or experiencing something, such as goodness, through nature, culture, or other human beings in their uniqueness. The other two ways he describes to discover meaning in life

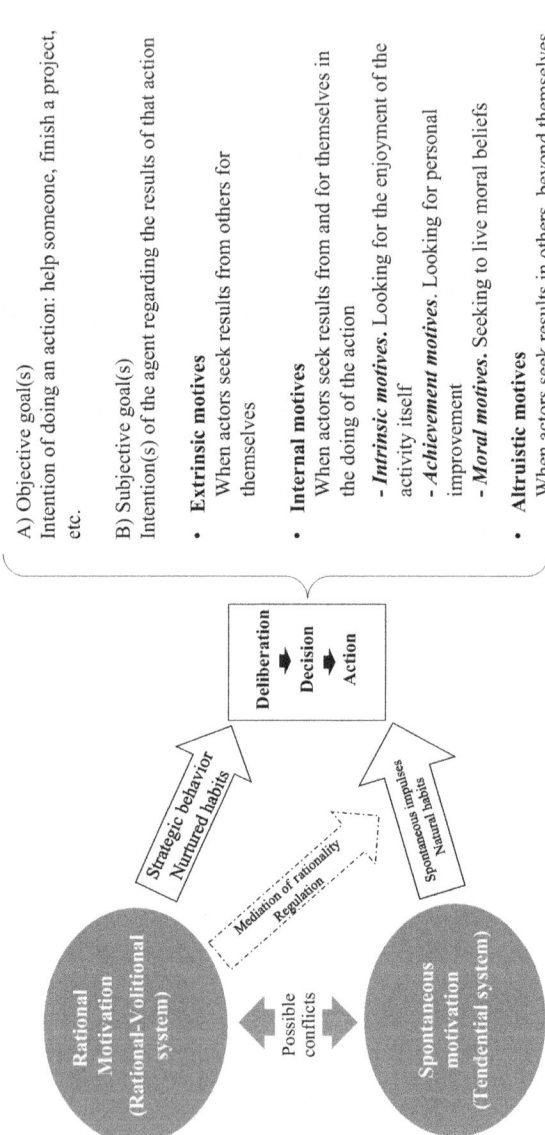

Figure 7.3 Human motivational structure: sources and purposes or motives.
Source: Own elaboration (Prats, 2020).

are through creating work or doing a deed, and through one's attitude toward unavoidable suffering.

Christensen, a Harvard professor, describes similar experiences in his article "How will you measure your life" in *Harvard Business Review*. He has observed his Harvard classmates from 1979 coming to meetings increasingly unhappy, divorced, and alienated from their children. None of the individuals had a deliberate strategy to arrive at those results. He considers that they did not keep the purpose of their lives front and center as they decided how to spend their time and focus their talents and energy (2010:8):

> People who are driven to excel have this unconscious propensity to underinvest in their families and overinvest in their careers—even though intimate and loving relationships with their families are the most powerful and enduring source of happiness. If you study the root causes of business disasters, over and over you'll find this predisposition toward endeavors that offer immediate gratification. If you look at personal lives through that lens, you'll see the same stunning and sobering pattern: people allocating fewer and fewer resources to the things they would have once said mattered most.

Christensen proposes that if one is not guided by a clear sense of purpose, one is likely to waste time and energy in obtaining the most tangible, short-term signs of achievement, but not what is really important. He addresses a critical aspect of our lives: finding a balance between our work and personal life within personal vital projects. He contemplates gift-love not only in personal relationships but also at work, which involves another type and intensity yet is gift-love (Christensen, 2010:4): "Management is the most noble of professions if it's practiced well. No other occupation offers as many ways to help others learn and grow, take responsibility and be recognized for achievement, and contribute to the success of a team."

The sense of meaning at work is also related to the Schwartz theory of basic values (S. H. Schwartz, 2012), which identifies ten basic personal values recognized across cultures, grouped into four dimensions: conservation, self-enhancement, openness to change, and self-transcendence. Within self-transcendence are the values of benevolence and universalism. They promote gift-love attitudes toward those with whom one is in frequent personal contact and humankind in general. Universalism is similar to Monroe's "shared humanity" described above. What we most value in life is closely related to our purpose and meaning in life.

In many cases, the meaning is found through the ones we love, at different levels, from family to the future planet we will leave to the next generations. Meaning and giving love at work is not only possible but also happens every day in some people's lives. Nevertheless, a combination of motives usually gives meaning to our work and they may include (a) love for one's family (using the retribution as a mean to cover the children and the family needs), (b) love for humanity (seeking improvement in an actor's area of expertise to make the world a better place), or (c) achievement purposes, such as realizing a professional dream (entering a medical specialty, producing an artistic performance, or starting a business), increasing scientific knowledge or pursuing art creation. In addition, collaboration in a long business project with a competent and consolidated team over time can generate a sense of purpose at work; it is something that is acquired through the relationship, throughout the ups and downs of the project, and that invokes a deep sense of companionship and in some cases true friendship.

Having gift-love at work could include expressions (we are not referring here to marketing strategies but real personal intentions) such as "leaving a better world to my children," "improve the living conditions for future generations through my work," or "doing work that matters." These purposes normally involve something affecting the well-being of part of the human community, such as having more comfortable furniture, more healthful food, or better medical services. From a motivational perspective, when the sense of meaning is related to the intention (directly or indirectly) to do good to others, it is a manifestation of altruistic motives.

Impact of Love Motives at Work

Looking for the good of others at work generates multiple positive effects. Altruistic motives affect not only the external results (the action itself and other people involved) but also the well-being and attitude of the actors themselves. The persons acting altruistically influence, directly or/ and indirectly, the performance at work in different dimensions (Bobocel, 2013; Bolino & Grant, 2016; Cardador & Wrzesniewski, 2015; De Dreu & Nauta, 2009; Grant & Berry, 2011; Hu & Liden, 2015). Studies have found that acting for the well-being of others enhances individual performance, productivity, and persistence (Bellé, 2014; Bolino & Grant, 2016; Thompson & Bunderson, 2003), commitment (Schaumberg & Wiltermuth, 2014), increase job satisfaction (Aknin, Sandstrom, Dunn, & Norton, 2011), and customer satisfaction (Podsakoff, Whiting, Podsakoff, & Blume, 2009), and thus creates ripple effects in organizations (Aknin et al., 2011), such as lower turnover and organization costs (Podsakoff et al., 2009).

Furthermore, when employee well-being grows, it results in decreased emotional exhaustion that otherwise appears from harming others (Grant & Campbell, 2007), and aids in negative task and self-evaluations (Grant & Sonnentag, 2010). In addition, the emotional benefits extend outside the workplace: when employees perceive high prosocial impact at work, they experience greater activated positive affect at home (Sonnentag & Grant, 2012). Evidence also indicates that when employees acknowledge that their actions benefit others, their prosocial motives are intensified, thus creating a virtuous circle (Bellé, 2013).

Nevertheless, an important consideration when studying the effects of well-being on altruistic agents is considering "reasonable altruism" (S. G. Post, 2005), that is, helping behavior that is not overwhelming. Those who are physically or mentally overwhelmed, or both, by the needs of others, experience stress that can have significant negative health consequences (Kiecolt-Glaser et al., 2003; Musick, Herzog, & House, 1999; C. E. Schwartz, Meisenhelder, Ma, & Reed, 2003).

Especially relevant is how motives affect the way managers lead and their relationship with their team members. In the following subsection, we enter into more detail regarding the relationship between (a) altruistic motives and leadership in organizations and (b) altruistic motives and organizational citizenship behavior.

Altruistic Motives and Leadership

A paradigmatic example of leading organizations mainly loving others is the servant leadership approach. The leaders who perform the servant leadership model present an altruistic perspective toward the members of the organization. Servant leadership emphasizes the leader's responsibility to the success of the organization as well as the moral responsibility toward subordinates, customers, and other organizationally relevant stakeholders (Greenleaf, 2002). It is centered on the followers, being the achievement of organizational objectives a subordinate outcome (Gregory Stone, Russell, & Patterson, 2004). In contrast, transformational leadership focuses on the organization's results: how leaders' behavior builds follower commitment toward organizational objectives. Gift-love has been considered a key aspect of servant leadership. Greenleaf, the father of servant leadership, has associated the relationship between leaders and followers with the concept of love (2002). The role of the leader is to serve the organization and its people. It is not centered on command and control. This gift-love is conceptualized from a moral and virtuous perspective (Patterson, 2010). The literature regarding servant leadership has revealed many distinguishable attributes of such leaders, including vision, credibility, trust, service, modeling, pioneering, appreciation of others, and empowerment (Russell & Stone, 2002). More specifically, Russell has depicted the profile of the leaders who care for their people at work (2001:81):

> Leaders who show appreciation for others reflect appropriate, unconditional love for their followers. Such leaders incorporate empathy, patience, and encouragement in their relational style. Empowerment of organizational members also grows out of a trusting environment.

It reflects the leadership values of equality and love. Overall, servant leadership succeeds or fails on the personal values of the people who employ it.

Research on servant leadership has largely emphasized its relationship with community citizenship behaviors, in-role performance, and organizational commitment (Ehrhart, 2004; Liden, Wayne, Zhao, & Henderson, 2008; Neubert, Kacmar, Carlson, Chonko, & Roberts, 2008; Walumbwa, Hartnell, & Oke, 2010). It also influences team performance through affect-based trust and team psychological safety. A study conducted by Schaubroeck and his colleagues (2011) observed that the management through servant leadership generates an additional 10% of the variance in team performance beyond the effect of transformational leadership.

But apart from a formal leadership style, as the formulation of Servant Leadership, love toward others is considered a key aspect in successful leadership. In a study for the book *The Leadership Challenge* (Kouzes & Posner, 2002), managers without identification of a specific leadership model were interviewed. The results highlighted that love is an integral part of leadership. Why love is considered important by managers is less frequently addressed. According to Charles McCoy (1985), good management requires technical knowledge, financial competence, innovative imagination, ethical understanding, discerning judgment, and moral courage. Some authors have considered love and courage virtue directly related: Courage is seen as a particular operation of wisdom and love (Murdoch, 1970), part of the meaning of love (Martin, 1996), or an element of love (Vincent, 1987). Dowrick describes courage, fidelity, restraint, generosity, tolerance, and forgiveness as acts of love (Dowrick, 1997). The Nietzschean aphorism "He who has a *why* to live can bear almost any how" is also applicable to courage and love in management leadership: the *how* (courage needed) is endurable when the *why* or the motivation is gift-love. If we think of Mother Teresa's activities in terms of a non-profit organization, we see a clear example of incredible courage overcoming hardships and difficulties, out of love. Would someone be prompted to exert the same level of effort and devoting life for other reasons? The power of gift-love seems to be among the strongest motives in humans.

Altruistic Motives and Organizational Citizenship Behavior (OCB)

OCB is defined by Organ (1988) as behavior that goes beyond job requirements and is not directly or formally rewarded. It is behavior that benefits the organization or its members in some way and accordingly has also been referred to as prosocial organizational behavior (Brief & Motowidlo, 1986). The literature on the person–organization fit (Kristof, 1996) suggests that employees are able to develop an extensive understanding of an organization's values and goals. Employees have emotions about the organization, including feeling sympathetic to its needs and values. Besides, they may care about the organization's future.

According to role identity theory, employees who strongly identify with their organizational role integrate OCB into their employee role definitions and enact OCB because their engagement with their organization induces feelings of altruistic motivation (Kamdar, McAllister, & Turban, 2006). Furthermore, employees may engage in OCB because of prosocial concerns, such as advancing the organization's mission (Callero, 1985; Finkelstein & Penner, 2004). When employees identify themselves with the organization, they have personal concerns for the organization because they care strongly about their relationship partner, and thus facilitate OCB to enhance the welfare of the organization (Pearce & Gregersen, 1991).

Given the multiple possible motives for the same OCB behavior, Rioux and Penner (2001) developed a scale to measure OCB motives. Based on an extensive literature review and professional consultations, they finally constructed a scale with three factors: organizational concern (OC), prosocial values (PV), and impression management (IM). For every factor, they selected ten items representing each factor. Some of the items reflecting PV motives are more directly related to altruistic motives: "Because I feel it is important to help those in need," "Because I believe in being courteous to others," "Because I am concerned about other people's feelings," "Because I want to help my co-workers in any way I can," and "Because I can put myself in other people's shoes." These items include the maximum detail of analysis attainable through a scientific method. Which of these are expressions of love? We do not know *a priori*, but we are inclined to suggest that the following three are more altruistic based on their descriptions: "Because I am concerned about other people's feelings," "Because I want to help my co-workers in any way I can," and "Because I can put myself in other people's shoes." Why be concerned about others? Why do I want to help? Why be concerned about other's feelings? These concerns imply the existence of some internal value related to the worth of others' lives as humans – that we identify someone worthy of consideration, concern, affection, and dedication. We can also call these experiences manifestations of gift-love.

Conclusion

In this chapter, we have contemplated different conceptualizations of love and it is proposed a conceptualization of altruistic motives rooted in gift-love. The altruistically motivated actor seeks the well-being of others out of selfless love. The different manifestations of altruistic motives show the different degrees and intensities that this love dwells in humans.

The external manifestations are multiple and not only include the ones we understand typically as prosocial behaviors, but more. This chapter also suggests an integration of altruistic motives within the human motivational structure, comments on the relationship between love and meaning at work, and considers the positive repercussions of altruistic motives in organizations.

Notes

1 We have an emotional reaction when hitting a squirrel with a car or when hitting a person with a car, but the intensity of the reaction and worry in the latter case is much higher. There is an implicit cognitive understanding of the different values of beings that permeates and affects our emotional reactions and manifestations.

2 I follow the philosopher Leonardo Polo's conceptualization of gift-love (denominated by him with the Spanish term "Amor donal").

3 This human reality is accepted in the legal and moral fields and has many repercussions. These fields can help to support the intentional decision argument in altruistic motives. In the legal world, the attenuation or increase of the penalty can be related to the intentionality or act voluntarily. A simple example could be someone who kills a person by accident hitting him/her with a car, in comparison with a person who wants to kill someone by hitting him/her with a car. In terms of behavior (external actions), the descriptions of the two actions would be exactly the same, but the repercussions would be different. What makes the difference is the intention of the actor. Furthermore, we could not speak, properly speaking, about the morality of a human act if there were not an intentional decision of the actor.

4 Moral philosophy has indicated that the first beneficiary of any beneficial action is the benefactor (Polo, 2015). And vice versa happens with wrong moral actions: Socrates noted many centuries ago that the first victim of injustice is the one who commits it.

5 Some authors name indistinctly altruistic motivations or prosocial motivations. But given that other authors consider them not necessarily equated (see Bolino & Grant, 2016), I prefer to use the terms "altruistic motives" or "transcendent motives" emphasizing the other-oriented approach.

References

Aknin, L. B., Sandstrom, G. M., Dunn, E. W., & Norton, M. I. (2011). It's the recipient that counts: Spending money on strong social ties leads to greater happiness than spending on weak social ties. *PLoS One*, 6(2), e17018. https://doi.org/10.1371/journal.pone.0017018

Aristotle. (2000). *Nicomachean ethics. The basic works of Aristotle* (Roger Cris). Cambridge: University Press.

Aronfreed, J. (1980). *Conduct and conscience: The socialization of internalized control over behavior*. New York, NY: Academic Press.

Bar-Tal, D. (1986). Altruistic motivation to help: Definition, utility and operationalization. *Humboldt Journal of Social Relations*, 13(1–2), 3–14. Retrieved from https://psycnet.apa.org/record/1988-23402-001.

Barberá Heredia, E. (2002). Modelos explicativos en psicología de la motivación. *Revista Electrónica de Motivación y Emoción, 5*(10), 6.

Batson, C. D. (1998). Altruism and prosocial behavior. In D. Gilbert, S. Fiske, & G. Lindzey (Eds.), *The handbook of social psychology* (4th ed., vol., pp. 282–316). New York, NY: McGraw-Hill.

Batson, C. D. (2011). *Altruism in humans.* New York, NY: Oxford University Press.

Batson, C. D., & Powell, A. A. (2003). Altruism and prosocial behavior. In T. Millon, & M.J. Lerner (Eds.), *Handbook of psychology: Vol. 5. Personality and social psychology* (pp. 463–484). Hoboken, NJ: John Wiley & Sons, Inc.

Batson, C. D., & Shaw, L. L. (1991). Evidence for altruism: Toward a pluralism of prosocial motives. *Psychological Inquiry, 2*(2), 107–122. https://doi.org/10.1207/s15327965pli0202_1

Bazerman, M. H., Tenbrunsel, A. E., & Wade-Benzoni, K. (1998). Negotiating with yourself and losing: Making decisions with competing internal preferences. *Academy of Management Review, 23*(2), 225–241. https://doi.org/10.5465/AMR.1998.533224

Bellé, N. (2013). Experimental evidence on the relationship between public service motivation and job performance. *Public Administration Review, 73*(1), 143–153. https://doi.org/10.1111/j.1540-6210.2012.02621.x

Bellé, N. (2014). Leading to make a difference: A field experiment on the performance effects of transformational leadership, perceived social impact, and public service motivation. *Journal of Public Administration Research and Theory, 24*(1), 109–136. https://doi.org/10.1093/jopart/mut033

Bellusci, David C. (2013). *Amor dei in the sixteenth and seventeenth centuries.* Amsterdam: Editions Rodopi.

Berkowitz, L. (1972). Social norms, feelings, and other factors affecting helping and altruism. *Advances in Experimental Social, 6,* 63–108.

Binswanger, H. (1991). Volition as cognitive self-regulation. *Organizational Behavior and Human Decision Processes, 50,* 154–178. https://doi.org/10.1016/0749-5978(91)90019-P

Bobocel, D. R. (2013). Coping with unfair events constructively or destructively: The effects of overall justice and self–other orientation. *Journal of Applied Psychology, 98*(5), 720–731. https://doi.org/10.1037/a0032857

Bolino, M. C., & Grant, A. M. (2016). The bright side of being prosocial at work, and the dark side, too: A review and agenda for research on other-oriented motives, behavior, and impact in organizations. *The Academy of Management Annals, 10*(1), 599–670. https://doi.org/10.1080/19416520.2016.1153260

Brief, A. P., & Motowidlo, S. J. (1986). Prosocial organizational behaviors. *Academy of Management Review, 11*(4), 710–725. https://doi.org/10.5465/amr.1986.4283909

Caldera, R. T. (1999). *Sobre la naturaleza del amor. Cuadernos de Anuario Filosófico.* Pamplona: EUNSA.

Callero, P. L. (1985). Role-identity salience. *Social Psychology Quarterly, 48*(3), 203. https://doi.org/10.2307/3033681

Cardador, M. T., & Wrzesniewski, A. (2015). Better to give and to compete? prosocial and competitive motives as interactive predictors of citizenship behavior. *Journal of Social Psychology, 155,* 255–273. https://doi.org/10.1080/00224545.2014.999019

Christensen, C. M. (2010). How will you measure your life? *Harvard Business Review, 88*(7/8), 46–51.

Clary, E. G., Snyder, M., Ridge, R. D., Copeland, J., Stukas, A. A., Haugen, J., & Miene, P. (1998). Understanding and assessing the motivations of volunteers: A functional approach. *Journal of Personality and Social Psychology, 74*(6), 1516–1530. https://doi.org/10.1037/0022-3514.74.6.1516

Colby, A., Sippola, L., & Phelps, E. (2001). Social responsibility and paid work in contemporary American life. In A. S. Rossi (Ed.), *Caring and doing for others: Social responsibility in the domains of family, work, and community* (pp. 463–501). Chicago, IL: University of Chicago Press.

Darley, J. M., & Latane, B. (1970). Norms and normative behavior: Field studies of social interdependence. In R. Macauly & L. Berkowitz (Eds.), *Altruism and helping behavior* (pp. 83–101). New York, NY: Academic Press.

De Dreu, C. K. W., & Nauta, A. (2009). Self-interest and other-orientation in organizational behavior: Implications for job performance, prosocial behavior, and personal initiative. *Journal of Applied Psychology, 94*(4), 913–926. https://doi.org/10.1037/a0014494

Deci, E. L., La Guardia, J. G., Moller, A. C., Scheiner, M. J., & Ryan, R. M. (2006). On the benefits of giving as well as receiving autonomy support: Mutuality in close friendships. *Personality and Social Psychology Bulletin, 32*(3), 313–327. https://doi.org/10.1177/0146167205282148

Deci, E. L., & Ryan, R. M. (2000). The "what" and "why" of goal pursuits: Human needs and the self-determination of behavior. *Psychological Inquiry, 11*(4), 227.

Dovidio, J. F., Piliavin, J. A., Schroeder, D. A., & Penner, L. A. (2006). *The social psychology of prosocial behavior.* New York, NY: Psychology Press. https://doi.org/10.4324/9781315085241

Dowrick, S. (1997). *Forgiveness and other acts of love.* Melbourne, Australia: Penguin Australia.

Ehrhart, M. G. (2004). Leadership and procedural justice climate as antecedents of unit-level organizational citizenship behavior. *Personnel Psychology, 57*(1), 61–94. https://doi.org/10.1111/j.1744-6570.2004.tb02484.x

Eisenberg, N. (1986). *Altruistic emotion, cognition, and behavior.* Hillsdale, NJ: Lawrence Erlbaum.

Eisenberg, N. (1991). Values, sympathy, and individual differences: Toward a pluralism of factors influencing altruism and empathy. *Psychological Inquiry, 2*(2), 128–131. https://doi.org/10.1207/s15327965pli0202_5

Eisenberg, N. (2000). Emotion, regulation, and moral development. *Annual Review of Psychology, 51*, 665–697.

Eisenberg, N., Fabes, R. A., & Spinrad, T. L. (2006). Prosocial behavior. In N. Eisenberg, W. Damon, & M. Lerner (Eds.), *Handbook of child psychology: Social, emotional, and personality development* (vol. 3, pp. 646–718). New York, NY: Wiley.

Eisenberg, N., Miller, P. A., Shell, R., McNalley, S., & Shea, C. (1991). Prosocial development in adolescence: A longitudinal study. *Developmental Psychology, 27*(5), 849–857. https://doi.org/10.1037/0012-1649.27.5.849

Eisenberg, N., & Spinrad, T. L. (2014). Multidimensionality of prosocial behavior. Rethinking the conceptualization and development of prosocial behavior. In L. M. Padilla-Walker & G. Carlo (Eds.), *Prosocial development. A multidimensional approach.* New York, NY: Oxford University Press. https://oxford.universitypressscholarship.com/view/10.1093/acprof:oso/9780199964772.001.0001/acprof-9780199964772

Eisenberg, N., VanSchyndel, S. K., & Spinrad, T. L. (2016). Prosocial motivation: Inferences from an opaque body of work. *Child Development*, 87(6), 1668–1678.

Epstein, S. (1998). Personal control from the perspective of cognitive-experiential self-theory. In M. Kofta, G. Weary, & G. Sedek (Eds.), *Personal control in action*. The Springer Series in Social Clinical Psychology. Boston MA: Springer. https://doi.org/10.1007/978-1-4757-2901-6_1

Ferreiro, P., & Alcázar García, M. (2002). *Gobierno de personas en la empresa*. Barcelona: Ariel.

Finkelstein, M. A., & Penner, L. A. (2004). Predicting organizational citizenship behavior: Integrating the functional and role identity approaches. *Social Behavior and Personality*, 32(4), 383–398. https://doi.org/10.2224/sbp.2004.32.4.383

Frankl, V. E. (2006). *Man's search for meaning* (5th ed.). Boston, MA: Beacon Press (Original work published in 1946).

Frankl, V. E. (2014). *The will to meaning*. New York, NY: Penguin Random House Company (Original work published in 1969).

Garrido Gutierrez, I. (2002). La motivación: mecanismos de regulación de la acción. *Revista Electrónica de Motivación y Emoción*, 3(5), 5.

Gehlen, A. (1988). *Man. His nature and place in the world* (C. McMillan & K. Pillemer, Trans.). New York, NY: Columbia University Press.

Grant, A. M. (2007). Relational job design and the motivation to make a prosocial difference. *Academy of Management Review*, 32(2), 393–417.

Grant, A. M., & Berry, J. W. (2011). The necessity of others is the mother of invention: Intrinsic and prosocial motivations, perspective taking, and creativity. *Academy of Management Journal*, 54(1), 73–96.

Grant, A. M., & Campbell, E. M. (2007). Doing good, doing harm, being well and burning out: The interactions of perceived prosocial and antisocial impact in service work. *Journal of Occupational and Organizational Psychology*, 80(4), 665–691. https://doi.org/10.1348/096317906X169553

Grant, A. M., & Sonnentag, S. (2010). Doing good buffers against feeling bad: Prosocial impact compensates for negative task and self-evaluations. *Organizational Behavior and Human Decision Processes*, 111(1), 13–22. https://doi.org/10.1016/j.obhdp.2009.07.003

Greenleaf, R. K. (2002). *Servant leadership. A journey into the nature of legitimate power & greatness*. Mahwah, NJ: Paulist Press.

Gregory Stone, A., Russell, R. F., & Patterson, K. (2004). Transformational versus servant leadership: A difference in leader focus. *Leadership & Organization Development Journal*, 25(4), 349–361. https://doi.org/10.1108/01437730410538671

Guillén, M., Ferrero, I., & Hoffman, W. M. (2015). The neglected ethical and spiritual motivations in the workplace. *Journal of Business Ethics*, 128(4), 803–816. https://doi.org/10.1007/s10551-013-1985-7

Hackman, J. R., & Oldham, G. R. (1976). Motivation through the design of work: Test of a theory. *Organizational Behavior and Human Performance*, 16(2), 250–279. https://doi.org/10.1016/0030-5073(76)90016-7

Hackman, J. R., & Oldham, G. R. (1980). *Work redesign*. Reading, MA: Addison-Wesley.

Hawley, P. H. (2014). Evolution, prosocial behavior and altruism: A roadmap for understanding where the proximate meets the ultimate. In M. Laura

Padilla-Walker & G. Carlo (Eds.), *Prosocial development. A multidimensional approach* (pp. 43–69). New York, NY: Oxford University Press.

Hu, J., & Liden, R. C. (2015). Making a difference in the teamwork: Linking team prosocial motivation to team processes and effectiveness. *Academy of Management Journal, 58*(4), 1102–1127. https://doi.org/10.5465/amj.2012.1142

Hurlbut, W. B. (2002). The science of altruism. Introduction. In S. Post, L. Underwood, J. Schloss, & W. Hurlbut (Eds.), *Altruism and altruistic love: Science, philosophy, and religion in dialogue*. Oxford: Oxford University Press.

Kamdar, D., McAllister, D. J., & Turban, D. B. (2006). "All in a day's work": How follower individual differences and justice perceptions predict OCB role definitions and behavior. *Journal of Applied Psychology, 91*(4), 841–855. https://doi.org/10.1037/0021-9010.91.4.841

Kehr. (2004). Integrating implicit motives, explicit motives, and perceived abilities: The compensatory model of work motivation and volition. *The Academy of Management Review, 29*(3), 479–499.

Khalil, E. L. (2004). What is altruism? *Journal of Economic Psychology, 25*(1), 97–123. https://doi.org/10.1016/S0167-4870(03)00075-8

Kiecolt-Glaser, J. K., Preacher, K. J., MacCallum, R. C., Atkinson, C., Malarkey, W. B., & Glaser, R. (2003). Chronic stress and age-related increases in the proinflammatory cytokine IL-6. *Proceedings of the National Academy of Sciences of the United States of America, 100*(15), 9090–9095. https://doi.org/10.1073/pnas.1531903100

Kouzes, J. M., & Posner, B. Z. (2002). *The leadership challenge* (3rd ed.). San Francisco, CA: John Wiley & Sons, Inc.

Krebs, D. L. (1970). Altruism: An examination of the concept and a review of the literature. *Psychological Bulletin, 73*(4), 258–302. https://doi.org/10.1037/h0028987

Krebs, D. L., & Hesteren, F. Van. (1994). The development of altruism: Toward an integrative model. *Developmental Review, 14*(2), 103–158. https://doi.org/10.1006/DREV.1994.1006

Latham, G. P., & Pinder, C. C. (2005). Work motivation theory and research at the dawn of the twenty-first century. *Annual Review of Psychology, 56*(1), 485–516. https://doi.org/10.1146/annurev.psych.55.090902.142105

Leeds, R. (1963). Altruism and the norm of giving. *Merrill-Palmer Quarterly of Behavior and Development, 9*(3), 229–240. https://doi.org/10.2307/2092623

Lewis, C. S. (1960). *The four loves*. New York, NY: Harcourt Brace Jovanovich.

Liden, R. C., Wayne, S. J., Zhao, H., & Henderson, D. (2008). Servant leadership: Development of a multidimensional measure and multi-level assessment. *Leadership Quarterly, 19*(2), 161–177. https://doi.org/10.1016/j.leaqua.2008.01.006

Locke, E. A., & Schattke, K. (2019). Intrinsic and extrinsic motivation: Time for expansion and clarification. *Motivation Science, 5*(4), 277–290. https://doi.org/10.1037/mot0000116

Loewenstein, G. (1996). Out of control: Visceral Influence on behavior. *Organizational Behavior and Human Decision Processes, 65*(3), 272–292.

López Moratalla, N. 2021. *Bioética desde la corporalidad*. Pamplona, Spain: EUNSA.

Martin, M. W. (1996). *Love's virtues*. Lawrence, KA: University of Kansas Press.

McCoy, C. S. (1985). *Management of values*. Marshfield, MA: Pitman.

Metcalfe, J., & Mischel, W. (1999). A hot/cool-system analysis of delay of gratification: Dynamics of willpower. *Psychological Review, 106*(1), 3–19.

Monroe, Kristen R. (1996). *The heart of altruism. Perceptions of a common humanity.* Princeton, NJ: Princeton University Press.

Monroe, Kristen R. (2002). Explicating altruism. In S. Post, L. Underwood, J. Schloss, & W. Hurlbut (Eds.), *Altruism and altruistic love: Science, philosophy, and religion in dialogue.* Oxford: Oxford University Press.

Murdoch, I. (1970). *The sovereignty of good.* London: Routledge & Kegan Paul.

Musick, M. A., Herzog, A. R., & House, J. S. (1999). Volunteering and mortality among older adults: Findings from a national sample. *The Journals of Gerontology Series B: Psychological Sciences and Social Sciences, 54B*(3), S173–S180. https://doi.org/10.1093/geronb/54B.3.S173

Nagel, T. (2016). *The possibility of altruism.* Princeton, NJ: Princeton University Press.

Neubert, M. J., Kacmar, K. M., Carlson, D. S., Chonko, L. B., & Roberts, J. A. (2008). Regulatory focus as a mediator of the influence of initiating structure and servant leadership on employee behavior. *Journal of Applied Psychology, 93*(6), 1220–1233. https://doi.org/10.1037/a0012695

Organ, D. W. (1988). *Organizational citizenship behavior: The good soldier syndrome.* Lexington, MA: Lexington Books.

Patterson, K. (2010). Servant leadership and love. In D. Van Dierendonck & K. Patterson (Eds.), *Servant leadership: developments in theory and research.* London: Palgrave Macmillan.

Pearce, J., & Gregersen, H. B. (1991). Task interdependence and extrarole behavior: A test of the mediating effects of felt responsibility. *Journal of Applied Psychology, 76*(6), 838–844.

Pérez López, J. A. (1991a). El poder... ¿Para qué? *Nota Técnica IESE Business School, TDN-85,* 1–13.

Pérez López, J. A. (1991b). *Teoria de la acción humana en las organizaciones. La acción personal.* Madrid: Rialp.

Pérez López, J. A. (2014). *Foundations of management* (ebook). Madrid: Rialp.

Podsakoff, N. P., Whiting, S. W., Podsakoff, P. M., & Blume, B. D. (2009). Individual- and organizational-level consequences of organizational citizenship behaviors: A meta-analysis. *Journal of Applied Psychology, 94*(1), 122–141. https://doi.org/10.1037/a0013079

Polo, L. (2012). *Presente y futuro del hombre* (2nd ed.). Madrid: Rialp.

Polo, L. (2015). *Introducción a la filosofía. Obras completas de Leonardo Polo* (4th ed., vol. XII). Pamplona: EUNSA.

Post, S. G. (2005). Altruism, happiness, and health: It's good to be good. *International Journal of Behavioral Medicine, 12*(2), 66–77. https://doi.org/10.1207/s15327558ijbm1202_4

Post, S., & Underwood, L. (2002). Concluding summary. future research needs on altruism and altruistic love. In S. Post, L. Underwood, J. Schloss, & W. Hurlbut (Eds.), *Altruism and altruistic love: Science, philosophy, and religion in dialogue.* Oxford: Oxford University Press.

Prats, M. (2020). *Altruistic Motives: Conceptualization, nature, sources, and their repercussions on human well-being and organizations.* University of Navarra.

Read, D., & Van Leeuwen, B. (1998). Predicting hunger: The effects of appetite and delay on choice. *Organizational Behavior and Human Decision Processes, 76*(2), 189–205. https://doi.org/10.1006/obhd.1998.2803

Reichmann, J. B. (1985). *Philosophy of the human person.* Chicago, IL: Loyola Press.

Rioux, S. M., & Penner, L. A. (2001). The causes of organizational citizenship behavior: A motivational analysis. *Journal of Applied Psychology, 86*(6), 1306–1314. https://doi.org/10.1037/0021-9010.86.6.1306

Rosso, B. D., Dekas, K. H., & Wrzesniewski, A. (2010). On the meaning of work: A theoretical integration and review. *Research in Organizational Behavior, 30*, 91–127. https://doi.org/10.1016/j.riob.2010.09.001

Russell, R. F. (2001). The role of values in servant leadership. *Leadership & Organization Development Journal, 22*(2), 76–84. https://doi.org/10.1108/01437730110382631

Russell, R. F., & Stone, G. A. (2002, May 1). A review of servant leadership attributes: Developing a practical model. *Leadership & Organization Development Journal.* https://doi.org/10.1108/01437730210424

Ryan, R. M., & Deci, E. L. (2000). Intrinsic and extrinsic motivations: Classic definitions and new directions. *Contemporary Educational Psychology, 25*(1), 54–67. https://doi.org/10.1006/ceps.1999.1020

Schaubroeck, J., Lam, S. S. K., & Peng, A. C. (2011). Cognition-based and affect-based trust as mediators of leader behavior influences on team performance. *Journal of Applied Psychology, 96*(4), 863–871.

Schaumberg, R. L., & Wiltermuth, S. S. (2014). Desire for a positive moral self-regard exacerbates escalation of commitment to initiatives with prosocial aims. *Organizational Behavior and Human Decision Processes, 123*(2), 110–123. https://doi.org/10.1016/j.obhdp.2013.10.012

Schindler, D. C. (2018). *Love and the postmodern predicament: Rediscovering the real in beauty, goodness, and truth.* Eugene, OR: Cascade Books.

Schroeder, D. A., & Graziano, W. G. (2015). The field of prosocial behavior: An introduction and overview. In D. A. Schroeder & W. G. Graziano (Eds.), *The Oxford handbook of prosocial behavior.* New York, NY: Oxford University Press.

Schwartz, C. E., Meisenhelder, J. B., Ma, Y., & Reed, G. (2003). Altruistic social interest behaviors are associated with better mental health. *Psychosomatic Medicine, 65*(5), 778–785. https://doi.org/10.1097/01.PSY.0000079378.39062.D4

Schwartz, S. H. (2012). An overview of the Schwartz theory of basic values. *Online Readings in Psychology and Culture, 2*(1), 11. https://doi.org/10.9707/2307-0919.1116

Singer, I. (1984). *The nature of love* (vol. 2). Chicago, IL: University of Chicago Press.

Slade, F. (2000). On the ontological priority of ends and its relevance to the narrative arts. In A. Ramos (Ed.), *Beauty, art, and the polis* (pp. 58–69). Washington, DC: The Catholic University of America Press.

Sonnentag, S., & Grant, A. M. (2012). Doing good at work feels good at home, but not right away: When and why perceived prosocial impact predicts positive affect. *Personnel Psychology, 65*(3), 495–530. https://doi.org/10.1111/j.1744-6570.2012.01251.x

Sorokin, P. A. (1954). *The ways and power of love.* Boston, MA: Beacon Press.

Spaemann, R. (2000). *Happiness and benevolence* (J. Alberg, Trans.). Notre Dame, ID: T&T Clark Ltd.

Staub, E. (1978). *Positive social behavior and morality.* New York, NY: Academic Press.

Thompson, J. A., & Bunderson, J. S. (2003). Violations of principle: Ideological currency in the psychological contract. *Academy of Management Review, 28*(4), 571–586. https://doi.org/10.5465/amr.2003.10899381

Vincent, J. (1987). The five virtues of St Thomas Aquinas. *Sociology and Social Research, 71,* 174–182.

Walumbwa, F. O., Hartnell, C. A., & Oke, A. (2010). Servant leadership, procedural justice climate, service climate, employee attitudes, and organizational citizenship behavior: A cross-level investigation. *Journal of Applied Psychology, 95*(3), 517–529.

Weinstein, N., & Ryan, R. M. (2010). When helping helps: Autonomous motivation for prosocial behavior and its influence on well-being for the helper and recipient. *Journal of Personality and Social Psychology, 98*(2), 222–244. https://doi.org/10.1037/a0016984

Wilson, D. S., & Sober, E. (2002). The fall and rise and fall and rise and fall and rise of altruism in evolutionary biology. In S. Post, L. Underwood, J. Schloss, & W. Hurlbut (Eds.), *Altruism and altruistic love: Science, philosophy, and religion in dialogue.* Oxford: Oxford University Press. https://oxford.universitypressscholarship.com/view/10.1093/acprof:oso/9780195143584.001.0001/acprof-9780195143584-chapter-17

8 Toward a Systematic Approach to Building a Loving Organization

The Humanistic Organizational Development Matrix

William A. Andrews

Introduction

Can an organization love? If so, how does an organization love, and how would that love manifest itself to its organizational participants? What would be the managerial implications of building a Loving Organization? Can organizational love be identified through assessment? To address these questions, this chapter is organized into four parts: (1) *The Love Challenge* considers why the promotion of human flourishing is difficult, (2) the *Loving Organization* examines whether an organization can love, (3) *Essential and Developmental Humanness* explores the precise nature of human flourishing, and (4) *The Humanistic Organizational Development Matrix* blends these conceptual foundations with a management model of psychosocial development creating a new paradigm for organizational development and offering a new way to assess employee development and integration in an organizational context. This framework provides a practical approach to building a Loving Organization systematically while also identifying a developmental path for individual human flourishing.

For the purpose of this chapter, it is worthwhile to define "love," as the word has become almost meaningless in the English language, invoking notions of everything from teenage infatuation to sexual love to self-sacrificing commitment. Simply stated, love is that which promotes ethical human flourishing (Pirson 2017, p. 135). Notions of human flourishing and dignity require a conceptualization of Essential Humanness. Pirson (2017, p. 170) further notes, "A core endeavor of humanistic management should therefore be to produce a better understanding of the notion of dignity." To better understand human dignity, it is helpful to understand what it means to be essentially human so as to identify the attributes that need to "flourish" and be "dignified" – a pursuit that has been approached from both ancient philosophical and theological reasoning, as well as from contemporary research.

DOI: 10.4324/9781003254034-9

The Love Challenge

Why would building a Loving Organization or the promotion of human flourishing be a challenge to an organization if goodness is rooted in human nature? Why would it not be instinctive…the normal course of interaction? Two streams of thought converge on this question: First, overlaying all the magnanimous dimensions of one's individual human-ness is a Darwinian bent toward advantaging oneself at the expense of others. Second, institutional or systemic effects can moderate beneficent aspects of human behavior. Institutional or societal rules can reward base or predatory behavior while suppressing or even oppressing noble virtues and aspirations.

An Individual's Contribution to the Love Challenge

Regarding the individual's contribution to why human flourishing does not flourish, Dawkins (2016), the renowned evolutionary biologist, suggests that infecting our Essential Humanness is a strong bias toward self-enhancement at the expense of others, coupled with at least the pos-sibility of desire-sets that are insatiable. He notes,

> Let us try to teach generosity and altruism, because we are born selfish. Let us understand what our own selfish genes are up to, because we may then at least have the chance to upset their designs, something that no other species has ever aspired to do.

Especially noteworthy is the fact that Dawkins grounds his assertions in an epistemology of genetics-based evolutionary biology, implying that no human is beyond the influence of selfish genes. He also suggests that both as individuals and as co-creators of systems, one fights against essential selfish nature in doing anything that is not self-serving. This suggests a slight modification of our definition of love: love is that which promotes ethical human flourishing without reference to an advantage gained. To put it in Pirson's (2017, p. 135) terms, "economism" in all its forms (pure, bounded, or enlightened) fails to provide a motive for self-giving beyond instrumental gratuity aimed at overall personal benefit.

Cooperative Arrangements and the Love Challenge

Among the various types of systems capable of suppressing human flourishing, economic systems readily demonstrate the point; one of the fundamental presuppositions of capitalist, neo-classical economics is the scarcity of resources. This doctrine underlays the supply and demand curves, and hence the pricing mechanism. It fuels competition for scarce resources, which flows from the systemic to the organizational level and then to the personal level as organizations compete for customers and resources, and individuals compete among themselves for institutional inclusion (employment) and goods and services.

The oppressive nature of systems toward human flourishing is a prominent feature of Marxist and Anarchist theory (Garrison 2004, Marx and Engles 2002, Goldman 1910) as well as contemporary libertarianism (Sciabarra 1987). Indeed, no shortage of oppressive organizations and systems has existed across either time or cultures. Global slavery and 20th-century Nazism serve as archetypal reminders. Less alarming forms can be found in systemic overwork impacting mental health and longevity (cf. Milner et al. 2015, Dermot and Rosato 2013). Social systems inherently generate winners and losers, establish a power hierarchy, and promulgate measures of success (Marx 2017; Acemoglu and Robinson 2012) supportive to survival of the system. Such systems tend to subjugate human flourishing to the extent that individuals surrender their dignity embodied in their humanness either by seduction (the winners) or by oppression (the losers).

Marx and Engles (2002) and Guevera (1965) assert that systemic effects – and essentially private property (Giddens 1981) – create class conflict which exacerbates and institutionalizes selfishness at the individual, institutional, and systems levels. Capitalism is joined to selfishness as both a medium and an outcome.

However, Christensen (2012) commented on what Gueverra (1965) saw as the necessary condition for Marx's socialism to work:

> Guevara promoted the idea that Cubans had to become hombres nuevos, or "new men", *fundamentally changed in their nature to desire the welfare of the whole over the individual* [emphasis added]. This type of man would be willing to sacrifice his life in order to liberate his brothers…

In effect, Gueverra admitted that Marxism would not work given the extant human condition.

Dawkins (2016, p. 140) further cautions about the vulnerability of such a system: "Any altruistic system is inherently unstable, because it is open to abuse by selfish individuals ready to exploit it." Thus, Marxist oppression of human flourishing assumes two forms: (1) the heavy hand of the state actors curtailing unsanctioned ("selfish") thought or action and (2) the corruptible nature of state actors who would appropriate collective resources for personal benefit (Sowell 1985; Friedman 1912–2006).

Marxism and capitalism differ as to solutions. However, whether at the societal or institutional level, systems are designed to solve social problems – not (generally) to be oppressive (at least that is the way they are presented to constituents). Nevertheless, both systems tend to reflect the values and protect the dignity of those in power, often at the expense of the others.

Dropping down from the system level to the institutional level, agency theory is built on the premise that much organizational behavior is predicated on tactics for minimizing self-dealing. Leavitt and Sluss (2015) identified threats to personal, interpersonal, and organizational identity as institutionally based factors increasing organizational deception by employees. Hewlin (2003) recognized the correlation between dissimulation needed for personal survival at work, and stress, job satisfaction, and resignation. Grover (1993) identified this willingness to use deception to disadvantage the other party in a negotiation.

To summarize, the Love Challenge identifies two hurdles to human flourishing: first, humans have a bent toward advantaging themselves by disadvantaging others; second, structures that organize society can reinforce and perpetuate selfish tendencies while suppressing more generous instincts. Can stable systems be built based on self-giving so as to foster and develop self-giving in individuals? If so, the possibility and potential of a Loving Organization emerges, led and influenced by those who are systematically mastering their own selfishness – an outcome implied by both Erikson's (1950) and Kohlberg's (1984) models of human development. By creating policies, processes, and systems that reify and perpetuate the selfless values in its members, a virtuous cycle might be created. The Love Challenge is how to overcome the systemic and individualistic capacity for self-dealing that pervades individuals and all of the collaborative structures in which they may participate.

The Loving Organization

Having proposed the Love Challenge as an uphill battle against selfish aspects of our systems, organizations, and our individual human natures, the question remains whether an organization can love in the sense of promoting human flourishing. Some have argued that only humans can love since organizations are impersonal and cannot reciprocate love in a meaningful way. Hume (1985) argues for the prominent role of "sentiment" (motives) in moral choice generally. Likewise, Kant insisted that motives or intentions are at the heart of an altruistic act (Kant 2017; Korsgaard 2009). Organizations are unable to produce sentiments – only outcomes. Others object to the notion of an intentionally Loving Organization on the basis of theory of the firm. Neither transaction cost theory (Coase 1988; Williamson 1975) nor agency theory (Daily et al. 2003; Eisenhardt 1989) provides constructs that might serve as integration points for organizational love. The former views organizations as developing around cost efficiencies, while the latter assumes self-dealing as the driver of organizational behaviors. Evolutionary theory can do little better, asserting only that humans learned that cooperating and helping others could facilitate survival – a form of Pirson's (2017, p. 135) *bounded economism.*

Apart from whether an organization *can* love, one must ask if organizational motives might matter? Logically consistent utilitarian approaches would insist that considering motives adds a distinction that makes no difference since motives convey little utility given a particular outcome. If while pursuing utilitarian goals such as "creating a customer" (Drucker 1954) or "maximizing profit" (Friedman 1970), an organization happens to promote human flourishing, why should it matter to the "flourished" employee?

The fact that motives do matter can be deduced from the viewpoint of the recipient of a perceived act of self-giving: If giving (of manager's time, permission, development opportunity, etc.) is always instrumental, the receiver will not have a basis for relational confidence in the event of a mistake, failure, or personal crisis (Elangovan and Shapiro 1998). The psychological and relational implications of this should not be overlooked: "Betrayal" is only one misstep away. According to Reina and Reina (2006, p. 37), perceived betrayal increases in seasons of organizational change, and "Betrayal destroys the fabric of relationships that keep ... organizations operating." If, however, instrumental giving is supplemented by selfless giving (on the part of the organization or the manager), a more durable basis for trust is perceived. "Early" Lululemon and Zappos (prior to being acquired by Amazon) both offered employees significant personal development opportunities that were only indirectly related to their performance at work, and both had unparalleled retention rates for their respective industries and enviable corporate cultures. Exemplifying the Loving Organization, these firms supported broadly construed human development and flourishing without regard for a "return" beyond the satisfaction of having helped employees live more effectively with integrity in their various spheres of influence.

Beer et al. (2015) provides a perspective from the study of leadership training effectiveness that suggests that not only *can* organizations love, but that they are the necessary vehicle through which individuals can express and perpetuate the human face of love at work. The organization, through its culture, polices, and processes, mediates love between individuals in the organizational context. In their study, they assert that leadership training has not produced organizational improvements commensurate with the enormous investment because of structural (bureaucratic) barriers. Fixing the structural barriers, rather than focusing on improving the training or the individuals, proved to be the pathway toward meaningful organizational change. Beer's finding would suggest that the organization itself – as a collection of its values, processes, policies, structure and systems – can amplify or suppress its capacity to create human flourishing generally. An organization that intentionally facilitates human flourishing through its various mechanisms can be thought of as a Loving Organization because its systems, once in place, can shape its future toward human flourishing. Taleb (2018) describes the process generally:

> Systems don't learn because people learn individually... Systems learn at the collective level by the mechanism of selection: by eliminating those elements that reduce the fitness of the whole.... Food in New York improves from bankruptcy to bankruptcy, rather than the chefs' individual learning curves. Compare the food quality in mortal restaurants to that in an immortal governmental cafeteria.

It is individuals that reify the loving culture, but culture can outlast the individuals who reify it, forming a virtuous cycle capable of self-perpetuation. Individuals entering such an organization will be shaped by the human flourishing they experience through humanistic processes, policies, and commitments of the organization, and become the next generation of leaders embodying and protecting these commitments. Critical to the success of this organizational regeneration and the survival of a Loving Organization are (1) building a "mechanism of selection" mentioned by Taleb (above) and (2) identifying the general nature of processes, policies, and practices that would align humanistic values with this "mechanism of selection." For example, Taleb saw bankruptcy as being a mechanism of selection for New York restaurants.

In an economistic organization, a selection mechanism might be something as simple as achieving sales targets consistently. Related processes and policies might include sales training and merit-based compensation schemes. In a humanistic organization, continuance in the organization might be predicated on achieving appropriate development in important categories of human flourishing. It would need to ensure that those who continue with the organization are committed to its distinctive humanistic values, and less likely to fall prey to Dawkins' warning of selfishness overwhelming altruistic systems.

How have social scientists conceived of human flourishing in a developmental framework? Such a model might provide a "mechanism of selection" by suggesting humanistic developmental milestones. Once identified, these targets would in turn suggest processes and policies supporting these milestones.

Both Erikson's (1950) model of psychosocial development and Kohlberg's (1984) construal of moral development view the apex of human development (psychosocially and morally, respectively) as the capacity to self-give for the welfare of others without regard to instrumental benefits. As shall be developed below, Kohlberg describes his sixth (highest) stage as the adoption of universal moral principles by which one abides regardless of the cost to oneself (Kohlberg 1984). Kant (2017) articulated this same principle in his famous Categorical Imperative. Likewise, in successfully managing Erikson's seventh stage, the psychosocially mature individual focuses his or her efforts on "giving back" without expectation of reciprocity. So according to both Kohlberg and Erikson, the capacity for selfless motivation is the byproduct of a long series of developmental successes. Progress through these developmental stages could serve as milestones for employee development in a humanistic organization. Collectively, they would become the "mechanism of selection" by which the whole institution acculturates the values of humanistic management.

Ironically, the benefit of reaching the highest levels of development is the ability to serve others without expecting reciprocity – it is *not* the attainment of power *per se*. Moreover, there is something in human nature that *knows* self-giving is both noble and desirable. Nietzsche (2010) recognized this tendency, though he condemned it thoroughly as perpetuating weakness in others. The humanist would make the opposite case; self-giving seeks to enhance dignity and well-being of others (Pirson 2017), strengthening weaknesses and promoting human flourishing. Yet Kohlberg suggests that only "ten to fifteen percent" of humankind achieves this self-giving, sixth level of moral development. Erikson was similarly cautious about most humans achieving the higher levels of psychosocial development. Nevertheless, Kohlberg's estimate suggests that a significant core of humanity possesses the capacity to take leadership roles in pursuit of the Loving Organization.

It is neither likely nor necessary that one will be able to exorcize completely the lower tendencies of human nature, either from the individual or from the organization. Nor is it likely that every vestige of instrumentalism could be removed – either from individuals or systems. Guevara's (1965) New Man is at least partially out of reach. Nevertheless, individuals who for a variety of reasons and employing a variety of methods can *substantially* identify and overcome their self-serving biases can build organizations and systems that *substantially* promote ethical human flourishing from noninstrumental motives.

Essential Humanness

What is the Essential Humanness that should be developed by organizations? Before one can cause it to "flourish," one must have at least some sense of what "it" is.

Aristotle and Plato identified rationality and morality as the primary distinctives of humanness, and that morality was consequent to rationality. They tended to view passions and feelings as contrary to rationality and hence the source of foolishness, evil, and oppression. Importantly, Plato saw the material world as mere shadows and images of the essential reality which existed in the immaterial realm. The consequence of this was to substantially neglect the importance of one's physical constitution on Essential Humanness; by contrast, Aristotle asserted that physiology was inseparable from the rational and moral aspects of human nature.

The ancient Judeo-Christian scriptures, beginning with the Creation Account, affirmed that man was made in the image of God and was thus by nature a secondary co-creator, while also corroborating Aristotle's and Plato's construal of the rational and moral features of humanness. The

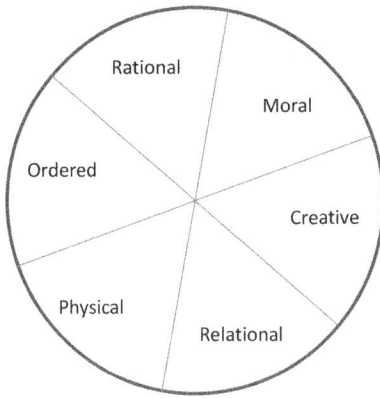

Figure 8.1   Six dimensions of essential humanness.

Creation Account further emphasized the relational aspect of humanness: "It is not good for man to be alone." In agreement with Aristotle, the Creation Account gave place for recognizing the essential nature of our physical existence as Adam suffered the loss of immortality through moral failure, incurring a physical curse on both work and childbirth (Genesis 3:16,19).

So peering briefly into ancient literature one can identify six dimensions of humanness: the rational, moral, creative, order seeking, physical, and relational.

This development of Essential Humanness corroborates, refines, and expands on Pirson's (2017, pp. 63–64) "four drives" of human nature – acquiring, bonding, learning, and defending. "Bonding" and "learning" correspond directly with relational and rational dimensions. "Acquiring" and "defending" are best conceived as drives that surround all aspects of Essential Humanness, that is, we seek to acquire (cause to flourish) or defend Essential Humanness.

Corroborating and expanding on the ancient synthesis of Essential Humanness, modern research proposed well-received models of human development. For example, Kohlberg (1984) developed a robust theory of moral development. Erikson's (1950) model of psychosocial development identified a path-dependent model of developing relational capacity. Entire fields of research have developed around the implications of characteristics such as age, gender, and disability – aspects of the physical dimension of Essential Humanness (cf. Rosenthal 1995; Marcus et al. 2016; Ozawa and Yeo 2006). Piaget's (1952) work on cognitive development sought to track the emergence of rationality from birth to adulthood. Creativity has been linked to cognitive and social development (Gilliford 1950; Unsworth 1996). The need for order-seeking is strongly implied by Maslow's (1987, 1943) hierarchy of human motivation since

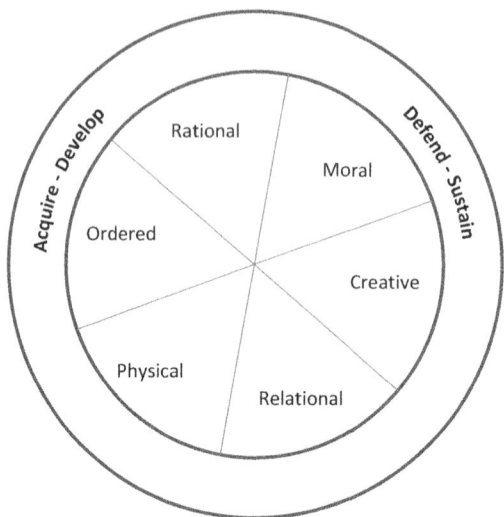

Figure 8.2 Essential humanness and moderating <u>drives</u>.

the attaining of the three first levels of need (physical, security, and social) suggests the importance of building durable, coordinated social systems. Nevertheless, implications of the developmental nature of Essential Humanness have been largely overlooked in the Management literature.

Essential Humanness presents a target by which organizations might measure the potential impact of management policies, practices, or initiatives on its six dimensions: relational, rational, moral, physical, order-seeking, and creative. Research implies, however, that *methods* of development *and* developmental goals vary according to the subject's stage of development in each of the several dimensions. For example, Maslow spoke of a *hierarchy* of needs. Appealing to higher-order needs would not tend to be effective if lower-order needs remained neglected. Piaget (1977), Erikson (1964, 1950), and Kohlberg (1984; Kohlberg and Hersh 1977; Kohlberg 1969) (representing rational, social, and moral development, respectively) all theorized that future development would be suppressed by deficiencies in prior stages of development. Within the organizational context, the implications of this are profound for managerial theory and practice. In every dimension of Essential Humanness, whether an organizational intervention creates flourishing or suppression will depend on understanding the individual's stage of development. As organizational participants move through successive stages of development, their capacities and goals will change, as should an organization's methods to stimulate the next round of human flourishing and development. Thus, Humanness has both a static (Essential Humanness), timeless framing and a developmental process that dictates stage-dependent needs which suggest particular developmental goals and methods. Conceptualized this way, Essential Humanness and Developmental Humanness provide a foundation for supporting Pirson's (2017) conceptualizations of intrinsic dignity and conditional dignity:

- Intrinsic dignity respects the six universal categories of Essential Humanness.
- Conditional dignity relates to one's progress through the developmental stages of each of the various categories of Essential Humanness.

These two framings provide potential organizational targets for expressions of organizational love. For example, how can an organization intentionally promote the engagement of employees' creativity? When does the use of 360-degree evaluations promote better relational capacity? When does it cause relational dysfunction and mistrust in the organization? Who will find corporate social outings relationally significant, and who will find them threatening and isolating? For those who find outings threatening, what managerial interventions could help the employee resolve their fears and continue their psychosocial development and integration into the organization? Answers to these types of questions would be expected to vary depending on the employee's stage of development. To assess an employee's stage of development and an organization's responses, the Humanistic Organizational Development Matrix (HODM) is proposed.

The Humanistic Organizational Development Matrix

Erikson's stages of psychosocial development have putative associations with all six dimensions of Essential Humanness. For this reason, the HODM framework can provide insights into the developmental nature of human flourishing in individuals, while simultaneously building systems, processes, and organizational culture indicative of a Loving Organization.

The HODM is derived from Erikson's model of psychosocial development as an indicator of human flourishing, defining stage-dependent developmental targets ("selection mechanisms") and stage-appropriate management praxis. Erikson (1950) studied psychosocial development in humans from childhood through adulthood. His research has generated several validated assessment tools (cf. Darling-Fisher 2018; Wood et al. 1998; Darling-Fisher and Leidy 1988; Kline Leidy and Darling-Fisher 1995), prescriptive models for achieving developmental milestones (Manning 1988), and follow-on articles refining and developing his original work (Christiansen and Palkovitz 1998). It has been applied to normal development (Rosenthal, Gurney, and Moore 1981), classroom management (Wood 1986), identifying and remediating developmental pathologies (Ya-Yu et al. 2002; Huberty et al. 1973), self-management strategies (Perry et al. 2015), but surprisingly *never* to organizational development or management theory.

The premise behind adapting Erikson's model as a management tool to gauge human flourishing is that employees entering and maturing in an organization face the same "crises" (sic) that Erikson noted in children as they developed from infancy into adulthood and then through old age. For example, in the initial Trust stage, employees are trying to determine if the organization is a fundamentally safe, cooperative place that will support their development, or whether it is fundamentally an adversarial "...if- you-can-survive- we-will-keep-you" environment. In the Competence stage (Stage 2), the employee "crisis" revolves around being able to perform the demands of the job to an acceptable level; Stage 3 involves a growing sense of agency or voice – a concept which has received much attention in the management world from Bandura's (1997) seminal work on the topic; the fourth stage crisis relates to one's ability to achieve mastery of one's responsibilities. In stages 5 and 6, the emphasis shifts to a more external orientation: first, a willingness to identify with the company, and then to confirm meaningful personal relationships beyond what the work itself demands. Whitten and Godfrey (1998) found that employees encountered an identity crisis associated with work similar to individual identity crises associated with coming of age. In Stage 7, the employee becomes self-giving in attitude toward the company and aspires toward leadership to perpetuate its success apart from benefits received. In the final stage, the employee reflects with gratitude or satisfaction for having shaped and been shaped by the organization.

According to Erikson (1950), inability to master demands of the immediate stage would disadvantage the employee in mastering the demands of successive stages. For example, an employee who does not master the third stage – Agency – and feels that his or her ideas are not valued will have difficulty identifying with the organization in Stage 5, and will tend to self-identify as an outsider until such time as the Agency stage can be revisited and mastered. Organizations that can accurately assess the developmental stages of their employees and target initiatives that support stage-specific development will be resourcing their employees' development of Essential Humanness. Table 8.1 illustrates how organizational analogues and stage-appropriate employee milestones can be derived from Erikson's model and how these milestones would relate to Essential Humanness.

The HODM identifies the successive targets of human flourishing, provides a humanistic "selection mechanism" for advancement or continuance in the organization, and channels managerial decisions toward policies that collectively create a Loving Organization.

By clarifying the nature of developmental milestones, the matrix allows managers to propose initiatives to further the employee's or cohort's development ("stage-appropriate interventions"), and provides evaluative criteria for examining current or prospective policies and processes

Table 8.1 Translating Erikson's Individual-Focused Framework into an Organization-Focused Framework

Stage	Erikson's descriptor	HODM organizational equivalent	Erikson's failure state	HODM successful employee milestone	Associated essential humanness
1	Trust	Trust	Distrust	"The company is on my side."	Moral
2	Autonomy	Competency	Self-doubt	"I can do this."	Rational
3	Initiative	Personal Agency	Guilt/Shame	"My ideas are good. I have voice."	Relational, Creative
4	Industry	Focused Engagement	Inferiority/"B-Team"	"I do my work with distinction."	Order-seeking
5	Identity	Organizational Identification	Role Confusion	"I identify with my company."	Relational Moral
6	Intimacy	Interpersonal Caring	Isolation	"I care about the 'whole person' of those I work with."	Relational
7	Generativity	Leadership Development	Stagnation	"I help shape the next generation of leaders."	Relational, Order Seeking, Creative
8	Integrity	Gratitude	Despair	"I both owe and have paid a debt of gratitude for our mutual shaping."	Moral

that could be supportive or suppressive to employees at particular stages (See Table 8.2, common stage-inappropriate mistakes).

Table 8.2 shows the HODM development matrix, orienting the stages of development with stage-critical employee milestones, illustrating effective and ineffective strategies for employee development.

Using the matrix for employee development requires that the supervisor assess employees progress through the Organizational Milestones and engage each employee with stage-appropriate resources for development. For example, Digital Ocean greets new employees with a balloon (so other employees can greet them), a bottle of Champaign, a personal note, and some company swag. This is intended to send a "welcome to the family" message – a good start toward assuring the employee that "the company is on my side." Twitter situates new employees in close proximity to colleagues who are likely to be instrumental in helping them master the tools and processes associated with their job. This kind of forethought supports employee achievement of Level 2 milestone of Competence. Facebook approaches building Competence more directly by putting all new software engineers into an intensive six-week bootcamp so that when they engage their first projects, they do so with substantial confidence. Each stage requires its own tactics for meeting the new HODM milestones as shown in Table 8.2, column 2. It is unlikely that a six-week bootcamp would work for building holistic caring of others. A more longitudinal modeling of care would be more effective. While it is possible to insert such practices into companies that are not concerned with human flourishing, companies committed to building Essential Humanness can intentionally and systematically accelerate human development with practices such as these, in pursuit of building the Loving Organization.

Implications for Research

The HODM provides a theoretically based framework by which organizations can develop a set of metrics focused not on financial or operational outcomes, but on human development. A first order of research might be to construct and validate an instrument that identifies the respondent's company-specific level of psychosocial development. Such an instrument could perhaps be an extension of the Modified Erikson Psychosocial Inventory (MEPSI) (Darling-Fisher 2018) and would be expected to provide insights into hiring, training, and promoting practices. Second, a more comprehensive set of "interventions" could be validated to remediate employees' company-specific psychosocial deficiencies. Table 8.2 provides examples of interventions, but certainly more could be considered. Understanding which interventions work best in which organizational contexts (culture, industry, etc.) and with which types of individuals (age, race, religion, gender, educational

Table 8.2 Humanistic Organizational Development Matrix (HODM)

HODM Stage	HODM individual milestones and assertions	Individuals' questions for organizations to assess	Stage-appropriate organizational interventions	Common stage-inappropriate organizational mistakes
1	Trust "The company is on my side."	"Are my colleagues friends or adversaries? Are they here to support me or expel me?"	* Provide mentor or "concierge" * Provide general training * Provide socialization opportunities	* Overemphasis on performance-based evaluations * "Sink or Swim" culture substitutes for training. EE feels no support.
2	Competence "I can do this."	"Am I competent at essential tasks?"	* Training in task specifics "Badges" * Clear expectations	* Unclear expectations * Feedback not frequent enough. * Feedback lacks supportive feel.
3	Agency "My ideas are good. I have voice."	"Do I have voice? Is my creativity valued? Can I shape what goes on here?"	* Acculturation training * Structured opportunity to voice suggestions about immediate task environment	* Only opportunity for input is through organization-wide channels. * Organization structure and budget processes suppress good ideas.
4	Engagement "I do my work with distinction."	"Can I do my job to a high standard?"	* Deliberate exposure to best practices/ high performers * Recognition of successes	* Formal recognition only awards "the winner," other high-performing employees not recognized, sending plethora of "wrong signals".
5	Organizational Identification "I identify with my company."	"Do I identify with my company's ethos or values? Do I want to see it succeed?"	* Provide opportunities to represent the company publicly * Inclusion in decision-making/leadership groups	* Participants in leader groups chosen based on financial performance metrics only rather than a broader set of organization values. Sends contradictory message about real values.

(continued)

Table 8.2 Cont.

HODM Stage	HODM individual milestones and assertions	Individuals' questions for organizations to assess	Stage-appropriate organizational interventions	Common stage-inappropriate organizational mistakes
6	Interpersonal Caring "I care for about colleagues holistically."	"Do I demonstrate to sensitivity and care for 'whole person' without seeking improvement in overall firm performance.?"	* Modeling * Meaningful retreats, etc. where leaders build bonds * Empathy training * Supportive performance reviews	* Culture separating personal and professional life rigorously maintained. * Performance review process is primarily evaluative w/o personal support for needed improvement.
7	Leadership Development " I have formal and informal influence."	"Can I perpetuate the organization values in the next generation of leaders?"	* Development/ mentoring opportunities * Values spokesperson * Input on level-appropriate decisions	* Leadership development program offers no opportunity for more responsibility. * Stated values subordinated to intense pressure for financial returns.
8	Gratitude: "I appreciate other's contributions to my success?"	"Has the organization helped me become some-thing I value, and have I left my values imprinted on the organization?"	* Helping employees find perspective on the meaning of their work.	* Culture of treating employees as "factors of production". * Permitting a hyper-competitive culture where one rises only at the expense of another.

level, etc.) could contribute to an organization's adoption of the instrument as a development tool and to subsequent employee flourishing.

By extending the application of Erikson's model from the individual to the organization, this research challenges one of Erikson's core assumptions: that psychosocial development is portable from one life context (or organization) to another. In keeping with social capital theory (Adler and Kwon 2002; Levi et al. (2018), Putnam's (1995) "re-potting hypothesis" (that social integration decreases with mobility), our research assumes that each social context presents a new environment where the organization must invite employees into increasing levels of psychosocial development, and the individual must respond by demonstrating a willingness and capacity to integrate psychosocially with the organization. The organization can influence the individual's willingness and capacity through effective policies, processes, and initiatives. The HODM provides a framework for evaluating current practices and processes, and how they would impact employees at different stages. This could potentially identify practices that have been unwittingly forced on employees to their detriment.

Practical Proposals

In an effort to illustrate how the HODM could influence management practice and organizational culture, the following practices are offered.

Performance Reviews

Formal performance reviews are disdained by supervisors and subordinates alike, and fraught with challenges (Adler et al. 2016; Mathison and Vinja 2010; Murphy 2008). In addition to tracking job-specific performance metrics, an emphasis could be placed on contributions to the psychosocial development of colleagues. Rather than have the employee or supervisors self-report on psychosocial development of the employee being evaluated, the firm could require each employee to comment on anyone in the organization who contributed to his or her development along the HODM dimensions. Collectively, the resulting body of qualitative data would identify the "who" and "how" of building Essential Humanness within the organization. It would capture an employee's impact outside of the formal reporting structure – consistent with self-giving. This instrument would in effect be a call to the members of the organization to respond to questions like the following:

- Which employees were instrumental in helping you feel a part of the organization?
- Which employees helped you develop tacit knowledge requisite to your job?
- Which employees have been generally supportive and encouraging in doing excellent work?

- Which employees inspired you to expand your own vision of your capabilities?
- Which employees went the "extra mile" for you?
- Which employees showed you small kindnesses?

By rewarding employees for self-giving behaviors without regard for whether the kindness shown was instrumental in accelerating sales or profits, companies begin to demonstrate a commitment to fostering loving behavior.

Mentoring and Training

Formal mentoring programs where a subordinate is assigned a mentor have struggled to persist in many organizations due to the perceived extra work on the mentor's part, asymmetric values between the mentoring dyad, personality clashes, and the like (Johnson and Smith 2019; Straus et al. 2013). Once performance evaluation takes on the character described above, Johnson and Smith's (2019, p. 3) proposal of replacing formal mentoring with "mentors-of-the-moment" could be institutionalized:

> Mentors-of-the-moment help to promote a mentoring culture where all members of the organization — especially those in the middle to upper ranks — seek opportunities in daily interactions to develop or grow junior colleagues and peers. The mentor-of-the-moment model flips the script on mentoring, from an onerous, formal, add-on obligation, to a delightful opportunity to use shorter exchanges to enhance self-esteem, self-confidence, and sense of belonging in someone junior. In this culture, trips to the coffee room, passing a colleague in the corridor, or lingering in the wake of meetings all become moments to greet an unfamiliar person, commend them on an excellent contribution, ask them about their career aspirations, or counter imposter syndrome symptoms with a well-timed affirmation.

This notion of mentorship is perhaps best expressed as an "organizational concierge." A concierge knows the local landscape and resources, and is available on an as-needed basis. Traditional mentor relationships function more like a tour guide – under his or her control and on a short leash. In addition, informal mentorship in self-giving behavior could be supplemented with more formal training in related skill sets such as active listening, empathy, and cross-cultural training.

Diversity and Inclusion (D&I)

The HODM can provide insights into where and how D&I failures occur in an organization, and may shed light on the extent to which such failures stem from unconscious bias or simply poor management. The notion of social inclusion is central to Erikson's model of psychosocial development; his model predicts that one's sense of exclusion will grow with time as subsequent stages of development are delayed for lack of development in previous stages. Companies can ask themselves diagnostic questions like the following:

- Do minorities have a basis for believing we are not as committed to their success as to majority-culture hires? (Level 1)
- Do minorities receive the training, assistance, affirmation, and mentoring needed to feel competent in their work? Is the majority culture affirming the competent work of minorities? (Level 2)
- Do minorities feel that their voice is heard? Is the majority culture perpetuating unconscious bias in meetings or discussions with minorities? (Level 3)
- Do minorities feel they have been treated fairly (equitably) so as to feel value-congruence with the company? Is the majority culture aware of extra burdens unwittingly placed on the minority culture? (Level 5)

The HODM recognizes the importance of the sequencing of these items. Attempting to fix higher-stage problems before lower-stage competencies are achieved may be ineffective and squander resources.

Conclusion

Perhaps the most inspiring aspect of this research is that it offers a pathway by which a company can systematically support the development of its employees in a manner that can substantially impact their Essential Humanness. It implies a sort of organizational humanist manifesto by which organizations commit themselves to the development of Essential Humanness in their employees, and design and track development through the HODM. It envisages managers who, as part of their responsibilities, are charged with grooming subordinates toward becoming self-giving people and who are evaluated on the basis of their demonstration of and their subordinates' progress in Essential Humanness. It invites debate about how to remain competitive while affording employees dignity through development. It outlines the shape of the Loving Organization – one committed to a systematic approach to building relational, moral, and rational capacity – regardless of the direct return to the company. In this way, it confronts the Love Challenge by recognizing "what our selfish genes are up to" (Dawkins 2016) and works toward developing a system of support and accountability to perpetuate the development of Essential Humanness.

References

Acemoglu, D., & Robinson, J. (2012). *Why nations fail: The origins of power, prosperity, and poverty*. New York, NY: Crown Publishing, a division of Random House.

Adler, P., & Kwon S. (2002). Social capital: Prospects for a new concept. *The Academy of Management Review, 27*(1), 17–40.

Adler, S., Campion, M., Colquitt, A., Grubb, A., Murphy, K. R., Ollander-Krane, R., & Pulakos, E. D. (2016). Getting rid of performance ratings: Genius or folly. *Industrial and Organizational Psychology: Perspectives on Science and Practice, 9*, 219–252. https://doi.org/10.1017/iop.2015.106

Bandura, A. (1997). *Self efficacy: The exercise of control.* New York, NY: W. H. Freeman.

Beer, M., Boselie, P., & Brewster, C. (2015). Back to the future: Implications for the field of HRM of the multi-stakeholder perspective proposed 30 years ago. *Human Resource Management, 54*, 427–438.

Christenson, R. (2012). Che Guevara and the Hombre Nuevo in Cuba. *Historia: The Alpha Rho Papers*, p. 86. file:///C:/Users/wandrews/Downloads/616-1-2345-2-10-20120622.pdf (Accessed Dec. 9, 2020).

Christiansen, S. L., & Palkovitz, R. (1998). Exploring Erikson's psychosocial theory of development: Generativity and its relationship to paternal identity, intimacy, and involvement in childcare. *The Journal of Men's Studies, 7*(1), 133–156. https://doi.org/10.3149/jms.0701.133

Coase, R. (1988). The nature of the firm: Meaning. *Journal of Law, Economics, & Organization, 4*(1), 19–32.

Daily, C. M., Dalton, D. R., & Cannella, A. A. (2003). Corporate governance: Decades of dialogue and data. *Academy of Management Review, 28*(3), 371–382.

Darling-Fisher, C. (2018). Application of the modified Erikson Psychological Stage Inventory: 25 years in review. *Western Journal of Nursing Research*, 2018 Apr 1:193945918770457. doi: 10.1177/0193945918770457.

Darling-Fisher, C. S., & Leidy, N. K. (1988). Measuring Eriksonian development in the adult: The modified Erikson Psychosocial Stage Inventory. *Psychological Reports, 62*(3), 747–754. https://doi.org/10.2466/pr0.1988.62.3.747

Dawkins, R. (2016). *The selfish gene* (p. 140). Oxford: Oxford University Press.

Dermot, O., & Rosato, M. (2013). Worked to death? A census-based longitudinal study of the relationship between the numbers of hours spent working and mortality risk. *International Journal of Epidemiology, 42*(6), 1820–1830.

Drucker, P. (1954). *The practice of management.* New York, NY: Harper.

Eisenhardt, K. M. (1989). Agency theory: An assessment and review. *Academy of Management Review, 14*(1), 57–74.

Elangovan, A. R., & Shapiro, D. L. (1998). Betrayal of trust in organizations. *Academy of Management Review, 23*(3), 547–566.

Erikson, E. (1950). *Childhood and society.* New York: W.W. Norton Company.

Erikson, E. (1964). *Insight and responsibility.* New York: W.W. Norton Company.

Friedman, M. (1970). The social responsibility of business is to increase its profits. *New York Times Magazine*, September 13.

Friedman, M. (1912–2006). *Capitalism and freedom.* Chicago, IL: University of Chicago Press.

Garrison A. (2004). Defining terrorism: Philosophy of the bomb, propaganda by deed and change through fear and violence. *Criminal Justice Studies, 17*(3), 259–279.

Genesis 3:16,19. *New American standard bible.* Grand Rapids, MI: Zondervan.

Giddens, A. (1981). *A contemporary critique of historical materialism* (p. 105). University of California Press.

Goldman, E. (1910). *Anarchism and other essays.* New York, NY: Mother Earth Publishing Association.

Grover, S. (1993). Why professionals lie: The impact of professional role conflict on reporting accuracy. *Organizational Behavior and Human Decision Processes, 65,* 251–272.

Gueverra, E. (1965). Socialism and man in Cuba. *The Che Reader.* Ocean Press: North Melbourne, Australia.

Guilford, J. P. (1950). Creativity. *American Psychologist, 5,* 444–454. doi:10.1037/h0063487

Hewlin, P. F. 2003. And the award for best actor goes to . . .: Facades of conformity in organizational settings. *Academy of Management Review, 28,* 633–642.

Huberty, C., Quirk, J., & Swann W. (1973). An evaluation system for a psychoeducational treatment program for emotionally disturbed children. *Educational Technology, 13,* 73–80.

Hume, D. (1985). *Essays: Moral, political and literary.* Indianapolis, IN: Liberty Press.

Johnson, W. B., & Smith, D. G. (2019). Real mentorship starts with company culture, not formal programs. *Harvard Business Review Digital Articles, 2–5.* https://hbr.org/2019/12/real-mentorship-starts-with-company-culture-not-for mal-programs (Accessed December 14, 2020).

Kant, E. (2017). *Groundwork of the metaphysics of morals* (trans. by Abbott, T.). Overland Park, KS: DigiReads.com.

Kline Leidy, N., & Darling-Fisher, C. (1995). Reliability and validity of the Modified Erikson Psychosocial Stage Inventory (MEPSI) in diverse samples. *Western Journal of Nursing Research, 17*(2), 168–187.

Kohlberg, L. (1969). Stage and sequence: The cognitive developmental approach to socialization. In D. A. Goslin (Ed.), *Handbook of socialization theory and research* (pp. 347–480). Chicago, IL: Rand McNally.

Kohlberg, L. (1984). *The psychology of moral development: Moral stages and lifecycle. Essays on moral development* (Vol. 2). New York, NY. Harper Collins.

Kohlberg, L., & Hersh, R. (1977). Moral development: A review of theory. *Theory and Practice, 16,* 53–58.

Korsgaard, C. (2009). Natural motives and the motive of duty: Hume and Kant on our duties to others. Harvard University. www.people.fas.harvard.edu/~korsgaar/CMK.Motive.of.Duty.pdf (Accessed May 15, 2020).

Leavitt, K., & Sluss, D. (2015). Lying for who we are: An identity-based model of workplace dishonesty. *Academy of Management Review, 40,* 587–610. https://doi.org/10.5465/amr.2013.0167

Livi, S., Theodorou, A., Rullo, M., Cinque, L., & Alessandri, G. (2018). The rocky road to prosocial behavior at work: The role of positivity and organizational socialization in preventing interpersonal strain. *PLoS One, 13*(3), e0193508. https://doi.org/10.1371/journal.pone.0193508

Manning, L. (1988). Erikson's psychosocial theories help explain early adolescence. *NASSP Bulletin, 72*(509), 95–100.

Marcus, J., Fritzsche, B. A., Le, H., & Reeves, M. D. (2016). Validation of the work-related age-based stereotypes (WAS) scale. *Journal of Managerial Psychology, 31*(5), 989–1004. doi:http://dx.doi.org.stetson.idm.oclc.org/10.1108/JMP-11-2014-0320

Marx. K. (2017). *Capital.* Overland Park, KS: DigiReads.com Publishing.

Marx, K., & Engels, F. (2002). *The communist manifesto.* New York, NY: Penguin.

Maslow, A. (1943). A theory of human motivation. *Psychological Review, 50*(4), 370–396.

Maslow, A. (1987). *Motivation and personality* (3rd ed.). New York, NY: Harper Collins.

Mathison, D., & Vinja, L. (2010). The annual performance review as a positive source for employee motivation? *Journal of Business & Economics Research*, 8(12), 111–120.

Milner, A., & Smith, P., & LaMontagne, A. (2015). Working hours and mental health in Australia: Evidence from an Australian population-based cohort, 2001-2012. *Occupational and Environmental Medicine*, 72(8), 573–579.

Murphy, K. R. (2008). Explaining the weak relationship between job performance and ratings of job performance. *Industrial and Organizational Psychology: Perspectives on Science and Practice*, 1, 148–160. https://doi.org/10.1111/j.1754-9434.2008.00030.x

Nietzsche, F. W. (2010). *The anti-Christ*. Auckland, NZ: Floating Press.

Ozawa, M. N., & Yeo, Y. H. (2006). Work status and work performance of people with disabilities: An empirical study. *Journal of Disability Policy Studies*, 17(3), 180–190. doi:http://dx.doi.org.stetson.idm.oclc.org/10.1177/10442073060170030601

Perry, T. E., Ruggiano, N., Shtompel, N., & Hassevoort, L. (2015). Applying Erikson's wisdom to self-management practices of older adults: Findings from two field studies. *Research on Aging*, 37(3), 253–274.

Piaget, J. (1952). *The origins of intelligence in children*. New York, NY. International Universities Press.

Piaget, J. (1977). *The development of thought: Equilibrium of cognitive structures*. New York, NY: Viking Press

Pirson, M. (2017). *Humanistic management* (p. 170). Cambridge: Cambridge University Press.

Putnam, R. D. (1995). Bowling alone: America's declining social capital. *Journal of Democracy*, 6(1), 65–78. doi:10.1353/jod.1995.0002.

Reina, D., & Reina, M. (2006). *Trust and betrayal in the workplace: Building effective relationships in your organization* (vol. 37). San Francisco, CA: Berrett and Koehler Publishers.

Rosenthal, P. (1995). Gender differences in managers' attributions for successful work performance. *Women in Management Review*, 10(6), 26. doi:http://dx.doi.org.stetson.idm.oclc.org/10.1108/09649429510096006

Rosenthal, D. A., Gurney, R. M., & Moore, S. M. (1981). From trust to intimacy: A new inventory for examining Erikson's stages of psychosocial development. *Journal of Youth and Adolescence*, 10(6), 525–537. https://doi.org/10.1007/BF02087944

Sciabarra. C. (1987). The crisis of libertarian dualism. *Critical Review*, 1(4), 86–99. doi: 10.1080/08913818708459506

Sowell, T. (1985). *Marxism philosophy and economics* (p. 218). New York, NY: William Morrow & Company.

Straus, Sharon E., Johnson, Mallory O., Marquez, C., Feldman, Mitchell D. (2013). Characteristics of successful and failed mentoring relationships. *Academic Medicine*, 88(1), 82–89. doi: 10.1097/ACM.0b013e31827647a0

Taleb, N. (2018). What do I mean by skin in the game? my own version. *Incierto*, March 5, 2020. https://medium.com/incerto/what-do-i-mean-by-skin-in-the-game-my-own-version-cc858dc73260 (Accessed May 19, 2020).

Unsworth. M. (1996). A theory of individual creative action in multiple social domains. *Academy of Management Review*, 21, 1112–1142.

Whetten, D., & Godfrey, P. (Eds.) (1998). *Identity in organizations: Developing theory in through conversations.* Thousand Oaks, CA: Sage.

Williamson, J. (1975). *Markets and hierarchies: Analysis and antitrust implications.* New York, NY: Free Press.

Wood, M., Combs, M., & Swindle, F. (1998). *Documenting effectiveness.* Athens, GA: Developmental Therapy Institute.

Ya-Yu, L., Loe, S., & Cartledge. (2002). The effects of social skills instruction on the social behaviors of students at risk for emotional and behavioral disorders. *Behavioral Disorders, 27,* 371–385.

9 Putting Love First

Redefining Managing, Organizing, and the Future of Work

Elena P. Antonacopoulou

Introduction

While love has progressively featured as a "word" in the management and organization studies vocabulary as some research attests (Cunha et al., 2017; Barsade and O'Neil, 2014; Andersen and Born, 2008), it still hardly features in mainstream conversations and even when it does, it tends to be more likely perceived as a "dirty" word and "an idea," which is more likely to provoke discomfort. This response to "love" as an essential phenomenon in human affairs across contexts (not least of which organizations) may have been exacerbated due to the epidemic of the "#me too" debate, which has not only galvanized all possible defenses against sexual harassment at work (Williams, 2019). It has also "killed" what might have once been romanticized as a prospect that deep and meaningful relationships can be formed in organizations especially at a time when the workplace is the most dominant place where everyday life is played out. This remains critical despite the drastic redefinition of the notion of the workplace promulgated by the Covid-19 pandemic and measures of "stay at home" and "social distancing." Perhaps if anything, due to these new flexible working conditions, the meaning of workplace and its significance in the ways the "work-force" relate with one another becomes even more critical. It is precisely this "force" when working with and through "others" in the "place" where we do that which we call "work" that merits bringing closer to focus. I will call such a "force" love and I will explore in this chapter the "place" that love holds in our working lives (beyond our personal lives) to consider what might the future workplace look like if organizing and managing work give us not only more meaning but also more scope to "love what we do and do what we do with love" (Antonacopoulou and Bento, 2003).

In this chapter I entertain a radical form of reorganization by exploring *Putting Love First* as a governing principle enabling new ways of relating, working, and uniting in serving the common good, as an essential dimension for the future of work. I explore this repositioning of love as receiving more prominence in managing and organizing by posing

DOI: 10.4324/9781003254034-10

the question: *what might the impact be if love formed the basis for re-organizing and managing with a difference?* To address ways of embedding love in managing and organizing, I introduce new "love languages," extending previous references to the five love languages (Chapman, 2010) that have also been translated into the five languages of appreciation in the workplace (Chapman and White, 2012). The main thesis of previous references to love language in human affairs is the proposition that each person has the tendency to favor some over other gestures or expressions of love (gifting, appreciation, acts of service, touch, and quality time) that may be limited to a primary and a secondary language which may be developed if they seek to understand and respond to the other's needs and preferences.

I put forward the case that instead of a bilingual orientation toward love and its expression, a multi-lingual orientation can be promoted instead. The possibility of *Putting Love First* governing the connectivity and not only relationality underpinning management and organizational practices extends beyond merely the five languages and their integration in multiple ways of making others (be they employees, customers, or other stakeholders shaping any organization's ecosystem) feel appreciated or valued (Chapman and White, 2012; White and Mackenzie-Davey, 2003). Instead, the focus will be to place love as the main language – one that affords to transcend preferences, orientations toward loving and instead adopts additional fundamental principles that shape what will be referred to as *"Free Love"* and *"Higher Love."* By giving voice to these new love languages, the objective is to enhance the sense of safety in vulnerability that love ultimately calls for. I will show how placing love as a force for reorganizing and "managing work" with a difference can attend to the toxicity that has forced so many "workers" to remain silent, endure violations of dignity, and suffer forms of inequality and victimization. More powerfully, I will attend to the lack of "isothymia" (Fukuyama, 2019) – equal worth – underpinning the phenomenon of *"humane poverty"* that mankind exhibits not only in the workplace but in ways of being and becoming, that is, ways of living.

Humane poverty unlike references to "humane capital" (Hlupic, 2018) attends to advancing human potential positioning dignity and recognition of worth – "axia"[1] – as the core value proposition underpinning measures of "value." In this respect, evaluating and accounting for what matters in human affairs, which are at the core of what makes corporations arenas of collective growth, lies the equanimity that many notions of "capital" (social, cultural, humane, etc.) tend to ignore. In this respect, humane poverty calls for an uprising (rising up – elevating) in human affairs and ways of inter-connecting with each other and the ecology, such that the systems we contribute to creating not only recognize the importance of equality and diversity, but are also inclusive beyond tokenisms. Such inclusiveness marks our ways of interrelating enabling us to meet each other as equals and with equilibrium as a basis of aligning our actions with the common good (Antonacopoulou and Georgiadou, 2020). This means that inclusiveness is about "inter-being" (Nhat Hanh, 2015), which I will elaborate as a new place/positioning guiding our efforts to "build back better" and "fairer" (PHE, 2021) (post-Covid) by reorganizing and managing with solidarity, unity, and axiology.

Living and working have always been in a balancing act that was accepted as mostly out of balance, hence the work–life balance debate continuing to expose the tensions. Since the Covid-19 pandemic, work life and nonwork life have become so entangled that it now becomes even more critical to address this balancing act, as we pave the future of work. This calls for greater investment in advancing human potential to avert humane poverty and this means that there is a need to attend to "isothymia" that underpins the otherwise "bystander"[2](Paull et al., 2012) positioning that has made acceptable inaction and what Bauman (1989) recognizes as "adiaphoric." As Fukuyama (2019: 23) explains, "thymos is the part of the soul that seeks recognition." This struggle to be seen and to feel honored, he further explains, acknowledges the worthiness that already exists. And such worthiness, I would add, replaces isothymia with *isotimia*, defined as *inclusiveness of shared worth through love* and not just empathy nor compassion that otherwise can advance human affairs in work organizations and beyond in the wider civic renewal that love's force has the power to propel.

Such a repositioning of love explicates the significance of *altruism*, the act of giving love without an expectation for it to be returned and *dignity*, an essential source defining what being human means as key principles (axies) of what it would practically require *Putting Love First*. This is especially if we recognize that these principles are also critical foundations on which humanity rests alongside other established critical love elements such as respect, trust, kindness, joy, and equanimity.

It is these axies that I draw on to propose an *axiology of love* in managing and organizing. Such axiology elevates the significance of love not only as a key language but also as a connecting tissue and energy force aligning both the multiplicity of linguistic genres and acts of love, while liberating love in the process. Such an axiology also addresses the central tenet of this book to invite us to ponder if "love is all we need." The analysis of *Free Love* and *Higher Love* as foundations for new ways of managing and organizing shows in practice what it takes to put love first as an *axia*. As a mark of worth (value), love as an axia elevates our appreciation of its value/significance enabling managing and organizing to acquire new purpose – serving the common good. The latter is positioned as a foundation for redesigning work not only to restore meaningfulness, but inclusiveness as central tenets of the future humanity deserves to be afforded.

The chapter explores these ideas in three sections. Following the introduction, a brief overview of ways love has featured in hitherto management and organization studies is provided to distil not only the treatment of the phenomenon but also why embedding it in the mainstream workplace discourse will take more than just learning the language of love. This is explicated by extending the current love languages – or languages of appreciation – in introducing two other languages – *Free Love* and *Higher Love*. In the second section, each of these new love languages is elaborated on the basis of two guiding principles: altruism and dignity. The third section elaborates the axiology of *Putting Love First* in explicating the implications for repurposing managing and organizing to serve the common good. There are no conclusions to round up this analysis as the objective is to leave open, unfinished. In doing so, the objective is to invite continuity in the conversation and the elaboration and extension of the thesis presented. By leaving the thesis in this chapter as a work in progress, the invitation is to also appreciate that love is not fixed nor a matter of attaining, but an ongoing pursuit in search of arresting moments where love in its full complexity is also why pondering the question *what is love?* must necessarily remain central to the governing question of this book as well – Is Love all we need? Our "need" to experience "love," share it and place as a central tenet to our ways of managing and organizing work and life, beyond the workplace, remains essential to our effort to define as central to the future of work, the commitment to practicing learning to love.

The Language of Love in the Management and Organization Studies Discourse

Although "love" does not feature prominently in the management and organization studies discourse, it has nonetheless commanded some attention in accounts addressing themes such as the importance of psychological needs of belonging, relatedness, care for and being cared by others, not least through the enrichment of employee experience in the provision of services that maintain employee morale, shape professional collaborations, and support learning (Ulus, 2019; Vanderstukken et al., 2016; Cunha et al., 2016; Walker, 2011; Antonacopoulou and Gabriel, 2001). And while love as a concept has attracted multiple interpretations and distinctions of "kind" or "version of love" (Agape – unconditional, Eros – romantic, Philia – affectionate, Philautia – self-protection, Storge – familiar, Pragma – pragmatic, Ludus – playful, and Mania – obsessive), what continues to fascinate and puzzle is not just the feelings and emotional reactions that love as a phenomenon provokes (Barsade and O'Neil, 2014; Argandoña, 2011). It also bewilders us to confront the ways we "see" each other, what matters to us individually and collectively and brings things to focus in terms of what we pay attention to as the poet J.D. McClatchy (2001) wrote contrasting love and lust (desire) stating that "Love is the quality of attention we pay to things." I would also suggest following Levinas (1972) that our quality of attention to "the other" is even more critical to our efforts to learn how to love and to attend to love itself. That is why drawing on Haraway (2016) I want to emphasize "the other" as "making kin" – being in and caring for that multispecies world; and that "staying with the trouble" is a way to understand it and why love matters. To use her words:

> It matters what matters we use to think other matters with; it matters what stories we tell to tell other stories with; it matters what knots knot knots, what thoughts think thoughts, what descriptions describe descriptions, what ties tie ties. It matters what worlds make worlds, what worlds make stories.
>
> (p. 12)

This for me returns to the thesis I placed as integral to changing, learning, and knowing, namely, that beyond autopoises (self-organization) there is, as Haraway attests, "sympoiesis" (co-creation and not only coexistence – symbiosis) this is why I sought to bring attention to *syschetisms* (interconnections) (Antonacopoulou, 1997). The quality of such connections and the character of the connection of connections themselves goes beyond unidirectional or bidirectional relationships and modes of relating, be those through inter-action, intra-action or trans-action (see Emirbayer and Mische, 1998; Barad, 2010). It addresses the essence of what it means to inter-connect what Nhat Hanh (2015) refers to as "interbeing." Hence, returning to rethink syschetisms is no less a labor of love (in my own scholarship) and an integral part of what love and loving also calls for – laboring – staying with – entangled. Such entanglement is not being averse to disentanglement nor recognizing "others" in the ecology. It is an emplacement, a positioning (Antonacopoulou and Fuller, 2020) toward the connections that energize the force, that is love holding us together and, as I will also explain, driving us also apart. Attending to love in this way is an invitation to show up in our everyday experiences as we navigate not knowing what our next move might be. Such openness and readiness to absorb the vulnerability that love and loving present us with provoke fear. Such fear some commentators (Chapman, 2010) have sought to arrest by formulating a "language code" that can guide how we choose to attend to love.

It is worth noting that this already presents a challenge in empirically arresting love as a phenomenon if we note that potentially tautologically love affords both the way experiences are attended to and defines the quality of the experience itself as it too is the experience. As Kahlil Gibran (1923) eloquently accounts for this puzzle, "Love gives naught but itself and takes naught but from itself. Love possesses not nor would it be possessed; For love is sufficient unto love." A point that perhaps is brought home to us by the teaching of Thich Nhat Hanh in his treatise of "How to Love" (2015) guiding us to recognize love as an informed practice that requires deliberate practice – to hone the "skill of loving" – if we are to master a potentiality in pursuit of human excellence.

And it is this almost impenetrable complexity that may well have guided some of the linguistic simplification that has otherwise dominated the management and organization studies discourse. On the one hand, we are perforce to surrender to love's power to conquer everything and, on the other hand, we are invited to commit to learning one of life's finest lessons, understanding (not merely making sense) how to love (ourselves and each other as part of the wider ecology) means and entails, because what essentially matters if we commit to *learning to love,* as Thich Nhat Hanh reminds us, is to avoid being the cause of harm and pain. In his words, "To love without knowing how to love wounds the person we love. To know how to love someone, we have to understand them."

This understanding is more than interpreting and perceiving what "the other" needs or prefers. It calls for listening and speaking their love language claims Chapman (2010) as he makes the case for the five love languages which he subsequently adapts as five languages of appreciation (Chapman and White, 2012) to extend the basic principles from personal to professional relationships in the workplace. These languages of appreciation collectively seek to provide recognition and through making employees feel valued, this enhances their commitment and job satisfaction, as well as the connectedness between the organization's members and wider engagement in realizing organizational priorities. Although they are presented as "languages" they comprise of acts that those to whom they are extended to would value most. And the main thesis is that as in personal so too in professional relationships, there is a disposition toward some actions that we value and perceive as more important and clear indications of other's recognition of who we are and how we contribute to defining and serving the common good.

The invitation Chapman and White (2012) therefore extend is to "master" the other's love language so that the love and appreciation offered are received rather than risk missing the mark. In this respect, each of the love languages offers tangible and visible ways to speak out loud through the actions another person takes, their love and appreciation to another. This means that if one's preferred language – "native tongue" – of appreciation is words of affirmation, quality time, acts of service, gifting or physical touch, then "speaking their language" is critical for love to find its place. I provide a brief overview of what each of these love languages/languages of appreciation means in placing love in the workplace.

Appreciation/Love Language #1: Words of Affirmation

Providing verbal praise for achievements and recognizing accomplishment in meeting or exceeding expectations by acknowledging a job well done are basic examples of this love language. It can also be an affirmation of character qualities that is demonstrated by a person, such as their honesty, humility, compassion, and integrity. It can also constitute a praise for one's personality traits such as their optimism, spontaneity, and immaculate presentation. These expressions of admiration of another person's qualities to themselves directly and in private, in the presence of others, or in writing, are an active way of "*seeing*" the person as they are. They are also affirming to the person that they are accepted and included as they are. This is why words of affirmation can also entail comments about how one looks, what they wear that makes them beautiful in the other's eyes, is more than a passing compliment. It is an act of recognition – perceiving again – that this person is noticeable as are their contributions.

Appreciation/Love Language #2: Quality Time

If one's preference is for quality conversation – focused one-to-one attention – so that they feel safe to be vulnerable, share frustrations, concerns and feel understood, is integral to this language of appreciation. It extends to the other, an affirmation that they are heard, they are listened to, and that their version of reality matters. This is why empathy can be an act of love in demonstrating one appreciates how the other person experiences a given situation. It is not just a matter of sympathy in how one feels. It is "*listening*" that affirms feelings, thoughts and is less concerned with offering advice or solutions and perhaps more concerned with seeing the issue from the other's gaze, recognizing and sharing in the feelings they are experiencing. Such listening is seeing with the other's eyes the impact a situation has on them. Making time for such conversations over coffee or a meal buys quality time to show one genuinely cares about the other person's well-being. Equally, making time to do a fun activity together actively demonstrates the willingness to share an experience – from doing a sport both enjoy, to reading and discussing topics of shared interest, the essence is to do something that brings joy with someone who we care to show we care.

Appreciation/Love Language #3: Acts of Service

Irrespective of how capable one is to fulfill the work tasks, the opportunity to have someone offer to help is not only an act of kindness but also a mark of respect in the choice to share the load. Volunteering to help others or to undertake tasks (and that includes mundane chores like cleaning the shared kitchen at work) that involve community participation signals the desire to support and express the value attributed to what is being shared. It shift the onus from "someone else can do this" to one where "serving the collective is an honor." As discussed in the previous paragraphs, in the same way "*seeing*" and "*listening*" to the other matter, "*holding*" the other by offering support in actively contributing to activities that can free them up from other tasks, give them more free time or just support them in getting things done, all these gestures matter. They are symbolic and active marks of appreciation and care for what needs to be done and why sharing and contributing to the workload matters to good citizenship as much as to good relationships with others. It might only take just offering a glass of water or a cup of coffee to a colleague to show such caring.

Appreciation/Love Language #4: Receiving Gifts

The active forms of recognition that present tangible offers unlike the example of a glass of water or a cup of coffee can also take the form of a gift. Such gifts and the value of what is being extended can assume different degrees of significance and translate into different messages, which is also why gifting is a sensitive matter and one that needs to be handled with extra care. For the purpose of this analysis and drawing on the way this language of appreciation has been conceived of originally by Chapman and White (2012), the focus is on gifts that form acts of respect. However, as a general principle, gestures like offering flowers, a basket of fruits, a voucher for a meal, books, an experience, etc., are indicative illustrations of appreciation that seek not to "compensate" for what one does or who one is in the workplace. They are illustrations that beyond "*seeing*" someone, "*hearing*" their perspective, or "*holding*" them when offering support, gifting is "*valuing*" them and indicating to them that who they are is worthy and valuable to others.

Appreciation/Love Language #5: Physical touch

Perhaps the most delegate of areas of expressing appreciation and love are the boundaries of physical interaction and what these may entail or be interpreted as, especially when extended in the workplace. Notwithstanding, the opening remarks in the chapter's introduction about the implications of the "me too" campaign and the very real and serious implications of sexual harassment cannot be ignored, as Chapman and White (2012: 101) point out, "...physical touch can have a positive impact in the workplace when done appropriately. A firm handshake of greeting or congratulations, a high five in celebration, a fist bump – all are used frequently in work-orientated relationship." Marks of affection can still be a respectful way of expressing care beyond "*seeing*," "*hearing*," "*holding*," and "*valuing*" the other, by "*embracing*" (literally and metaphorically) as a mark of accepting them and crediting them with their worth. Such embracing we have learned to do during the Covid-19 pandemic in our socially distancing ways by not only connecting in conversation through our computer screens while "zooming," "teaming," and "skyping." We mark clearly if we are in a "good" or "bad" place (feeling happy or sad) when we reach out to each other to receive each other's life challenges and not only work priorities. Such "embracing"

I have personally learned to activate through intentionally smiling. In our socially distances and progressively remote modes of working as the norm, smiling can act as a "hug" 2 meters apart! Try it and witness the effects of a smile's touch.

These examples of expressing love and appreciation as a "language" that could govern our ways of communicating and relating in the workplace remind us of the centrality of love and appreciation in human affairs. Yet, much as the case is made of how critical it is to recognize our and the other's preferred language, as well as investing the time to learn the "dialects" with which such languages can be "spoken," there is more that can enrich the role of love in our lives (in and out of) work. To present the love/appreciation languages as "rules" governing our ways of connecting, relating, and working together does not fully serve the need to also understand and serve love in its own terms. This calls for extending the current portfolio of languages to provide not only greater scope to refine our capacity to communicate better. This means not only learning to speak each other's language of appreciation. I would argue that love itself is a language that we all choose to learn how to converse in with different degrees of fluency.

If we explore love itself as a language, we may need to go beyond our appreciation of what boundaries and rules define language. This is because love itself is not a language because it is spoken or signed, encoded into secondary media using auditory, visual, or tactile stimuli. Nor is it a language, because we can master the rules of phonology, morphology, syntax, semantics, and pragmatics in justifying it being a language. Love is a language that liberates us from the boundaries that otherwise can hold us back to express our humanity. It is a form of expression with which we communicate as well as rise above the otherwise unhealthy environment the workplace is also becoming when toxicity dominates instead of love. I introduce two new love languages to attend specifically to this challenge and to provide the foundation for exploring love's axiology that shifts the focus on its elements not as a language per se but as a life force.

New Love Languages – Free Love, Higher Love

Whether we relate to others in the workplace on a personal or professional way, the idea that love and appreciation have languages of expression may do little to secure the healthy relationships we might seek. In the book that followed their work on the five languages of love and appreciation, Chapman, While and Myra (2014) account for the toxic workplace and ways of rising above it. Notably, they draw attention to "poisonous environments" where "conflict, hurt, anger, poor communication, lack of appreciation" are rife. They capture the kinds of behaviors that are only too common among those especially in roles where the power they are afforded does not meet neither their competence nor character, and hence unsurprisingly do more harm than good. These are examples not only where love and appreciation are absent. They are the "places" (at work, in social interactions, and in personal relationships) that thrive on fear, the latter being the opposite of love as pointed out earlier. Such fear is especially prominent when envy, greed, and insecurity fuel the way one chooses to conduct themselves abusing their power and enforcing their control on others.

Typical of the incidents that Chapman et al. (2014) account to describe, the resulting toxicity includes language (both spoken and enacted) that undermines, belittles, and violates dignity, not least because the pickering, criticism, lack of support, fuel conflict, fear and anger supported by misinformation, rumors and gossip only energize blame than responsibility. Indicative illustrations of toxicity include the following:

> "you have no future in this school."
>
> "we all got used to thinking we were inept losers who didn't really deserve to be paid."
>
> "I couldn't please her. No matter what I did, it was never enough...I tried talking with her and asking what I needed to do to improve... she eventually accused me of cheating the company. God knows, I was not guilty!...She had no evidence but was convinced... So, I was fired."
>
> "...her attitude communicates I'm useless."
>
> "...conversations with HR ...got me nowhere!... they're not there to help or protect you from your mean boss. They are there to ensure the company doesn't get sued."
>
> "the tension is so thick I hate to go to work.... I hate my life."
>
> "It's so unhealthy to bottle up my emotions, but I'm forced to keep my mouth shut."
>
> "this is killing me."

Taking these examples together, it is easy to sum them up as clear illustrations of what happens when a "bully [is] in sight," the title Tim Field (1996) gave to a book dedicated to accounting for bullying as a phenomenon and disease (a pathological disorder) that underpins toxic environments. Understandably and rightly so it comes with a "health warning" in that the stories and accounts provided drawn from lived experiences and their impacts can be disturbing. Disturbing they are, because what they do reveal among other things is not that the toxicity accounted is fed by and expressed in acts of bullying. It is an act of war that violates human dignity. As indicative quotes below neatly sum this up:

> Each day going to work was like going to war – the office was a battle zone where a group of managers would take it in turns to

humiliate and denigrate staff. I would not have believed that this type of behaviour could happen in a civilised society on a daily basis and be accepted had I not seen and experienced it myself.

(p. 4)

I was bullied severely over a period of three years and eventually dismissed on a thumped-up charge. The dismissal and appeal hearings were a foregone conclusion. A year later, having been let down repeatedly by the legal system, I still feel like I've been accused of a crime whilst the real criminals are off galivanting about, probably bullying someone else. My only 'crime' was to take pride in and enjoy my job.

(p. 6)

Recognizing that there is no clear remedy to attend to this challenge that derives from human misconduct, it is puzzling to know how to respond when evidence shows that *"Bullying is… for the perpetrator's pleasure, can be regarded as a form of psychological rape because of its intrusive and violational nature"* (Field, 1996: 5). Summing up the challenge in a flyer (see Figure 9.1), Field's (1996) analysis stands out for the provocation it presents us to ponder not only if we are being bullied but more so, if we might unintentionally be a bully and worse still, remain bystanders to the massacre of human dignity that such toxic acts reflect (Mulder et al., 2017). There are plenty of other recent accounts of bullying or mopping in the workplace (Monzani et al., 2016; Aleassa and Megdadi, 2014; Lutgen-Sandvik and McDermott, 2011), and I choose to draw on Field's work because of the vivid quotations that express the sentience and pain that violations of dignity inflict.

BOX 9.1 A Leaflet on Bullying

I didn't realise I was being bulled:

Bullying is constant criticism, nit-picking, fault-finding and undermining, ostracised and excluded, being singled out, belittled, threatened, overloaded with work and unrealistic goals, twisting everything you say and do, abuse of disciplinary procedures to present you in bad light and undermine your integrity.

The purpose of bullying is to "hide inadequacy" and "divert attention away from their inadequacy. In an insecure workplace this is how incompetent people, keep their jobs".

Serial Bully – can be a "selfish, insensitive, insecure, immature but plausible individual… who is convincing and convulsive liar, lacks conscience and is drawn to positions to power".

I am off work with stress:

Bullying causes high negative stress resulting in anxiety, sleepless-ness, fatigue, trauma, tearfulness, poor concentration, panic attacks, fragility, shattered self-confidence, low self-esteem, isolation.

It can also prompt other medical conditions like: hyperventila-tion, hypervigilance, hypersensitivity, headaches, skin problems, depression, palpitations.

Adapted from Field, T. (1996)

The reality of working life is such that the existence of love languages may not only fail to deliver the antidote to toxicity, it may also fail to stop the bullying that it is often accompanied by. This calls not only for new ways of addressing these human indignities at work and the experi-ence of working. It also calls for learning to love differently not only work and working but also workers and the workplace. This is what motivates making the case for two new love languages in professional (and personal) relationships. Each of these love languages is discussed in turn and together they provide the foundation for an axiology of love in human conduct reconstituting the meaning of managing and organizing if we choose to put love first.

Free Love

A sixth love language – *Free Love* – is introduced to embrace the uncon-ditional nature of love implicated in "agaph." It seeks to show how a var-iety of other love languages (discussed in the previous section) could be combined to enable human growth. This means recognizing that instead of assuming that there is one love language that we may be versed more than others, we are invited to recognize that love itself is changing, and hence the love languages we need to learn to become better versed at, in our unique ways of connecting with each other, also need to become broader. Therefore, it is proposed that *Free Love* is the freedom to express love in multiple ways simultaneously connecting different aspects (gifting, appreciation, acts of service, touch, and quality time) and by implication transcending the limits imposed by focusing on a primary and secondary language.

The notion of freedom to love in multiple ways extends the meta-phor of language beyond the "grammar of action" that is implicated in the previous accounts of love languages. It seeks to transcend, but not replace the scope for what needs to be attended to when expressing love and appreciation in our interactions with one another. It offers as the foundation of "speaking" love's languages the scope for multiple accents, not least because as Chapman (2010) also affirms *love is a choice.* And it is not just that love as the active choice to love the other can "create the climate where we can deal with our past conflicts and failures." It is acknowledged that "love doesn't erase the past, but it makes the future different" as Chapman (2010) proclaims, yet what love also does is that it changes over time and so does the choice of who and how to love. This is perhaps why one of the most fundamental aspects of learning a language is not the language itself but the learning process.

Learning to love is the least and yet most important parts of commanding the language of love. And learning to love is liberating knowledge to enable the organic growth of the individual and the relationships that they choose to enter. This also means that learning and loving go beyond a code of conduct, and invite us to grow our humanity. Being human we couldn't learn to understand and speak the languages of love, by limiting our repertoire to a set of guidelines. We should not approach learning itself with a vision of a step-by-step process. If we seek learning by "painting in numbers," we only develop the capacity to follow instructions. Learning to love is not an instructional or didactic process. It is a liberating process where improvization, creativity, and innovation enrich our experience of learning and loving, together serving love's purpose to help us grow to our full human potential.

No wonder when we approach learning to love as an instructional process, the very instructions followed are unlikely to guarantee a safe and sustainable relationship. This is not least, because when a crisis presents itself the panic, fear, resentment, and many more reactions not only fail to nurture love, but can kill love all together. This is not least because instructions can imprison love into a version of what it owed to be, based on what is previously known. We learn to love, when we surrender to not knowing. Crisis therefore offers the opportunity to transcend a language *per se* and to start focusing on love's native tongue. This introduces beyond *"seeing," "hearing," "holding," "valuing,"* and *"embracing" "the other,"* also *"tasting"* the other.

Taste here is a way of expressing a native tongue in numerous dialects (e.g., English is spoken very differently across the UK and across other countries and continents, e.g., United States and Australia). Taste here is freeing the limits of language to start versing in ways that touch the essence of what brings us together sometimes when we do not speak the same language at all. This is when we drop "language" restrictions in words and acts. We engage instead, in sensing like one would, when experiencing a new taste which challenges our taste buds in the levels of heightened sensitivity we can afford, in our efforts to understand before we demonstrate appreciation and love to the other. This very experience of putting the taste of love to the test as opposed to the spoken language and the grammar of action it dictates is a process of freeing ourselves and each other to connect in ways that know no boundaries. They are essentially returning us to our essence of being human but certainly not Neanderthals in our conduct.

Just as a child navigates learning their world by tasting, feeling, and touching, so too *Free Love* invites us to connect with each other by revealing and bringing the child in us alongside the adult and not always fully matured person that our experiences may suggest we may be. If we endeavor to see the child in each other, we learn to love with heightened sense of vulnerability in protecting the other and ourselves while loving. That may not avert the pain love can also cause, but it liberates the other to feel safe to be loved and to love as a child would, not knowing fully the consequences of their actions. That is not to say that *Free Love* is childlike and childish, irresponsible and innocent. It means, exercising consciously loving in ways that are liberating the other and can nurture each other's growth and the growth of the love that is shared.

Such freedom is essential in the constantly unfolding nature and quality of love that relationships are defined by. Changing love is not least triggered by the changing relationships and the changing love agents that define the quality of love and commit to growing and sustain it. And while *Free Love* accounts for multiple ways of loving at the same time, it also recognizes that there is still scope to grow out of love and to outgrow the very source where love received may be drawn from.

In other words, this would be the language of freedom to use multiple symbols, gestures, methods, and expressions of love and in doing so allowing love to find its own way of speaking to the other not expecting it to be expressed in a prescribed way, but ensuring that the other feels loved by tasting the love given with the freedom to express what this taste feels like to them. This would be analogous to imagining how might one connect with others if they did not share the same language (e.g., one could only speak Greek and English and the other couldn't speak either languages but could only understand Italian). One would then consider using other forms of communicating their love that would be part of the universal language of humanity. The following example is illustrative of *Free Love*.

In the course of doing voluntary work on a "house project," I worked alongside a co-worker who I did not share a common language with. During less than a handful of occasions when we met and worked together, our communication of love and respect for each other as coworkers was not limited to words and certainly not restricted by the absence of a shared language to communicate with each other. I spoke English and Greek, she spoke only Italian. And yet, in the course of working together, we were singing together, we joked and laughed together, we worked hard to complete the project together and we have remained in contact since the end of that phase of the "house project," because we gave each other love in the way we respectively felt recognized and appreciated as coworkers and now as friends.

This is simply because neither of us limited our connection to each other to one set of gestures, words, or actions – nor languages. We both became multilingual in our capacity to relate with each other by recognizing that the love of seeing this "house project" completed enabled us to work well with each other to get the job done. We self-organized and managed the deadlines imposed on us by continuing to have fun in the process, because we "listened" to the sentiments that connected us and enabled us to see this project through successfully.

And distance has not interfered in our capacity to remain in dialogue and connected sustaining and growing our friendship. Even if we have mostly due to physical distance relied, on social media platforms and emoticons to express our appreciation toward each other, we were still able to meet each other as humans. We respectively come from different social backgrounds and professional work. We met face-to-face after several months and the same force of energy which connected us then was present in the joy we took, spending time in the mundane activities which nonetheless cemented our mutual trust, respect in each other, and our equanimity in preserving our shared humanity and each other's dignity, something that the "house project" itself as an experience and place of work had in some instances undermined.

What this example aims to explicate is that multilingualism in the use of a variety of love languages simultaneously provides the foundation for growing our humanity by sharpening the choices we make in constructing and reconstructing our identity in relation to the other. "The other" does not provide affirmation that we are being valued and hence "rewarded" by being loved. It offers instead a basis for aligning as Fukuyama (2019: 9–10) puts it explicating identity, "one's inner self and an outer world of social rules and norms that does not adequately recognize the inner self's worth or dignity." By elevating dignity as our mutual worth as different people, with different skills and expertise, different spoken languages, we related to each other by placing our individual dignity and *isotimia* (equal worth) as the linchpin that fuels our mutual care and love for each other.

Free Love then offers to the repertoire of love languages an invitation to adjust to the dialect that connecting to the other calls for. It is a love language in its own right, because it shifts the focus from acts of appreciation in work to transcend work and give it new meaning to the quality of connections when they fuel our individual and collective identity which remains our ongoing work in progress. In practical terms what this means is that in *putting love first* we go beyond compassion and kindness in recognizing and accepting each other as we are. We shift to our shared commitment to make our work meaningful as a basis enabling each other to nurture our growth as humans. We actively take steps to liberate love's capacity to nurture our humanity and support our alignment of our inner self with the world and each other. It provides us with a basis for rebuilding our personal and professional identity. This is when we strip off our titles and qualifications as evidence of the credentials we bring to qualify ourselves to do our work. It provides instead a certification that we come to work with *philotimo* – the commitment to honor each other's worth – dignity.

By introducing *Free Love* as a love language and within that complex notions like "isotimia"[3] and "philotimo"[4] both of which are recognized for the difficulty they present to "translate" accurately the meaning, I aim to make two further principles more clear. First, I draw attention to the importance of balance and poise in the workplace. This goes beyond inclusiveness, equality, and diversity. It brings to the fore the power of inter-relating with each other not just through our shared interests but making that which rests between us (in this example, "the house project"), that which also enables us to meet each other not only as equals, but with *equilibrium* as the basis of aligning in our work not only self-interest but the common good as well.

This focus on the common good liberates love from the boundaries of the exchange (if you like this and I do that for you, then I show my love and you have to do this which I like to show you love me) that otherwise we are in danger of entrapping ourselves and love itself into. The focus on the common good liberates us and our love to serve a higher purpose. The common good shifts us beyond a transactional approach to loving which defies the essence of love. Instead, it focuses on our "inter-being" as Thich Nhat Hanh (2015) explains by placing also equanimity as a principle of loving. This point goes beyond considering every being in its "infinite otherness" as Levinas (1972: 49) attests. It is about freeing ourselves and our love not only with acts but with our presence in and for each other's "suffering." This is the basis for a *Higher Love*, discussed next.

Higher Love

By liberating love in ways where our inter-being with and for each other not only elevates our work to serving our vocation – the common good, it presents us with the gift of knowing how to love by liberating love to find expression in multiple ways and often not spoken or enacted in specific gestures. It allows love to be given and received beyond exchange. It is gifted to each other with the knowledge that it may not be reciprocated and in fact may be the very cause of pain and suffering that we may be perforce to endure.

This higher altitude of loving becomes a foundation for the seventh love language what will be termed *Higher Love* to suggest that it is only when one learns to set love and those to whom love is directed to free, that one actually *puts love first* – over their own needs and interests. It would be akin to a "letting be" as much as a "letting go." This means enabling and allowing love to be present, not measured, accounted for or spoken, but sensed in all the invisible ways that it can be experienced and appreciated for the power it has to create hope, harmony, and a healthy way of managing and organizing. This would be the case when the orientation is the service of the "higher purpose" that love represents. This love language is of a higher altitude because it extends beyond boundaries and transcends time and space. It introduces to the power of managing and organizing beyond temporality, the here and now of goal attainment, the commitment to believe that each person has something valuable to give, when given the confidence to believe they can.

Illustrations of this love language can be found in moments when conflict at work is not resolved but allowed to be, accepting that this is an integral part of inter-relating and inter-acting that may or may not foster our inter-being. If we dig deeper into what lies beneath disagreements and the disconnections that these represent, it is not only a matter of competing perspectives and world views, preferences, and personal interests. Conflict at its core is about the stance different parties take in preserving their dignity. As Donna Hicks (2018), expert in international politics, highlights, most wars, other political conflicts (and that includes terrorism) are all expressions of fighting both for what we believe in and what we stand for as we preserve our dignity. Hicks invites leading in organizations, with greater sensitivity to what constitutes dignity. This means including and accepting the other's identity, recognizing and honoring their unique qualities, offering understanding and acknowledgment in who they are and the unique qualities they bring. These are not only testaments of love, but expressions of *sentiments* that preserve dignity and foster also the advancement of humanity.

To understand *Higher Love* is not to limit our focus on acts and symbols of love, but it is to understand love as a life force, a source fueling human dignity. For if as Laura Hillenbrand explains: "Dignity is as essential to human life as water, food, and oxygen," we also then appreciate that "the stubborn retention of it, even in the face of extreme physical hardship, can hold a man's soul in his body long past the point at which the body should have surrendered it." Dignity then can only be fully engaged with if we literally and metaphorically *come to our senses*.

This is not just about engaging all of our senses (seeing, hearing, smelling, touching, and tasting) even if implicated in the love languages discussed in earlier paragraphs. What I seek to draw attention to is returning to the issue of understanding the other and attending to the other as an expression of love. I want to suggest that in order to do so we are compelled and propelled to go beyond reason and emotion in extending our love. Loving is more than sensemaking (Maitlis and Christiansen, 2014). Foresight and hindsight (Sandberg and Tsoukas, 2015) are not sufficient to engage with the dynamic complexities when navigating the unknown. Loving, like living, is a constant leap into the unknown and that couldn't be more relevant to the volatility, uncertainty, complexity and ambiguity (VUCA) conditions that characterize the nature of working life and the challenge for leadership when managing and organizing (Antonacopoulou, 2018a).

This framing extends beyond sensemaking as a cognitive and emotional process. It introduces beyond interpretation (which may be inaccurate in representing the other's reality and truth) the commitment to understanding the other and the love they need and not only how we feel they should be loved by us. Such understanding can be served beyond our sensibility (reason) or sensitivity (emotions), by the *sensations* that underpin the *sentiments* of loving (as a love language). In this respect, the *sensuousness* accounted for in coming to our senses is a *way of knowing* that is in movement and the making of sense is not only guided by the senses, but by the emerging *sensations* formed in the midst of *practicing* (Antonacopoulou, 2018b).

Learning to love and the art of loving in working life is also precisely about practicing loving. Practicing reflects the knowing in movement (as conditions change and new insights are generated) as "deliberate, habitual and spontaneous repetition" (Antonacopoulou, 2008: 224). Practicing is a way of making sense that fosters rehearsing, refining, learning, and changing actions. Practicing is therefore "a leap of faith" (Antonacopoulou and Fuller, 2020) as new possibilities in everyday action are created when connecting what is known with the unknown and unknowable. In short, practicing is a movement, enabling returning to make sense afresh through ways of knowing that are *sensible, sensitive,* and *sentient,* but also enriched with *sentiment*. Practicing accounts for the commitment to learn to love as the other understands and recognizes love in sentiments – felt energy vibrations.

Such practicing is where inter-connectivity/inter-being becomes possible, not least because it extends beyond projections and desirable outcomes founded on probabilities or plausibility (both based on existing knowledge). Instead, I would argue that *Higher Love* is the ultimate call for a leap of faith in the realm of potentiality where no certainty is possible and yet a multiplicity of possibilities are within our reach (even if we can't predetermine how to attain them).

Higher Love signals that a love language that goes beyond words and actions is an endless array of vibrations that constitute a *CORE intelligence (CQ)* (Antonacopoulou, 2019) when learning to love. Reference to *CORE* encapsulates *Centeredness, Oneness, Reflex,* and *Energy* as critical dimensions in what defines who one is and what one does (in their personal and professional identity). Hence, *Higher Love* invites accessing and working from our CORE, to not only provide a safe home for the otherwise vulnerable dignity that defines our identity and need to be loved. It also elevates our work in serving the common good to retain *freedom of choice* embedding *sensuousness – sensibility, sensitivity,* and *sentience* – as integral to managing and organizing.

Illustrations of *Higher Love* are to be found in both personal and professional relationships where disagreement unavoidably becomes a way of negotiating not only our boundaries with the other, but defending our dignity in remaining true to who we are. This must not be confused as self-love only as this is not about being selfish. I will draw again on personal experience and I will place *Higher Love* in the context of workplace toxicity to draw out more clearly how it can serve a vital source of improving managing and organizing.

With nearly 30 years of employment experience I have had more than my fair share of incidents of exclusion, marginalization, humiliation, undermining, or simply put my dignity violated. I choose not to take the position of the victim in analyzing these incidents, but offer these as examples of how mainstream bullying has become in everyday life (and beyond the workplace), almost to the extent that we are at risk of becoming immune to the otherwise indignity epidemic that it fuels, and hence my reference to "humane poverty." The toxicity virus can find expression in more deliberate attempts to cause harm in the psychological injury that is inflicted on those who experience a bully as Field (1996) attests and Hicks (2018) elaborates. This analysis, however, is less about the causes of bullying and the unjustified ways in which organizations and society permit this to become integral to working life, not least because the bystander effect more often than not means that it remains unaddressed when silence prevails (Detert and Edmondson, 2011; Morrison, 2012). Perhaps most disturbing is that more and more passive onlookers of bullying acts and toxic conduct become also perpetrators of the same undignified ways of managing and organizing work. These perpetrators sadly assume their positional power permits them to exercise control without anyone questioning their actions echoed in other experiences and not just mine (Pheko, 2018).

And precisely because I have not been immune to such undignified treatment, by students who I have gone out of my way to support, personally and professionally, in their development; colleagues who I have nurtured and played a critical part in their development and promotion, only to have them shut the door in my face as soon as they assumed power, removing me from committees, taking my work and presenting it as their own. Equally, I have had line managers who have set unrealistic goals, intentionally set me up to fail, by assigning problematic tasks to complete, told me point blank to look for work elsewhere and made malicious allegations against me directed toward not only undermining my professional integrity, but also destroying me professionally and forcing me out of the profession altogether. My working life has been anything but easy and every single moment of rising up in achievement has a trail of pain and suffering in being subjected to treatment that at times has felt inhuman and uncivilized considering the "educated" otherwise place of work I am privileged to be part of and represent.

Mastering the strength to acknowledge these incidents in my professional life is testament to the fact that denying them would be to also undermine their significance in enabling me to reach the level of understanding that this very chapter is founded upon. For I do not promote here CORE intelligence to advocate for intellect. Instead, I promote the growing capacity of becoming more "intelligent" – in touch with our sensations – that lies at the core of being human, the essence of who we are – our dignity. Hence, "core" here is used both to explicate dignity and to ignite curiosity in exploring how to awaken and draw on

CORE intelligence as the – *Centeredness, Oneness, Reflex,* and *Energy* – that marks a "place" (feeling safe being vulnerable – a home – a "good" place) – aligning personhood, practice, and purpose to serve the common good. When we are *centered* with our intuitive instincts, *one* with the ecosystem we are co-creating, *reflexive* in our thoughts and actions and *energized* and *energizing*, this is a state of vibrational awakening. This is a state from which *Higher Love* emanates and flows.

Recognizing abuse and bullying, and it is important to name it and admit that this is what it is and that it is actually happening and its effects are real, is an important aspect of *CORE intelligence*. What such recognition provokes is the scope to also meet the challenge that the impact of bullying presents. Field (1996) outlines many of the costs and consequences of bullying to health, social structures, and finances for all those implicated – victims, perpetrators, their families and communities. None comes out of bullying as a winner (not even the bullies themselves, even if it appears that they might do so initially) (Zawadzki and Jensen, 2020). Life has a way of attributing justice even if the socio-political system and organizational structures that support it remain fundamentally unjust.

Hence, I promote *CORE intelligence* as the state of searching, re-searching, and reflexively critiquing which I see as integral to practicing and inseparable from the use of practical judgment, if one chooses to place the common good as a priority. In this regard, I recognize that even if on the outside my professional life and career may seem to some as unparalleled in growth, achievement and impact (be it the awards and indicators of esteem, and the level of respect and trust earned in the international community professionally and standing in the local communities one actively participates), I might not have grown to be able to understand what *Higher Love* is, let alone conceptualize, theorize, and promote it had it not been for the suffering that bullying and toxicity I have been subjected to provided me the opportunity to learn about. Simply put, I would not have become the human being able to remain human in growing my humanity. I would have not learned what love means, let alone, how to love and better still choose to put love first.

This is why my focus here is to extend beyond the remedies to bullying that many popular books and victims provide that rightly range from cooperation and conciliation through mediation, negotiation, confrontation, and legal action (Field, 1996). I will propose instead to meet bullying with love as I want to show that while love as it is often claimed, may conquer all, it is also the antidote to the pain that only love causes. To paraphrase Mother Teresa's insightful paradox, "*...if you love until it hurts, there can be no more hurt, only more love.*"

Higher Love is that love where the pain endured has no room for vindictiveness and defensiveness and certainly no longer anger or resentment. It leaves only room for gratitude for the learning to love and loving to learn what love is. And this is the purpose that *Higher Love* ultimately is intended to serve. Ironic as this may sound, I choose to meet my bullies with love as I have learned to sit with the pain that violations of dignity cause. I have also learned to listen to the reactions in my body not only the physical ones and they have been many (that called for numerous medical procedures) with little or no physical healing. What the sensations in the language of the body reveal is exactly why I introduced earlier *CORE Intelligence*.

The vibrations and sensations send signals in the body that heighten sensibility, sensitivity, and sentience. This means that the focus shifts beyond mental capacity to engage intellectually with the experience (here I focus on bullying but it is relevant to both positive and other types of negative experiences including trauma) but learning to remain curious and confident to wonder when exercising the essential critique (practical judgment) that defines the freedom to choose how to respond.

CORE Intelligence then is a conscious engagement with experiences when navigating the unknown (and both experiences of loving and dealing with crisis hold a lot of unknowns) to master the art of remaining *centered*, grounded in the moment and fully present. Bullies need love and understanding more than anyone else. Provoking them to see what they are doing can blind them by the ego-driven response and their narcissistic pathologies. Retaining *oneness* with the ecosystem provides sources of restoring balance in the reality that governs the bullying (and that goes for enduring bullying). Maintaining *reflexivity* is critical. It is so easy to fall in the trap of reviewing events in ways that not only one becomes more confused, but blinded by the manipulation. Reflexivity unlike reflection or review of experience extends beyond merely taking another look at one's actions – taken for granted assumptions, emotions, perceptions, and the sociopolitical environment in which one operates in (Cunliffe, 2016). Reflexivity is not just about being critical or skeptical about the meanings that inform actions or the actions themselves (Antonacopoulou 2010). Reflexivity is *in-sight* – a capacity to see deeply within – inside – but also to see in a fresh light/sight over and beyond – a panoramic view, a new gaze. Reflexivity is a way of seeing simultaneously inside (within) and outside (above and beyond) the actions constitutive of one's conduct in relation to that of others and directed toward others (Antonacopoulou, 2019). This is why *reflex* is more than a reaction. It is a measured/informed, responsible response, which also has the potential to energize and be energizing.

Creating the necessary psychological (and where possible the essential physical distance) provides the foundation for healing to emerge in time. It is typical, for example, for disagreements to fuel gossip in the workplace and that fosters marginalization and victimization. Mediation and coaching can facilitate breaking such boundaries and restoring dialogue so that the differences in perspective can be worked when the time is right. In other words, *Higher Love* is not pushing one's love or perspective (love language preference through certain gestures – gifting, appreciation, acts of service, touch, and quality time). Instead, if love is not received the way one needs at any given point in time, or if the love offered does not make the other feel loved (but undermined, used, unvalued), it is more prudent to step back let go of the connection either temporarily (create the necessary distance so as to experience other connections) or permanently. This is because this *Higher Love* guides the appreciation that it is not possible to have the connection necessary to nurture and soothe all parties implicated in this relationship.

Setting love free in this way allows not only for virtuousness but for humanity too. It is recognizing that even if we assume that "love is all we need," the way others need to be loved may not be the way we know how to love them or can love them. This also implies having the courage to let go – move on and move out – of current work relationships and seek other places where to place the love being offered to nurture more healthy connections to be formed. This does not necessarily mean exiting the organization, although that too may be the prudent thing to do. Instead, it is possible to position different parties in different roles that will not demand nor call on them to interact or support each other given the relationship is not nurturing to them personally or the tasks that need to be performed.

Taken together *Free Love* and *Higher Love* offer a foundation for returning to the governing question of this book: *Is love all we need?* I turn to this next as a foundation for inviting an axiological repositioning of the place of love in the workplace and why the future of work invites us to do just that – put love first.

Is Love All We Need? An Axiology of Putting Love First

I have set out in this chapter to explore *Putting Love First* as a governing principle enabling new ways of relating, working, and uniting in serving the common good. I have introduced two additional love languages – *Free Love* and *Higher Love* – to explore this repositioning of love as receiving more prominence in managing and organizing by pondering the question: *What might the impact be if love formed the basis for re-organizing and managing with a difference?* These new love languages seek to highlight that love in organization is not just about love in the workplace. It is about giving love the place it deserves in human affairs in work and beyond so that it is emplaced – positioned – in ways that enable its work to happen. When we put love first, we can be courageous to disagree, strong to admit our capacity to give love in the ways we and the other need and bold in accepting that the love we receive may not be sufficient. *Putting love first* liberates us to remain "human" – a never-ending "work in progress." Our humanity then is about living to learn what is love and how to love. And in this learning and loving we live differently and when we do so, our capacity to organize and manage fosters continuous learning from which our personal and collective growth depend and love in its varied forms can flourish.

What the love languages explored in this chapter also promote is the invitation to understand not only the value of love, but that everything in the ecosystem (not just people, but also plants and animals, and even mundane objects) merits love being extended in the way they are treated. If love is a gift that any act of kindness essentially extends, then it is extended without any expectation or demand. Love is altruistic by nature. It finds us and binds us and grows the version of ourselves that makes us worthy of the other if we chose to love freely, and selflessly.

There is no code for loving, but what the love languages also suggest is that the language of love may find expression in multiple accents, and dialects and "mother tongues" and yet there is no universal grammar that governs it for it is not just spoken for and listened, looked for, and seen. Love touches all of us in ways we have no code to fully comprehend, which is why it invites us to use the eyes of our soul – our CORE intelligence – to come to our senses. It invites us to look beyond the joy and pain when loving and heighten attentiveness to the sensations that guide our ongoing learning and exploration to unite as one, to develop shared interests, to serve the common good. Doing so also energizes us and others to remain reflexive always in search of learning to love more and to love differently, for love too changes.

This is why to comprehend the *axiology* of love is not just to account for true love's elements. Undeniably Thich Nhat Hanh (2015) rightly points to "kindness, compassion, joy and equanimity" as love's elements. These alongside trust, respect, and altruism form essential tenets that accentuate the foundations for love to exist. If we choose to put love first as a place from which we come to meet each other in our workplace interactions and collaborations, then the ways we manage and organize work will not only make work meaningful and fulfilling. It will more likely make that work feel genuinely *interesting*. In the same way I have introduced inter-being as a basis for *Free Love*, I invite us to reconsider what interesting could also mean. For if we accept that which rests between us (*inter-rest* – what rests between two) is the common good, then *philotimo* and *isotimia* can restore the balance, equilibrium that can nurture not only inclusiveness and equanimity, but restore joy in working together to serve our vocation and calling and the higher purpose that work and working are designed to fulfill.

Aiming higher (beyond the bottom line targets, shareholder interests, and short-term productivity goals) elevates work and working beyond the scope for it to be the basis of meeting our life's needs as employees. It can also make working to live and not only living to work a more intelligent way of managing and organizing. This is not only because we recognize each other and our worth and honor our dignity and shared humanity. In doing so, we begin to respond more clearly to the connection between the "*I*" and the "*we/the Other*." The other is an extension of the self, because if who I am provokes enough insecurity and fear for bullying and toxicity to become the norm, then I have a choice to extend my support but I also have a choice to protect myself and honor my dignity. And here lies the essence of axia – the value of love.

An axiology of putting love first is not about valuing love or e-valuating how we extend and receive love. An axiology of love is about the ways we value ourselves, each other and the value we attach to being worthy. Worthiness is more than value (irrespective of measure). Worthiness and the essence of axia is about the honor that defines philotimo and isotimia. Both words hold "timi" – honor at the core. This is to remind us that honoring ourselves and each other in our ecology is the logos (not just the language, but the end, the meaning) of why an axiology is itself a mark of honor life and all that is living.

Higher Love can help us align closer what it means to live and to love. After all, both words have the same foundation but only a letter differs – I and O (L-I-ve and L-O-ve). If in managing and organizing the I and O (me and others) become the connecting forces uniting and driving us to achieve what serves us all well – the common good – then working offers a platform for learning to live and love what we do, do what we do with love and allow for working life to be lived well with love as a critical component elevating our humanity.

Idealistic as this may sound, it also offers an axiology of *Putting Love First*, as an axia – a measure of our worth. In managing and organizing we have ways of measuring growth in size and volume (width and height). We are lacking a *measure for depth* and assessment of *substance*. Hence, if *Putting Love First* was a marker for our depth as human beings presenting ourselves to work with the best possible scope to serve the common good, then we do not need a code or set of rules to guide our conduct. The substance of our humanity is also our moral compass. An axiology of love is an assessment not "measure" of worth and worthiness that the art of loving can be accounted for when present. This transforms our need for love and the question of whether love is all we need into a question of learning. *Can we learn to put love first and engage in such learning in a mode of practicing the art of loving not only informed and in command of its languages, dialects and sensibilities, sensitivities and sentience that it provokes?*

If we ponder on the question, then recognizing the role of love in managing and organizing with a difference becomes a commitment to practicing loving and loving differently shifting our focus beyond questions of love as a need but if we are left wanting of love, what kind of love do we need? As our needs change, so does our love, and as love changes, so does our capacity to love differently and in multiple ways guided by the commitment to put love first. This offers also the basis for loving what we do and doing what we do in the workplace a way of redefining the future of work, by restoring interest and inter-being, isotimia and philotimo as central to working. Doing so invites us to come to work not only for our living but to make our living the place where we also place our love. And as what we do is an expression of the essence of who we are, our dignity, character and CORE intelligence, putting love first as a way of working, this forms a stance – an emplacement – an invitation to explore what becoming love entails (Antonacopoulou, 2018a). This is why perhaps for the first time I can proudly "sign" authorship by revealing that my professional surname – Antonacopoulou – is not what I would best be known by. Those who choose to know me call me "L1."[5] What I offer in this chapter is not just my perspective or position on the subject. This chapter marks my speaking out (free love) and speaking up (higher love), not just as a scholar or an axiologist, but as a human being committed to do the work to become human in the humanity we can cocreate when we put love first.

Acknowledgments

I hold full responsibility for the ideas in this chapter, but remain grateful for the "love" extended to me in the feedback and conversations I had with a number of friends and colleagues, including Jim Walsh, Regina Bento, Woon Gan Soh, Silvana Gaffurini, Isabel Beydag, Dan Parnell, Phil Unworth, and others who will remain anonymous.

My sons – Alexandros and Aristotelis Antonacopoulos – remain my best teachers and critics, helping me learn to love in my penultimate of roles – becoming and being their mother.

Notes

1 Axia here is used to expand the references to principles and virtues to also recognize value as a measurement instrument. Hence, isotimia means equal worth, not only equal value in currency terms. This brings to the fore that central to economy is also axiology and not only the monetary instruments of accounting for value. The value of values is a mark of the kind of human one chooses to be. Such axiology assesses worthiness based on humanity starting from the basis that all human are born equal.

2 Bystander is the unresponsiveness to emergency events or malpractice. Such inaction may be deemed as a mark of indifference (adiaphoria) when events witnessed are not scrutinized as good, evil, or morally relevant.

3 Isotimia (Greek ισοτιμία – ἴσος (isos), "equal" and τιμή (timi) "worth/axia" is introduced here not in the typical treatment of the word in the economic vocabulary to denote the exchange rate of currency. Instead, it draws on the same principles of Isonomia (Greek: ἰσονομία from the Greek ἴσος (isos), "equal" and νόμος nomos, "law" to highlight the importance not only of equivalence and equality but also equilibrium (balance, poise – ισορροπία).

4 *Philotimo* (also spelled *filotimo*; Greek: φιλότιμο) is a Greek word that is without definition, but impacts the world beyond imagination. The word *philotimo* comes from the Greek root words *filos*, meaning "friend," and *timi*, meaning "honor." The meaning of philotimo extends far beyond the words "friend" and "honor," for the "love of honor" is almost impossible to translate sufficiently as it describes a complex array of virtues.

5 L1 has been my nick name in my various coaching engagements where I redefined my work and myself – El-ena – El (sound L) ena (number 1 in Greek) as L1 to mean that the ways I choose to live and work so that I put love first.

References

Aleassa, H., and Megdadi, O. (2014). Workplace bullying and unethical behaviors: A mediating model. *International Journal of Business and Management, 9*(3), 157–169.

Andersen, N. Å., and Born, A. W. (2008). The employee in the sign of love. *Culture and Organization, 14*, 325–343.

Antonacopoulou, E. P. (1997). *A study of interrelationships: The way individual managers learn and adapt and the contribution of training towards this process.* Unpublished PhD Thesis.

Antonacopoulou, E., and Bento, R. (2003). Methods of 'Learning Leadership': Taught and Experiential. 10.13140/2.1.5052.7369.9.

Antonacopoulou, E. P. (2008). On the practise of practice: In-tensions and extensions in the ongoing reconfiguration of practice. In D. Barry and H. Hansen (Eds.), *Handbook of new approaches to organization studies* (pp. 112–131). London: Sage.

Antonacopoulou, E. P. (2010). Making the business school more 'critical': Reflexive critique based on phronesis as a foundation for impact. *British Journal of Management* – Special Issue 'Making the Business School More "Critical" ', *21*(1), 6–25.

Antonacopoulou, E. P. (2018a). Organisational learning for and with VUCA: Learning leadership revisited. *Teoria e Práctice em Administração (Theory and Practice Management Journal* – Leading Brazilian Journal) Special Issue, *8*(2), 10–32.

Antonacopoulou, E. P. (2018b). Energising critique in action and in learning. The GNOSIS 4R framework. *Action Learning: Research and Practice, 15*(2), 102–125.

Antonacopoulou, E. P. (2019). Sensuous learning: What is it and why it matters in addressing the Ineptitude in professional practice. In E. P. Antonacopoulou and S. S. Taylor (Eds.), *Sensuous learning for practical judgment in professional practice: Volume 1: Arts-based methods* (pp. 13–44). London: Palgrave Macmillan.

Antonacopoulou, E. P., and Fuller, T. (2020). Practising entrepreneuring as emplacement: The Impact of sensation and anticipation in entrepreneurial action. *Entrepreneurship and Regional Development Journal, 32*(3–4), 257–280.

Antonacopoulou, E. P. and Gabriel, Y. (2001). Emotion, learning and organisational change: Towards and integration of psychoanalytic and other perspectives. *Journal of Organisational Change Management*, Special Issue on 'Organisational Change and Psychodynamics', *14*(5), 435–451.

Argandoña, A. (2011). Beyond contracts: Love in firms. *Journal of Business Ethics, 99*(1), 77–85.

Barad, K. (2010). Quantum entanglements and hauntological relations of inheritance: Dis/continuities, space time enfoldings, and justice-to-come. *Derrida Today, 3*(2), 240–268.

Barsade, S. G., and O'Neill, O. A. (2014). What's love got to do with it? A longitudinal study of the culture of companionate love and employee and client outcomes in a long-term care setting. *Administrative Science Quarterly*, 59(4), 551–598.

Chapman, G. D. (2010). *The 5 love languages: The secret to love that lasts.* Chicago, IL: Northfield Pub.

Chapman, G. D., and White, P. E. (2012). *The 5 languages of appreciation in the workplace: Empowering organizations by encouraging people.* Chicago, IL: Northfield Pub.

Chapman, G. D., White, P. E., and Myra, H. (2014). *Rising above a toxic workplace: Taking care of yourself in an unhealthy environment.* Chicago, IL: Northfield Pub.

Cunha, M. P., Clegg, R. S., Costa, C., Leite, A. P., Rego, A., Simpson, A. V., Sousa, M. O., and Sousa, M. (2017). *Gemeinschaft* in the midst of *Gesellschaft*? Love as an organizational virtue. *Journal of Management, Spirituality & Religion*, 14(1), 3–21.

Cunha, V., Santos, M.M., Moradas-Ferreira, P., Castro, L.F.C., and Ferreira, M. (2017). Simvastatin modulates gene expression of key receptors in zebrafish embryos. *Journal of Toxicology and Environmental Health. Part A*, 80(9), 465–476.

Cunliffe, A. (2016). On becoming a critically reflexive practitioner redux: what does it mean to be reflexive? *Journal of Management Education*, 40(6), 747–768.

Detert, J. R., and Edmondson, A. C. (2011). Implicit voice theories: Taken-for-granted rules of self-censorship at work. *Academy of Management Journal*, 54(3), 461–488.

Emirbayer, M., and Mische, A. (1998). What is agency? *American Journal of Sociology*, 103, 962–1023.

Field, T. (1996). *Bully in sight: How to predict, resist, challenge and combat workplace bullying – Overcoming the Silence and denial by which abuse thrives.* Wantage: Success Unlimited.

Fukuyama, F. (2019). *Identity: Contemporary identity politics and the struggle for recognition.* London: Profile Books.

Gibran, K., & Rouben Mamoulian Collection (Library of Congress). (1923). The prophet.

Haraway, D. J. (2016). *Staying with the trouble: Making kin in the Chthulucene.* New York, NY: Duke University Press.

Hicks, D. (2018). *Leading with dignity: How to create a culture that brings out the best in people.* London: Yale University Press.

Hlupic, V. (2018). *Humane capital: How to create a management shift to transform performance and profit.* London: Bloomsbury Business.

Levinas, E. (1972). *Totality and infinity.* Dordrecht: Springer.

Lutgen-Sandvik, P., and McDermott, V. (2011). Making sense of supervisory bullying: Perceived powerlessness, empowered possibilities. *Southern Communication Journal*, 76(4), 342–368.

Maitlis, S., and Christianson, M. (2014). Sensemaking in organizations: Taking stock and moving forward. *The Academy of Management Annals*, 8(1), 57–125.

McClatchy, J. D. (2001). *Love speaks its name.* New York, NY: Knopf.

Monzani, L., Braun, S., and van Dick, R. (2016). It takes two to Tango. The interactive effect of authentic leadership and organizational identification on employee silence intentions. *German Journal of Human Resource Management*, 30(3–4), 246–266.

Morrison, E. W. (2012). Employee voice behavior: Integration and directions for future research. *Academy of Management Annals*, 5, 373–412.

Mulder, R., Bos, A. E. R., Pouwelse, M., and van Dan, K. (2017). Workplace mobbing: How the victim's coping behavior influences bystander responses. *The Journal of Social Psychology*, 157(1), 16–29.

Nhat Hanh, T. (2015). *How to love*. Berkeley, CA: Parallaro Press.

Paull, M., Omari, M., and Standen, P. (2012). When is a bystander not a bystander? A typology of the roles of bystanders in workplace bullying. *Asia Pacific Journal of Human Resources*, 50, 351–366.

Pheko, M. M. (2018). Rumors and gossip as tools of social undermining and social dominance in workplace bullying and mobbing practices: A closer look at perceived perpetrator motives. *Journal of Human Behaviour in the Social Environment*, 28(4), 449–465.

Public Health England (PHE). (2021). Inclusive and sustainable economies: Leaving no-one behind. Supporting place-based action to reduce health inequalities and build back better. Report. Available online at: Inclusive and sustainable economies: leaving no-one behind – GOV.UK (www.gov.uk) (Accessed April 2021).

Sandberg, J., and Tsoukas, H. (2015). Making sense of the sensemaking perspective: Its constituents, limitations, and opportunities for further development. *Journal of Organizational Behavior*, 36(1), 6–32.

Ulus, E. (2019). Transferential loss: Unconscious dynamics of love, learning, and grieving. *Academy of Management Learning and Education*, 1–44. doi.org/10.5465/amle.2017.0404

Vanderstukken, A., Van den Broeck, A., and Proost, K. (2016). For love or for money: Intrinsic and extrinsic value congruence in recruitment. *International Journal of Selection and Assessment*, 24(1), 34–41.

Walker, A. (2011). Creativity loves constraints: The paradox of Google's twenty percent time. *Ephemera*, 11(4), 369–386.

White, M., and Mackenzie-Davey, K. (2003). Feeling valued at work? A qualitative study of corporate training consultants. *Career Development International*, 8(5): 228–234.

Williams, J. (2019). The misery of the post-#MeToo workplace: Myths about rampant sexual harassment have led to calls to police everyday interactions. *Spiked*, July. Available online at www.spiked-online.com/2019/07/10/the-misery-of-the-post-metoo-workplace/ (Accessed April 2020).

Zawadzki, M., and Jensen, T. (2020). Bullying and the neoliberal university: A co-authored autoethnography. *Management Learning*, 51(4), 398–413.

10 Socio-Emotional Resources and the Principle of Human Dignity in the Workplace

The Case of Workplace Romance

Coralie Fiori-Khayat

10.1 Introduction

In November 2019, the press reported the dismissal of the then serving McDonald's CEO on the grounds that he had been involved in a romantic relationship with another employee of the company – the fully consensual nature of which was in no way ever disputed. In the United States, the revelation of this relationship caused a scandal. On this side of the Atlantic, the dismissal caused consternation among lawyers. The workplace, of course, is generally acknowledged to be relatively conducive to romantic relationships (Anderson & Fisher, 1991). Historically, a "workplace romance" was defined as "*a relationship between two members of the same organization that is perceived by a third party to be characterized by sexual attraction*" (Quinn 1977, p. 30). Sometime later, this definition evolved to refer to "*mutually desired relationships involving sexual attraction between two employees of the same organization*" (Pierce & Aguinis, 2001, p. 206). In the United States, ten million relationships in the workplace are formed or developed each year (Black et al., 2013, p. 36); in France, about 16% of employees have at some stage become romantically involved with a colleague, according to an Institut français d'opinion publique (IFOP) survey conducted in 2018 (IFOP, 2018). Despite the frequency of this phenomenon, it remains a relatively secretive and taboo subject in both the New World and Europe. It has previously aroused the interest of researchers, but still remains an understudied and neglected area. Generally speaking, when considering the existence of workplace romances, the emphasis is often placed on the perceived organizational risks and difficulties associated with such a relationship, particularly in relation to the reactions of other members within the organization (Alder & Quist, 2014; Biggs et al., 2012; Boyd, 2010; Bradford, Sargent, & Sprague, 1980). Romance, however, can also be the product of a very special relationship between two individuals, which is typically marked by a sense of mutual respect – at least in postmodern societies, where a woman is able to separate from a partner who might be disrespectful to her. Romance, therefore, can be a key factor in the construction and

DOI: 10.4324/9781003254034-11

development of the two involved partners' sense of dignity. Exploring the issue of workplace romances through this concept of human dignity has not previously been attempted – despite the fact that it often represents an integral component of these relationships. Here, we define "love" as a socio-emotional resource, one that forms a part of human dignity. Romance carries a socio-emotional value linked to dignity, which is then confronted with express or implicit rules within an organization, bringing the relationship into conflict with the workplace. Why this tension emerges and how it might be overcome are two questions that have so far, to our knowledge, remained unanswered. This chapter tries to address this oversight. First, we begin by setting out the theoretical background by contextualizing the wider subject of romantic relationships in the workplace and, then, by developing the ethical framework in which they take place. From there, we attempt to expand and develop upon this theoretical model before finally moving toward our concluding remarks, where implications, limitations, and further directions are discussed.

10.2 Theoretical Background

10.2.1 A Taboo Subject but One That Exists in Every Workplace

The existence of romantic relationships in the workplace comes as no surprise to anyone (Burke & McKeen, 1992; Clarke, 2006; Crail, 2006). A significant part of our collective time is spent in the workplace (Pierce, Byrne, & Aguinis, 1996; Worrall & Cooper, 2001) with colleagues, subordinates, superiors, or partners (customers or suppliers). The workplace is a place of sociability and is, therefore, an environment conducive to interpersonal exchanges (Gautier, 2007; Mano & Gabriel, 2006; Pierce, Byrne, & Aguinis, 1996). These exchanges are likely to lead to personal relations (Pinel, Long, Landau, Alexander, & Pyszczynski, 2006; Salvaggio, Hopper, Streich, & Pierce, 2011), whether these are simply friendly in nature or more romantically charged (Anderson & Fisher, 1991; Furnham, 2012; Kakabadse & Kakabadse, 2004; Peak, 1995). Moreover, many cultures are very accepting of love-based relationships in the workplace, attributing such incidences to a force of destiny or to a situation divinely willed (Mano & Gabriel, 2006). In these cases, both society and the organization itself can really only take note of the situation, which is considered as being imposed by an external and superior power – by divinity or providence. As a universal rule, romance cannot in any practical way be banned from the workplace. Quantitative surveys have confirmed this. In France in 2018, 35% of French employees had, or were having, a romantic relationship with a person from their professional environment (IFOP, 2018). This can be compared to more than half of UK employees a decade earlier (Clarke, 2006), or indeed employees of various other nationalities (Kakabadse & Kakabadse, 2004). In France, this proportion rises to 42% for managers, and 14% of employees involved in relationships met their current partner as part of (or during) their professional activities. This makes working together the most frequent means of meeting a potential partner – ahead of dating sites and personal ads or socializing activities (both at 11%) (IFOP, 2018). The quantitative data in the United States is even more remarkable, and clearly demonstrates that having a romantic life in the workplace is a common phenomenon (Burke, 2010; Mainiero & Jones, 2013).

The fact remains, however, that despite how universal it may be, the notion of such personal relationships existing in the workplace is generally viewed quite poorly (Brown & Allgeier, 1995; Burrell, 1984; Dillard, Hale, & Segrin, 1994; Quinn, 1977; Roy, 1974). The desire to regulate romantic relations in the workplace goes back, in concrete terms, to the arrival of women into the labor market when men were off at war (Alder & Quist, 2014). As such, the phenomenon is relatively recent. Historically, the professional and private spheres were clearly separated and had relatively little overlap (Zelizer, 2009). Although new technologies, new ways of working, and an increased level of services being available to employees, in order to help them in their private lives (e.g., concierge services), have led to a seepage of the professional sphere into private life, any movement in the opposite direction tends to be very poorly perceived (Schultz, 2003, 2006). Romantic relationships have been argued to put the organization at risk of an increase in deviant behavior (Anderson & Hunsaker, 1985) and a decline in the professional performance of the individuals concerned (Dillard & Broetzmann, 1989).

Several companies claim to prohibit employee romances for the sake of protecting women from sexual harassment (Mainiero & Jones, 2013). However, the reality may not be quite as clear-cut (Pierce, Aguinis, & Adams, 2000), and it has even been suggested that many organizations are more concerned with avoiding liability if an incidence of harassment be committed against one of their members (Boyd, 2010). This type of prohibition (McDonald & Noble, 2011) seems to mainly concern US companies and their foreign subsidiaries – or, at least, in countries that allow such infringements of fundamental freedoms. Under French law, any clause in an employment contract, or in policies that are applicable to employees, which has, either directly or indirectly, the purpose (or effect) of limiting the rights of employees to have personal relationships (whether friendly, amorous, sexual, extramarital, or otherwise) with each other would be illegal and deemed not fit for purpose. In the United States, where companies do not systematically prohibit relationships between employees (Lickey, Berry, & Whelan-Berry, 2009), most managers believe that any such incidences should be handled on a case-by-case basis (Biggs, 2012). Most of the time, however, workplace relationships are kept secret by the people involved and are only later revealed through gossip (Mano & Gabriel, 2006). This would suggest that the relative taboo pertaining to such relationships is widely acknowledged and keenly felt. Some authors have even gone so far as to compare romantic relationships between colleagues to incest (Mead, 1980) – though this particular interpretation has clearly not aged well (Anderson & Fisher, 1991). One can even speak of a form of self-censorship related to managing perceptions (Snyder, 1974). Knowing themselves to be vulnerable to gossip (Farley, Timme, & Hart, 2010; Kurland & Hope-Pelled, 2000), individuals engaged in a workplace romance might tend toward controlling any displays of mutual attachment in front of their coworkers (Brown & Allgeier, 1996) and even to attempt to demonstrate an increased level of professionalism (Dillard, 1987). However, romantic relationships can introduce disruption into an organization (Mainiero, 1986), even if the individuals involved adopt entirely neutral behaviors when they are in each other's presence at work. The employment relationship is an asymmetrical relationship, marked by a contract in which the employee is subordinate to his or her employer (Mainiero, 1986) – in other words, to the organization and those who run it. Such professional relationships can exhibit varying degrees of cordiality; however, even if these relations are warm, by their very nature they exclude any type of attachment akin to that which presides over a romantic relationship (Brady & Hart, 2006; Burrell, 1984; Ehrhardt & Ragins, 2019; Salvaggio, Hopper, Streich, & Pierce, 2011). When such a romantic relationship emerges within an organization, the lines become blurred (Schultz, 2003; Roy, 1974). As soon as a third party to the couple, another member of the organization, learns of this relationship, a redefinition of roles soon takes place (Brown & Allgeier, 1996) where each half of the couple assumes, in addition to his or her professional capacity, the function of "X's partner." The respective roles of the individuals involved influence the smooth functioning of the group of employees within the organization (Brown & Allgeier, 1996). If the individuals work in separate departments and are not expected to interact professionally on a regular basis, the organization is little affected. The situation is quite different when the two partners work on the same team. In this case, other members of the group may feel a sense of injustice, which is known to lead to negative reactions of anger and retaliation (Barclay, Skarlicki, & Pugh, 2005; Baumert & Schmitt, 2012; Gollwitzer & Denzler, 2009). The situation is worse when a relationship develops between two members of the same department where there is a hierarchical link between them (Jones, 1999; Powell, 2001). Still, the passionate nature of reactions to romantic relationships in the workplace is well established. This lively reaction is, undoubtedly, due to the fact that love is a socio-emotional resource which is exchanged in the workplace.

10.2.2 The Workplace, a Place for the Exchange of Socio-emotional Resources

As a place of socialization and interpersonal exchange, the workplace is the preferred terrain for developing social exchange theory (SET) generally and socio-emotional resource theory in particular.

SET borrows from social psychology (Gouldner, 1960), sociology (Blau, 1964), and anthropology (Emerson, 1976). It has developed significantly over the past 50 years or so. It is rooted in the notion of reciprocity in interactions that lead to interdependent, contingent, and implicit obligations. For Gouldner (1960), the transactional path remains central. Foa and Foa (1974, 1980, 2012), on the other hand, show that symbolic exchanges partially shape relationships in the workplace. According to Foa and Foa, *"the assumption that every transaction, both economic and emotional, follows the same rules"* is misleading, which explains why *"specifying and classifying exactly what is exchanged"* has received little attention (2012, p. 16) because interactions between people do not follow the same pattern as economic exchanges. Socio-emotional resource theory outlines six major classes of resources: love, status, information, money, goods, and services. While the definition of money, goods, and services is conventional and does not call for further explanation, the first three classes all have very specific meanings. Foa and Foa define "love" as *"an expression of affectionate regard, warmth or comfort"*; "status" as *"an evaluative judgement that conveys prestige, regard or esteem"*; and "information" as a category that *"includes advice, opinions, instruction or enlightenment but excludes those behaviors that could be classed as love or status"* (2012, p. 16). Expanding on interpersonal relationships in the workplace, Foa and Foa (2012, p. 19) emphasize two propositions: first, *"interpersonal behavior consists of giving and/or taking away one or more resources"*; and, second, behaviors involving *"allied resources"* are more common than those involving *"less closely related resources."* Love, in this classification, is the resource involving an extremely frequent behavior and is, therefore, a long-term process; this resource is highly particular, highly symbolic, and is, among all resources, the one that brings the highest gain to the giver. In a quantitative analysis, Foa and Foa (2012) showed that 96% of respondents prefer to exchange love for love (rather than love for another resource). The symmetrical nature of the exchange, therefore, presents a universal character.

One criticism that has been leveled at this taxonomy is that it does not seem to take into account moral resources – which Folger (2012) addresses. Moral resources are widely accepted norms whose authority is disconnected from any transactional basis but comes from an authority external to and superior to the parties. Here, the experience that anyone can make of a universal sentiment is likely to run up against sometimes implicit rules, of a moral or regulatory nature (if the organization has prohibited romantic relations between colleagues). We then observe a competition between two types of socio-emotional resources: love and status. The love relationship is likely to jeopardize the position of each member of the couple in the organization, whether the partners are of equal rank or not, whether they work in the same department or not. Gossip, innuendo, and implicit messages can completely undermine a leader's authority or lead to a deleterious atmosphere within the peer group. The establishment of a romantic relationship between colleagues, even if it is secret, therefore carries a high risk of jeopardizing the professional status of both members. The durability of a romantic relationship in such a context therefore presupposes the primacy of love over status. This competition is superimposed on an ethical distortion.

10.2.3 An Ethical Distortion (Rights Ethics vs. Duties Ethics)

Historically, the role of the modern state, born out of the philosophy of the Enlightenment, is to guarantee the right of everyone to, among other things, the pursuit of happiness. In the aftermath of the Second World War, an implicit sharing of responsibilities was established between companies and the State, with the former guaranteeing an improvement in living conditions due to increased wealth. The increase in wealth (which was a burden on companies) and its fair distribution (which was the responsibility of the state) were thereby the basis of a new type of social contract (Cragg, 2000). However, it is often in the name of risk to employee performance (and therefore risk to wealth generation) that organizations try to discourage romantic relationships between colleagues. If there is a social contract, its implementation highlights leonine clauses.

The fact is that the general principles of ethical theories are only an abstract general framework (Smith & Dubbink, 2011). They prove to be relatively disconnected from the concrete situations in which decisions have to be made in real life. These frameworks are rich in ideas, values, notions, but are not recipes for making the right decision – or the least bad one. However, they help organizations to progress in the recognition of their ethical responsibilities, particularly with regard to human rights and fundamental freedoms. It is true that the ethics of rights has progressed in most companies and the most blatant discriminations (based on skin color, philosophical or religious orientation, or even health status) are in principle no longer in existence – or, at least, no longer claimed to be. However, the fact remains that the fundamental freedoms of employees and in particular their right to privacy, including in the workplace, are subject to major limitations, particularly in the United States.

These limitations are sometimes justified by the idea that the employee is accountable to the employer for the proper performance of his or her professional obligations (Werhane, 1983). But what is meant by professional obligations? For a lawyer – or, at least, in continental law – the answer is relatively simple: it is the obligation to perform the duties required by the employer in the manner prescribed by the employer, and to perform them in good faith, with due care and diligence. The prerogatives that the employer derives from the relationship of subordination do not go beyond this; and, more specifically, an employer who attempts to regulate the privacy of its employees would be at fault. Business ethics, however, takes a broader scope and tends to include, in the obligations that the employment contract has created, implied obligations to meet implicit, culturally determined expectations related to the role an individual plays in the workplace. In other words, the role played by the employee is not limited to the performance of his or her tasks, but encompasses culturally and socially established postures, rooted in implicit rules and norms, from social and moral sources (Persson & Hansson, 2003).

For these postures to be acceptable, they must be perceived as fair and just. It is first of all organizational justice (Colquitt, 2001) that is summoned and, within it, interactional justice and, more precisely, interpersonal justice. Interactional justice refers to the fairness and equity of how individuals feel they are treated when implementing procedures and protocols within the organizational framework (Colquitt et al., 2001). Interpersonal justice refers to the level of respect, courtesy and dignity with which the individual is treated by those responsible for implementing organizational procedures and protocols, or in carrying out the results that these procedures and protocols achieve (Greenberg, 1987). However, the sense of justice and fairness in treatment is subjective in two ways. On the one hand, even if there is a common ground that is rooted in a cultural and social construct, perceptions of justice vary from one individual to another and what seems right to one person may not necessarily seem right to another. Thus, Karl and Sutton (2000), in a qualitative survey, show that managerial actions aimed at sanctioning love relationships between employees are perceived, by peers, as legitimate on condition that the professional performance of at least one of the parties involved decreases and, conversely, that managerial abstention is legitimate only on condition that the professional performance of the couple improves. Where none of these conditions are met, it would be legitimate for management to try to discourage romance, without necessarily proceeding with disciplinary proceedings against the persons concerned. This study was conducted in the United States and is rooted in the theory of organizational justice. It shows a strong support among the employees interviewed for a form of interference by management in the private lives of employees, in the name of professional performance. In fact, this reaction shows much more a triumph of utilitarian thinking, in which the general interest is made up of the sum of individual interests. In France, such interference would be worth criminal proceedings against its perpetrator, with the risk of imprisonment, without prejudice to civil actions for damages. The same seems to be true in Germany (Boyd, 2010). If we accept that law is the normative translation of the functioning of a given society at a given time, we can measure the divergences that exist in the two modes of social construction aimed at answering the same question. On the other hand, even in the case of an identity of social construction, the sense of justice or equity varies according to the role assigned to the subject. Thus, what seems "fair" in the eyes of management (e.g., sanctioning both members of the couple) may seem questionable to colleagues (who do not observe a decrease in the professional performance of the individuals concerned) and profoundly unfair to the individuals concerned (who have been careful to exercise absolute discretion in the workplace). This double subjectivity makes it necessary to look for an anchor point, an invariant in variation, which will make it possible to determine the balance between the organization's desire to preserve a framework conducive to work and the equally legitimate desire of employees to seek their happiness.

The ethics of duty, and more particularly the Kantian school, could provide a nuanced response. The categorical imperative (Borowski, 1998), theorized in the *Foundations of the Metaphysics of Morals* (1785), is declined in several formulations. The most famous is found in the second section, §421: "Act only according to the maxim that you may want it to become a universal law." Applied to the question of the possible prohibition of romance between employees, one could conceive that in view of the difficulties that such a situation is likely to engender, a universal law prohibiting relations between employees anywhere in the world would relieve many managers. This project comes up against the second formulation of the same categorical imperative (Arnold & Bowie, 2003), centered on the notion of humanity: "*Act in such a way that you always treat humanity, whether in your own person or in the person of any other, never simply as a means, but always at the same time as an end*" (Kant, 1956, p. 96). For Kant, the human being has the right to be respected and treated with dignity. This right derives directly from the capacity of the human being to behave as a rational being, capable of discernment and therefore able to carry out moral actions. However, the major risk of idyllic behavior in the workplace is not sexual harassment, but the reduced productivity of one or the other member of the couple (Boyd, 2010), as well as an increase (or appearance) of a sense of injustice (Pierce, Karl, & Brey, 2012). In other words, the motive behind the restrictive policies in question is organizational performance, not respect for individuals. Such policies ultimately result in treating the human being not as an end in itself but as a means to serve the organization's development – thereby denying the consubstantial dignity of humanity. Humanity may have been understood as proceeding from a metaphysical dimension (this is the case in Aristotelian thought), but Kanticism sees dignity as a consequence of the rationality of the human being (Dierksmeier, 2015). It is on the basis of his or her ability to think of himself or herself as a rational and free, and therefore a responsible, being that the human being is accorded a dignity that is inherent in his or her humanity (Dierksmeier, 2016). Rationality and dignity are therefore inseparable in Kanticism, as is responsibility. Moreover, proscription policies deal with the life of employees outside the workplace, in the personal sphere, understood in its most intimate aspects. Limiting their free choice of romantic partner, on the grounds of an economic or legal risk for the organization, amounts to treating them as beings deprived of reason. The lack of respect (Arnold, Audi, & Zwolinski, 2010) is undeniable and excludes the possibility of giving a morally binding value to such a rule. Ensuring the healthy growth and development of the organization is perfectly legitimate, but this objective cannot be the basis for a rule with a universal purpose. Put another way, postures may possibly constitute hypothetical imperatives (devoid of binding moral force) but by no means categorical imperatives.

Therefore, it may be asked whether respect for cultural and moral rules should prevail over the pursuit of happiness on the one hand and whether it can justify infringements of the privacy of the persons concerned on the other hand. Such respect presupposes a justification that is all the more solid as it affects fundamental freedoms, in particular the right to private and family life, which is enforceable against all, including employers. The challenge is, therefore, to understand how a specific socio-emotional value (love) being exchanged fits into an organizational ethical framework. If love is part of the sense of human dignity, then how does it form the basis for the measure and the limit, not so much of the relationship, but of its publicity?

10.3 Socio-emotional Exchanges within an Ethical Framework

By combining elements from the literature on workplace relationships and socio-emotional resources with analyses rooted in three major ethical theories, we have developed our model of dignity as a cornerstone of the rights of employees to have their privacy respected – even if their behavior appears, at first glance, to offend morality and logic. Our analyses of ethics and socio-emotional resources show that third parties may act for essentially destructive motives and are likely to make value judgments subject to substantial ideological bias. We discuss our model and related proposals in three parts. In the first part, we consider the circumstances in which the relationship comes to the knowledge of third parties. In the second part, we examine the biases and reactions underlying the judgments made by third-party colleagues about the relationship, and the consequences (usually negative) induced by these judgments, rather than by the relationship itself. In the third, we discuss the organizational effects when one member of the couple moves away from the organization or from the partner.

Before further developing the model, however, two introductory clarifications on the delimitation of its scope of application are sought. The model only covers consensual relationships between adults (thus excluding sexual harassment, sexual assault, rape, and acts on minors in the workplace); it also excludes "one-night stands," which may well never be known to anyone in the workplace. Of course, such relationships may subsequently lead to a deterioration of relations within the teams, especially when they are called upon to work together. More often than not, however, such brief relationships are covered up in the workplace, and the break-up of any relationship occurs too soon to have aroused the suspicions of others.

10.3.1 *How Third-Party Colleagues Learn about the Relationship*

Occasionally, the individuals themselves will communicate the existence of their relationship; but this is rare, according to the existing literature on the subject. This might also be seen as a sign of a serious relationship, one that is intended to last and is formalized in the various circles in which the persons concerned live, including the family and the workplace. Revealing the existence of such a relationship has the value of transparency; and, more often than not, the persons concerned may take it upon themselves to take appropriate precautions – taking care not to work in the same department, for example, especially when there is a difference in hierarchical levels between them. Such an initiative allows the persons concerned to have control over the moment when the disclosure occurs, not to mention the context in which it is revealed, and enables the hierarchy to anticipate any possible consequences – and, if necessary, to take internal action to avoid difficulties. Several authors have observed that when the relationship is serious enough to be announced by the persons concerned, the organizational reaction is generally positive, especially when family values are promoted.

The overwhelming majority of empirical analyses, however, demonstrate that the couple involved tend to keep the relationship private for as long as possible. With the exception of one case, where an employee had revealed her pregnancy by her manager at a company staff party (Mano & Gabriel, 2006), qualitative surveys suggest that couples are generally very discreet. It is most often by chance – by seeing them in their private lives (in restaurants, for example) – that colleagues accidentally discover the existence of a personal relationship. This can then result in a chain of gossip that enables other members of an organization to become aware of a situation they did not previously suspect (Bencsik, Juhasz, & Seben, 2019). This type of process merits a number of observations.

On the one hand, when members of the couple are caught together in an activity outside the workplace and outside working hours, they are by definition operating in the context of their private lives. It can be assumed from the outset that what is private does not concern their employer or their colleagues. It is, therefore, an intrusive action for an individual (a member of the organization) to reveal to third parties (other colleagues) the actions of other members of the organization when committed in an extra-professional context. Assuming that there are restrictive rules imposed within that organization, the question of compliance with established social standards of discretion remains. In the Kantian system, dignity is based on the principle of rationality. Man is dignified because he has an intrinsic capacity to behave rationally – to do what he must – and this rationality gives him access to freedom. However, it is difficult to see how one might behave rationally and freely, and therefore responsibly, whilst being under constant supervision by third parties. Third-party supervision is a sign of infantilization; therefore, when applied to adults, it amounts to a denial of dignity and a challenge to their ability to be free, rational, and responsible beings. Whatever justification may be given by any third party who has taken a direct interest in the relationships of other colleagues, the fact remains that the dignity of the persons concerned has been violated and the actions of this third party are, therefore, morally unconscionable. A similar conclusion can be drawn in reference to theories of organizational justice and, more particularly, those concerning interpersonal justice. There is an element of profound injustice in seeing events and actions that occur and are visible only in the private sphere be brought to public knowledge. It is reasonable to assume that if adults have made their relationship invisible to their colleagues, it is because they intend it to be private – and the intrusion of third parties into that private sphere cannot be argued as just, precisely because the necessary precautions to ensure privacy have been taken.

Furthermore, there are questions as to what motivates an involuntary witness to private events to become the voluntary author of such disclosures to third parties. A workplace is an environment where gossip is common (Ellwardt, Wittek, & Wielers, 2012; Kurland & Hope-Pelled, 2000). Gossip about the private lives of other colleagues is a frequent occurrence. However, it is rare for rumors to spread quickly and widely about fairly trivial matters. For example, if one learns that someone has a particular passion for Schubert's trios, it is unlikely that colleagues will make it a priority topic in front of the coffee machine. On the other hand, secrets about a potential office romance might well whet the appetites of peers. Gossip is a way for the gossiper to establish his or her power (Fiset, Al-Hajj, & Vongas, 2017; Kurland & Hope-Pelled, 2000). This power manifests itself in several ways. First of all, there is the power that is perceived by third parties: whoever is seen to hold valuable information becomes a person of considerable interest. In this case, such gossip makes it possible to better understand the interplay of alliances, rivalries, and power relations that exist within a team, a department, or an organization – given that it is reasonable to assume that the two members of the couple are allies in intra-organizational power relations (Xie, Huang, Wang, & Shen, 2020). Being privy to this information makes it possible, if necessary, for a third party to pass on messages through the partner of the intended recipient of a communication – that is to say, through an unofficial channel. Both the romantic and sexual dimensions of interpersonal relations have been known to make organizations uncomfortable: in these circumstances, a form of transgressive curiosity might arise within an organization, which is further amplified when there is an internal desire for a secretive relationship to be revealed. The gossiper can, therefore, significantly expand his or her network of potential supporters (Farley, Timme, & Hart, 2010; Kurland & Hope-Pelled, 2000). Power might also be exercised over the members of the couple through innuendoes or thinly veiled threats, particularly when a relationship is perceived as very high risk due to it being adulterous (Wilson, 2015) or homosexual in nature

(Bowring & Brewis, 2009; Powell & Foley, 1998; Rumens, 2008). This is very close to an implicit form of blackmail or harassment. The third party may even intend to monetize his or her silence – or, at least, discretion – by using the threat of disclosure as a retaliatory tool or as a means of asserting his or her power. In this case, the third party is intruding into the symmetrical exchange of love (understood as a socio-emotional value) between the two members of the couple. This individual is seeking "status" (in the sense of Foa & Foa, 1980), whether in the form of more power, a promotion, or higher consideration. Their interference is disruptive in that it introduces a transactional dimension (status vs. discretion) into a private relationship. Whatever the consequences on the couple's relationship, this intrusion causes a deterioration of intra-organizational relations.

We can, therefore, make the following proposals:

> *Proposition #1a: Insofar as the persons concerned announce the existence of their relationship themselves, leading to its formalization within the organization, this relationship is perceived as serious enough for them to draw the relevant organizational consequences and the reaction within the organization is generally positive overall, which preserves the dignity of the members of the organization (persons concerned and colleagues).*

> *Proposal #1b: Insofar as the persons concerned have shown their affection for each other in their private lives and outside the place and hours of work, any disclosure of this element by third parties, incidental witnesses, violates the dignity of the lovers.*

> *Proposition #1c: To the extent that the witness communicates these facts, which are part of the privacy of others, intra-organizational relationships deteriorate.*

> *Proposition #2a: The third-party witness who spreads rumors about the affair acts to increase his or her intra-organizational power over other third parties, who are fond of rumors, in order to build a network of allies in the context of actual or potential power struggles.*

> *Proposition #2b: The third-party witness who spreads rumors about the affair acts by letting implicit threats of blackmail hang over the lovers.*

3.2 Peer Judgments and Their Consequences on Intra-organizational Relationships

Sometimes the organizational response to a workplace relationship is neutral or even benevolent. Several factors may explain this attitude: the organizational context and the type of profession practiced may lead to a more liberal attitude toward privacy. The relative youth of the members of the organization or when the consequences for the proper functioning of the organization are limited or nonexistent (e.g., because the two persons concerned work in different departments, there is no conflict of interest or risk of favoritism) may have a similar effect. In such cases, the dignity of all is preserved and there are no difficulties.

The publicity given to the relationship (without the knowledge of the principal parties involved) is the direct cause of the judgments, most often negative, made by peers toward their colleagues involved (Pinel, Long, Landau, Alexander, & Pyszczynski, 2006; Salvaggio, Hopper, Streich, & Pierce, 2011). Peers are most often informed by rumors in the hallway and then subsequently pay more attention to acts and behaviors that they would otherwise not have noticed. Some authors (Anderson & Hunsaker, 1985; Quinn, 1977; Mainiero, 1986) indicate that peers are particularly attentive to the time spent in discussions (possibly behind closed doors) between the two partners, the duration of their lunch breaks, and even their comings and goings outside the workplace and working hours. Such curiosity evidences a form of suspicion toward the behavior of their colleagues. The judgment is, therefore, tainted by an implicit and perhaps even unconscious pejorative dimension. An attempt has been made to identify the reasons for the emergence of a relationship between colleagues (Anderson & Fisher, 1991; Anderson & Hunsaker, 1985). It is striking, however, that third parties are asked to comment on the reasons why two other people are in an intimate relationship (Brown & Allgeier, 1996; Dillard & Broetzmann, 1989). This is an aporetic quest. Even two lovers might not be able to explain the reasons for their romantic involvement any better than Michel de Montaigne did about Joachim du Bellay: "If I am urged to say why I loved him, I feel that it can only be expressed by answering: 'Because it was him, because it was me'" (Montaigne (de), 1595, reprinted 2019) (I, 28). Third parties can, therefore, only have a fragmented and prejudiced view, influenced by their bias, of the underlying motives. The authors of various empirical analyses on this subject observe one consistent element: the disapproval that is attached to such a relationship (Dillard, 1987) (Dillard, Hale, & Segrin, 1994). Women are often considered to be seeking professional gratification, such as a promotion (Ford & McLaughlin, 1987; Swartz, Warfield, & Wood, 1987; Jones, 1999; Quinn, 1977). As such, women are often assigned the role of seductresses, who attract men more through their physical appearance than by their professional aptitudes (Bradford, Sargent, & Sprague, 1980), or viewed as individuals who pursue strategic objectives (Baskerville-Watkins, Smith, & Aquino, 2013). Other studies suggest that a woman who is emotionally involved with one of her colleagues can sometimes be the victim of social conditioning; can sometimes be a person primarily concerned with ensuring a certain standard of living for themselves by marrying their boss; can sometimes even be a vengeful woman, who is ready to stand up against an unequal system and will seize their chance to do so by any means possible (Backhouse & Cohen, 1978). The first two possibilities envisaged by Backhouse and Cohen are, in fact, components of the same paternalistic social determinism. A woman, assigned to the role of good wife, good mother, and good colleague, is also expected to marry a good partner; and, for the proponents of this conception, marrying one's boss is certainly a means of social fulfillment. All these analyses have one thing in common: they implicitly or explicitly deny women their status as human beings, denying them their dignity and burdening them with all the evils of the world (Riach & Wilson, 2007). Indeed, if women act under the yoke of social determinism, they do not behave as rational beings capable of choosing and assuming the consequences of their decisions – in other words, as free and dignified beings. The subjection to determinism, which seems to be an important explanatory factor for some authors, is nothing more than a negation of women's free will, because she is a woman. Similarly, if the woman supposedly acts in order to obtain professional favors, in other words engages in an asymmetrical "love for status" type of exchange, she is effectively assigned the role of a prostitute. Under these conditions, the professional successes that concern this woman (and, to a lesser extent, the man) are attributed more to the relationship she is having rather than to her professional skills.

Reprobation increases when there is a hierarchical element in the relationship (Jones, 1999; Powell, 2001). Peers who are equal to the lowest ranked partner in the hierarchy tend to perceive, rightly or wrongly, a strong sense of unfairness and mistrust. As a result, peers may tend to seek blame for the injustice they feel. However, the way in which responsibility is assigned by those who witness or, *a fortiori*, are victims of a sense of injustice generally influences their reactions to negative events that occur within the organization (Kent & Martinko, 1995; Weiner, 1985; 1995). They attribute their feeling of injustice to the workplace romance itself, and, therefore, to a voluntary and potentially long-lasting act: as a socio-emotional resource, love is built over time and has the highest and most lasting frequency of exchange (Foa & Foa, 2012). Tolerance of a perceived injustice tends to be low when the victim considers that the perpetrator acted deliberately and that the cause of the behavior is a desire for stability – because such behavior is, in principle, intended to last (Martinko & Zellar, 1998). Moreover, if peers consider that they are being harmed as a result of an existing relationship, they logically infer that they are being confronted with a breach of either explicit rules (in the case of a restrictive internal policy) or implicit moral norms. In both cases, it is an internal fault of the organization and, more specifically, of two of its members. And in cases where an intra-organizational transgression is sensed, the virulence of any reaction to an alleged or proven injustice is increased (Cohen, 1982; Greenberg, 1984; Martinko, Gundlach, & Douglas, 2002). It does not matter, therefore, that this notion of injustice is only felt, nor even that it is only perceived after the fact. A sense of rage becomes the default emotional response of peers who themselves feel aggrieved. In the dyadic relationship between the two lovers (symmetrical exchange of love), a negative correlate (hatred) emerges in a disruptive way, carried by peers outside the relationship (Paetzold, Dipboye, & Elsbach, 2008). Similarly, a negative correlate of "status" in the sense of Foa and Foa (1980; 2012) emerges, which can deprive people of their dignity through a denial of their status. Gossip and innuendo are well documented in the literature, where they are mainly targeted at women, who are then assigned the role of seductresses (Bradford, Sargent, & Sprague, 1980). Their reputation is at stake and the repercussions on their career can be very negative (Teo et al., 2012). High levels of disapproval can also lead to less professional engagement – although other emotional factors may come into play – in that involvement in the romantic relationship can reduce the work rate of the person concerned (Shuck et al., 2016). It is certainly legitimate to question the injustice that can result from a romantic relationship between two colleagues, especially when one of them occupies a hierarchically important position. It is tempting to see a promotion or recognition for the lowest lover in the hierarchy as a reward for extra-professional performance. However, it should be noted that very strong friendships can exist, without a sexual dimension, between two people of different hierarchical rank (Ehrhardt & Ragins, 2019). Such relationships can lead to judgments and assessments that are distorted, at least in part, by this friendship – or, at least, third parties might imagine so. But unless one conceives of an organization that is entirely deprived of any emotion, in other words an organization that is totally dehumanized, it seems impossible to prohibit two members of an organization from maintaining intense, regular, and lasting exchanges of socio-emotional resources. A manager's respect for the professional skills of one of his subordinates can be extremely strong and lasting: in such a case, the socio-emotional resource mobilized is status, more than love, but the result remains the same. The person concerned may benefit from being rewarded in such cases, which arouses the jealousy of their peers. It is striking to note that the stigma of preferential treatment will commonly be thrown at the individual who is promoted or rewarded because of any recognized romantic relationships (Bradford, Sargent, & Sprague, 1980; Dillard, Hale, & Segrin, 1994; Jones, 1999). Though this does not appear to be the case for individuals who, through his or her interpersonal skills or qualities as a diplomat, will have been able to get into the good books of the hierarchy.

We can, therefore, make the following proposals:

> *Proposal #3a: Insofar as the organizational climate does not condemn and may even welcome liaisons between colleagues, and as long as a romantic relationship does not create favoritism or conflict of interest, such relationships receive neutral or benevolent reactions, capable of safeguarding everyone's dignity.*

Proposal #3b: Insofar as the lovers had not spoken about their relationship within the organization, it is the publicity made by third parties that is the cause of the judgments made by the other members of the organization.

Proposal #3c: Peers make negative judgments about the motivations behind the relationship, reducing the woman to the role of seductress and denying her dignity.

Proposal #3d: When there is an element of organizational verticality in the relationship, the peer reaction is even stronger. A strong sense of unfairness is experienced, even if it is not factually objectified. These reactions can result in the deprivation of dignity by denying them their professional status and skills.

10.3.3 The Organizational Effects of Separation on One of the Two Members of the Couple

Failed workplace romances can be found in two types of scenarios (which are not exclusive): one of the two members may choose to end the relationship (Horan, Cowan, & Carber, 2019), or he/she might leave the organization. The termination of the relationship may occur at the behest of one of the two members. In such cases, the major risk for peers is that the workplace itself may become a stage for ensuing arguments, which might jeopardize the dignity of not only the former lovers but also other members of the organization, who may be witnesses to disputes or even encouraged to take sides in any conflict (Verhoef & Terblanche, 2015). This presents a major organizational risk, for which the main countermeasure is typically the call for a sense of responsibility. Some people may leave the organization or request a transfer to a distant location. For example, in one case where an employee announced her pregnancy, which had resulted from her relationship with a particular colleague, at a party organized by the company, she subsequently discovered that this colleague was also involved with other employees in the same team. The employee, a foreign national, asked to be repatriated to the head office in her home country (Mano & Gabriel, 2006).

The situation becomes much more complicated when the organization intends to end the relationship by relocating one of the parties to a distant geographic area (Horan, Cowan, & Carber, 2019). Normally, mobility clauses in employment contracts give the employer very broad powers. However, there are limitations: on one hand, the infringement of private and family life and, on the other hand, the abuse of rights. The right to private and family life is constitutionally guaranteed in France, and conventionally guaranteed in the Council of Europe member states. In the United States, it is guaranteed by the US Constitution. It is, therefore, a universal human right, enforceable by the employee against their employer. However, this does presuppose that the employee has made his or her relationship public to their superiors – something which is not always necessary, particularly when the relationship is potentially scandalous (Bowring & Brewis, 2009; Rumens, 2008), perhaps because of its adulterous or homosexual nature. The process of transferring one of the members can be seen as a means of organizational pressure. This type of approach clearly constitutes an infringement on the right to private and family life, and it denies dignity to the employees concerned. They are faced with a dilemma: to accept the transfer and forcibly end their relationship, or to refuse the transfer and leave the organization. It may also be the case that, from a legal standpoint, enforced transfers may be challenged on the grounds of being disproportionate and unnecessary. The intention may be to increase organizational performance, but such transfers may also be designed to put an end to a situation that is perceived to be detrimental to the proper functioning of the organization. Therefore, it can be questioned whether the underlying intentions behind these transfers justify the measures under consideration, especially when a transfer to another department or to a closer location (not involving a change of residence) is possible. Such a solution should only be reserved for extreme situations, when favoritism for the partner is blatant and detrimental to the functioning of the group. It should not merely be the consequence of any irritation felt by peers, or a form of jealousy on the part of other colleagues. It is, therefore, important that the facts are properly documented and that any decision taken, for example, as part of a sanction for managerial misconduct, follows the rules applicable to disciplinary proceedings, without the emotional context intervening. In other words, the question is whether a member of the organization has been undeservedly benefitted, in a professional sense, by virtue of a private relationship at the expense of other more deserving colleagues. In such a sensitive context, objectivity and factual documentation must be particularly high, lest it would open the door not only to litigation but also to a form of arbitrariness and organizational censorship. However, when the relationship leads to a tension in intra-organizational relations, the most frequent reaction is to dismiss one of the partners. It has been established in critical studies on the subject that dismissal mainly affects the lowest hierarchical member. In practice, this is generally the woman. This means that women lose out on both a professional and a personal level, especially when the emotional investment of the man is shown to have been limited. Moreover, the decision to terminate an individual's employment on account of a now dissolved private relationship poses an undeniable problem in terms of justice and dignity. As far as organizational justice is concerned, regardless of whether a relationship has irritated certain third parties, the decision to terminate a person's employment effectively represents a form of banishment from the organization. It is not always clear whether the ban is proportionate to the harm (actual or alleged) caused to the proper functioning of the organization. Moreover, the virulence of peer reaction, and the resulting deterioration of professional relationships, is most often linked to a sense of injustice, especially when the lowest ranking partner receives a professional reward that is considered undeserved by his or her peers. By definition, however, any reward has been decided upon by that individual's superiors – albeit for reasons unrelated to the individual's competence. Sanctioning the latter, *a fortiori* by dismissal, does not seem logical: while it is true that the person concerned has benefited from a professional reward without necessarily deserving to do so, the fault lies with those responsible for the decision (who cannot be the beneficiary). This person is usually high-up enough in the organizational hierarchy to avoid any sanction. In such cases, the sanction taken constitutes a violation of the status (in the sense of Foa & Foa, 2012) of the person concerned. By banning him or her from the organization, his or her dignity and humanity have been violated (Binnin & Huo, 2012).

It is impossible, however, to predict the impact of organizational decisions on emotional relationships. Although the majority of peers consider the motivations for such a relationship to be unglamorous since between one-quarter and half of these relationships end in marriage (Furnham, 2012) – that is to say, the relationship itself is the realization of a desire to start a family. We can, therefore, only call on organizations to exercise the utmost caution and moderation when sanctions are envisaged in connection with the discovery or development of an emotional relationship between two colleagues.

We can, therefore, make the following proposals:

Proposal #4a: The risk of personal conflict related to separation spilling over into the professional sphere is an important explanatory factor for restrictive policies on romantic relationships between colleagues.

Proposal #4b: Insofar as the separation is conflictual, the departure of one of the parties (outside the organization or to another geographically distinct site) at their own request is one of the solutions to be favored. Conversely, the hierarchical decision to separate the couple (through transfer or dismissal), apart from a separation on their own initiative, constitutes an attack on the dignity of the persons involved.

Proposal #4c: The sanctions in the case of an affair between colleagues generally target the lowest person in the hierarchy, most often the woman, even when the person concerned is not directly at fault for securing a questionable promotion.

Proposition #4d: Neither the organization's reaction nor the pejorative judgments of colleagues can predict the future of a relationship between colleagues, which has a success rate equivalent to that of any other relationship between adults.

10.4 Implications, Limitations, and Directions

Although it is beginning to arouse the interest of researchers, the subject of romantic relationships within the workplace remains an underexplored area of scholarship. Neither ethical issues nor the influence of socio-emotional resources as an explanatory framework has, until now, been the subject of any conceptual study. A major contribution made by this chapter is to demonstrate that the violation of the dignity of the persons concerned, by the intervention of third-party witnesses (most often in the form of gossip), is a more disruptive element than the liaison itself – even and especially in the presence of restrictive policies. Our framework also explains why the discovery of a romantic relationship between colleagues is likely to trigger reprisals and value judgments based on *a posteriori* constructs. Therefore, we hope to have contributed to the existing literature by showing how and why the notion of dignity and its inscription in organizational justice are misused by both peers and even the hierarchy in the context of power struggles. Our analysis also contributes to the existing scholarly literature by demonstrating how reprisals and value judgments can be emotionally motivated. These reactions are influenced at the intrapersonal level, according to the feelings and emotions that peers and leaders tend to exhibit. We have integrated the results of previous studies within our framework, which is rooted in the notion of human dignity. The tension between dignity and power can be fundamental in explaining the sequence of reprisals against lovers in the workplace, and the framework utilized must account for these dynamics. By showing the interaction between socio-emotional resources, dignity, and organizational justice, we hope to have provided a useful tool for future research.

Why do third parties tend to express their opinions on private matters that are none of their business? We establish that they act within the dynamic of a power struggle, using gossip as a means of outreach (to third parties) or blackmail (to those concerned). Organizational justice, utilized to denounce the injustices that might result from any affair, serves as a convenient ideological pretext to discredit certain peers, especially if they belong to minority groups: women, visible minorities, and lesbian, gay, bisexual, transgender, and questioning (LGBTQ). We establish that the value judgments made result in denying one of the members of the couple (most often the woman) her professional status and, under these conditions, her dignity.

Like any theoretical framework, our model needs to be substantiated with empirical studies. It would be interesting, for example, to compare the value judgments made by third parties about lovers according to their gender and their possible minority status, using a critical and intersectional approach. Another avenue could be to analyze the feelings and reactions of the main parties involved: curiously, it is mainly third parties to the relationship that are asked for their opinions on the reasons why a workplace relationship may have blossomed, how it then developed, and what organizational consequences it brought about. The lovers themselves have generally been cast in an unseemly role – especially in the case of unconventional relationships and specifically when there is the possibility of adultery and/or hierarchical verticality. This is not to suggest, however, that these would be uninteresting areas to explore. Data collection can be complex: it would be advisable to give preference to qualitative interviews while ensuring strict anonymity.

Another possible direction for future research could be to integrate this framework into the study of humanistic management. Since human dignity is the very foundation of this school of thought, how is this particular value utilized when a romantic relationship is discovered, especially when it is deemed as unconventional? To what extent would leaders give precedence to human dignity and the right to privacy?

10.5 Conclusion

Previous research on relationships in the workplace has tended to focus on its negative aspects, most often consigning women to the role of seductresses. Here, we have integrated the existing academic literature within a framework based on socio-emotional resources, organizational justice, and the notion of dignity, which helps us understand the tension between two antagonistic imperatives: organizational well-being and the right of each individual to have their life choices preserved and respected. We have shown how a fuller delineation of these issues allows us to better understand the struggle against social stereotypes and, as such, contributes to current scholarly debate. We have analyzed how the concept of dignity, sometimes used to justify retaliations against colleagues who are found to be in love, is in fact misused, as most disclosures usually result from an invasion of an individual's privacy, thereby demonstrating that it is not necessarily the couple themselves who should be accused of a lack of dignity.

Throughout this chapter, we have put the existing literature and our own framework into perspective. Its conceptual elements have yet to be confirmed with empirical examples from real life. Qualitative studies on couples working in the same company could provide a better understanding of this complex managerial reality.

References

Alder, S., & Quist, D. (2014). Rethinking love at the office: Antecedents and consequences of coworker evaluations of workplace romances. *Human Resource Management*, 53(3), 329–351.

Anderson, C., & Fisher, C. (1991). Male–female relationships in the workplace: Perceived motivations in office romance. *Sex Roles*, 25, 163–180.

Anderson, C., & Hunsaker, P. (1985). Why there's romancing at the office and why it's everybody's problem. *Personnel*, 62(2), 57–64.

Arnold, D., Audi, R., & Zwolinski, M. (2010). Recent work in ethical theory and its implications for business ethics. *Business Ethics Quaterly, 20*(4), 559–581.

Arnold, D., & Bowie, N. (2003). Sweatshops and respect for persons. *Business Ethics Quaterly, 13*(2), 221–242.

Backhouse, C., & Cohen, L. (1978). *The secret oppression: Sexual harassment of working women.* Canada, Toronto: The MacMillan Company.

Barclay, L., Skarlicki, D., & Pugh, S. (2005). Exploring the role of emotions in injustice perceptions and retaliations. *Journal of Applied Psychology, 90,* 629–643.

Baskerville-Watkins, M., Smith, A., & Aquino, K. (2013). The use and consequences of strategic sexual performances. *Academy of Management Perspectives, 27*(3), 173–186.

Baumert, A., & Schmitt, M. (2012). Some hypotheses on cross-cultural differences in the impact of resource type on the preferred principle of distributive justice. In Dans K. Törnblom, & A. Kazemi (Eds.), *Social resource theory* (pp. 273–281). New York, NY: Springer.

Bencsik, A., Juhasz, T., & Seben, Z. (2019). The importance of informal knowledge sharing (workplace gossip) in organisations. *38th International scientific conference on economic and social development* (pp. 46–57). Varadzin, HR: VADEA.

Biggs, D.M., Matthewman, L., & Fultz, C. (2012). Romantic relationships in organizational settings. *Gender in Management: An International Journal, 27*(4), 271–285.

Binnin, K., & Huo, Y. (2012). Understanding status as a social resource. In Dans K. Törnblom, & A. Kazemi (Eds.), *Social resource theory* (pp. 133–148). New York, NY: Springer.

Blau, P. (1964). *Exchange and power in social life.* New York, NY: Wiley.

Black, D.A., Kolesnikova, N., Sanders, S.G. and Taylor, L.J. (2013). Are children "Normal"?. *The Review of Economics and Statistics, 95*(1), 21–33. doi: https://doi.org/10.1162/REST_a_00257.

Borowski, P. (1998). Manager–employee relationships: Guided by Kant's categorical imperative or by Dilbert's business principle. *Journal of Business Ethics, 17,* 1623–1632.

Bowring, M., & Brewis, J. (2009). Truth and consequences: Managing lesbian and gay identity in the Canadian workplace. *Equal Opportunities International, 28,* 361–377.

Boyd, C. (2010). The debate over the prohibition of romance in the workplace. *Journal of Business Ethics, 97,* 325–338.

Bradford, D., Sargent, A., & Sprague, M. (1980). The executive man and woman: The issue of sexuality. In D. Neugarten, & J. Shafritz (Eds.), *Sexuality in organizations.* Oak Park, IL: Moore Publishing Company.

Brady, F., & Hart, D. (2006). An aesthetic theory of conflict in administrative ethics. *Administration & Society, 38*(1), 113–134.

Brown, T., & Allgeier, E. (1995). Managers' perceptions of workplace romances: An interview study. *Journal of Business and Psychology, 10*(2), 169–176.

Brown, T., & Allgeier, E. (1996). The impact of participants characteristics, perceived motives and job-behaviors on co-workers' evaluations of workplace romances. *Journal of Applied Social Psychology, 26*(7), 577–595.

Burke, R. (2010). Psychologically intimate, romantic and sexually intimate relationships in the workplace. In Dans R. Burke, & C. Cooper (Eds.), *Risky business: Psychological, physical and financial costs of high risk behaviour in organizations* (pp. 205–238). Farnham, UK: Gower Publishing Limited.

Burke, R., & McKeen, C. (1992). Social-sexual behaviours at work: Experiences of managerial and professional women. *Women in Management Review, 7*, 22–31.

Burrell, G. (1984). Sex and organizational analysis. *Organization Studies, 5*(2), 97–118.

Clarke, L. (2006). Sexual relationships and sexual conduct in the workplace. *Legal Studies, 26*, 47–368.

Cohen, R. (1982). Perceiving Justice: An attributional perspective. In Dans J. Greenberg, & R. Cohen (Eds.), *Equity and justice in social behavior* (pp. 119–160). New York, NY: Academic Press.

Colquitt, J. (2001). On the dimensionality of organizational justice: A construct validation of a measure. *Journal of Applied Psychology, 86*(3), 386–400.

Colquitt, J., Conlon, D., Wesson, D., Porter, C., & Ng, K. (2001). Justice at the millennium: A meta-analytic review of 25 years of organizational justice research. *Journal of Applied Psychology, 86*(3), 425–445.

Cragg, W. (2000). Human rights and business ethics: Fashioning a new social contract. *Journal of Business Ethics, 27*, 205–214.

Crail, M. (2006, July 25). Rise in workplace liaisons no longer a danger. *Personnel Today*, p. 51.

Dierksmeier, C. (2015). Human dignity and the business of business. *Human Systems Management, 34*, 33–42.

Dierksmeier, C. (2016). What is 'humanistic' about humanistic management? *Humanistic Management Journal, 1*, 9–32.

Dillard, J. (1987). Close relationships at work: Perceptions of the motives and performance of relational participants. *Journal of Social and Personal Relationships, 4*, 179–193.

Dillard, J., & Broetzmann, S. (1989). Romantic relationships at work: Perceived changes in job-related behaviors as a function of participant's motive, partner's motive, and gender. *Journal of Applied Social Psychology, 19*, 93–110.

Dillard, J., Hale, J., & Segrin, C. (1994). Close relationships in task environments: Perceptions of relational types, illicitness, and power. *Management Communication Quaterly, 7*, 227–255.

Ehrhardt, K., & Ragins, B. (2019). Relational attachment at work: A complementary fit perspective on the role of relationships in organizational life. *Academy of Management Journal, 62*(1), 248–282.

Ellwardt, L., Wittek, R., & Wielers, R. (2012). Talking about the boss: Effects of generalized and interpersonal trust on workplace gossip. *Group & Organization Management, 37*(4), 521–549.

Emerson, R. (1976). Social exchange theory. *Annual Review of Sociology, 2*, 335–362.

Farley, S., Timme, D., & Hart, J. (2010). On coffee talk and break-room chatter: Perception of women who gossip in the workplace. *Journal of Social Psychology, 150*(4), 361–368.

Fiset, J., Al-Hajj, R., & Vongas, J. (2017, September). Workplace ostracism through the lens of power. *Frontiers in Psychology*, 1528.

Foa, E., & Foa, U. (2012). Resource theory of social exchange. In Dans K. Törnblom, & A. Kazemi (Eds.), *Social resource theory* (pp. 15–32). New York, NY: Springer.

Foa, U., & Foa, E. (1974). *Societal structures of the mind*. Springfield: Charles C. Thomas.

Foa, U., & Foa, E. (1980). Resource theory: Interpersonal behavior as exchange. In Dans K. Gergen, M. Greenberg, & R. Willis (Eds.), *Social EXCHANGE: Advance in theory and research*. New York, NY: Plenum.

Folger, R. (2012). Moral RESOURCES. In K. Törnblom, & A. Kazemi (Eds.), *Social resource theory* (pp. 149–160). New York, NY: Springer.

Ford, R., & McLaughlin, F. (1987, October). Should Cupid come to the workplace? An ASPA survey. *Personnel Administrator*, 100–110.

Furnham, A. (2012, Feb 12). On your head: Don't be surprised to find cupid among the cubicles. *The Sunday Times*. Récupéré sur www.thesundaytimes. co.uk/sto/public/Appointments/article870552.ece.

Gautier, C. (2007, 1st quarter). Managing romance in the workplace. *Journal of Employee Assistance*, 7–9.

Gollwitzer, M., & Denzler, M. (2009). What makes revenge so sweet: Seeing the offender suffer or delivering a message? *Journal of Experimental Social Psychology*, *45*, 840–844.

Gouldner, A. (1960). The norm of reciprocity: A preliminary statement. *American Sociological Review*, *25*, 161–178.

Greenberg, J. (1984). On the apocryphal nature of inequity distress. In Dans R. Folger (Ed.), *The sense of injustice* (pp. 167–188). New York, NY: Plenum.

Greenberg, J. (1987). A taxonomy of organizational justice theories. *Academy of Management Review*, *12*(1), 9–22.

Horan, S., Cowan, R., & Carber, E. (2019). Spillover effects: Communication involved with dissolved workplace romances. *Communication Studies*, *70*(5), 564–581.

IFOP. (2018). Retrieved from https://www.ifop.com/en/#.

Jones, G. (1999). Hierarchical workplace romance: An experimental examination of team member perception. *Journal of Organizational Behavior*, *20*, 1057–1072.

Kakabadse, N., & Kakabadse, A. (2004). *Intimacy: International survey of the sex lives of people at work*. Basingstoke: Palgrave.

Kant, I. (1956). *Groundwork of the metaphysic of morals* (Trans. H. J. Paton). New York, NY: Harper & Row Publishers.

Karl, K., & Sutton, C. (2000). An examination of the perceived fairness of workplace romance policies. *Journal of Business and Psychology*, *14*(3), 429–442.

Kent, R., & Martinko, M. (1995). The development and evaluation of a scale to measure organizational attribution style. In Dans M. Martinko (Ed.), *Attribution theory: An organizational perspective* (pp. 53–75). Delray Beach, FL: St Lucie Press.

Kurland, N., & Hope-Pelled, L. (2000). Passing the word: Toward a model of gossip and power in the workplace. *Academy of Management Review*, *25*(2), 428–438.

Lickey, N., Berry, G., & Whelan-Berry, K. (2009). Responding to workplace romance: A proactive and pragmatic approach. *Journal of Business Inquiry*, *8*(1), 100–119.

Mainiero, L. (1986). A review and analysis of power dynamics in organizational romances. *Academy of Management Review*, *11*(4), 750–762.

Mainiero, L., & Jones, K. (2013). Workplace Romance 2.0: Developing a communication ethics model to address potential sexual harassment from inappropriate social media contacts between coworkers. *Journal of Business Ethics*, *114*, 367–379.

Mano, R., & Gabriel, Y. (2006). Workplace romances in cold and hot organizational climates: The experience of Israel and Taiwan. *Human Relations, 59*, 7–35.

Martinko, M., Gundlach, M., & Douglas, S. (2002). Toward an integrative theory of counterproductive workplace behavior: A causal reasoning perspective. *Journal of Selection and Assessment, 10*, 19–33.

Martinko, M., & Zellar, K. (1998). Toward a theory of workplace violence and aggression: A cognitive appraisal perspective. In Dans R. Griffin, A. O'Leary-Kelly, & J. Bolins (Eds.), *Dysfunctional behavior in organizations: Violent and deviant behavior* (pp. 1–42). Stamford, CT: JAI Press.

McDonald, R., & Noble, F. (2011). Romance in the workplace: Ethical and legal implications for employers. *Proceedings of the Northeast Business & Economics Association* (pp. 297–300).

Mead, M. (1980). A proposal: We need taboos on sex at work. In Dans J. Shafritz, & A. Neugarten (Eds.), *Sexuality in organizations*. Oak Park, IL: Moore Publishing Company.

Montaigne (de), M. (1595, reprinted 2019). *Essays*. Paris: Robert Laffont.

Paetzold, R., Dipboye, R., & Elsbach, K. (2008). A new look ar stigmatization in and of organizations. *Academy of Management Review, 33*(1), 186–193.

Peak, M. (1995). Cupid in a three piece suit. *Management Review, 5*.

Persson, A., & Hansson, S. (2003). Privacy at work – Ethical criteria. *Journal of Business Ethics, 42*, 59–70.

Pierce, C., Aguinis, H., & Adams, S. (2000). Effects of dissolved workplace romance and rater characteristics on responses to a sexual harassment accusation. *Academy of Management Journal, 43*(5), 869–880.

Pierce, C.A., & Aguinis, H. (2001). A framework for investigating the link between workplace romance and sexual harassment. *Group & Organization Management, 26*(2), 206–229.

Pierce, C., Byrne, D., & Aguinis, H. (1996). Attraction in organizations: A model of workplace romance. *Journal of Organizational Behavior, 17*(1), 5–32.

Pierce, C., Karl, K., & Brey, E. (2012). Role of workplace romance policies and procedures on job pursuit intentions. *Journal of Managerial Psychology, 27*(3), 237–263.

Pinel, E., Long, A., Landau, M., Alexander, K., & Pyszczynski, T. (2006). Seeing I to I: A pathway to interpersonal connectedness. *Journal of Personality and Social Psychology, 90*(2), 243 257.

Powell, G. (2001). Workplace romances between senior-level executives and lower-level employees: An issue of work disruption and gender. *Human Relations, 54*(11), 1519–1544.

Powell, G., & Foley, S. (1998). Something to talk about: Romantic relationships in organizational settings. *Journal of Management, 24*, 421–448.

Quinn, R. (1977). Coping with Cupid: The formation, impact, and management of romantic relationships in organizations. *Administrative Science Quaterly, 22*, 30–45.

Riach, K., & Wilson, F. (2007). Don't screw the crew: Exploring the rules of engagement in organizational romance. *British Journal of Management, 18*(1), 79–92.

Roy, D. (1974). Sex in the factory: Informal sexual relations between supervisors and work groups. In Dans C. Bryant (Ed.), *Deviant behaviour* (pp. 44–66). Chicago, IL: Rand McNally.

Rumens, N. (2008). Working at intimacy: Gay men's workplace friendship. *Gender, Work and Organization, 15*, 9–30.

Salvaggio, A., Hopper, J., Streich, M., & Pierce, C. (2011). Why do fools fall in love (at work)? Factors associated with the incidence of workplace romance. *Journal of Applied Social Psychology, 41*, 906–937.

Schultz, V. (2003). The sanitized workplace. *Yale Law Journal, 112*(8), 2061–2193.

Schultz, V. (2006). Understanding sexual harassment law in action: What has gone wrong and what can we do about it. *Thomas Jefferson Law Review, 29*(1), 1–56.

Shuck, B., Owen, J., Manthos, M., Quirk, K., & Rhoades, G. (2016). Co-workers with benefits: The influence of commitment uncertainty and status on employee engagement in romantic workplace relationships. *Journal of Management Development, 35*(3), 382–393.

Smith, J., & Dubbink, W. (2011). Understanding the role of moral principles in business ethics: A Kantian perspective. *Business Ethics Quaterly, 21*(2), 205–231.

Snyder, M. (1974). Self-monitoring of expressive behavior. *Journal of Personality and Social Psychology, 30*, 526–537.

Swartz, R., Warfield, A., & Wood, D. (1987). Co-worker romances: Impact on the work group and on career oriented women. *Personnel, 64*, 22–35.

Teo, L., Chan-Serafin, S., Minbashian, A., Chee-mun Cheng, D., & Wang, L. (2012). Hierarchical workplace romance: The role of social judgment and gender on career outcomes. *Academy of Management Proceedings*. doi:https://doi.org/10.5465/AMBPP.2012.12880abstract

Verhoef, H., & Terblanche, L. (2015). The effect of dissolved workplace romances on the psychosocial functioning and productivity of the employees involved. *Social Work, 51*(1), 287–310.

Weiner, B. (1985). An attributional theory of achievement motivation and emotion. *Psychological Review, 92*, 548–573.

Weiner, B. (1995). *Judgments of responsibility*. New York, NY: Guilford Press.

Werhane, P.H. (1983). Accountability and employee rights. *International Journal of Applied Philosophy, 1*(3), 15–26.

Wilson, F. (2015). Romantic relationships at work: Why love can hurt. *International Journal of Management Reviews, 17*, 1–19.

Worrall, L., & Cooper, C. (2001). Working patterns and working hours: Their impact on UK managers. *Leadership and Organizational Journal, 20*(1), 6–10.

Xie, J., Huang, Q., Wang, H., & Shen, M. (2020). Perish in gossip? Nonlinear effects of perceived negative workplace gossip on job performance. *Personnel, 49*(2), 389–405.

Zelizer, V. (2009). Intimacy in economic organizations. *Research in the Sociology of Work, 18*, 23–55.

11 Adapting a Ministry of Love for Workplace Transformation

A Case Study and The Chaplaincy of Centers for Wiser Leadership

Teresa J. Rothausen and
Thomas G. Maridada

Our Stories: The Surprising Power of Love at Work

When I (Rothausen) was an assistant professor, there was a senior full professor in my area who was a master teacher. As I was honing my teaching, I sought him out for advice as I became increasingly frustrated by the short-term thinking of many of my MBA students, who seemed to prefer "top ten lists" on how to lead to a thoughtful, self-reflective approach. I shared my frustrations with him, as well as what I had tried so far to reorient students toward life-long learning and away from quick fixes. We talked through some of the assignments we had each used, which turned out to be more similar than different. So why was he a master teacher whereas I was struggling? After an hour or so of conversation, he said something that carved itself into my heart and mind: "Of course, you have to love your students."

Though it is painful to recall now, my response was along the lines of sharing how I was already doing this. I'm sure I regaled him with all the many ways I demonstrated that I cared about what students wanted from the class. He listened patiently, then said something like, "Those are good techniques. But it's not about technique. You don't need them to 'have the impression' that you care. You actually need to love them." To my credit, I shut up at that point. It was one of those moments you remember, when your paradigm shifts.

Yet, I didn't fully absorb the message for another couple of years. When I did, student responses to my teaching changed dramatically. I took risks to customize the curriculum beyond the "scientific body of knowledge" in order to be responsive to needs I saw in my students, whether it was a fear of bringing their whole selves to leadership, hunger for deeper meaning and fulfillment through their leadership, or expanding their views of the purposes of the enterprise of business and commerce. I tried to infuse the curriculum with ideas from far beyond the typical textbooks on leadership. As I infused love more and more into my teaching, my students started asking me, "When are you going to write a book about

DOI: 10.4324/9781003254034-12

leadership? This approach is so much richer than any other leadership development I have taken." To this day, I remain grateful to this mentor for daring to say the word "love" in a situation in which it could have been seen as inappropriate or at best, odd. His words, "You actually need to love them," stay with me to this day.

When I (Maridada) was named superintendent of a failing school district in Michigan, let's call it Public School District (PSD), student achievement was at an all-time low, and so was the morale of the teachers and staff. When a district has been moved into a status of being in corrective action, many superintendents, in the name of reform, think that handing down an edict to do things a certain way "just because I said so," – the strongman approach to leadership – is necessary for accelerating reform. Yet, as I visited classrooms, observed teachers, met with parents, engaged with students, and collaborated with principals, it became clear to me that the abysmal performance – single-digit proficiency levels in math and reading, in some cases – was not about recalcitrance on the part of teachers. What was seen as a "negative attitude" by some was about something much deeper. Their dismay came from hurt, shame, disappointment, and hopelessness.

In my leadership classes, I had not been taught to address hurt, shame, or hopelessness. No one told me what to do to motivate people to be hopeful when they are leading in conditions where ceilings leaked on a daily basis and were falling down, fungus was growing through the carpet, and there was a constant dearth of supplies. I needed a different approach from the leadership approaches I had learned. I realized I needed to base my approach on love first.

I needed to embody care for those who, in turn, needed to care for our primary constituency, the children. Instead of strategic plans and models, I first focused on relationships, listening, asking respectful but tough questions, and being with the teachers in demonstrable ways. I took a chaplaincy approach, though I would not have used that term at the time. In response, one teacher said, "I have been teaching for 25 years and you are the first person who has ever asked me ... questions." Over time, asking questions, reflecting with teachers on their teaching practice, challenging old mindsets, and encouraging teachers resulted in a district transformation. As their leader, I had to love the teachers if I wanted them to love the children.

Though one of us came from business (Rothausen, I had a short finance career before becoming an academic and now am a professor of management) and one from education (Maridada, I was a teacher, principal, and superintendent in the public school system), we both migrated over time to leadership development, having seen how powerful the influence of leadership can be in our respective fields. At mid-career we each made some shifts in how we facilitate leader development. A primary reason for these shifts was our increasing dissatisfaction with the academic and practice literatures on organizational leader development. Though we were both teaching leadership courses and running programs that were meant to develop leaders, and though there is some research on "what works best," we also noticed considerable gaps.

Gaps in Leadership Development: Love and Wisdom

One gap is underdevelopment within the leadership literature on levels of adult human development toward wisdom (Bassett, 2011; Liebert, 2000). In their book on resistance to change, Kegan and Lahey (2009) note that in the field of leadership development, there is a lot of focus on leadership and little focus on development; by this they mean human development. Growth through the adult development stages toward wisdom requires self-awareness, reflection, and moral development. Yet experts agree that in business leadership development and education there is a general failure to develop self-aware, reflective, moral leaders (Bass, 2008; Bennis & O'Toole, 2005; Khurana, 2007) and to get beyond understanding and comprehension to application, reflection, and action (Avolio, 2010; Dierdorff et al., 2009).

One characteristic of wisdom is recognition of the interdependence of all of us with each other, other creatures, and the world, which is one form of love. Many faith and wisdom traditions emphasize the importance of love of others over fear of others. In fact, growth toward this orientation may be a key marker for development of wisdom (Bassett, 2011; Liebert, 2000; Rothausen, 2017). Yet, in institutions focused on economics and quantitative measurements of outcomes, rather than their meanings (see Rothausen & Henderson, 2019a), fear too often dominates – fear of not making the numbers, global competition, falling behind technologically, and personal fear of losing one's job. Leadership becomes oriented around fears, rather than growing in wisdom.

In Western faith traditions, certain figures are associated with Wisdom. For example, Judaism retains a personification of Wisdom in the book of Proverbs, which in Christianity became Jesus as "the Word" or "Wisdom" made flesh. In Islam, one of the Prophet's daughters is one figure associated with wisdom, as are the words or "Hadith" of the Prophet. In Christianity and Islam, these figures are also the central figures whose lives manifested perfect love, so we see that wisdom comes from love. Adult developmental psychology suggests this as well. Academics describe the highest stages of adult development in terms that are surprisingly similar to the lives of Jesus and Mohammed, as well as the Buddha and other figures who saw clearly that we are all interconnected. These people developed a preference for the poor in order to bring forward a world of greater justice. A thorough review of these descriptions is beyond the scope of this chapter, but here we review some findings briefly to build our argument for a new form of chaplaincy in the workplace.

Adult Development toward Love and Wisdom

Although our cultural marker suggests that we are "done" developing once we join the workforce after our primary education or training, in fact adults develop long beyond age 18 or 22. Given certain conditions, we grow and mature and can become wiser. Structural models of human development explicate levels of intellectual or cognitive, emotional or psychological, and spiritual or moral development that, if achieved, lead to higher planes of intellectual, emotional, and spiritual understanding across life domains. At these higher planes, people develop increasingly sophisticated processes for making meaning of reality that take into account higher levels of complexity.

Jean Piaget is the founding father of structural stage models, analogous to Erik Erikson's founding role for lifespan models, and many have built on their work including Loevinger on ego development, Kegan on evolving self, and Fowler on stages of faith, coalescing in a model of changing life patterns culminating in six generalizable stages that encompass cognitive, emotional, and spiritual development toward greater facility with complexity. Using Liebert's integrative work on structural stages, supplemented with other integrative sources (i.e., Hoare, 2011; Parks, 2011; Laloux, 2014), these stages can be characterized as comprising a first two stages that generally occur in childhood – the (1) impulsive and (2) self-protective stages (although these can and do carry forward into adulthood in some), and in healthy adulthood, development continues through stages of (3) conforming, (4) inner-dependence, (5) interdependence, and finally and rarely to (6) integrated (these labels are suggested in a number of works, including Leibert, 2000, but a number of other labels are used by different authors).

The highest two stages are where we start to develop wisdom. This development of the human person has also been written about by philosophers. For example, the American philosophers Emerson and Thoreau wrote about this same idea in depth, describing higher development in various ways, including that:

> Life must be lived on a higher plane. We must go up to a higher platform, to which we are always invited to ascend; there, the whole aspect of things changes.
>
> (Emerson, 1844)

> Most of the luxuries and many of the so-called comforts of life are not only not indispensable, but positive hindrances to the elevation of mankind.
>
> (Thoreau, 1989: 334)

Their essays, which focus on the essence of Nature rather than God or a human figure, suggest a "higher" vantage point that sees everything as interconnected such that love for any part of creation or nature, as well as love of any other being, is love of self and vice versa – we are all one at this level. There are several "paths" to this level of development, yet some argue that the spiritual element of our human nature must be engaged for this to happen.

In summary, our perspective is that love is fostered by fostering development to these higher stages. Spiritual development is a path to this development, and ministry is one way to foster spiritual development. In workplaces, then, ministry to leaders is one way to create conditions for wiser leadership to develop, and chaplaincy is a ministry that suggests itself as a form that occurs inside nonreligious organizations. Our conclusion is that love can be brought into workplaces through the fostering of these higher levels of adult development, and one way to do so may be chaplaincy, though we have explored other ways as well (see Rothausen, 2017).

In this chapter, we use our experiences in business and education as leaders ourselves, as scholars of leadership, and having both been in roles charged with developing leaders, to build our argument that one way to reorient organizations away from fear-based and toward love-based motivations, or toward wisdom through wiser leadership, through supplementing existing leader development methods with a specific set of practices associated with chaplaincy, adapted to workplaces as Centers for Wiser Leadership. In addition to building a model, we illustrate the impact of the model elements in my (Maridada) experiences as a superintendent in PSD, and argue for the institutionalization of chaplaincy as an office or department within in business organizations and other workplaces

PSD Case Study Introduction

My (Maridada) first superintendent role was in the first-ever district to be placed in corrective action by the State Department of Education. In this district, 100% of students lived below the federal poverty index. In part, I was asked to lead in this district because I had previously been part of a leadership team recognized for transforming a school that became a US Department of Education National Blue Ribbon School of Excellence. I had worked closely with teachers to modify and adapt our practices to meet the learning needs of students, building internal capacity to solve problems of practice, and working in teams to analyze data and using that data to re-teach to mastery while taking steps to close and eradicate achievement and opportunity gaps.

Everything I was told before taking on the role as superintendent indicated that the teachers in that district were very difficult to work with, did not care about children, and would wage war on anyone who is in the executive leadership position. I was told that anyone taking on this challenge would have to go in and be like a "bull in a china shop" if they wanted to lead change, that I should be prepared to wear a bullet-proof vest if I wanted to lead change there.

Even with that warning, I was stunned by what I saw on day one. I was appalled by the level of decay in the physical plant in each of the school buildings and what appeared to be an overall disdain by teachers and the administrative staff about the work they were undertaking. The combination of these factors, quite frankly, made any speculations about transformation appear implausible. Before I arrived in the district, student attendance had dramatically shrunk from 5,000 students in the district's heyday to 1,000 students or less, depending on the day. One of the challenges that the district encountered was open enrollment, which gave parents permission to choose the school they thought best for their child even if it was outside the district. However, losing students to open enrollment was, by far, the least of the district's concerns.

Arguably, improving teacher quality and providing children with consistent and sustained access to highly effective teachers is one of the most meaningful investments and undertakings that any educational leader can make, given that the goal is to both close and eradicate achievement and opportunity gaps. Most often when problems are discussed, quick fix, "microwave" approaches are championed, which in my experience seldom work, and when they do it is only for a short period of time.

Often quick fixes result in temporary increases in test scores or short-term improvements to student discipline. There is a fallacy of equivocation that exists here; it would be a false-equivalent to assume that inconsistent bumps in test scores are the correlate to achieving mastery. A one-year bump in test scores is a shallow outcome, as compared to swimming in the deep end as a school leader must do to ensure that rigorous instruction takes place in every classroom, every day. Despite being strongly encouraged to consider such quick fixes in this district, I insisted on taking a different approach, one rooted in love, using key elements central to organizational chaplaincy.

As a result, at the end of my five years as superintendent we had achieved levels I had been told were impossible. Some of the outcomes were as follows: enrollment in the district increased by more than 400% (to over 4,000 students); the district was working to close opportunity gaps by creating extended learning opportunities for students to travel abroad (to France, Spain, and Portugal); some students participated in theater training on Broadway and others attended master classes with the Detroit Symphony Orchestra and the Alvin Ailey Dance Troupe; the district was one of the first in the state to start an Early College Cohort Initiative, which allowed students to earn an Associate of Arts degree concomitant with their High School diploma and allowed them to graduate from high school and enter their undergraduate college journey as juniors, with two years of college credit completed.

By using these deeper, relational elements of chaplaincy over quick fixes, in my fifth and final year, nearly 90% of the graduating class was accepted into college, and two years later, the district was featured in publications and on TV morning shows. One report shows that at end of my term as superintendent, proficiency levels far exceeded districts in counties throughout the state with much higher average student socio-economic status. So what are the key elements of chaplaincy?

Introduction to Chaplaincy

Ministry exists in many forms beyond what often comes to mind, such as priest or pastor, imam, rabbi, or monk. These roles exist within specific faith traditions. However, many other forms of ministry exist both within and outside of a faith tradition or institution, including ministries of spiritual education, pastoral care, pastoral counseling, spiritual direction, and chaplaincy, among others (Snodgrass, 2015).

According to one definition, a "chaplain is an individual who provides religious and spiritual care with an organizational setting" (Gilliat-Ray et al., 2013: 5). As such, this form of ministry is well suited to workplaces and organizations. Just as pastoral counseling emerged as a "bilingual" blend of counseling and ministry in the mid-20th century (Snodgrass, 2015: 6), chaplaincy is bi- or even trilingual because chaplains must blend languages of spiritual care, theology, and the "business" of the organization in which they are embedded.

Newitt (2011) reviewed job descriptions for chaplains and found three primary duties: spiritual *care* of members of the embedding organization (including spiritual care, spiritual support, and spiritual leadership), leading spiritual *rituals* for and within the embedding organization (including rituals and practices, e.g., from a Western tradition this may include worship, prayer, devotional time, and services for various occasions), and spiritual and religious *education*, including training and development programs of various kinds related to religion and spirituality, including religious diversity. As part of these duties, chaplains become aware of a set of concerns operating in the embedding organization that other leaders may not hear about, and therefore they can "... raise, and in some respects answer, the questions that religion and faith pose for an institution" (Gilliat-Ray et al., 2013: 43). To this we would add also questions of meaning and purpose as well as matters of development of wisdom.

Globally, models of spiritual care are rapidly evolving, and chaplaincy is no exception. For example, pastoral counseling is in a period of profound transformation (Snodgrass, 2015: 6), and Spiritual Directors International reports rapid expansion of direction relationships within and between faith traditions and with those whose spiritual practice transcends or ignores faith traditions (e.g., Rahman, 2007). Chaplaincy, too, is evolving in at least two ways.

First, it has long been common to find chaplaincies embedded in hospitals, prisons, military units, and universities (Threlfall-Holms &

Newitt, 2011), but more recently, chaplaincy is expanding into arts organizations, shopping centers, airports, courts, police forces, fire services, sports organizations, agricultural institutions, and leisure attractions (Gilliat-Ray, Mansur, & Pattison, 2013; Threlfall-Holms & Newitt, 2011). Second, chaplaincy is evolving rapidly from Christian-based to a multi-(and no-) faith professional position or role (Gilliat-Ray et al., 2013; Threlfall-Holms & Newitt, 2011). These trends suggest that chaplaincy is perfectly poised to become a structural center for spiritual growth toward wisdom within work organizations in a new way.

Corporate chaplaincies have existed for decades but have tended to be based in one faith tradition – Christianity (e.g., see Shellenbarger, 2010). For example, Corporate Chaplains of America (CCA) claims 4,000 chaplains across the United States embedded in workplaces (chaplain. org). CCA defines chaplains as care providers in a way similar to other employee assistance benefits an organization may provide, and their introductory video lists their services as involving hospital, marriage and family, budgeting, jail and court visits, funerals, and grief care (https:// chaplain.org/what-is-chaplaincy/). Their emphasis on being "non-denominational" hints at CCA's Christianity, which its mission statement makes explicit: to "build caring relationships with the hope of gaining permission to share the life-changing Good News of Jesus Christ in a non-threatening manner" (https://chaplain.org/mission/). This organization is staffed by ordained chaplains, which extends legal confidentiality protections into the workplace.

This organization illustrates how chaplaincy has been conceptualized in workplaces in the past, and it will likely remain one active manifestation. However, this form of organizational chaplaincy has a number of limitations. Most obviously, though chaplains themselves may minister to people of other faith and to atheists and agnostics, it is explicitly Christian rather than being explicitly for multi-, inter-, or no-faith people. In addition, this concept limits the impact of chaplaincy to individualized care for employees.

We believe that chaplaincy's foundation of personal care, alongside the evolution into an inter-, multi-, and no-faith ministry, and expansion to care for both individuals and the organization as a whole and its leadership is what is needed now. We suggest that in the form of Centers for Wiser Leadership (or something similar), this adapted chaplaincy could be very powerful beyond caring for individuals, to orient an organization toward love and the common good. Centers for Wiser Leadership, then, involve a new form of ministry growing from chaplaincy.

Models of the Chaplain's Role in Organizational Transitions toward Love

There are several models of chaplaincy, and as we outline above they are in a period of rapid evolution. These models often rely on metaphors to describe chaplaincy, while differentiating it from other forms of spiritual care, though there are overlaps between different forms of ministry. Some of the metaphors used for chaplaincy include more religious metaphors such as missionary, pastor, prophet, rabbi, imam, or activist, and others are more secular, such as spiritual care or inclusion (Todd, 2011; Threlfall-Holmes, 2011: 118). One area in which the models are most rapidly evolving is around diversity and inclusion, including particular forms of multi-faith and inter-faith as well as multi-religious-belonging (Clooney, 2010; Patel: 2016; Todd, 2011).

Despite this complexity, there is some agreement about chaplaincy, including its location within a secular organization and the qualities required of the chaplain. In his review, Newitt (2011) notes an emphasis on spiritual care often being needed at times of transition, whether it is adapting to hardship, phases of spiritual growth and development, or changes in the organization in which the chaplain is embedded. In human development toward wisdom, periods of transitions are opportunities for growth (Bassett, 2011; Liebert, 2000) and are triggered by internal and external cues related to the maturation of people's identities and as well as their pursuit of a more holistic sense of meaning and well-being in work organizations (e.g., Rothausen, Henderson, Arnold, & Malshe, 2017; Rothausen & Henderson, 2019). We argue that this is true not only for individuals, but also for organizations as a whole.

Transitions often raise spiritual issues of transcendence and meaning. It is important to be explicit about the meaning of the words "spiritual" and "spirituality" here. Sheldrake (2013) reviewed the study of spirituality and concluded that it arises out of many religions and wisdom traditions but is not the same as religion. In fact, spirituality precedes religion and may be facilitated by it. Spirituality is a complex concept but generally includes at least some or all of a set of five defining factors (Sheldrake, 2013: 3–4): it is holistic; it involves a quest for the sacred or "deserving veneration" (*New Oxford American Dictionary*); it is understood to involve a quest for meaning, which "implicitly suggests an understanding of human identity and of personality development"; it is linked to human thriving, which also resonates with conclusions in the adult development literature, and it relates to "the quest for ultimate values in contrast to an instrumentalized or strictly materialistic approach to life."

There is significant debate about the extent to which separating spirituality from the wisdom traditions in which it was carried for millennia is possible or desirable (see Schneiders, 2000). This debate is beyond the scope of the current work. Spirituality and religion have a complex and subtle interrelationship that bears further exploration in work literatures, which I (Rothausen, 2017) discuss elsewhere.

Newitt (2011) explored the skills or competencies underlying spiritual care, spiritual leadership, and spiritual education in secular organizations, finding attentiveness to people, theological knowledge, knowledge and skill with religious ritual and practice, and reflexive, critical, creative thinking to be core, along with communication and administrative tasks in the organization. Similarly, in an undated 88-page review of the literature on the efficacy of chaplaincy that includes research through 2010, the HealthCare Chaplaincy Network cited research that suggests by extending a "ministry of presence," chaplains assist those who are hurting by helping them create new meaning (HealthCare Chaplaincy, undated: 23). They concluded that "the chaplain, through his or her presence, can help restore to the patient the opportunity to feel some control, a sense of power, and a sense of transcending purpose, to experience being loved and to express love" (HealthCare Chaplaincy, undated: 23). They also noted that "the wellspring from which all of our care arises is love" (HealthCare Chaplaincy, undated: 23–24).

In summary, this review suggests that in chaplaincy, love is manifested through presence to create a sense of control, power or agency, and transcending purpose. These three spiritual needs have parallels in psychology. For example, self-determination theory (Ryan & Deci, 2000) posits that, separate from external motivators, individuals are motivated by internal needs for autonomy (control), competence (agency), and relatedness. The relatedness in psychology is to others, and in spiritual matters to a larger or "higher" sense of transcendent "mattering," as well as serving others.

Case Study: PSD Leader as Chaplain

Although I (Maridada) was not aware of chaplaincy models explicitly at the time, I was intentionally using key elements of chaplaincy in my leadership of the district.

Presence. In the beginning of my tenure in the district, I met with every stakeholder in the organization. Taking a listening stance first, and sitting with the teaching staff, even in their discomfort when sharing their experiences, was one form of presence I used. Another symbol that I was there to hear all stakeholders was that a survey was sent from the Office of the Superintendent, to every parent, teacher, community leader, and employee in the district, and a series of biweekly town hall meetings were held to debrief with the community concerning the results of the survey. The survey results provided a long list of areas where improvement was needed. Many parents and community leaders were skeptical, saying this could just be another exercise in futility, as when other outsiders had come in and made promises but fallen short in delivering on any of the promises made for change.

As a newly appointed superintendent, I not only visited every school in the district, but also visited every classroom. I set up appointments to talk with every single teacher in the district. Every leader in that district had not only seen me from afar, but had the opportunity for me as their leader to be present with them in person. And I didn't hide from them my heartbreak at hearing them talk about wanting to be more effective and not having even the basic supplies needed or worse still, that they were using their own resources (e.g., their paychecks) to purchase supplies, despite the district already being ranked in the bottom quartile of districts with the lowest salaries in the state. They felt safe enough to share that they brought food to students who were hungry because those students, who had not eaten in days, found it difficult to be engaged in the learning process. I was present as a witness as teachers expressed understandable anger and sadness about the persistent rodent and bug infestations, or pointed out that there were bathrooms that were in disrepair which made for an inhumane existence every day for both them and the students they taught.

In previous assignments, I had implemented some of the most promising practices, which were informed by seminal research on improving schools (e.g., Darling-Hammond, 2000; Marzano, Pickering, & Pollock, 2001; Sanders & Rivers, 1996; Schmoker, 1999; Wright, Horn, & Sanders, 1997). However, I knew that in this role I had to start with a more fundamental element of personal transformation – building trust by using my own presence.

Instead of blaming teachers for abysmal performance, like a chaplain I listened to leaders' concerns. And this was hard, emotionally exhausting work. Only after establishing a trusting, caring (loving) relationship could steps toward improving the conditions be undertaken. After my debriefs with the teaching staff, I let them know that I did not blame them, that I too would have been mad as hell if I had to endure those conditions year after year! I would have been hurt and disappointed also, especially if people just kept pointing the finger at me in the name of accountability, while the basic care I needed as a professional, or even as a human being, remained unmet.

Creating Control and Autonomy. After listening to the leaders of the classrooms, I needed to act. Their sense of control came not only from being able to give voice to their challenges and have the witness of my presence, but to see that what they said mattered in the form of actions. They were not going through a union representative or their principal, but had an opportunity to sit directly, in person, with the leader – the one with whom the buck stopped, and tell me directly what their concerns were as well as suggest changes that they hoped would be made on my watch.

Creating Agency and Recognizing Competence. After hearing their concerns, I asked teachers, staff, parents, and students to name three areas that, if they saw improvements in those areas by the end of the year, it would restore their faith in the district, give them hope, and make them feel empowered as change agents in the district. Here I also used my full presence, being vulnerable and brutally honest with them. I told them that one thing I never wanted to do was fall short in keeping my word. I told them that since our buildings in some cases are 50 years old, I could not promise new schools. I also told them I could not promise everyone a raise, because I inherited the budget. I told them that I could not wave a magic wand and ensure that all of their troubles would magically go away, because I was human just like they were. In addition, though, I did promise to remove the barriers that I could that caused their feelings of disappointment, marginalization, and hurt, and I told them they had the power to set the priorities that I would focus on in the first year.

Teachers identified three things that would give them hope: (1) fixing facilities, which included addressing the bug and rodent infestation; (2) instead of beating them over the head about test scores, to allow them access to the tools they needed to provide more effective instruction and then give them the opportunity to use professional dollars to improve their practice as teachers; and (3) commit to ensuring their students gain access to breakfast every morning. Does this sound like a group of people who do not care about children?

I followed through by listening and acting on their behalf, something we believe chaplains can do confidentially in organizations as well. We prioritized the budget in years one and two to fix buildings, including plumbing, heating and cooling, painting, replacing carpeting and windows, and more. We invited a university partner to work with teachers – analyzing data and identifying problems of practice, and collaboratively creating specific solutions including professional development. Our university partner created an on-site competency-based graduate program, which built capacity in our teachers, and we started to see immediate gains in student achievement. The on-site professional development program also included National Board Certified Teachers and university professors on-site, who conducted lesson studies, modeled lessons, and video-taped lessons to provide quality feedback to teachers concerning their instructional practice – every teacher in the district was required to participate in this initiative and we continued this practice every year that I was in the district.

Encouraging Transcendent Purpose and Relatedness. I asked teachers to please share with me what made them feel marginalized, besides the poor working conditions and lack of supplies. I asked them if I could do one thing, within reason that would ignite the spark for them to love teaching again, what would it be? I was surprised by their answer. I was expecting them to tell me something that was so far-reaching that it would not be within our grasp. Instead, they asked "When you make major decisions, could you please have a teacher at the table to hear our perspective and discuss how the decision will impact learning in the classroom?" They went on to say that they were not talking about traditional union meetings where someone from the union was at the table to discuss working conditions; instead, they wanted a different type of collaboration. They asked me to choose an elementary, middle, and high school teacher every month to have a conversation with so that I would never lose touch with how administrative decisions would impact students and teachers.

Every month for the remainder of the five years that I served as superintendent, I had a teacher from all grade levels at the table to discuss the impact of the decisions made in governing the district. I discovered how powerful "teacher voice" was in leading school transformation. I also realized that for some reason in our profession, in K-12 education, we have strayed from common sense standards of professionalism which govern other professions. Can you imagine the lawyers in a law firm making a decision for the firm which had not been vetted through the experience and expertise of other lawyers? Can you imagine that a group of surgeons would report to someone who has been given the title of Chief of Surgery, who not only has not been trained as a surgeon, but also has never performed a surgery? So, when we talk about teacher practice, would it not stand to reason that teachers should be at the table when critical decisions are made which involve teaching and learning? For some reason we believe that we should care about children, but do not think it is a moral imperative to care about the people who educate them.

It is critical to our democracy, and the posterity of our nation, that we understand that the greatest investment that we can make is the retention and development of highly effective and accomplished teachers. Using a spiritual vision, I was able to emphasize this connection and emphasize it in my interactions with teachers, asking them to partner with me on improving their practice. While, in my opinion, it takes time to become an accomplished teacher, we can create the conditions to foster a growth mindset which cultivates highly effective practice on a more ubiquitous scale by connecting leaders with their ultimate, higher purpose.

Spiritual Care, Leadership, and Education. Unfortunately, we have yet to view the teaching profession as a practice, in the same way that we view law or medicine. While we discuss our profession "as a practice" ethereally, pragmatically many of our current school districts continue to be stymied in tradition and the status quo. Not many school or district leaders are asked, "What investments do you make to ensure improvements in teacher quality?" A chaplain approaches each individual knowing they have value and care about their impact on the workplace. This attitude opens people up to their leader and to learning new things, including the model of everyone being a professional.

For example, professionals such as lawyers and doctors spend time "fact finding" before acting. For lawyers, it is important to put together the facts of the case and analyze it from multiple angles, including that of opposing counsel, so that they can best prepare and develop a strategy which will hopefully help them win the case. Similarly, medical doctors work within a web of complexities. They must take the time to find out the medical history of both the patient and their family, to find a path forward to address the patient's malady while minimizing the possible negative consequences from as many complications as possible to ensure a positive outcome for the patient. Although both doctors and lawyers try hard to conduct a risk analysis which will allow them to lead from a position of strength, unexpected complications arise. Although a surgeon may have performed the same operation thousands of times, while there is standardization around how to prep for the operation and knowledge of various strategies to use when performing the specific operation, each operation is different because it is informed by the medical history of the patient. While performing the operation, unexpected complications may arise, but a skilled surgeon alters the script and has within their arsenal multiple strategies to attempt to address the complications. Similarly, the most effective lawyers may be thrown for a loop when unexpected evidence is presented which could potentially alter the outcome of the case. However, they do more fact-finding so that they can pivot and find ways to improve their strategy to hopefully create a favorable outcome for their client.

In each of the aforementioned examples, we are spotlighting professions which rely on individuals to "think-through" complexities, strategize to mitigate risks and ultimately "lean in" despite the complications inherent in the case. In other words, the expertise of these professionals matters significantly, and without the cultivation of that expertise, success is not inevitable. So is the case with teachers, who should be among the most lauded of all professions, but have been acutely diminished in our country because we do not understand, or value, the critical role that they play in shaping our democracy.

During my first two weeks on the job as superintendent, of particular interest to me were the scores at one of our schools where student achievement had flat-lined over the last 6 years. I engaged teachers in a discussion about ways to significantly improve performance. I asked them to reflect on their pedagogy and share with me why they thought, despite incredible efforts being made on their part, the results did not reflect that the dial was being moved to significantly improve student achievement. This approach reflects the approach of the chaplain in being present and asking questions of the individual in order to educate them, rather than telling them what must be wrong.

After asking her many questions, one teacher said to me:

> I have been teaching 25 years and you are the first person who has ever asked me those questions. I am here before school and I stay after school just in case my students need extra help. I provide whole group instruction. I only have 55 minutes with them, so I don't have time for differentiated groups. I guess I have felt like if I covered the material, it is their responsibility to come prepared and be engaged. I would say I am a pretty effective teacher. What else do you want me to do?

After being present with this teacher to hear her side of things, I found that she cared about the children she served, but had not been challenged to think of herself as empowered to step out of her comfort zone to ensure students' academic success. I worked with her, and many others, to help them re-frame their work as a professional practice that they were, in part, responsible for their craft, telling them that we do not learn how to masterfully reach all students during your first year in the classroom, that skill set is cultivated over time.

In sum, by following a ministry-based process of presence and listening, honoring teachers' sense of autonomy and control over their professional practice, acting on what I heard, and connecting teachers to a higher purpose, I was able to provide the support, care, and education they needed to succeed. When they succeed, children succeed. This is true for all humans in community, but a chaplaincy approach sees this interconnectedness through using a love-based, rather than a fear-based approach.

The Chaplain versus a Chaplaincy

In this case study, we illustrate how a leader can serve as chaplain to other leaders in order to unleash their capacity to change, grow, and become wiser leaders. However, as I (Maridada) went through this process I realized that there needs to be a way to institutionalize these changes if they are to remain beyond the tenure of one leader. When I (Rothausen) consult to organizations wanting to make a change, I frequently use the analogy of the organization as a human person in order to illustrate the key systems that need to be healthy and reoriented in order to make change stick.

A person has a skeletal, cardio-vascular, and nervous system as well as a personality, spirit, or soul. Similarly, an organization has a structure on which the entire organizational messages are sent, a human resource system that feeds and oxygenates all the people and sends them to do different jobs in the system, a management and leadership system that determines direction and sends messages along the lines of the skeletal structure, and a culture that demonstrates its values.

In our case study, I (Maridada), as the "brain" of PSD, was able to redirect and send new messages of love and care throughout his school district in part by virtue of holding the office of the "chief brain" of the district, and as such I was able to reorient the other leaders in the district. However, in this model, if the changes were to outlast one leader, they need to be integrated as well into the various human resource systems that impact people (recruiting, hiring, training and development, performance assessment and coaching, and compensation) as well as in the structure and culture of the organization.

Rather than rely on one leader to enact love in an organization, we recommend a chaplaincy-type center. However, as we mentioned above, due to the word "chaplain" having certain traditional meanings, we suggest that organizations instead form a department or office that may include chaplains from more than one (and no) faith tradition, which could be called something such as a "Center for Wiser Leadership" where leaders could go to address the spiritual matters inherent in their work. Rather than viewing chaplaincy as caring for individuals through things that are happening primarily in their lives outside of the organization, this new chaplaincy would be oriented around listening and caring about leaders' actual work itself, creating a presence, a space to regain control and competence, and to connect with the transcendent purpose of their work, as well as to be spiritually cared for and educated as they enact change.

Regardless of the label, having a "center" or "department" gives this value a physical location within the structure of the organization. Thoughtfully grafting this office or department in an appropriate way to the existing structure is important and would be different in each organization. In addition to impacting the "skeleton" or structure, having such an office would be an additional place that people could go to get spiritually "fed and oxygenated" for their work and the work of leadership. Finally, the office itself would become a symbol of this value within the organization, and could hold events and provide educational opportunities that would further impact the culture and the "the way we do things around here."

Centers for Wiser Leadership: A New Chaplaincy for Workplaces

I (Maridada) was chosen to lead change in a place where few believed change, much less transformation, was possible. As a chaplain does, as the leader I first built relationships with classroom leaders who were hurting, by being present. I saw the spark come back into their eyes when I listened to them. As a result of being truly seen and heard, these teachers took ownership for the district being transformed.

Many business organizations today are also sites of hurt and trauma, and even short of trauma, there are high levels of psychophysiological strain (e.g., in qualitative research, see Rothausen et al., 2017). Many have written about record levels of disengagement from work. On the positive side, we are also seeing movements to address these crises, including increasing interest in purpose and meaning at work (e.g., Dik, Byrne, & Steger, 2013; Rosso, 2010; Rothausen & Henderson, 2019a), positive psychology (e.g., Snyder & Lopez, 2005), and spiritual leadership (see Fry, 2003 and Rothausen, 2017). Centers for Wiser Leadership, emphasizing human development and using spirituality as a path, fit well with these movements.

Fear-oriented motivations in organizations contribute to outcomes from staggering levels of disengagement to incivility and harassment. Levels of employee disengagement believe the fact that more people are looking for meaning in their lives, at least in part, through their work (Rothausen & Henderson, 2019a). I (Maridada) discovered that we have made it acceptable in our nation for teachers to be invisible. In far too many districts, the teachers who are the classroom leaders working directly with our nation's future have the least amount of autonomy yet carry the burden and bear the weight of the highest levels of accountability. I (Rothausen) hear regularly from MBA students who feel unseen and powerless to change the negative elements that touch their work and leadership in business organizations. Chaplains, through their emphasis on presence, listening, relationship trust, and connection with transcendence, could be a powerful tool to forward meaning, purpose, and positive psychological health in workplaces.

This redefined chaplaincy is for leaders at all organizational levels. It provides spaces and teaches practices that foster wiser leadership, that is, leaders who have developed to higher spiritual, emotional, and intellectual levels. One way, but far from the only way, to create conditions for wiser leadership is to develop this new form of chaplaincy. A Center for Wiser Leadership would be a physical space in an organization, staffed by those with expertise in spiritual development.

The change and transformation in PSD did not occur by first executing a ten-point strategic plan, or with a top-ten list of high-yield strategies to improve test scores. On the contrary, student achievement was improved because after we attended to the trauma of our teachers by really seeing it and listening to it, we were able to equip them with the tools they needed to facilitate learning and academic growth for our students. This phenomenon would transfer to many workplaces. After all, who cares if you know when to use data, how to analyze it, or if you are able to differentiate instruction if you are so distraught from hurt and despair that it blinds you to the reality of your true purpose.

Leaders need to know why our followers are hurting before we can go any further. Sometimes that starts with a conversation where we must just listen before suggesting a list of strategies for improvement, "lean in" and offer the ministry of presence, recognizing that the greatest gift that we can give to others as leaders is ourselves. A ministry of presence can facilitate a conversation that encourages self-disclosure on the part of those who are struggling to do better but who have experienced difficulties and challenges, without their disclosure compromising their dignity. There are those who will say that all of this sounds like the mantra of a 21st century New Age guru when it is suggested that leaders can glean and learn from the conceptual framework of the chaplaincy to inform how we lead organizational transformation.

However, based on our experience as well as our study of the spiritual development of leaders, we would argue that when you enter organizations, especially where mounting turbulence exists, rarely does dysfunction occur just because an item on a strategic plan has not been fully realized. There are underlying social, emotional, and psychological challenges which often exacerbate and cause dysfunction to fester in organizations. For the same reasons that doctors do not administer physical and occupational therapy to patients who are in cardiac arrest because the most immediate need is to save the patient's life and then stabilize them before they can work on improving the quality of their life; so too, leaders must be heard and their emotional, physical, and psychological needs must be addressed before we delve deeper to create a more sustainable form of organizational transformation.

Centers for Wiser Leadership as Instruments for Love

Organizations and institutions struggle with widespread loss of trust in leadership. In response, they often revive ethics programming, and this is important. Nonetheless, ethical, legal, and moral violations continue in organizations and professions with ethical codes, ethics training, and compliance departments. These are necessary but insufficient. It is time to get more holistic and personal. It is time to change the way we do leader development and start orienting our own and others' leader development toward the common good. It has often been suggested to me (Rothausen) that we should not use words such as "spiritual" in corporate America because people will not listen.

We have three responses to this point. First, this is directly contrary to our experience when we do talk to people. Overwhelmingly, individuals in one-to-one situations encourage us to continue our spiritual work with leaders because it is so important, once they understand that their own relationship to religion (positive or negative) is not impacted by this work. Second, we understand the push-back due to the association of ideas like ministry, chaplaincy, and spiritual direction with organized religion, and in particular with Christianity. But as we reviewed at the beginning of this chapter, all these disciplines are evolving across wisdom traditions, including the wisdom that exists in evolved atheism and agnosticism. These new, evolved versions of spiritual care, which include all, can be the versions of these practices we adopt to care for leaders and everyone in organizations. Throwing away the wisdom in wisdom traditions because some religious institutions have failed is like throwing the baby out with the bath water. Finally, think about corporate history. When I (Rothausen) started my professional career as a Certified Public Accountant (CPA) decades ago, anyone who wanted to bring up the concept of employee or leader "wellness" in corporate America would have heard similar advice not to mention such an "out there" concept. Now, corporate wellness centers and initiatives are ubiquitous.

Based on our work with leaders in business and education, we have developed alternatives to using "loaded" words like chaplaincy. Because one purpose of ministry is to foster growth in wisdom, one approach is to form Centers for Wiser Leadership that are centers for chaplaincy and spiritual direction. Another is to use the term "spiritual care." Whatever labels are used, however, it is important that the ministers themselves remain oriented toward love. It is easy for different functions in organizations originally oriented around care of workers and leaders to be appropriated as "strategic partners." Indeed, an organized chaplaincy within a corporation could be a partner but must also recognize different core missions and remain anchored in the value of love.

We know from philosophy, theology, and psychology what creates the conditions for wisdom, but this knowledge has not been "packaged for corporate consumption." This new form of chaplaincy – Centers for Wiser Leadership – could be this "package," creating multi- and no-faith, culturally inclusive corporate spaces with affiliated teams of people – specialists in the work of moral and spiritual development in leadership. These spaces function as centers to consult confidentially and teach practices that fuse: inner intention; intellectual, emotional, and spiritual learning; and action, customized to specific organizational settings.

A cornerstone of interfaith leadership and of interfaith chaplaincy practices is a conviction that religious differences can enrich ethical decision-making and strategy formation, in a truly interfaith consideration of the issues, challenges, problems, and opportunities that arise in businesses and other organizations.

In summary, what we need to heal leadership in our society is not only intellectual treatment of ethics, but also fostering the development of wise, mature, whole leaders at all levels – their minds, hearts, bodies, and souls, across wisdom traditions, toward the common good, that is, toward love. In this chapter, our thesis is that an expansion of key elements of chaplaincy into business organizations could not only be beneficial, but may be necessary if any fundamental change in the ways business organizations are led, how they function, and the ends they pursue, away from fear-based, economics-primary, transactional cultures, values, and ends, and toward love-based, prosocial, balanced cultures, values, and ends.

Conclusion

Many researchers have written about the need for change in organizational leadership to resolve complex challenges that result in spiritual pain, including social and environmental injustice. Yet few have suggested concrete ways to reorient organizational leaders. Practically, how can organizations reorient toward love while not losing sight of their economic functions and imperatives? For one answer to this question, we suggest the creation of Centers for Wiser Leadership, based on the specific form of spiritual care and development, or ministry, of chaplaincy.

References

Avolio, B. J. (2010). Pursuing authentic leadership development. In N. Nohria & R. Khurana (Eds.), *Handbook of leadership theory and practice* (pp. 739–768). Boston, MA: Harvard Business Press.

Bass, B. M., & Bass, R. (2008). *The Bass handbook of leadership: Theory, research, and managerial applications* (4th ed.). New York, NY: Free Press.

Bassett, C. L. (2011). Wisdom and its development: Learning to become wise(r). In C. Hoare (Ed.), *The Oxford handbook of reciprocal adult development and learning* (2nd ed., pp. 302–317). New York: Oxford University Press.

Bennis, W. G., & J. O'Toole. (2005). How business schools lost their way: Too focused on "scientific" research, business schools are hiring professors with limited real-world experience and graduating students who are ill equipped to wrangle with complex, unquantifiable issues - in other words, the stuff of management. *Harvard Business Review (May)*, 96–104.

Clooney, F. X. S. J. (Ed.). (2010). *The new comparative theology: Thinking interreligiously in the 21st century*. New York, NY: T & T Clark International.

Darling-Hammond, L. (2000). Teacher quality and student achievement: A review of state policy evidence. *Education Policy Analysis Archives, 8*(1). Retrieved January 22, 2004 from http//olam.ed.asu.edu/epaa/v8nl/.

Dierdorff, E. C., Rubin, R. S., & Morgeson, F. P. (2009). The milieu of managerial work: An integrative framework linking work context to role requirements. *Journal of Applied Psychology, 94*(4), 972–988. https://doi.org/10.1037/a0015456.

Dik, B. J., Byrne, Z. S., & Steger, M. F. (Eds.). (2013). *Purpose and meaning in the workplace*. Washington DC: American Psychological Association.

Emerson, R. W. (1844). *Lecture to the society in Amory Hall, March 3*. Retrieved September 10, 2016, from www.emersoncentral.com/newengland.htm.

Fry, L. W. (2003). Toward a theory of spiritual leadership. *The Leadership Quarterly, 14*, 693–727.

Gilliat-Ray, S., Mansur, A., & Pattison, S. (2013). *Understanding Muslim chaplaincy*. New York, NY: Routledge.

HealthCare Chaplaincy. (undated). *Literature review: Testing the efficacy of chaplaincy care*. Retrieved November 22, 2019, from www.healthcarechaplaincy. org/templeton-research/tr-literature-review/59-tr-.

Hoare, C. (Ed.). 2011. *The Oxford handbook of reciprocal adult development and learning* (2nd ed.). New York, NY: Oxford University Press.

Kegan, R., & Lahey, L. L. (2009). *Immunity to change: How to overcome it and unlock the potential in yourself and your organization*. Boston, MA: Harvard Business School Publishing.

Laloux, F. (2014). *Reinventing organizations*. Brussels: Nelson Parker.

Liebert, E. 2000. *Changing life patterns: Adult development in spiritual direction*. St. Louis, MO: Chalice Press.

Marzano, R. J., Pickering, D. J., & Pollock , J. E. (2001). *Classroom instruction that works: Research-based strategies for increasing student achievement*. Alexandria, VA: Association for Supervision and Curriculum Development.

Newitt, M. (2011). The role and skills of a chaplain. In M. Threlfall-Holms & M. Newitt (Eds.), *Being a chaplain* (pp . 103–115). London: Society for Promoting Christian Knowledge.

Parks, S. D. (2011). *Big questions, worthy dreams: Mentoring emerging adults in their search for meaning, purpose, and faith*. San Francisco: Jossey-Bass.

Patel, E. (2016). *Interfaith leadership: A primer*. Boston, MA: Beacon Press.

Rahman, J. (2007). What to expect in Islamic spiritual direction. *Presence: An International Journal of Spiritual Direction*, June (13,2), 35–41.

Rosso, B. D., Dekas, K. H., & Wrzesniewski, A. (2010). On the meaning of work: A theoretical integration and review. *Research in Organizational Behavior, 30*, 91–127.

Rothausen, T. J. (2017). Integrating leadership development with Ignatian spirituality: A model for designing a spiritual leader development practice. *Journal of Business Ethics, 145*(4), 811–829.

Rothausen, T. J., & Henderson, K. E. (2019a). Meaning-based job-related well-being: Exploring a meaningful work conceptualizations of job satisfaction. *Journal of Business and Psychology, 34*(3), 357–376.

Rothausen, T. J., & Henderson, K. E. (2019b). Two messages from the other side of the turnover coin: "Here to stay or go?" and "Should I stay or should I go?" Commentary in *Industrial and Organizational Psychology: Perspectives on Science and Practice, 12,* 306–309.

Rothausen, T. J., Henderson, K. E., Arnold, J. K., & Malshe, A. (2017). Should I stay or should I go? Identity and well-being in sensemaking about retention and turnover. *Journal of Management, 43*(7), 2357–2385.

Ryan, R. M., & Deci, E. L. (2000). Self-determination theory and the facilitation of intrinsic motivation, social development and well-being. *American Psychologist, 55,* 68–78.

Sanders, W. L., & Rivers, J. C. (1996). *Cumulative and residual effects of teachers on future student academic achievement (Research Progress Report).* Knoxville, TN: University of Tennessee Value-Added Research and Assessment Center.

Schmoker, M. (1999). *Results: The key to continuous school improvement.* Alexandria, VA: Association for Supervision and Curriculum Development, p. 70.

Schneiders, S. M. (2000). Religion and spirituality: Strangers, rivals, or partners? *Santa Clara Lecture, 6*(2), 1–26.

Sheldrake, P. (2013). *Spirituality: A brief history* (2 ed.). Chichester: Wiley-Blackwell.

Shellenbarger, S. (2010). Praying with the office chaplain. *Wall Street Journal,* June 23. Retrieved May 22, 2014, from www.wsj.com/articles/ SB100014240 52748704853404575322742500015642.

Snodgrass, J. L. (2015). Pastoral counseling: A discipline of unity amid diversity. In E. A. Maynard & J. L. Snodgrass (Eds.), *Understanding pastoral counseling* (pp. 1–15). New York, NY: Springer Publishing.

Snyder, C. R., & Lopez, S. J. (Eds.) (2005). *Handbook of positive psychology.* Oxford: Oxford University Press.

Todd, A. (2011). Responding to diversity: Chaplaincy in a multi faith context. In M. Threlfall-Holms & M. Newitt (Eds.), *Being a chaplain* (pp. 89–102). London: Society for Promoting Christian Knowledge.

Thoreau, H. D. (1989). *A Week—Walden—Maine Woods—Cape Cod.* Library of America edition, 978–0940450271.

Threlfall-Holms, M. (2011). Exploring models of chaplaincy. In M. Threlfall-Holms & M. Newitt (Eds.), *Being a chaplain* (pp. 116–126). London: Society for Promoting Christian Knowledge.

Threlfall-Holms, M., & Newitt, M. (Eds.) (2011). *Being a chaplain.* London: Society for Promoting Christian Knowledge.

Wright, S. P. , Horn, S. P., & Sanders, W. L. (1997). Teacher and classroom context effects on student achievement: Implications for teacher evaluation. *Journal of Personnel Evaluation in Education, 11,* 57–67, 63

12 "Tough Love" Characterizing Paternalistic Leadership

The Case of Family Firms

Nava Michael-Tsabari, Francesco Barbera, and Bart Henssen

"Love," as a depiction of relationships in organizations, is rarely found in the modern management literature (Barsade & O'Niell, 2014), and even more uncommon in Western world contexts (Pellegrini, Scandura, & Jayaraman, 2010). Yet, along with its more studied cognitive aspects, organizational culture[1] has critical emotional components, which include the various sentiments related to "loving relationships" in the workplace (Barsade & O'Niell, 2014). Focusing on feelings of affection, compassion, caring, and tenderness for others at work, Barsade and O'Niell (2014) suggest a construct of "companionate love," which characterizes relationships between coworkers. In their longitudinal study, they find that companionate love at work positively relates to employees' satisfaction and teamwork and negatively relates to their absenteeism and emotional exhaustion (Barsade & O'Niell, 2014). Based on warmth, connection, and sensitivity toward other coworkers, this form of love in organizations relates to horizontal relationships between equal parties.

However, warm emotional and sensitive relationships can also be present in hierarchical, vertical relationships between a superior and subordinate. Further, significant employee outcomes can occur as a result. Although this type of organizational love is less understood, an ideal context to explore vertical loving relationships is in *family* firms, that is, organizations that are owned and managed by family members. As family relationships often embody a type of love linked to particular feelings, behaviors, challenges, and rewards, family firms, and the loving relationships therein, are uniquely characterized by an overlap between family and business (Tagiuri & Davis, 1996). A fundamental hierarchical relationship observed in most, if not all, families is the love between parent and child. Known as storge love (based on an Aristotelian classification) (Masuda, 2003), this type of love is multifaceted and paradoxically exemplified by compassion, mutual respect, and commitment, as well as obligation, fear, and dependency (Aycan, 2006). In family firms, such love is inherent – and can manifest in various aspects of their organizational culture and leadership style – in the form of *paternalism*.

DOI: 10.4324/9781003254034-13

As one of the most intriguing, complex, and controversial constructs in the management literature (Aycan, 2006), paternalism refers to a "father-like" leadership style in which strong authority is combined with concern and considerateness (Pellegrini & Scandura, 2008), which reflects the idea of "tough love" – a combination of love and discipline or control. Specifically, paternalism has been defined as a "hierarchical relationship in which a leader guides [the] professional and personal lives of subordinates in a manner resembling a parent, and in exchange expects loyalty and deference" (Gelfand, Erez, & Aycan, 2007, p. 493). Although the concept has been utilized by scholars to explain family business dynamics (Ainsworth & Wolfram-Cox, 2003; Johannisson & Huse, 2000), it has only scarcely been studied in this context (Chirico, Nordqvist, & Colombo, 2012). As a whole, the family business literature deems paternalism as an implicit condition – without fully considering the extensive, stand-alone general literature on paternalism found in the organizational behavior literature. Further, the more established paternalism literature has not necessarily considered the unique antecedent relational conditions experienced by family firms that give rise to paternalism. Using 30 qualitative descriptions of employees in six family firms, this chapter integrates the family business and paternalism literatures. In doing so, we theoretically link known paternalism dimensions to family firms, and untimely present a conceptual model that outlines how and why family firms exhibit storge love in the shape of paternalism, as well as the various employee outcomes that can result from such behavior.

Our contribution is threefold. First, by exploring paternalistic leadership in family firms, we can shed light on both the antecedents and outcomes of paternalism, an issue troubling the extant paternalism literature (Pellegrini & Scandura, 2008). For example, we theorize how family ownership itself affects the paternalistic management style in family firms. Second, by more explicitly relating paternalism to the leadership style and organizational culture of family firms, we can more precisely understand how it functions as a unique employee control mechanism in such firms. By doing so, we describe the special employment setting characteristic of family firms where love and control paradoxically characterize their employer–employee relationships. Finally, by understanding the underling family drivers of a paternalistic management style, our chapter features the (potentially omitted) emotional aspects of organizational culture, not just in family firms, but in organizations in general. For example, through our understanding of family firms, in this chapter we show how love can also be a controlling mechanism in Western firms.

The structure of the chapter is as follows: first, we open with an in-depth description of paternalistic love and present the apparent gaps in its current literature. We then link the specific dimensions of paternalism and love to elaborate on paternalistic management in family firms, demonstrating them with employees' quotes. Finally, we present our conceptual framework about why paternalism is prevalent in family firms, how it affects employees, and conclude with a discussion of the implications to other types of organizations.

Paternalism and Love in Organizations

At least in Western societies, love is seen as the most important of all human needs, central to our close relationships, and socially constructed (Noller, 1996). More specifically, love can be defined as "an attitude toward a target person involving predispositions to think, feel and behave in certain ways towards that person" (Rubin, 1970, p. 265, cited in Noller, 1996). Among different kinds of love, familial love is known as "storge" love, which characterizes the relationships between parents and their children, in an asymmetrical way (Hendrick & Hendrick, 1986). In the organizational context, this love can be referred to as paternalism. As a management style, it involves treating employees as if they were part of the extended family, mediating the line between "humanity and economic exploitation" (Anthony, 1986, p. 77). Historically, paternalism described a form of traditional authority based on rights and obligations stemming out of the family (Padavic & Earnest, 1994). The paternalistic relationship between a leader and his or her subordinates is a combination of strong authority *and* caring (Pellegrini & Scandura, 2008), what we call love and control, as "the idea of paternalism at work and social life derives from the relationships between parents and children... where parental affection and control... can coexist" (Aycan, 2006, p. 454). These seemingly conflicting roles of caring and demanding are at the root of paternalism. In practice, paternalism humanizes the workplace and emphasizes more flexible management systems instead of rigid and contractual relationships between employers and employees (Aycan, 2006). The Weberian analysis of modernization theory predicts that, with progressive institutional development, paternalism should eventually be superseded by more rational-bureaucratic, "modern" industrial authority, in which codified rules and procedures govern employee–employer relations (Padavic & Earnest, 1994).

However, contrary to these predictions, paternalism has not disappeared from the modern employment setting. In fact, there is a rising interest in paternalistic leadership in developing societies (Martinez, 2003), as well as in Western contexts (Pellegrini et al., 2010). For example, national welfare programs in the United States have become *more* paternalistic due to polls which show that paternalism is the preferred social policy by majority of Americans regarding welfare and poverty (Aycan, 2006). In the organizational context, the recurring interest in paternalism restores human and moral elements in the workplace, replacing rigid and contractual relationships between employees and employers with more flexible management procedures (Aycan, 2006). With that said, paternalism is multifaceted and can have varying effects on employee–employer relationship.

The Multiple Faces of Paternalism

Chan, Huang, Snape, and Lam (2013) refer to the dual roles of a paternalistic leader as authoritarian *and* benevolent, and call it "The Janus face." The paternalistic manager exhibits absolute authority and control over subordinates and demands unquestioning obedience, while simultaneously demonstrating individualized and holistic concern for subordinates' personal well-being (Chan et al., 2013). This dual coexistence is exemplified in the "tough love" idea, referred to in the title of this chapter. Adapting the dual perspective of paternalism has led to defining a general construct based on authoritarian versus benevolent leadership (e.g., Chan et al., 2013). Farh and Cheng (2000) proposed a model of paternalistic leadership with three dimensions: *authoritarianism, benevolence*, and *morality. Authoritarianism* refers to paternalism's dimension describing leader behaviors that assert authority and control and demand unquestioning obedience from subordinates. *Benevolence* refers to leader behaviors that demonstrate individualized, holistic concern for subordinates' personal and family well-being. In return, these subordinates feel grateful and obliged to reciprocate. The third dimension, *morality*, refers to demonstrating superior personal virtues, self-discipline and unselfishness, which encourage subordinates to respect and identify with the leader.

The three dimensions of paternalism exert different effects on employees' perceptions and outcomes, and at the same time they coexist, interact, and form paternalistic leadership as a whole (Wu, Huang, Li, & Liu, 2012). For example, Chen, Eberly, Chiang, Farh, and Cheng (2014) found that while all three dimensions of paternalistic leadership are related to employee performance, the two dimensions of benevolence and morality had positive relationships with in-role (formal job requirements) and extra-role (outside of formal job requirements) performance, whereas authoritarianism had a negative relationship with extra-role performance. In an attempt to capture this complexity, Aycan (2006) developed a nuanced construct of paternalism, which still includes the tough and loving coexisting dimensions. She describes the following five paternalistic leadership roles: (1) creating a family atmosphere in the workplace, (2) establishing close and individualized relationships with subordinates, (3) getting involved in the nonwork domain, (4) expecting loyalty, and (5) maintaining authority/control.

In their review, Pellegrini and Scandura (2008) criticize the unclear scales and measures of paternalism, as well as the various and partial dimensions of the construct, which are all called paternalism. In addition to the definition and measurement issues impeding research on paternalism, Pellegrini and Scandura (2008) also identify several important knowledge gaps. As paternalism is an emerging area in leadership research, these unaddressed questions are fruitful directions for future research, namely, paternalism's (1) antecedents, (2) link to organizational structures, (3) practice in various contexts, and (4) potential changes over time. We contend that many of these gaps can be addressed by examining the paternalistic leadership style of family firms. In the following sections, we describe the antecedents; the link to the organizational structure of the owning family; the context of employer–employee relationships; and how this phenomenon may change over time. As a result, we believe that the family firm context may inform wider paternalism literature in various ways.

Paternalism and Love in Family Firms

A family firm is a business in which one or several families have effective control over the strategy of the firm and the business contributes significantly to the wealth and identity of the family (Astrachan & Shanker, 2003). The majority of firms around the world are family firms (La Porta, Lopez-de-Silanes, & Shleifer, 1999). Although many small- and medium-sized businesses are family owned, about one-third of the S&P 500 firms are family controlled as well (Anderson & Reeb, 2003). Many well-known brands around the world are family firms, including Wal-Mart, Ford, Fiat Crysler, Mars, Volkswagen, Aldi, BMW, and Roche Group, among many other global players (Pieper, Astrachan, & Neglia, 2016). This prevalence potentially deems the paternalistic organizing of "tough love" a widespread management style[2].

Family firms have been described as possibly gaining from the emotional bond that employees feel toward the organization as being part of an "extended family" (Chua, Chrisman, & Steier, 2003). In an archetypal family business, employees can constitute a "pseudo-family" (Tan & Fock, 2001, p. 128). Poza, Alfred, and Maheshwari (1997) describe a "family feeling" that nonfamily managers consider a nonmonetary reward and an advantage of working for a family firm. For example, Nicholson (2008) points to an inclusive culture with a communitarian size and structure where nonfamily employees at all levels feel the positive difference of working for a family firm. Guzzo and Abbott (1990) argued that this "family feeling" is a powerful mechanism of social identity in family firms. Describing this mechanism and the role of familial/storge love in the context of family firms' employment setting is the goal of this chapter.

Descriptions of organizational culture in family firms primarily portray paternalistic attributes (Ainsworth & Wolfram-Cox, 2003; Johannisson & Huse, 2000). Dyer (1986, 1988) describes how this paternalistic organizational form is created and owned by patriarchal families. Family, as a metaphor, can be described along two dimensions of cohesion and leadership style, referring to the high emotional closeness between group members and the paternalistic and centralistic management roles enacted in these organizations (Michael-Tsabari & Tan, 2013). The positive associations invoked by the family metaphor include integration, harmony,

Table 12.1 Linking Paternalism Dimensions to Family Firm Literature

Aycan's (2006) paternalism dimension	Description of paternalistic dimension (Aycan, 2006)	Characteristics of family firms
Creating a family atmosphere in the workplace	Behaving like a father to employees, giving fatherly advice to subordinates in their professional as well as personal lives.	Family business employees become "part of the family" (Kets de Vries, 1996), employees constitute a "pseudo-family" (Tan & Fock, 2001, p. 128).
Establishing close and individualized relationships with subordinates	Establishing close relationships with every subordinate individually, knowing every one of them in person (personal problems, family life, etc.), being genuinely concerned with their welfare, taking a close interest in subordinates' professional as well as personal life.	Emotional bond of employees, who are part of an "extended family" (Chua et al., 2003), Poza et al. (1997) describe a "family feeling," members of family firms view interconnectedness and personal relationships as defining elements of their identities (Miller & Le Breton-Miller, 2005).
Getting involved in the nonwork domain	Attending important events (like weddings, funerals, graduations, etc.) of employees, providing help and assistance (e.g., financial) to subordinates if they need it, acting as a mediator between an employee and their spouse if there is a marital problem.	Family firms are found to have a stronger sense of community at work, and an inclusive culture (Miller, Le Breton-Miller, & Scholnick, 2008).
Expecting loyalty	Expecting loyalty and commitment from subordinates, expecting them to immediately attend to an emergency in the company even if this requires employees to do so at the expense of their private lives and time.	Loyalty and seniority important for success (Lansberg, 1999), members are expected to cooperate obediently (Dyer, 1986).
Maintaining authority/control	Giving importance to status differences (position ranks), and expecting employees to behave accordingly; believing that the leader knows what is good for subordinates and their careers; not wanting anyone to doubt his authority.	Family members depend on the family leader (i.e., the founder) (Dyer, 1986), the founder sets the goals for the family (Dyer, 1986), a controlling owner controls the business and family affairs (Lansberg, 1999).

and loyalty. Like the paradoxical combination of love and authority embedded in paternalism, the family firm's organizational culture also includes more negative implications of "family," such as hierarchical and repressive social relationships (Ainsworth & Wolfram-Cox, 2003).

Demonstrating how paternalism describes the relationship with employees, a family firm owner said, "I'm a father figure rather than a boss" (Ainsworth & Wolfram-Cox, 2003, p. 1476). As captured in the seminal description by Dyer (1986) opening this chapter, paternalism and fatherly love relationships with nonfamily employees are common in family firms. With that said, paternalism is also linked to undesirable outcomes, such as reduced firm-level entrepreneurship (Chirico & Nordqvist, 2010), reduced control in family firm governance (Cicellin, Mussolino, Martinez, & Iacono, 2013), and a negative perception of nepotism in hiring practices (Erden & Oetken, 2019; Lubatkin, Durand, & Ling, 2007).

In this chapter, we explore how the "tough love" management style associated with paternalism exemplifies what is currently known about family firms. By connecting the general literature on paternalism with anecdotal descriptions of paternalistic leadership in family firms, Table 12.1 summarizes the links between Aycan's (2006) five dimensions of paternalism and family firm descriptions of paternalistic leadership.

A Pilot Study: Interviews with Nonfamily Employees in Family Firms

To explore how nonfamily employees describe the relationship with family owners, we held qualitative interviews with 30 nonfamily employees from six family firms which have been done as a pilot study for this chapter. Averages are as follows: participants' age 39.3 years, their work tenure 10.2 years, and 53.3% were female. Firm age was, on average, 58 years, and firm size included 193.3 employees. Participants were asked to describe the organizational culture in their employment setting. All interviews were held by the first author, recorded and transcribed. Love as a dominant characteristic of employment was evident in these testimonials, as described by an employee, "They (the firm owners) love me and I love them, like family" (Employee 9), and also with other coworkers, "I love the people that I work with" (Employee 14). Encouraged by this, the following sections present a selection of these data and relate them to paternalism in family firms.

The Family Firm Difference

Comparing the organizational culture in a family firm with a different culture in a previous nonfamily organization he worked for, an employee described the emotional component, leading to positive and negative outcomes:

I came [in my previous employment] from a very cold and rigid organization where it was very clear what the hierarchy was, and the owner wouldn't greet you with a 'good morning', and something was missing for me…. Here it was nicer for me. Somedays it is not so nice, because some days are less nice, when people are angry, where there is more stress, when something wasn't executed like it should have. Because everything is on an emotional basis, it also has disadvantages, it is clear…. You can get hurt more. Because if it is someone [a boss] who is estranged, and once in 6 months he gets to speak with you and tell you that you were wrong doing A, B, C, [you don't mind as much as] when he [my current owner] tells me so, I take it home, I am personally involved and I have a personal responsibility.

(Employee 22)

A nonfamily manager specifically described how this emotional/loving management style is created by the owner and cascaded down to the top management and employees:

We transmit the love that [the owner] gives to his management, his top management team, you transmit it down, like you don't come and say, well if the CEO receives every person and listens to everyone, so who am I not to listen to my people? Like he listens [to us], I have to listen to them [my employees]. And this is like the management that he transfers to us and we transfer it to the people below us.

(Employee 23)

"Tough Love" – A Combination of Caring and Control

The paternalistic management style combines strong authority with concern and considerateness (Pellegrini & Scandura, 2008). These two seemingly contradicting dimensions embody a control mechanism via "tough love." The employees described how management in family firms does not include direct protocols, but rather an expectation based on the family feeling. In this context, owners care and create an inclusive employment environment while employees are expected to reciprocate with loyalty and execution of work tasks. Trust, devotion, and loyalty are common descriptions of the outcomes of the "tough love" atmosphere. For example, this description:

In general, here they [owners] quite trust the employees, they give them tools but kind of let them do their work in a way, I won't tell you that it is with no control, because this is completely untrue, but in a freer way than in other places. It is this thing of feeling like a family, because they trust a lot. Whoever gets in is being trusted, he is given tools to succeed.

(Employee 27)

The employees we spoke to specifically tied together the organizational feeling instilled by owners and their care of employees with a control mechanism:

> It is fun coming to a place of employment and to give all that you can. I think it is important. And it is fun to see that other people after 7,8,10 years, 12 years, they work with devotion, like no one has to come and control them. Not like other places where people work and you come and you see there are cameras everywhere and the boss calls you every second. Here they don't have to do it, because the employees they are devoted any way…. I can really see it, the devotion that you can trust them [the employees] that it is on their shoulders and that they'll do anything to make it work. Like it comes to their pocket.
>
> (Employee 19)

Loyalty Expectations and Outcomes

Loyalty is the result of the loving and caring dimension of the owners' paternalistic management style, and is directly referred to as the mechanism invoked by the owners to influence outcomes in the firm:

> This loyalty, I don't think that you have it elsewhere. The caring. I need to work; I need to do the assignments related to my work. We do here much beyond [that]…We really care about the firm, if they'll [the owners] decide that people should help at the storage, then we will get down and help, not because I have to, and it happens here a lot, and I don't think it happens in other places.
>
> (Employee 14)

The owners' "tough love" results with a love from their employees toward them and the firm:

> Because I love this place, I live this place…. when you live your work, it is easier for you, more fun, you enjoy your work. Not many [people] go to work enjoying it…. And I come to a place I love, I grew up here, which is more important.
>
> (Employee 10)

Summing up, this cycle of love expressed in a working relationship between owners and their nonfamily employees replaces other organizational control mechanisms, as expressed by Employee 9: "They (owners) love me and I love them, like family."

A Model of Paternalistic Leadership in Family Firms

Given the links outlined in Table 12.1, we apply our understanding of paternalistic leadership in family firms to outline both the antecedents

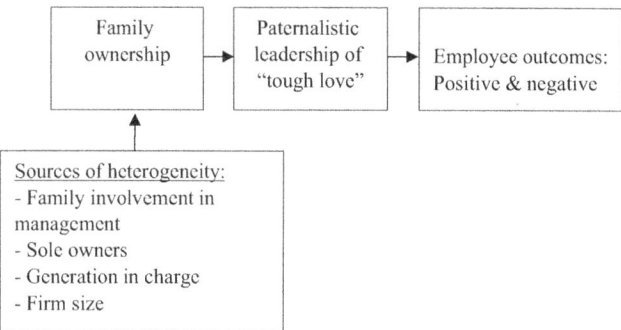

Figure 12.1 A model of paternalistic leadership in family firms.

and outcomes to this kind of employment setting. Figure 12.1 describes a prospective model of paternalistic leadership in family firms. These concepts are explored in the following sections.

Antecedents of Paternalism in Family Firms

Organizational culture stems from ownership, as business leaders establish the culture and organizing mode of their organization (Pettigrew, 1979; Schein, 2004). As Schein (2004, p. 2) described, leaders do this by imposing their "own values and assumptions on a group." Leaders create the ideologies, beliefs, and rituals of their organization via "the translation of individual drive into collective purpose" (Pettigrew, 1979, p. 573). In family firms, with a longer tenure of family CEO's (McConaughy, 2000), founders not only establish the values and goals that guide their enterprise, but they also "have ample time on the job to ensure that their beliefs and preferences are imbued deep into the culture and systems of their firms" (Gagné, Sharma, & De Massis, 2014, p. 647). In a broader sense, a family's involvement in the top management team has been suggested to create and enforce its values on the larger managerial collective (Barnett, Long, & Marler, 2012). In this way, we support the notion that patriarchal owners create paternalistic organizations (Dyer, 1986).

Heterogeneity of Family Firms

Family firms are no homogeneous group and can be defined in various ways. Historically, the distinctive qualities of family firms have been established by focusing on pure ownership (Barry, 1989), qualitative descriptions of family management (Dyer, 1986), and multiple family member involvement (Rosenblatt, de Mik, Anderson, & Johnson, 1985). More recently, researchers have pointed out a lack of consensus regarding exactly how to operationalize family involvement (O'Boyle, Pollack, & Rutherford, 2012). Adding to the complexity, the current state of the family firm field is increasingly highlighting the heterogeneity among such firms, and the various outcomes that can result from multiple definitions (Nordqvist, Sharma, & Chirico, 2014). We refer to the heterogeneity of the different types of family firms as the various influences on ownership.

Influences on Ownership

Ownership vs. Management: There are two main ways in which a family can exert influence on their firm: influence on ownership and influence on management. Family influence on *ownership* includes measures such as the proportion of a family's shareholding (e.g., Maury, 2006), the extent to which two or more shareholders share the same surname (e.g., De Massis, Kotlar, Campopiano, & Cassia, 2015), chief executive officer (CEO) and board chair positions filled by same family member (e.g., Zahra, 2003), and family representation on the board of directors (e.g., Zahra, 2003). With respect to a family's influence on its firm via *management*, most studies have focused on the direct influence, for example, the number of family employees (Ling & Kellermanns, 2010), whether the CEO is a family member (Gomez-Mejia, Larraza-Kintana, & Makri, 2003), or the extent to which family members are represented on the top management team (TMT) (Mishra & McConaughy, 1999). The latter denotes as Family Involvement in Management (FIM), defined as family percentage in the TMT (Mishra & McConaughy, 1999).

Sole Owners: In a complementary study distinguishing among family firms, family founders, and lone founders among Fortune 1000 firms, "lone founder firms" were most inclined to growth strategies and therefore were best at providing returns to the owners (Miller, Le Breton Miller, & Lester, 2011). Similarly, Fahlenbrach (2009) found that Founder-CEOs tend to invest more in research and development, have higher capital expenditures, and make more focused mergers and acquisitions. These findings indicate the possible heterogeneity among sole owners and the rest of family firms.

Generations: Another key distinction that can explain performance differences is generational leadership. For example, firm performance for founder-CEO-led firms was found to be significantly superior to those of successor-CEO-led firms (Bennedsen, Nielsen, Pérez-González, & Wolfenzon, 2007; Fahlenbrach, 2009; Villalonga & Amit, 2006). More generalized comparisons also reveal performance advantages for first, compared to later, generations in family firms (Molly, Lavern, & Deloof, 2009).

Size: Firm size has also been found to influence family firm performance. Family involvement generally has a positive effect for large public firms and an insignificant or negative effect for smaller private firms (Stewart & Hitt, 2010). Meyer and Rowan (1977) point at the link between firm size and increased formality and rationality in organizing, claiming that size increases the complexity of internal relations and the need to coordinate

(Penrose, 2009). On the other hand, smaller firms allow for a community feeling (Ariely, 2008; Nicholson, 2008), which conforms to our goal of studying family-like paternalistic leadership in organizations. Research has shown that firms that deliberately restrict unit sizes to around or below 150 employees are better able to maintain a unitary and strong communitarian[3] culture, which is explained by evolutionary theory as the maximum size at which individuals can function as self-organizing social communities (Ariely, 2008; Nicholson, 2008). Based on this discussion, we contend that firm size can significantly influence the paternalistic management style of family firms, leading to a change in the organizational culture when firms grow in size.

Outcomes of Paternalistic Management: Positive and Negative

The vast majority of research on paternalistic leadership has mainly focused on various employee outcomes, such as decreased turnover intentions (Cheng, Huang, & Chou, 2002), increased job performance (Chou, Cheng, Chen, Jen, & Hsu, 2005), and organizational commitment (Farh, Cheng, Chou, & Chu, 2006). Studies have shown that different dimensions of the paternalism construct (e.g., benevolent, moral, and authoritarian) can have both positive and negative outcomes (Pellegrini & Scandura, 2008). For example, moral and benevolent dimensions have been positively related to job performance, job satisfaction, and psychological health (Chao & Kao, 2005), as well as the organizational citizenship behavior (OCB) of employees (Farh et al., 2006). On the other hand, authoritarian dimensions have been negatively related to job performance and OCB (Aryee, Chen, Sun, & Debrah, 2007; Liang, Ling, & Hsieh, 2007), and job satisfaction and psychological well-being (Chao & Kao, 2005; Erden & Otken, 2019).

Similar outcomes were also found in family firm contexts. For example, positive paternalism outcomes (related to moral and benevolent dimensions) were driven by the benefits linked to high-quality relationships between family business leaders and their employees, while an authoritarian leadership style can compromise the trust, reciprocity, altruism, and clan-based collegiality between family leaders and employees (Corbetta & Salvato, 2004; Lambrechts, Koiranen, & Grieten, 2009; Lambrechts, Koiranen, Grieten, & Bouwen 2009).

When employees are treated as "quasi family" (e.g., Karra, Tracey, & Phillips, 2006), family and nonfamily members are treated in a similar fashion. Such treatment can stimulate "a similar set of altruistic behaviors toward blood and non-blood relations, this behavior is 'rewarded' with a reciprocal set of altruistic behaviors in return" (Karra, 2018, p. 23). The literature suggests that building fruitful quasi-family relationships is dependent on personal relationships between employees and family leaders (Ward, 2004). In time, these relationships encourage reciprocal generosity and loyalty (Miller, Le Breton-Miller, & Scholnick,

2008), shared ties or shared experiences (Karra et al., 2006), and generative relational practices that are characterized by a high degree of joint psychological ownership – i.e., the feeling that the family business is "mine" or "ours" (Lambrechts, Koiranen, & Grieten, 2009; Lambrechts et al., 2009; Pierce, Kostova, & Dirks, 2001), thereby contributing to employees' affective commitment and stewardship behavior (Henssen, Voordeckers, Lambrachts, & Koiranen, 2014).

The organizational literature also supports the notion that the quality of relationships is one of the most important factors in a firm's ability to organize and manage change (e.g., Bouwen, 1998; Lambrechts, Koiranen, & Grieten, 2009; Lambrechts, Koiranen, Grieten, & Bouwen 2009; Shotter, 1993). For example, Lambrechts et al. (2009, p. 10) state that:

> If actors are able to continuously engage in high quality or generative relational practices, characterized by dialogical interpersonal behavior and supportive meaning making, they will experience a high degree of joint psychological ownership, and an ongoing willingness to invest in continuous improvement, innovation and learning.

Therefore, as paternalism increases, it is expected that employee loyalty and commitment also increase as a result of reciprocal altruistic behavior. However, an important footnote has to be made. It can be reasoned that an excess of employee reciprocal behavior (as a result of paternalism) could in some cases lead to employees' burnout and stress. This excess of compliance with expectations, or in other words a "moral obligation" to reciprocate leader's caring behavior, may ultimately result in negative effects, such as burnout, stress, and miscommunication. This is in line with findings that an excess of organizational commitment may result in negative outcomes both for the organization and the individual [see Randall (1987) for an overview of positive and negative effects of commitment].

Conclusion

In this chapter, we link together the general literature on paternalism and its "tough love" character with the leadership style characteristic of family firms. Using qualitative testimonials leading to a conceptual model, this chapter aims to understand the antecedents of "tough love" manifested in paternalism and its potential outcomes concerning the nonfamily employees in these organizations. By doing so, we demonstrate how love in horizontal relationships between owners and their employees is a prevalent phenomenon widely experienced in many firms across the globe. The duality expressed in the benevolent and the authoritarian sides of paternalism belongs and extends the hybrid nature of firms owned and managed by families.

We show that paternalism is a specific management style, affecting not just employee–employer relationships, but all facets of organizational culture. To illustrate this, and utilizing our linkage of the family business literature, Table 12.2 contrasts paternalism with more traditional "bureaucratic" manners of organizing along various dimensions of organizational culture.

Table 12.2 Comparison of Traditional Bureaucratic and Paternalistic Organizations

Dimensions – Degree to which:	Traditional bureaucratic	Paternalistic/Family firms*
Hierarchy is emphasized	**High**: Hierarchical; authority at the top	**High**: Hierarchical; authority at the top
Division of labor is formal and specialized	**High**: Formalized. specialized	**Low**: Informal, non-specialized
Employment is based on expertise	**High**: Employment based on technical qualifications; previous thorough training in a specialized area; little or no job rotation	**Low**: Employment based on commitment to the founder; training on the job; job rotation
Jobs are segregated by gender	**High**: Not explicitly addressed, but norm is high segregation by job title, women clustered at bottom	**High**: Not explicitly addressed, but norm is high segregation by job title, women clustered at bottom
Leadership style is authoritarian	**High**: Authoritarian leadership emphasized; autocratic	**High**: Authoritarian leadership emphasized; autocratic
Control is direct	**High**: Control is direct	**Moderate-low**: Control is partly direct and partly unobtrusive through internalized values reflecting loyalty to founder
Decision-making centralized and concentrated at high levels	**High**: Centralized decision making at higher levels, decisions final	**High**: Centralized decision making at higher levels, decisions final
Emotion treated as acceptable form of expression	**Low**: Emotional expression generally discouraged, devalued as irrational	**High**: Emotion openly expressed, personal and work related
Work and private life regarded as separate	**High**: Private life presumed to be separate from work activity, private adapted to work	**Moderate**: Private life concerns are relevant to work activity; private adapted to work

*Characteristics are based on this chapter as well as entrepreneurial/family firm literature (Dyer, 1986; Davis, Hampton, & Lansberg, 1997; Lansberg, 1999; Ward, 1997).
Source: Adapted from Martin, Knopoff, and Beckman (1998).

Table 12.2 demonstrates that, like bureaucracy, paternalism is also a viable control mechanism. The main differences between the two mechanisms are the emotional and unobtrusive way that control is being exercised and manifested in paternalistic practices. Reinforcing this, sociology research defines paternalism as an ideological persuasion used as a means of control within relations of power inequality (Martinez, 2003). Organizational studies view paternalism as a disguised control mechanism, as "a way of controlling employees through the pretense of family imagery, thus providing space for the manager to act as 'caring' and 'protective' head of the industrial 'household'" (Kerfoot & Knights, 1993, p. 665). This description demonstrates once again the dual quality of the two sides of the paternalistic leadership style of "tough love."

With that said, we have shown that both positive and negative outcomes can result from paternalism. Therefore, the style is not suitable for all firms or employees. Although we argue that family firms are particularly inclined to practice paternalistic controls, we also conceptualize differences among those firms, leading to the notion that heterogeneous family firms will practice paternalism in various ways. Further, not all employees will be attracted to paternalistic firms. Looking closer at the fit idea between organizations and their employees, Schneider (1987) – in his seminal study in which he concluded that "the people make the place" – explained that the attributes of people, not the nature of the external environment, are the fundamental determinants of organizational behavior. This perspective rests on the idea that people are not randomly assigned to different employment settings; rather, people are attracted to, are selected by, and remain in a setting that determines the work environment. Schneider calls this the Attraction-Selection-Attrition (ASA) framework (Schneider, 1987; Schneider, Goldstein, & Smith, 1995). The ASA model gained wide empirical support (Holcombe-Ehrhart & Ziegert, 2005) building on previous evidence and reasoning showing the match between individuals and their work environment. Although we do not explore these relationships further in our chapter, we set the stage for future work that explores the fit between paternalistic organizations and their employees.

Although paternalism has not received considerable attention in western management research, similar concepts have been put forth in the leadership literature, for example, "servant leadership." While the authoritarian leadership dimension of paternalism is found to be negatively related to job performance and OCB (Aryee et al., 2007; Erden & Otken, 2019; Liang et al., 2007), the so-called "servant leadership," i.e., a leadership style that perceives the leader as a giver and receiver of help (Schein, 1983), could be an alternative leadership style in line with the moral and benevolent dimensions of paternalism. Servant leadership promotes the valuing and development of people, the building of community, the practice of authenticity, and the providing of leadership for the good of those led. On that note, future research should explore the extent to which paternalism can achieve such outcomes, as well as how paternalism might be related to other leadership styles like servant leadership. On top of these future directions, this chapter expands our understanding of *how* love depicts relationships in organizations. We have also explained *why* paternalism can become prevalent in certain contexts. Not only that love exists in the organizational setting of family firm employee–employer relationships, but it is the core of their unique control mechanism. More specifically, organizational culture contains under-researched emotional elements, paternalism being the basis of the emotional bond between family owners and their employees.

Notes

1 Organizational culture is defined as the "climate and practices that organizations develop around their handling of people, or to the espoused values and credo of an organization" (Schein, 2004, p. 7). Therefore, it refers to how firms "do things" around practices such as their power structure, employer–employee relationships, and decision-making.

2 Unlike other organizations, the *family* influence in family firms is not limited to just work or management realms, rather family influence can also extend to governance and ownership matters. As a result, family issues, values, and culture can permeate the organization, affecting its strategy, policies, programs, goals, culture, and behavior (Pieper et al., 2015). This interaction between the two systems of family and firm has led to family business definitions such as: "[A] family business is a unique form of business organization since it involves the overlap of a system structured on rational economic principles with a system organized and driven by emotions" (Kets de Vries, Carlock, & Florent-Treacy, 2007, p. 26).

3 Communitarianism is a philosophy that emphasizes the connection between the individual and the community. Its overriding philosophy is based upon the belief that a person's social identity and personality are largely molded by community relationships, with a smaller degree of development being placed on individualism.

References

Ainsworth, S., & Wolfram-Cox, J. (2003). Families divided: Culture and control in small family business. *Organization Studies, 24*(9), 1463–1485.

Anderson, R. C., & Reeb, D. M. (2003). Founding-family ownership and firm performance: Evidence from the S&P 500. *The Journal of Finance, 58*(3), 1301–1328.

Anthony, P. (1986). *The foundation of management* (vol. 324). Oxfordshire, England: Routledge Kegan & Paul.

Ariely, D. (2008). *Predictably irrational.* New York, NY: Harper Audio.

Aryee, S., Chen, Z. X., Sun, L. Y., & Debrah, Y. A. (2007). Antecedents and outcomes of abusive supervisor: Test of a trickle-down model. *Journal of Applied Psychology, 1,* 191–201.

Astrachan, J. H., & Shanker, M. C. (2003). Family businesses' contribution to the US economy: A closer look. *Family Business Review, 16*(3), 211–219.

Aycan, Z. (2006). Paternalism: Towards conceptual refinement and operationalization. In U. Kim, K. S. Yang, & K. K. Hwang (Eds.), *Indigenous and cultural psychology*. New York: Springer Science & Business Media, LLC.

Barnett, T., Long, R. G., & Marler, L. E. (2012). Vision and exchange in intra-family succession: Effects on procedural justice climate among nonfamily managers. *Entrepreneurship Theory and Practice*, 36(6), 1207–1225.

Barry, B. (1989). The development of organization structure in the family firm. *Family Business Review*, 2(3), 293–315.

Barsade, S. G., & O'Neill, O. A. (2014). What's love got to do with it? A longitudinal study of the culture of companionate love and employee and client outcomes in a long-term care setting. *Administrative Science Quarterly*, 59(4), 551–598.

Bennedsen, M., Nielsen, K. M., Pérez-González, F., & Wolfenzon, D. (2007). Inside the family firm: The role of families in succession decisions and performance. *The Quarterly Journal of Economics*, 122(2), 647–691.

Bouwen, R. (1998). Relational construction of meaning in emerging organizational contexts. *European Journal of Work and Organizational Psychology*, 7, 299–319.

Chan, S. C., Huang, X., Snape, E., & Lam, C. K. (2013). The Janus face of paternalistic leaders: Authoritarianism, benevolence, subordinates' organization-based self-esteem, and performance. *Journal of Organizational Behavior*, 34(1), 108–128.

Chao, A. A. and Kao, H. S. R. (2005). Paternalistic leadership and subordinate stress in Taiwanese enterprises. *Research in Applied Psychology*, 27, 111–131.

Chen, X. P., Eberly, M. B., Chiang, T. J., Farh, J. L., & Cheng, B. S. (2014). Affective trust in Chinese leaders: Linking paternalistic leadership to employee performance. *Journal of Management*, 40(3), 796–819.

Cheng, B. S., Huang, M. P., & Chou, L. F. (2002). Paternalistic leadership and its effectiveness: Evidence from Chinese organizational teams. *Journal of Psychology in Chinese Societies*, 3, 85–112.

Chirico, F., & Nordqvist, M. (2010). Dynamic capabilities and trans-generational value creation in family firms: The role of organizational culture. *International Small Business Journal*, 28(5), 487–504.

Chirico, F., Nordqvist, M., & Colombo, E. (2012). Simulating dynamic capabilities and value creation in family firms: Is paternalism an "asset" or a "liability"? *Family Business Review*, 25(3), 318–338.

Chou, L. F., Cheng, B. S., Chen, C. H., Jen, C. K., & Hsu, C. T. (2005). Particularistic ties and interpersonal affection within Chinese high-level manager networks: Effects of deep-level psychological fitness and formal working relationships. *Indigenous Psychological Research in Chinese Societies*, 23, 201–257.

Chua, J. H., Chrisman, J. J., & Steier, L. P. (2003). Extending the theoretical horizons of family business research. *Entrepreneurship Theory & Practice*, 27(4), 331–338.

Cicellin, M., Mussolino, D., Martinez, M., & Iacono, M. P. (2013). Towards the construct of paternalism to investigate control in family business governance. *Corporate Ownership & Control*, 317–328.

Corbetta, G., & Salvato, C. (2004). Self-serving or self-actualizing? Models of man and agency costs in different types of family firms: A commentary on "Comparing the agency costs of family and non-family firms: Conceptual issues and exploratory evidence". *Entrepreneurship Theory & Practice, 28*(4), 355–362.

Davis, J. A., Hampton, M. M., & Lansberg, I. (1997). *Generation to generation: Life cycles of the family business.* Boston: Harvard Business Press.

De Massis, A., Kotlar, J., Campopiano, G., & Cassia, L. (2015). The impact of family involvement on SMEs' performance: Theory and evidence. *Journal of Small Business Management, 53*(4), 924–948.

Dyer, W. G. (1986). *Cultural change in family firms.* San Francisco, CA, & London: Jossy-Bass Inc. Publishers.

Dyer, W. G. (1988). Culture and continuity in family firms. *Family Business Review, 1*(1), 37–50.

Erden, P., & Otken, A. B. (2019). The dark side of paternalistic leadership: Employee discrimination and nepotism. *European Research Studies, 22*(2), 154–180.

Fahlenbrach, R. (2009). Founder-CEOs, investment decisions, and stock market performance. *Journal of Financial and Quantitative Analysis, 44*(2), 439–466.

Farh, J. L., & Cheng, B. S. (2000). A cultural analysis of paternalistic leadership in Chinese organizations. In J. T. Li, A. S. Tsui, & E. Weldon (Eds.), *Management and organizations in the Chinese context* (pp. 84–127). London: Palgrave Macmillan.

Farh, J. L., Cheng, B. S., Chou, L. F., & Chu, X. P. (2006). Authority and benevolence: Employees' responses to paternalistic leadership in China. In A. S. Tsui, Y. Bian, & L. Cheng (Eds.), *China's domestic private firms: Multidisciplinary perspectives on management and performance* (pp. 230–260). New York, NY: Sharpe.

Gagné, M., Sharma, P., & De Massis, A. (2014). The study of organizational behaviour in family business. *European Journal of Work and Organizational Psychology, 23*(5), 643–656.

Gelfand, M. J., Erez, M., & Aycan, Z. (2007). Cross-cultural organizational behavior. *Annual Review of Psychology, 58*, 479–514.

Gomez-Mejia, L. R., Larraza-Kintana, M., & Makri, M. (2003). The determinants of executive compensation in family-controlled public corporations. *Academy of Management Journal, 46*(2), 226–237.

Guzzo, R. A., & Abbott, S. (1990). Family firms as utopian organizations. *Family Business Review, 3*(1), 23–33.

Hendrick, C., & Hendrick, S. (1986). A theory and method of love. *Journal of Personality and Social Psychology, 50*(2), 392.

Henssen, B., Voordeckers, W., Lambrechts, F., & Koiranen, M. (2014). The CEO autonomy-stewardship behavior relationship in family firms: The mediating role of psychological ownership. *Journal of Family Business Strategy, 5*(3), 312–322.

Holcombe-Ehrhart, K., & Ziegert, J. C. (2005). Why are individuals attracted to organizations? *Journal of Management, 31*(6), 901–919.

Johannisson, B., & Huse, M. (2000). Recruiting outside board members in the small family business: An ideological challenge. *Entrepreneurship & Regional Development, 12*(4), 353–378.

Karra, N. (2018). *Family entrepreneurship in emerging markets.* London and New York, NY: Routledge.

Karra, N., Tracey, R., & Phillips, N. (2006). Altruism and agency in the family firm: Exploring the role of family, kinship, and ethnicity. *Entrepreneurship Theory & Practice, 30*, 861–877.

Kerfoot, D., & Knights, D. (1993). Management, masculinity and manipulation: From paternalism to corporate strategy in financial services in Britain. *Journal of Management Studies, 30*(4), 659–677.

Kets de Vries, M. F. R. (1996). The dynamics of family controlled firms: The good and the bad news. In C. E. Aronoff, J. H. Astrachan, & J. L. Ward (Eds.), *Family business sourcebook II* (vol. 2, pp. 312–323). Marietta, GA: Business Owner Resources.

Kets De Vries, M. F. R., Carlock, R., & Florent-Treacy, E. (2007). *Family business on the couch.* West Sussex: John Wiley & Sons, Ltd.

La Porta, R., Lopez-de-Silanes, F., & Shleifer, A. (1999). Corporate ownership around the world. *The Journal of Finance, 54*(2), 471–517.

Lambrechts, F., Koiranen, M., & Grieten, S. (2009). Co-creating psychological ownership for the changing family firm: Applying a relational practice perspective. Paper presented at the *9th IFERA World Family Business Research Conference,* Limassol, Cyprus, June 24–27, 2009.

Lambrechts, F., Koiranen, M., Grieten, S., & Bouwen, R. (2009). Co-creating psychological ownership for change: Applying a relational practice perspective in family business. *Proceedings of the 5th EIASM Workshop on Family Firm Management Research,* Hasselt, June 7–9, 2009.

Lansberg, I. (1999). *Succeeding generations: Realizing the dream of families in business.* Boston, MA: Harvard Business School Press.

Liang, S. K., Ling, H. C., & Hsieh, S. Y. (2007). The mediating effects of leader-member exchange quality to influence the relationships between paternalistic leadership and organizational citizenship behaviors. *Journal of American Academy of Business, 10,* 127–137.

Ling, Y., & Kellermanns, F. W. (2010). The effects of family firm specific sources of TMT diversity: The moderating role of information exchange frequency. *Journal of Management Studies, 47*(2), 322–344.

Lubatkin, M. H., Durand, R., & Ling, Y. (2007). The missing lens in family firm governance theory: A self-other typology of parental altruism. *Journal of Business Research, 60*(10), 1022–1029.

Martin, J., Knopoff, K., & Beckman, C. (1998). An alternative to bureaucratic impersonality and emotional labor: Bounded emotionality at The Body Shop. *Administrative Science Quarterly, 43*(2), 429–469.

Martínez, P. G. (2003). Paternalism as a positive form of leader-subordinate exchange: Evidence from Mexico. *Journal of Iberoamerican Academy of Management, 1,* 227–242.

Masuda, M. (2003). Meta-analyses of love scales: Do various love scales measure the same psychological constructs? *Japanese Psychological Research, 45*(1), 25–37.

Maury, B. (2006). Family ownership and firm performance: Empirical evidence from Western European corporations. *Journal of Corporate Finance, 12*(2), 321–341.

McConaughy, D. L. (2000). Family CEOs vs. nonfamily CEOs in the family-controlled firm: An examination of the level and sensitivity of pay to performance. *Family Business Review, 13*(2), 121–131.

Meyer, J. W., & Rowan, B. (1977). Institutionalized organizations: Formal structure as myth and ceremony. *American Journal of Sociology, 83*(2), 340–363.

Michael-Tsabari, N., & Tan, W. L. (2013). Exploring family features in non-family organizations: The family metaphor and its behavioral manifestations. *Entrepreneurship Research Journal, 3*(3), 391–424.

Miller, D., & Le Breton-Miller, I. (2005). Management insights from great and struggling family businesses. *Long Range Planning, 38*(6), 517–530.

Miller, D., Le Breton-Miller, I., & Lester, R. H. (2011). Family and lone founder ownership and strategic behaviour: Social context, identity, and institutional logics. *Journal of Management Studies, 48*(1), 1–25.

Miller, D., Le Breton-Miller, I., & Scholnick, B. (2008). Stewardship vs. stagnation: An empirical comparison of small family and non-family businesses. *Journal of Management Studies, 45*(1), 51–78.

Mishra, C. S., & McConaughy, D. L. (1999). Founding family control and capital structure: The risk of loss of control and the aversion to debt. *Entrepreneurship Theory & Practice, 23*(4), 53–64.

Molly, V., Lavern, E., & Deloof, M. (2010). Family business succession and its impact on financial structure and performance. *Family Business Review, 23*(2), 131–147.

Nicholson, N. (2008). Evolutionary psychology, organizational culture, and the family firm. *Academy of Management Perspectives, 22*(2), 73–84.

Noller, P. (1996). What is this thing called love? Defining the love that supports marriage and family. *Personal Relationships, 3*(1), 97–115.

Nordqvist, M., Sharma, P., & Chirico, F. (2014). Family firm heterogeneity and governance: A configuration approach. *Journal of Small Business Management, 52*(2), 192–209.

O'Boyle Jr, E. H., Pollack, J. M., & Rutherford, M. W. (2012). Exploring the relation between family involvement and firms' financial performance: A meta-analysis of main and moderator effects. *Journal of Business Venturing, 27*(1), 1–18.

Padavic, I., & Earnest, W. R. (1994). Paternalism as a component of managerial strategy. *The Social Science Journal, 31*(4), 389–405.

Pellegrini, E. K., & Scandura, T. A. (2008). Paternalistic leadership: A review and agenda for future research. *Journal of Management, 34*, 566–593.

Pellegrini, E. K., Scandura, T. A., & Jayaraman, V. (2010). Cross-cultural generalizability of paternalistic leadership: An expansion of leader-member exchange theory. *Group & Organization Management, 35*(4), 391–420.

Penrose, E. (2009). *The theory of the growth of the firm*. Oxford University Press.

Pettigrew, A. M. (1979). On studying organizational cultures. *Administrative Science Quarterly, 24*(4), 570–581.

Pieper, T. M., Astrachan, J. H., & Neglia, J. (2016). Work–family issues in family business: Pertinent aspects and opportunities for future research. In T.D. Allen & L.T. Eby (Eds.), *The Oxford Handbook of Work and Family*, 431.

Pierce, J. L., Kostova, T., & Dirks, K. T. (2001). Toward a theory of psychological ownership in organizations. *Academy of Management Review, 26*(2), 298–310.

Poza, E. J., Alfed, T., & Maheshwari, A. (1997). Stakeholder perceptions of culture and management practices in family and family – A preliminary report. *Family Business Review, 10*(2), 135–155.

Randall, D. M. (1987). Commitment and the organization: The organization man revisited. *Academy of Management Review, 12*(3), 460–471.

Rosenblatt, P. C., De Mik, L., Anderson, R. M., & Johnson, P. A. (1985). *The family in business: Understanding and dealing with the challenges entrepreneurial families face*. San Francisco, CA: Jossy-Bass Inc.

Schein, E. H. (1983). The role of the founder in creating organizational culture. *Organizational Dynamics*, 12(1), 13–28.

Schein, E. H. (2004). *Organizational culture and leadership* (3rd ed.). San Francisco, CA: John Wiley & Sons, Inc.

Schneider, B. (1987). The people make the place. *Personnel Psychology*, 40(3), 437–453.

Schneider, B., Goldstiein, H. W., & Smith, D. B. (1995). The ASA framework: An update. *Personnel Psychology*, 48(4), 747–773.

Shotter, J. (1993). *Conversational realities: Constructing life through language*. London: Sage.

Stewart, A., & Hitt, M. A. (2010). The Yin and Yang of kinship and business: Complementary or contradictory forces? (And can we really say?). In A. Stewart, G.T. Lumpkin, & J. A. Katz, (Eds.), *Advances in entrepreneurship, firm emergence and growth* (vol. 12, pp. 243–276). Bingley: Emerald Group.

Tagiuri, R., & Davis, J. (1996). Bivalent attributes of the family firm. *Family Business Review*, 9(2), 199–208.

Tan, W. L., & Fock, S. T. (2001). Coping with growth transitions: The case of Chinese family businesses in Singapore. *Family Business Review*, 14(2), 123–139.

Villalonga, B., & Amit, R. (2006). How do family ownership, control and management affect firm value? *Journal of Financial Economics*, 80(2), 385–417.

Ward, J. L. (1997). Growing the family business: Special challenges and best practices. *Family Business Review*, 10(4), 323–337.

Ward, J. L. (2004). *Perpetuating the family business: 50 lessons learned from long lasting, successful families in business*. Marietta, GA: Family Enterprise Publishers.

Wu, M., Huang, X., Li, C., & Liu, W. (2012). Perceived interactional justice and trust-in-supervisor as mediators for paternalistic leadership. *Management and Organization Review*, 8(1), 97–121.

Zahra, S. A. (2003). International expansion of US manufacturing family businesses: The effect of ownership and involvement. *Journal of Business Venturing*, 18(4), 495–512.

13 An Exploratory Study of Leaders' Expression of Love and Followers' Perceptions of Satisfaction and Engagement in the Workplace

Franklin Alexander Markow

Love: we all need and want it, but is there a place for such an ideal in the workplace? Is love something followers should feel from leaders? Does love have any place in the pantheon of leadership and management theory as a variable of interest, one leading to demonstrable positive organizational outcomes? Moreover, can we move beyond love as an emotion and aspiration, to a behavior and practice which enhances people's experience as organizational members? Love is perhaps one of the most written-on subjects in all literature, from the Greeks and Romans, through the Victorian era to contemporary times. Yet little is known about love as a leadership practice, or how it is enacted in appropriate ways in an organizational context, and little empirical research has been conducted connecting matters related to leaders, love, and organizational outcomes.

The overall arch of management and leadership studies suggests a sweep from scientific management, to human relations, emotions at work, emotional intelligence, to the *spirit at work* movements. In other words, we see a development from tangible, measurable, "hard" outcomes to more subjective "soft" yet nevertheless critical components of the human psyche. If we want to help the whole person in an organizational context, why not address a fundamental and primary need that we all have, to be loved? This is not to imply that an individual can get all their deep-seated love needs from their organizational leaders; but if leaders can learn to express and practice love in an organizational context, there may be something beneficial to them and the organization.

While there are ample love-related concepts in the leadership literature, and positive benefits seem to abound, there is no apparent higher-order, theoretically grounded approach that theorists or leaders can use to operationalize or make the behaviors distinct or explicit. It is thus proposed that Laaser and Laaser's (2013) and Satir et al.'s (2006) *Seven Desires* model, primarily used by those in the people-helping professions, can serve as an overarching framework to bring together several leadership concepts and can be useful for both theory-building and practice. The *Seven Desires* framework includes the need to be heard, affirmed, safe, touched, chosen, appreciated, and accepted. The hope is that this

DOI: 10.4324/9781003254034-14

coherent and memorable model can help leadership and organizational theorists, as well as leaders, define and express an admittedly subjective and nebulous ideal such as love. Following Satir and Baldwin's (1983) ideal of the *healing power of love* in a family context, love can be seen as a virtue of significance in an organizational context, one which values the well-being and wholeness of the community of those who join together as a work family.

We can see love-related ideas in the organizational literature, but it is often not described in ways that are tangible and practical. Rather it is an amorphous ideal, something that we should have or feel or aspire to. The *Seven Desires* model can give us an overarching framework for examining the *presence of loving behaviors*, and thus it can help us know if love is in fact present in a leader–follower relationship. Moreover, it can help us determine whether or not love can lead to positive organizational outcomes.

This chapter will address the connection between love and leadership as seen in the extant organizational leadership literature and offer a model to unify various ideas embedded throughout that literature. It also shares the results of a basic exploratory study that showed the efficacy of expressed leadership on followers in terms of their job satisfaction and work engagement.

Literature Review

Family Systems, and Laasers' and Satir's Contribution

Family systems theory in general is foundational to the practice of family counseling, addressing the latent seated webs of familial relations and feelings toward members of the family, both positive and negative, that keep us bound in certain roles. It is also considered one of the most influential of all the family conceptual frameworks (Broderick, 1993). It has been used as a way to understand how individuals interact with one another in an organizational context (Segal, 1996), with the view that organizational groupings are similar to the web of family relationships.

Mark and Debbie Laaser, who coined the term phrase the "Seven Desires of Every Heart" in their 2013 book of the same name, developed their work from over 30 years of practice as marriage and family counselors (Faithful and True: Welcome, n.d.). They took their influence from Virginia Satir, who has been called the "mother of family systems therapy" (Social Work Hall of Distinction, n.d.) and whose work is foundational to social work practice curriculum (Wretman, 2016). Satir and colleagues developed their *iceberg* model/metaphor for understanding human behavior in a family counseling setting (Satir et al., 2006). Similar to the proverbial iceberg, they posited that human behavior could be better understood and addressed by understanding the mass of feelings, perceptions, and coping strategies that lay beneath the surface. One of those underlying factors they labeled *yearnings*. These yearnings are the desires to be heard, affirmed, blessed, safe, touched, chosen, and included. These can often be unmet and unspoken expectations individuals have, which can explain certain behaviors or patterns of behavior. Thus, the phrase "seven desires of every heart" (Laaser & Laaser, 2013) refers to these seven underlying needs humans have which allow them to feel the deepest of connections with others.

Satir's work has previously been used to describe behavior in a workplace context. Her model for change has found its way into transformational change theory (Gross, 1994). Chen et al. (2001) have developed a process change model of unmet expectations based on the model. Ferch and Mitchell (2001) refer to Satir's approach when describing interpersonal relational leadership and need for intentional forgiveness. Banmen (1986) reviews the scope of Satir's work and orientation, citing her keen insights and ability to innovate in the field of family therapy, and her insights continue to inform counseling and, as this chapter suggests, perhaps leadership studies.

According to Lassrr and Laaser (2013) and Satir et al. (2006), the desires we all need to feel loved are:

1. To be heard and understood: Our ideas, thoughts, and feelings are listened to.
2. To be affirmed: What we do well, our accomplishments are noticed; the truth of our accomplishments is seen by others.
3. To be unconditionally accepted: Different than affirmation, not based on performance. To be appreciated and accepted for who we are, *not what we do.*
4. To be safe: To be free from fear and anxiety, to know that others are reliable.
5. To be touched: (appropriate) physical contact with other human beings.
6. To be chosen: To be selected by others in a special relationship, to be desired.
7. To be included: To belong to a special group or community, part of something larger than ourselves.

Culture: The Context of Leadership

Before examining love in leadership, it is appropriate to examine the larger context in which leadership is enacted, as seen through the lens of culture, and how culture can support love from a leadership perspective. Cameron and Quinn (2011) describe various types of organizational cultures. One such culture is referred to as the *clan culture*. The clan culture is characterized as a close-knit group with a strong sense of loyalty to the organization, and values close relationships and commitment. Moreover, leaders are seen as mentors or even parental figures, ensuring that the needs of "family members" are taken care of. In this sense, love by a leader would seem to be a central value and aspiration, as a way of expressing commitment and connection with followers, in the same way we expect parental figures to have love for their children.

Similarly, Bolman and Deal (2013) refer to the *human resources frame* as a way of understanding organizations. This frame sees organizations as webs of human relationships and emphasizes support and responsiveness to human needs. As a fundamental human need, fulfilling the need for love in an organizational context vis-à-vis culture can engender commitment and be part of the cohesion that binds a group together. Love can promote a sense of inclusion and belonging to organizational members, and engender positive emotional affect, in turn leading to a better employee experience, job satisfaction, engagement, and well-being.

Barsade and O'Neill (2014) assert that cultures have an (often overlooked) *feeling* dimension to them. For example, we can feel warm and accepted, or we can feel cold and isolated in the organizational context and culture. They describe a *culture of companionate love*, that is, feelings of affection, compassion, caring, and tenderness for others at work. They found that "an emotional culture of companionate love at work positively relates to employees' satisfaction and teamwork and negatively relates to their absenteeism and emotional exhaustion". (p. 551). Companionate love is an other-focused emotion, promoting interdependence and sensitivity toward other people. They also argue that emotion is mostly neglected in the study of organizational culture, and that while we know much about organizational culture, there has been a neglect of the affective side of people in most studies.

Love and Leadership

Part of the author's premise here is that ideals related to love, as defined in the *Seven Desires* model – the need to be heard, affirmed, safe, touched, chosen, appreciated, and accepted – can be seen embedded in various extant leadership and organizational literature. The next section will briefly explore several prominent leadership theories that feature love as a key variable. It will then show the discrete ideas of the model embedded in broader organizational and leadership-related constructs in order to clarify the rationale for using this model as a concise, overarching framework for a practical expression of love by organizational theorists and leaders.

There have been several contemporary leadership theories and writers who have placed love as part of their models and conceptions of what effective leadership look like. Concepts such as spiritual leadership (Fry, 2003; Fry & Eleftheria , 2017) and servant leadership (Greenleaf, 2002; Patterson, 2010) prominently include love as a component in their leadership models. Fry (2003) describes spiritual leadership as a leadership that not only enacts "typical" leadership behavior such as vision and direction, but also creates organizational cultures characterized by altruistic love, places where both leaders and followers express care, concern, and appreciation for others. He states,

> The ultimate effect of spiritual leadership is to bring together or create a sense of fusion among the four fundamental forces of human existence (body, mind, heart, and spirit) so that people are motivated for high performance, have increased organizational commitment, and personally experience joy, peace, and serenity.
>
> (p. 727)

Khandelwal and Mehta (2018) developed a leadership construct of *divine love* consisting of other extant ideas, such as accepting, appreciating, being altruistic, being humble, being open, being authentic, giving, setting free, taking action, treating equal, and valuing others.

Ferris (1988) stated that "although authors writing on leadership seldom make it explicit, love is the fundamental value that supports the concepts that many of them promote" (p. 41). Caldwell and Dixon (2010) posited that love, along with forgiveness and trust, represents critical leadership values which can help them maximize the value for the organization. Furthermore, Nur and Organ (2006) showed some evidence that spiritual leadership and *management by virtues* can lead to positive organizational outcomes such as organizational commitment, job satisfaction, and organizational citizenship behaviors.

Kouzes and Posner's (2017) book *The Leadership Challenge* has become a classic work in its own right and has impacted our thinking and practice of transformational leadership. Their *touch a heart* practice of exemplary leaders (Kouzes & Posner, 2017) speaks about the need for leaders to make an emotional connection with followers. They state about the ethics of love and leadership, contending that leadership is as much of an affective/emotionally driven proposition as it is a rational one, and that leaders are to love others as an ethical imperative. Bolman and Deal (2017) also describe love as an ethical leadership contribution of the caring extended family of organizations.

Caldwell (2019a) describes *transformative leadership* as a higher-order leadership construct which links love in various leadership theories, including transformational, servant leadership, Level 5 leadership, principle-centered leadership, covenantal leadership, and charismatic leadership. Similarly, Caldwell (2019b) describes *transformative ethics*, and affirms love as a leadership obligation, perceived by others through the ethical lens of those whom leaders serve. Parry and Kempster (2013) posit that charismatic leadership involves a "love story" between the leader and the follower. We love a certain leader because there is an emotional resonance between us and them.

Other Love-Related Needs Theories

There are of course other human needs theories which include an emotional/affective element. For example, though contested (e.g., Tay & Diener, 2011) Maslow's (1943, 1954) classic *hierarchy of needs* asserts that lower-order needs must be met before higher-order ones can be considered. These needs are physiological/physical needs, the need for safety, for belonging, for esteem, and for self-actualization. Note that the need for belonging includes the need for love, both sexual and non-sexual. McClelland's (1987) *learned needs theory* suggests that humans are primarily motivated by a need for achievement, affiliation, or power. Affiliation can include the need for love and acceptance. Max-Neef et al. (1989) describe a list of *needs and satisfiers*. These include the need for affection, creation, recreation, freedom, identity, understanding, participation, protection, and subsistence. Sirota and Klein (2013) describe three motivators in the workplace, which include equity/fairness, achievement, and camaraderie. In summation, we can see that the need for belonging (Maslow), affiliation (McCleland), affection (Max-Neef and Hevia) and camaraderie (Sirota) all imply emotional affect relating to one's need for love. As a foundational need, we can posit that the need for love, as expressed in the *Seven Desires* model, would be a key motivator in a workplace context, and that having that need met would lead to positive organizational outcomes.

Individual Aspects of the Seven Desires Model Embedded in the Leadership and Organizational Literature

The following section reviews the specific aspects of the *Seven Desires* model and shows connections with various concepts currently embedded in the leadership and organizational literature. The purpose is to show the relevance of each of these, to support the rationale for including them into a new coherent model of love and leadership.

To Be Heard and Understood

In an organizational context, this is the practice of listening to the thoughts, ideas, and aspirations of followers. Augsberger superbly stated that "being heard is so close to being loved that for the average person, they are almost indistinguishable" (Augsberger, 1982). We know about several positive benefits of listening in an organizational context. For example, we know that listening enhances trust and e organizational relationships (Brunner, 2008; Reed et al., 2016; Sherman & Cohen, 2006). Listening to *dissent* can be an act of servant leadership, and if we listen to those with outside opinions, without judging or critiquing them out of hand, we are serving them (Sprague, 2012). Listening is also a way to learn, and of discovering innovation (Heifetz et al., 2009).

To Be Affirmed

This implies that what followers do well – their accomplishments – are noticed and seen by others. Kouzes and Posner (2012) discuss the *Pygmalion effect*, and the importance of expecting the best, giving personalized recognition acknowledging good results, and reinforcing positive performance. Fry's spiritual leadership (2003) posits that members who are appreciated, along with their own sense of calling to an organization, will also be committed to the organization and contribute to its overall success.

To Be Unconditionally Accepted

This is different than affirmation, as it is not based on performance. This is to appreciate followers and accept them for who we are, *not what they do*. The Laasers (2013) and Satir (2006) originally refer to this as to be *blessed*, the biblical concept of accepting someone unconditionally, of receiving favor regardless of the circumstances. For this variable, it is admittedly difficult to see a connection in the current leadership literature. However, one can intuitively understand that being accepted for who they are, regardless of accomplishment, would translate into feelings of positive emotional affect, if not a sense of love from another person. The challenge to this from a leadership perspective is the typical *performance and reward* structure of most leader/follower (perhaps manager/subordinate) relationships. If someone does not perform their job well, there is typically an implicit questioning of their value to the organization. Unconditional acceptance is not what typically happens at performance evaluation time!

To Be Safe

Safety means that followers are free from fear and anxiety, to know that their leaders are reliable. There is a growing body of evidence on the importance of psychological safety in the organizational literature as seen in a systematic review of the literature done by Newmanl et al. (2017). These authors describe the positive impact of psychological safety on communication, knowledge sharing and voice behavior, learning behavior, performance, innovation and creativity, and employee attitudes. In a popular treatment, Coyle (2018) refers to *belonging cues*, those behaviors that signal safety to group members, that help create safe connections in groups in and among one another. Safety can be engendered by supportive leadership behaviors and organizational practices that lead to freedom of fear, reprisal, or reprimand for expressing oneself. This can also include protection from workplace bullying and harassment of any sort.

To Be Touched

This may be the most sensitive of all the *Seven Desires* constructs in an organizational context. Clearly, in our contemporary environment, we are not advocating unwanted sexual advances or intimacy gestures. Yet, the need to connect physically with other human beings has long been an indicator of mutual affection. Can touch have an appropriate role in the workplace to help leaders connect? For example, handshakes have been a staple gesture of safety and connection for centuries. Current gestures such as *high fives, fist bumps, shoulder taps*, etc., are informal workplace-appropriate gestures of connection between individuals who are connecting on an emotional level. In some organizational cultures, *hugs* are given and are accepted ways of connecting in the workplace. As embodied beings, humans need to connect with others, and this can have important, affirming effects in an organizational context.

Several studies have asserted the role of workplace touch. Spiegelman (2017) contends that there are consequences on a person's mental and physical health when this desire (for affection) is not met. The objective of her study was to understand if affection in the workplace could be beneficial on an employee's perception of stress, depression, and job satisfaction. She found that personality characteristics play a role in perceptions of received coworker affection, and that affection does have an impact on stress, depression, and job satisfaction. Fuller et al. (2011) introduced the concepts of *workplace touch self-efficacy* and *workplace touch initiation anxiety*. They also showed that there is a relationship between supervisors' use of touch and social effectiveness, which is an important competency for leadership. Bathurst and Cain (2013) described *embodied leadership* and the *aesthetics of gesture*. They posited that physical gestures engender important leader and follower relationship qualities and develop community as each responds to one another through (workplace appropriate) physical interaction. These physical interactions give organizational members ways to respond moment-by-moment to one another, which can develop stronger commitments and bonds.

There are also known benefits of physical proximity to improved communications and group performance. Coyle (2018) posited that high-performing cultures should more intentionally incorporate physical proximity in order to engender collaboration, serendipitous meetings, etc., by leveraging the *Allen curve*. The Allen curve refers to research which suggests that physical proximity to one another in the workplace leads to higher levels of meaningful communication and interaction.

In today's technologically mediated workplace, the logistical need for physical proximity seems to have diminished, yet the fundamental human need for closeness persists. And as of this writing, the literature was still catching up on this topic (e.g., Hoff, n.d.) during the Covid-19 pandemic, yet one can posit the deleterious effects that this lack of physical connection will have in the long term on the well-being of organizational members and outcomes, and leaders who lose close proximity with followers may jeopardize important communal connections.

To Be Chosen

This implies being selected by others in a special relationship, to be desired by others. Admittedly, this was perhaps the least strongly reflected in the extant organizational literature in this current examination. A couple of examples though can be conjectured. We can see that friendship in entrepreneurial teams can lead to superior performance (Francis & Sandberg, 2000) , and to *not* be chosen can be seen as a violation of equity (Adams, 1965). But these aside, little evidence was found of a *selection* concept that is germane. Nevertheless, being chosen instinctively engenders feelings of connection with and affection for others, hence its inclusion here. Any kid chosen last (i.e., not chosen) to be on the playground team can attest to this!

To Be Included

This is the idea that we belong to a special group or community, part of something larger than ourselves. One of the staples of the relational leadership literature is the *leader-member exchange theory* (LMX), which states that those with *in-group status/inclusion* are afforded greater levels of trust and confidence from their leaders, and this in turn leads to higher levels of job commitment, satisfaction, turnover, etc., from followers (Graen & Uhl-Bien, 1995). Edwards (2015) describes leadership and community, whereby community is foundational to our sense of belonging. Thus, leadership is about developing strong communities and inclusive cultures. Parry et al. (2019) posit that followers of a charismatic leader have an emotional connection with that leader in the form of a *sense of belonging* and links to their community.

Having reviewed the literature on both love in leadership and how ideas expressed in the *Seven Desires* model are reflected in a variety of other organizational concepts, we now turn to an investigation of how well these ideas hold together as a single construct, and their impact (if any) on followers' job satisfaction and work engagement.

Research Method

For this research the *Seven Desires* were considered as a higher-order construct, and a practical approach for leaders to express *love*, a seemingly subjective and amorphous ideal, to their followers, which in turn can lead to important organizational benefits, such as employee engagement and job satisfaction. These will be the independent variables in this study.

The outcome/dependent variables used in this study include job satisfaction and work engagement. Job satisfaction or employee satisfaction is a measure of workers' contentedness with their job, whether or not they like the job or individual aspects or facets of jobs, such as nature of work or supervision (Spector, 1997). Work engagement is "the harnessing of organization member's selves to their work roles: in engagement, people employ and express themselves physically, cognitively, emotionally and mentally during role performances" (Kahn, 1990, p. 694). These outcomes were chosen as proven beneficial outcomes, and easily assessable for purposes of a brief study.

Based on the literature reviewed here, the following hypotheses are postulated:

1. H1: The *Seven Desires* will factor together as a single construct.
2. H2: There will be a positive and significant correlation between *job satisfaction* and the *Seven Desires* by followers who express that their leader (direct supervisor) satisfies these.
3. H3: There will be a positive and significant correlation between *work engagement* and the *Seven Desires* by followers who express that their leader (direct supervisor) satisfies these.
4. H4: For each independent variable, as each measure (i.e., score on the instrument) increases, there would be a positive increase in the degree to which the variable impacts the dependent variables (job satisfaction and work engagement).

Sample

A web-based survey was distributed via social media. Respondents were asked to take the surveys and also forward the survey to their friends and associates using a snowball sampling technique. Additional surveys were sent to the researchers' associates, many of whom are involved in not-for-profit and higher education management and leadership roles. A total of 79 surveys were returned complete and usable.

Of the respondents, 53% were males, 47% were females, 76% were white, 6% were African-Americans, 6% were Latinos, 3% were Asians, 8% were multiracial, and 1% were Native Americans. The age range of the respondents was as follows: 13% were 18–24 years of age, 10% were 25–34 years, 29% were 35–44 years, 25% were 45–54 years, 18% were 55–64 years, and 5% were 65 years and older. Regarding the respondents' work organization type, 35% were from for profit/business, 35% were from non-profit/ministry, 20% were from education, 1% were from government, and 9% were identified as "other."

Measures

An instrument was developed with 16 questions. The questions of the instrument were related to perceptions of leaders' behavior and attitude by followers. There were 14 questions related to the *Seven Desires* model, with two questions for each subconstruct (heard, included, etc.). Respondents were asked to respond based on a five-point Likert-type scale, choosing either "Strongly Agree," "Agree," "Neither," "Disagree," or "Strongly Disagree." An example of a question measuring *being heard and understood* is "In conversations, my leader takes the time to listen to me, my thoughts and concerns." An example of a question measuring *safety* would be "I feel safe in the presence of my leader to be myself and openly share my ideas and thoughts without fear." Work engagement and job satisfaction were measured with one question each. The convenience sample consisted of $n=79$ respondents. See Table 13.1 for the question set.

Results

A factor analysis of the *Seven Desires* scale, using a principal component analysis, showed that 71% loaded on one factor, proving H1. Results from a factor analysis of the seven independent variables are presented in Table 13.2. Correlations for each of the variables all showed positive and significant correlations with one another. Further, the correlations between each of the seven variables and both job satisfaction and work engagement were positive and significant, proving H2 and H3. Table 13.3 presents the mean, standard deviation, variance, and correlations of the independent variables.

To test H4, a linear multiple regression model (LMR) with a set of control variables (age, gender, ethnicity, and job sector), coded either "yes" or "no," as well as the sum of the questions for each independent variable, was run against each of the dependent variables (job satisfaction and work engagement). The confidence level was set to 95%. A robustness check was also performed by running the LMR with individual questions, instead of the sum of the answers. Testing the substantive effects of the variables did not show the expected positive results. The overall results of the linear regression model indicated that these variables had no significant impact on the dependent variables – thus H4 was not proved. Tables 13.4a and 4b present the results of the multiple regression test.

Discussion

This chapter introduced readers to Laaser and Laaser's (2013) and Satir's (1986) concept of the *Seven Desires of Every Heart*, and proposed connections with other important variables in the organizational literature. It was proposed that this can serve as a model by which leaders can tangibly express *love* to followers, proposedly leading to important organizational outcomes, such as job satisfaction and work engagement. It also showed through an exploratory study an empirical connection between the components of the model with the organizational outcomes of commitment and engagement. The hypothesis that there would be a correlation between these seven variables was proved, and that these seven factors held together in a factor analysis. However, using linear multiple regression, it was shown that these individual items did not contribute significantly to the effect, thus bringing into question the efficacy of these variables alone in terms of followers' outcomes. Indeed, this demonstrated clearly the research dictum, "correlation is not the same as causation," and that a leader's expression of love to followers will not alone lead to their satisfaction or engagement in the workplace.

While it was not expected that expression of these behaviors exclusively would contribute to followers' perceptions of work engagement and/or job satisfaction, it was surprising and admittedly disappointing to see relatively no impact statistically, considering the ample connections that love and its intersection with many extant ideas embedded in the leadership literature would suggest. Methodological limitations could account for this, as there was a small sample size and limited question set. But how else can we account for this apparent lack of connection?

The *Seven Desires* may be mediating or moderating variables, which could possibly enhance other factors leading to job satisfaction and work engagement, such as the classic motivators and hygiene factors (Halpern, 1966), cognition and attitude (Tett & Meyer, 1993), and congruence and personality (Tokar & Subich, 1997).

The study did not look at other possible outcomes of leaders who express love in the workplace. For example, leader effectiveness, team cohesion, trust, motivation, organizational commitment, healthy culture development, and a host of other outcomes could be explored to see how leader's expression of love could affect outcomes. A more robust model, perhaps using the *Seven Desires* model as a mediator of some other extant variables which are connected to interpersonal, group or organizational outcomes, could provide more promising and positive results. As Barsade and O'Neill (2014) suggest, cultures of compassionate love do in fact lead to worker satisfaction and teamwork. Perhaps the *Seven Desires* need a *place* to exist, vis-à-vis organization cultures, or perhaps they themselves are ways to drive healthy cultures.

Another possible way to see love and its role is to see how it may contribute to other known theories of leadership. For example, transformational leadership (e.g., Bass, 1990; Avolio, 1999) emphasizes the interrelatedness of leader and follower, as does leader member exchange (Graen & Uhl-Bien, 1995) Uhl-Bien and other relational approaches to leadership. Perhaps love and the seven expressions of love as seen in this model are mediators and/or moderators of these various approaches to leadership. Further research is needed to see if and how the *Seven Desires* model could contribute to and enhance our understanding of current approaches to leadership.

Or to go the other direction, perhaps we should acknowledge the limited role that leaders actually do play in organizational success and follower outcomes. Meindl et al. (1985) through their *romance of leadership* construct (ironically) suggest that organizational success which is typically attributed to leaders may in fact be a *halo effect*, and that the followers' contributions may reflect the belief of followers in the leaders rather than actual actions of the leaders themselves. While leaders may act in loving ways toward followers, the overall impact on the success of the organization may be due to other factors. This and other follower-centric approaches to leadership may suggest that leaders' actions, including expressions of love, are only one way to understand the nature of leadership. Followers should not be seen as passive recipients of leaders, and thus their love (Collinson, 2006). Constructs such as shared leadership (Pearce et al., 2008), followers as co-producers and co-constructors of leadership (Uhl-Bien & Pillai, 2007), and other social constructivist and post-heroic views of leadership suggest that what leaders do may not be the epicenter of organizational outcomes or effectiveness, or follower satisfaction for that matter. In summary, not only do we need more than love, we need more than an understanding of leadership behavior to truly understand what brings people satisfaction and engagement with their work.

Conclusion

While the *Seven Desires* model can unify a myriad of extant leadership variables into a cohesive theory and can aid practitioners who seek to positively impact the lives of organizational members and enhance their experience, this study cannot empirically demonstrate that it directly has a significant impact on two important outcomes: work satisfaction or work engagement. Perhaps the old stanza "all you need is love" is not entirely correct, at least from an organizational leadership perspective (with apologies to all the Beatles aficionados). While there is ample support here and elsewhere that love can be a variable of significance for organizations and leaders, we should perhaps bracket our enthusiasm, put it into context, and seek to understand how expressions of love can demonstrate improved follower outcomes.

Or perhaps love is a virtue of such significance, leaders should seek to understand and practice it regardless. St. Francis de Sales wisely wrote, "Those who love to be feared fear to be loved, and they themselves are more afraid than anyone, for whereas other men fear only them, they fear everyone" (Camus, 2016 p. 58). Perhaps leaders can learn to help themselves by learning to love their followers, thus making the practice of leadership a more rewarding, enjoyable and authentic experience for everyone. Your mileage may vary...

Table 13.1 Question Items for Survey Instrument

Construct	Instrument questions
Accepted	I feel that I am accepted for who I am as a person, not just for the work that I do by my leader
Accepted	My leader accepts me for who I am, not just what I do
Acknowledged	I feel that my accomplishments at work are acknowledged and appreciated by my leader
Acknowledged	My leader regularly lets me know that I am a valued member of the organization
Chosen	At my work, I am often chosen to be on different groups or assignments by my leader
Chosen	My leader selects me for interesting and important assignments
Heard	In conversations, my leader takes time to listen to me, my thoughts, and concerns
Heard	I know that I have access to talk to my leader if needed
Included	I am part of the "in-group" of the leadership in my department or area.
Included	My leader makes me feel part of a special group or community
Safe	I feel safe in the presence of my leader to be myself and openly share my ideas and thoughts without fear
Safe	My leader never makes me feel threatened or fearful at work (e.g., yell, ridicule me, etc.)
Touched	My leader often shows affection in appropriate ways (hand shakes, shoulder pats, fist-bumps, etc.)
Touched	At my work, I am typically in close proximity to my leader and can easily walk around and connect with him or her.
Job Satisfaction	Generally speaking, I am satisfied with my job (e.g., it is a good fit for me, I am content where I am, etc.)
Work Engagement	Generally speaking, I feel truly engaged with my work and my workplace (i.e., I am strongly involved in my work, am enthusiastic about my work, happily engrossed in my work, etc.)

Table 13.2 Results from a Factor Analysis of the Seven Desires Independent Variables

Seven desires variable	Factor loading	Communality
To be Heard	0.89	0.79
To be Acknowledged	0.94	0.87
To be Accepted	0.92	0.84
To be Safe	0.85	0.71
To be Touched	0.73	0.53
To be Chosen	0.75	0.56
To be Included	0.82	0.67
Variance	4.97	4.97
% of Variance	71.03	71.03

Note: N = 79, Extraction method = Principal component analysis.

Table 13.3 Mean, Standard Deviation, Variance, and Correlations of Variables Measured

Variable	M	SD	Var	1	2	3	4	5	6	7	8
1. Heard	3.2	1.5	2.3	1							
2. Acknowledged	4.0	2.1	4.3	0.83*	1						
3. Accepted	3.7	2.2	4.8	0.86*	0.87*	1					
4. Safe	4.0	2.4	5.5	0.75*	0.77*	0.79*	1				
5. Touched	2.3	1.3	1.6	0.57*	0.63*	0.64*	0.49*	1			
6. Chosen	4.0	2.0	4.0	0.52*	0.67*	0.54*	0.50*	0.51*	1		
7. Included	4.5	2.1	4.6	0.65*	0.70*	0.65*	0.63*	0.49*	0.72*	1	
8. Work Satisfaction	2.0	1.1	1.2	0.68*	0.63*	0.65*	0.58*	0.45*	0.47*	0.55*	1
9. Work Engagement	2.0	0.9	0.8	0.51*	0.50*	0.53*	0.45*	0.46*	0.48*	0.54*	0.70*

*Correlation is significant at the 001 1.0 level (two-tailed).

Table 13.4a Multi-Linear Regression Analysis: Dependent Variable = Job Satisfaction

Effect	Estimate	SE	95% CI	
			LL	UL
Intercept	1.251	1.210	–1.175	3.677
Demographics:				
Age Groups (year)				
18–24	0.016	0.650	–1.286	1.318
25–34	–0.722	0.723	–2.170	0.727
35–44	–0.123	0.629	–1.385	1.138
45–54	–0.139	0.612	–1.367	1.088
55–64	0.189	0.617	–1.048	1.427
White	–0.007	0.498	–1.006	0.991
African-American	–0.069	0.709	–1.490	1.353
Native American	–0.312	1.023	–2.362	1.738
Asian	0.678	0.769	–0.864	2.220
Multirace	0.062	0.626	–1.192	1.316
Female	0.031	0.241	–0.453	0.515
For Profit	–0.588	0.770	–2.132	0.957
Not for Profit	–0.901	0.821	–2.547	0.746
Government	–0.321	1.201	–2.728	2.086
Education	–0.779	0.856	–2.496	0.938
Other	–0.887	0.776	–2.443	0.669
Independent Variables:				
Heard	0.298	0.157	–0.016	0.613
Acknowledged	–0.081	0.145	–0.371	0.210
Touched	0.032	0.119	–0.206	0.270
Accepted	0.142	0.156	–0.171	0.454
Safe	–0.005	0.077	–0.158	0.149
Chosen	0.067	0.086	–0.106	0.240
Included	0.054	0.087	–0.120	0.228

Note: N= 79, SE = standard error, CI = confidence intervals, LL = lower limits, UL = upper limits.

Male has been deleted from the model as it was too highly correlated with other variables. All demographic variables coded 1=Yes, 0=No.

Table 13.4b Multi-Linear Regression Analysis: Dependent Variable = Work
Engagement

Effect	Estimate	SE	95% CI	
			LL	UL
Demographics				
Intercept	0.33070819	1.141741	−1.9583446	2.619761
Age Groups (Year)				
18–24	0.597	0.613	−0.631	1.826
25–34	0.132	0.682	−1.235	1.499
35–44	0.530	0.594	−0.660	1.720
45–54	0.437	0.578	−0.721	1.595
55–64	0.431	0.582	−0.737	1.598
White	−0.181	0.470	−1.123	0.761
African-American	−0.158	0.669	−1.499	1.183
Native American	−0.444	0.965	−2.378	1.491
Asian	0.443	0.726	−1.011	1.898
Multirace	−0.185	0.590	−1.368	0.998
Female	−0.003	0.228	−0.459	0.454
For Profit	0.012	0.727	−1.446	1.469
Not for Profit	−0.147	0.775	−1.700	1.407
Government	0.148	1.133	−2.124	2.419
Education	0.084	0.808	−1.536	1.704
Other	0.582	0.732	−0.887	2.050
Independent Variables:				
Heard	0.129	0.148	−0.168	0.426
Acknowledged	−0.052	0.137	−0.326	0.222
Touched	0.027	0.147	−0.268	0.322
Accepted	−0.004	0.072	−0.149	0.141
Safe	0.084	0.112	−0.141	0.309
Chosen	0.087	0.081	−0.076	0.250
Included	0.133	0.082	−0.031	0.297

Note: N = 79, SE = standard error, CI = confidence intervals, LL = lower limits, UL = upper
limits.

Male has been deleted from the model as it was too highly correlated with other variables.
All demographic variables coded 1=Yes, 0=No.

References

Adams, J. S. (1965). Inequality in social exchange. *Advanced Experimental Psychology, 62*, 335–343. http://dx.doi.org/10.1016/S0065-2601(08)60108-2

Augsberger, D. W. (1982). *Caring enough to hear and be heard.* Baker Publishing Group.

Avolio, B. J. (1999). *Full leadership development: Building the vital forces in organizations.* Sage.

Banmen, J. (1986). Virginia Satir's family therapy model. *Individual Psychology, 42*(4), 480.

Bass, B. M. (1990). From transactional to transformational leadership: Learning to share the vision. *Organizational Dynamics, 18*(3), 19–31. https://doi.org/10.1016/0090-2616(90)90061-S

Bathurst, R., & Cain, T. (2013). Embodied leadership: The aesthetics of gesture. *Leadership, 9*(3), 358–377. https://doi.org/10.1177/1742715013485851

Bolman, L. G., & Deal, T. E. (2013). *Reframing organizations: Artistry, choice, and leadership* (5th ed.). Jossey-Bass.

Broderick, C. B. (1993). *Understanding family process: Basics of family systems theory.* Sage.

Brunner, B. R. (2008). Listening, communication and trust: Practitioners' perspectives of business/organizational relationships. *International Journal of Listening, 22*(1), 73–82. https://doi.org/10.1080/10904010701808482

Caldwell, C. (2019a). *Love and transformative leadership.* www.researchgate.net/publication/332538735_Love_and_Transformative_Leadership

Caldwell, C. (2019b). *Leadership and love: Insights through transformative ethics.* www.researchgate.net/publication/332567681_Leadership_and_Love_Insights_through_Transformative_Ethics

Caldwell, C., & Dixon, R. D. (2010). Love, forgiveness, and trust: Critical values of the modern leader. *Journal of Business Ethics, 93*(1), 91–101. https://doi.org/10.1007/s10551-009-0184-z

Cameron, K. S., & Quinn, R. E. (2011). *Diagnosing and changing organizational culture: Based on the competing values framework.* Wiley.

Camus, J. P. (2016). *The spirit of St. Francis de Sales.* CreateSpace Independent Publishing Platform.Chen, P., Tsai, S., & Lai, N. (2001). The construction of a process-change model of unmet expectations based on the Satir model. *Asian Journal of Counselling, 8*(1), 5–34.

Collinson, D. (2006). Rethinking followership: A post-structuralist analysis of follower identities. *Leadership Quarterly, 17*(2), 179–189. https://doi.org/10.1016/j.leaqua.2005.12.005

Coyle, D. (2018). *The culture code: The secrets of highly successful groups.* Bantam.

Edwards, G. (2015). *Leadership and a sense of belonging.* Edward Elgar Publishing.

Faithful and True. (n.d.). *Welcome.* Retrieved October 15, 2019, from https://faithfulandtrue.com/

Ferch, S. R., & Mitchell, M. M. (2001). Intentional forgiveness in relational leadership: A technique for enhancing effective leadership. *Journal of Leadership Studies, 7*(4), 70–83. https://doi.org/10.1177/107179190100700406

Ferris, R. (1988). How organizational love can improve leadership. *Organizational Dynamics, 16*(4), 41–51. https://doi.org/10.1016/0090-2616(88)90011-3

Francis, D. H., & Sandberg, W. R. (2000). Friendship within entrepreneurial teams and its association with team and venture performance. *Entrepreneurship Theory and Practice, 25*(2), 5–26. https://doi.org/10.1177/104225870002500201

Fry, L. W. (2003). Toward a theory of spiritual leadership. *Leadership Quarterly, 14*, 693–727. https://doi.org/10.1016/j.leaqua.2003.09.001

Fry, L. W., & Eleftheria, E. (2017). Spiritual leadership: Embedding sustainability in the triple bottom line. *Graziadio Business Review, 20*(3). https://gbr.pepperdine.edu/2017/12/spiritual-leadership/

Fuller, B., Simmering, M. J., Marler, L. E., Cox, S. S., Bennett, R. J., & Cheramie, R. A. (2011). Exploring touch as a positive workplace behavior. *Human Relations, 64*(2), 231–256. https://doi.org/10.1177/0018726710377931

Graen, G. B., & Uhl-Bien, M. (1995). The relationship-based approach to leadership: Development of LMX theory of leadership over 25 years: Applying a multi-level, multi-domain perspective. *Leadership Quarterly, 6*(2), 219–247. https://doi.org/10.1016/1048-9843(95)90036-5

Greenleaf, R. K. (2002). *Servant leadership: A journey into the nature of legitimate power and greatness*. Paulist Press.

Gross, S. J. (1994). The process of change: Variations on a theme by Virginia Satir. *Journal of Humanistic Psychology, 34*(3), 87–110. https://doi.org/10.1177/00221678940343007

Halpern, G. (1966). Relative contributions of motivator and hygiene factors to overall job satisfaction. *Journal of Applied Psychology, 50*(3), 198–200. https://doi.org/10.1037/h0023421

Heifetz, R., Grashow, A., & Linsky, M. (2009). *The practice of adaptive leadership: Tools and tactics for changing your organization and the world*. Harvard Business Press.

Hoff, T. (n.d.). *AMD special research theme: Individual health, well-being, and work lives in the age of pandemic*. Academy of Management. https://aom.org/events/event-calendar/event-detail/2021/08/01/higher-logic-calendar/amd-special-research-theme-individual-health-well-being-and-work-lives-in-the-age-of-pandemic

Kahn, W. A. (1990). Psychological conditions of personal engagement and disengagement at work. *Academy of Management Journal, 33*(4), 692–724. https://doi.org/10.5465/256287

Khandelwal, N., & Mehta, D. (2018). *Leadership by "love": A divine paradigm*, 6. www.scmspune.ac.in/journal/pdf/current/Paper%204%20-%20Nishant%20Khandelwal.pdf

Kouzes, J., & Posner, B. (2012). *The Leadership Challenges: How to Make Extraordinary Things Happen in Organizations*. San Francisco, CA: The Leadership Challenge—A Willy Brand.

Kouzes, J. M., & Posner, B. Z. (2017). *The leadership challenge: How to make extraordinary things happen in organizations* (6th ed.). Jossey-Bass.

Laaser, M. & Laaser, D. (2013). *Seven desires: Looking past what separates us to learn what connects us*. Zondervan.

Maslow, A. H. (1943). A theory of human motivation. *Psychological Review, 50*(4), 370–396. https://doi.org/10.1037/h0054346

Max-Neef, M., Hevia, A., & Hopenhayn, M. (1989). Human scale development: An option for the future. *Development Dialogue, 1*(7), 80.

McClelland, D. C. (1987). *Human motivation*. University of Cambridge.

Newman, A., Donohue, R., & Eva, N. (2017). Psychological safety: A systematic review of the literature. *Human Resource Management Review, 27*(3), 521–535. https://doi.org/10.1016/j.hrmr.2017.01.001

Nur, Y. A., & Organ, D. W. (2006). Selected organizational outcome correlates of spirituality in the workplace. *Psychological Reports, 98*(1), 111–120. https://doi.org/10.2466/pr0.98.1.111-120

Parry, K., Cohen, M., Bhattacharya, S., North-Samardzic, A., & Edwards, G. (2019). Charismatic leadership: Beyond love and hate and toward a sense of belonging? *Journal of Management & Organization, 25*(3), 398–413. https://doi.org/10.1017/jmo.2019.28

Parry, K., & Kempster, S. (2013). Love and leadership: Constructing follower narrative identities of charismatic leadership. *Management Learning, 45*(1), 21–38. https://doi.org/10.1177/1350507612470602

Patterson, K. (2010). Servant leadership and love. In D. van Dierendonck & K. Patterson (Eds.), Servant leadership: Developments in theory and research (pp. 67–76). Palgrave Macmillan UK. https://doi.org/10.1057/9780230299184_6

Pearce, C. L., Conger, J. A., & Locke, E. A. (2008). Shared leadership theory. *The Leadership Quarterly, 19*(5), 622–628. https://doi.org/10.1016/j.leaqua.2008.07.005

Reed, K., Goolsby, J. R., & Johnston, M. K. (2016). Extracting meaning and relevance from work. *International Journal of Business Communication, 53*(3), 326–342. https://doi.org/10.1177/2329488414525465

Satir, V., Gomori, M., Gerber, J., & Banmen, J. (2006). *Satir model: Family therapy and beyond*. Science & Behavior Books.

Segal, M. (1996). *Points of influence: A guide to using personality theory at work* (1st ed.). Jossey-Bass.

Sherman, D. K., & Cohen, G. L. (2006). The psychology of self-defense: Self-affirmation theory. *Advances in Experimental Social Psychology, 38*, 183–242. https://doi.org/10.1016/S0065-2601(06)38004-5

Sirota, D., & Klein, D. (2013). *The enthusiastic employee: How companies profit by giving workers what they want* (2nd ed.). Pearson FT Press.

Social Work Hall of Distinction. (n.d.). Retrieved October 15, 2019, from https://web.archive.org/web/20071010234128/http://www.socialworkhallofdistinction.org/honorees/item.php?id=33.

Spector, P. E. (1997). *Job satisfaction: Application, assessment, causes and consequences*. Sage. http://dx.doi.org/10.4135/9781452231549

Spiegelman, S. (2017). *Affection in the workplace: Personality, perceptions & affection*. Oregon State University. https://ir.library.oregonstate.edu/concern/graduate_thesis_or_dissertations/s7526j151

Sprague, R. F. (2012). Organizational dissent and servant leadership. *International Journal of Servant Leadership, 8/9*(1). www.gonzaga.edu/school-of-leadership-studies/departments/ph-d-leadership-studies/international-journal-of-servant-leadership

Tay, L., & Diener, E. (2011). Needs and subjective well-being around the world. *Journal of Personality and Social Psychology, 101*(2), 354–365. https://doi.org/10.1037/a0023779

Tett, R. P., & Meyer, J. P. (1993). Job satisfaction, organizational commitment, turnover intention, and turnover: Path analyses based on meta-analytic findings. *Personnel Psychology, 46*(2), 259–293. https://doi.org/10.1111/j.1744-6570.1993.tb00874.x

Tokar, D. M., & Subich, L. M. (1997). Relative contributions of congruence and personality dimensions to job satisfaction. *Journal of Vocational Behavior, 50*(3), 482–491. https://doi.org/10.1006/jvbe.1996.1546

Uhl-Bien, M., & Pillai, R. (2007). The romance of leadership and the social construction of followership. In B. Shamir (Ed.), *Follower-centered perspectives on leadership: A tribute to the memory of James R. Meindl.* IAP.

Wretman, C. J. (2016). Saving Satir: Contemporary perspectives on the change process model. *Social Work, 61*(1), 61–68. https://doi.org/10.1093/sw/swv056

14 Psychopathy and an Absence of Love in Organizations

Clive Boddy and Louise Boulter

Psychopathy and Psychopaths

Psychopaths have no emotion, empathy or love for others and in criminal populations are commonly associated with the most dangerous types of behavior and high degrees of recidivism (Laurell & Dåderman, 2005; Shaw & Porter, 2012). Psychopathic personality is marked by a constellation of features captured by a number of different psychopathy measures such as Lilienfeld's Psychopathic Personality Inventory (Ross, Benning, Patrick, Thompson, & Thurston, 2009), Cooke and colleague's Comprehensive Assessment of Psychopathic Personality (Hoff, Rypdal, Mykletun, & Cooke, 2012; Kreis & Cooke, 2011; Kreis, Cooke, Michie, Hoff, & Logan, 2012), or the Psychopathy Measure-Management Research Version (C. Boddy, 2019; Boddy, 2016; Boddy, Ladyshewsky, & Galvin, 2010). These features are commonly recognized as including a lack of empathy, guilt and remorse, emotional shallowness, glibness, egocentricity, and pathological lying (Cleckley, 1941/1988) and they increasingly appear to be correlated with brain chemistry and connectivity issues as illustrated by neuro-imaging studies. Such neuro-scientific studies in management have been described as promising but not without their limitations in terms of sample size, accessing appropriate subjects, consistency in findings, and ethical issues (Lindebaum, 2013). In psychology psychopaths are one of the more frequently studied populations but sample sizes tend to be low because of their relative rarity (circa 1%).

Since Patrick (1994) first implicated the role of the amygdala in psychopathy, there is growing evidence that the regions of the brain implicated in psychopathy are the prefrontal cortex and amygdala (Anderson & Kiehl, 2012; R. Blair, 2008; Glenn, Raine, & Schug, 2009; Weber, Habel, Amunts, & Schneider, 2008). Data from functional magnetic resonance imaging (fMRI) scans have also observed neurobiological differences in (mainly criminal) psychopaths.

Psychopathy is associated with brain abnormalities in a prefrontal, temporo-limbic circuit, in other words within the regions of the brain that are involved in emotional processing, among other things (Nickerson, 2014; Weber et al., 2008). There is thus evidence that psychopaths exhibit

DOI: 10.4324/9781003254034-15

deficits in the regions of the brain that are essential to moral judgment in normal individuals (Glenn, Raine et al., 2009).

Deficiencies in these areas of the brain have been associated with affective impairment and amoral behaviour and constitute a reoccurring theme in existing neuroscience studies on psychopaths (J. Blair, Mitchell, & Blair, 2005; R. Blair, 2008; R. James R. Blair, 2001; R. J. R. Blair & Cipolotti, 2000; Glenn, Raine et al., 2009; Intrator et al., 1997; Kiehl, Laurens, Bates, Hare, & Liddle, 2006; Motzkin, Newman, Kiehl, & Koenigs, 2011). Criminal and successful psychopaths are found to be less influenced by the emotional content of stimuli than non-psychopaths (Intrator et al., 1997; Steuerwald & Kosson, 2000). Further, evidence from one neuro-imaging study found that psychopathy was negatively correlated with medial prefrontal activity in response to pictures depicting moral violations, suggesting a reduced emotional response to moral stimuli in individuals with high levels of psychopathic traits (Harenski, Kim, & Hamann, 2009). A more recent analysis found that seven of 11 prior studies put forward evidence of deficits in criminal psychopaths' facial affect processing. Overall there is supportive evidence of psychopaths having issues with the processing of affective material (Brook & Kosson, 2013).

It was noted by Cleckley (1941/1988) that most psychopaths are not in prison and that psychopaths occupy positions of power in a corporate context. However, it was Babiak's (1995) case study of an industrial psychopath that essentially paved the way for the still emerging literature on the non-criminalised, successful corporate psychopath. In relation to this there is emerging evidence to suggest parallels between criminal and successful psychopaths. Osumi et al. (2012) summarize similarities as including "reduced amygdala volume, decreased amygdale activation during emotional and social task and impaired amygdale function, including a deficit in the recognition of the startle blink response" (Osumi et al., 2012). Findings from neuroscience studies thus primarily concern deficits in the amygdala that are linked to affective emotion, trust, ethical and moral decision-making in both criminal and successful psychopaths, and this, in part, contributes to an understanding of psychopath leaders' unemotional behavior.

Successful psychopaths, or corporate psychopaths as they are now known, may not be incarcerated, yet the consequences of their reported behavior in a workplace context are potentially pernicious. Corporate psychopaths, those people identified as being without conscience or empathy with others (Hare, 1999; Stout, 2005), have been connected to significant lapses in business ethics (C R Boddy, 2013; Marshall, Ashleigh, Baden, Ojiako, & Guidi, 2014) and moral decision-making (Seara-Cardoso, Neumann, Roiser, McCrory, & Viding, 2012). Corporate psychopaths may be said to break the social contract (Robertson & Ross Jr, 1995) between business and society because they are associated with lower levels of corporate social responsibility (Boddy et al., 2010).

Psychopaths, for example, are willing to engage in the illegal dumping of toxic waste (Ray & Jones, 2011).

Psychopaths have also been linked to the global financial crisis (Boddy, 2011a; Cohan, 2012; Mulhern, 2010; Spencer & Wargo, 2010) and have been described as being ultimately destructive (Babiak, 1995; Babiak & Hare, 2006; C R Boddy, 2010a, 2011b). Because of this, corporate psychopaths have been described as being perhaps the most significant threat to ethical corporate behaviour around the world (Marshall et al., 2014). They can be envisaged as being the opposite of the responsible leader (Maak, 2007; Maak & Pless, 2009; Maak & Stoetter, 2012; Voegtlin, 2012; Voegtlin, Patzer, & Scherer, 2010; Voegtlin, Patzer, & Scherer, 2012) and indeed as irresponsible and uncaring (C R Boddy, 2013).

It has been found that core psychopathic personality traits do not differ between successful and unsuccessful psychopaths (Benning, Patrick, & Iacono, 2005; Iria & Barbosa, 2009; Ishikawa, Raine, Lencz, Bihrle, & Lacasse, 2001). Moreover, the deficit in affective processing is shared (Osumi et al., 2012). However, the antisocial manifestations of these traits may differ. For example, successful psychopaths may be better at impulse control (Osumi et al., 2012), with unsuccessful psychopaths not as proficient at it (Murphy & Vess, 2003).

Love in Organizational Life

According to dictionary definitions, love is a strong affection for another arising out of kinship or personal ties, an attraction based on sexual desire or admiration associated with affection and tenderness, or a warm attachment or unselfish loyal and benevolent concern for the good of another. Within organizations the primary emotions driving action are reported to be fear and love, with Machiavelli claiming that it is better for a leader to be feared than loved because people are fickle, lying, and deceitful and more easily kept in line by fear. Lowney, on the other hand, claims that love is a better motivator because it binds teams together (e.g., p. 32) with ties of loyalty and affection enabling them to work seamlessly toward the common goal (Lowney, 2003) envisioned by their leader. Leaders who are driven by a love for their colleagues see the unique potential in each person and attempt to realize that potential by encouraging, mentoring, and motivating them.

Love and Psychopathy

With their emotional poverty, lack of affection (Nadis, 1995; Stout, 2005b) and entirely selfish orientation, psychopaths would appear incapable of feeling love for anyone and this lack of care or concern for others manifests in an unlovely and unlikeable workplace environment. This is explored in detail further on in this chapter.

Psychopaths, with their brain connectivity-related affective deficiency, have therefore been described as "outsiders to love" and as living outside the social and emotional fabric of society with no need for emotional attachments to others and a desire to destroy such attachments when they are seen in other people's relationships (Howell, 2018). When the psychopath is in a leadership position with an organization, this makes for a loveless and joyless workplace environment (C R Boddy, 2011b).

Etiology of Individual Psychopathy

In terms of the etiology or causes of psychopathy, a predominant view has emerged that a genetic predisposition is elemental in its formation whereas environmental factors determine the criminal or more societally successful course of the disorder. Some commentators go so far as to say that psychopaths are born that way (Cowan, 2014) and psychopathic traits do appear to be heritable (Unrau & Morry, 2019). Additionally, links between brain abnormalities and lack of emotional responsiveness, which is a characteristic of psychopathy, have been made (J. Blair et al., 2005). However, other researchers consider that environmental factors are critical and that negative childhood experiences can, for example, profoundly affect emotional functioning in adulthood (Porter, 1996). Thus, people who are severely traumatized or disillusioned by loved ones, argues Porter, or are deprived of any love, may learn to disengage their emotions as an effective coping mechanism, eventually emerging as psychopathic.

Similarly, an argument has been put forward that in terms of the genesis of psychopathy, it can originate as a result of deliberate human decisions to live one's life in a ruthless, selfish, unemotional, and materialistic manner (Levenson, 1992, 1993; Levenson, Kiehl, & Fitzpatrick, 1995). Such a choice is seen as entailing the decision to be uncompromising, callous and unfeeling, and to disregard any damage done to others as a result of a ruthless pursuit of mammon, dominance, and supremacy.

Thus, being unloved and abused or deciding that materialism and power trumps love may be antecedents to becoming psychopathic. Whatever the origins, psychopathy is a heartless, unfeeling, and pitiless condition. Organizational leaders with this personality may be expected to cause damage to their fellow employees and they do this, *inter alia*, through what they say and how they say it.

The Unlovely Speech of Psychopaths

An analysis of psychopaths' speech patterns reveals that relative to their contemporaries, they include more rational cause-and-effect descriptors, focus on material needs (e.g., money), and use fewer references to social needs (e.g., family) and find emotional descriptors difficult (Hancock,

Woodworth, & Porter, 2011). Additionally, Hancock describes how psychopaths use more past tense and less present tense verbs, indicating psychological detachment and less emotional engagement. Hancock concludes that these unconscious language differences support the notion that psychopaths operate on a primitive but rational level. They appear to be the "rational economic man" so discussed by economists, where they interact with others in impersonal transactional economic relations (Lawrence & Pirson, 2015).

A study published in 1998 investigated the reasons for the ability of psychopaths to lie so convincingly and found that criminal male psychopaths were quieter spoken than non-psychopaths. The authors hypothesized that this quietness aimed to draw the listener into the personal space of the psychopath so that they could use their nonverbal communication skills involving hand gestures and prolonged eye contact to convince the listener of their sincerity (Louth, Wiliamson, Alpert, Pouget, & Hare, 1998). These authors also noted that psychopaths treat emotional words like non-emotional words in terms of their intellectual and affective response to them and that psychopath's voice levels do not differ when verbalizing emotive words whereas the voice levels of non-psychopaths did vary when verbalizing emotional words. The researchers hypothesize that the lack of emotional response in psychopaths allows them to lie without the tell-tale signs that a non-psychopath would display out of nervousness or fear of being caught out (Louth et al., 1998). This may facilitate their career progression.

Etiology of Corporate Psychopathy

The fact that an organization may be psychopathically ruthless, manipulative, remorseless, and self-interested in its actions has been recognized since at least 1985 (Daneke, 1985). As Daneke draws from Cleckley's work on psychopaths in society (Cleckley, 1941/1988) and refers to a "sociopathic firm," he is clearly using the word "sociopathic" synonymously with "psychopath." Thus, as defined by the *Encyclopedia of Business and Professional Ethics*: -

> Corporate psychopathy is the condition whereby a corporation acts in a ruthless, uncaring, self-interested, conscience-free manner with respect to its employees, other people, and to the wider society in which it operates. Corporate psychopathy is marked by a callous lack of care or concern for the feelings of others, an incapacity to maintain enduring relationships, a reckless disregard for others' safety, an incapacity to experience guilt and well as deceitfulness, and repeated lying and conning others for profit together with a failure to conform to social norms with respect to lawful behavior. The psychopathic corporation acts irresponsibly, harms the environment, damages employees, and places customers and society at risk in its attempts to

fulfill its goals of profit maximization. It accepts no responsibility for its actions and has no regrets or empathy.

(C. R. Boddy, 2019)

There are at least two circumstances where a corporation can be psychopathic. First, according to Bakan, western corporations are born with a predisposition to psychopathy because of their mandate or charter to create profit for shareholders above all other considerations (Bakan, 2004). A corporation is thus psychopathic because of its constitution and legal status. Senior organizational leaders and managers may take an exclusive orientation toward profit orientation at face value and operate as if nothing else matters. This is the case implied by Daneke and more elaborately set out by Joel Bakan in his book and in the documentary that was based on the book (Bakan, 2004). Bakan further elucidated this viewpoint in a recent interview wherein he stated that such a corporation is self-interested to the extent of being pathologically committed to the pursuit of profit and power.

The second case in which corporate psychopathy can occur is when corporate psychopaths (also known as primary psychopaths, successful psychopaths, executive psychopaths, industrial psychopaths, or organizational psychopaths) have taken over the leadership of a corporation or other type of organization. In this case, the corporation's aims are subverted and realigned toward the pathological pursuit of wealth, prestige, honors, and power for the individual corporate psychopaths rather than for the corporation. This can involve fraud, subversion of organizational aims, and extensive mismanagement.

The remedy for this second situation is to closely manage, ethically supervise, or just remove the corporate psychopaths before they can undertake too much damage through their immoral and self-interested behavior.

Corporate psychopathy thus originates in the lack of care or love within the corporate "DNA." It is legally established as merely a heartless profit-making machine. Alternatively, systemic or corporate psychopathy may also result from individual corporate psychopaths within an organization establishing a culture of ruthless indifference to other stakeholders.

Corporate Social Responsibility, Sustainability, and Psychopathy

Corporate social responsibility is the idea that firms should be more than just economic machines and should assume responsibility for and be accountable for the effects that their actions have on society and the environment. Cowan quite rightly points out that the natural world and the species within it are in danger from the psychopath, because lacking emotion and love, they have no care for the future of humanity or other forms of life (Cowan, 2014). This lack of love or care manifests in the willingness of psychopaths to despoil the environment by disposing of toxic waste illegally (Ray & Jones, 2011). The perception that organizations run by corporate psychopaths as leaders are lower in corporate social responsibility has also been reported on (Boddy et al., 2010).

Findings included that when working under corporate psychopath managers, employees perceived that their organization was significantly less likely to do business in an environmentally friendly manner, a socially desirable manner or in a way that benefits the local community, or in a way that displays commitment to its employees (Boddy et al., 2010). Nonetheless, early commentators on corporate psychopathy speculated that corporate psychopaths may engage in corporate social responsibility to draw attention away from other devious management practices (Boddy et al., 2010). More recently, a link between psychopathically managed organizations and the perception that corporate social responsibility actions are merely taken to make the organization look good has been made. Corporate psychopath managers are deemed by their subordinates to engage in fake corporate social responsibility to make organizations appear more caring than they are.

The Emotional Maelstrom Created by Psychopath Organizational Leaders

Although psychopaths themselves have a reduced emotional range linked to neurobiological constraints, they can create emotional turbulence all around them as their fellow employees attempt to deal with the ruthless behavior of the organizational psychopath. This pitiless behavior can include the serial seduction of other staff members who, because of the relentless attention initially given to them by the psychopath, can believe that genuine love and attraction is involved. Psychopathy is associated with a short-term mating strategy, exploitative-ness in relationships, game-playing, intention to cheat in relationships and infidelity (Jonason, Valentine, Li, & Harbeson, 2011; Unrau & Morry, 2019). The use of coercive and manipulative sexual tactics to gain casual, non-emotional sexual interactions are also associated with psychopaths (Harris, Rice, Hilton, Lalumiere, & Quinsey, 2007; Muñoz, Khan, & Cordwell, 2011) as is intimate partner violence (Kiire, 2017) and promiscuity together with a lack of commitment to sexual partners (Ali & Chamorro-Premuzic, 2010; Khan, Brewer, Kim, & Centifanti, 2017).

The psychopath may appear attractive because of their well-dressed persona and personal presentation skills (Holtzman & Strube, 2013) as well as their claimed power, success, and self-confidence. The victim ultimately falls for the flattering advances of the psychopath and eventually reciprocates with a real emotional connection or love. However, once seduction is achieved, this attention quickly wanes as the thrill seeking of the psychopath is satiated. Attention is then replaced by more exploitative and abusive activities.

The partner of the psychopath is then left bewildered as subsequent behavior, post-seduction, is out of synch with what was originally experienced. The partner may then be subject to manipulation and lies and is kept hanging by the psychopath until the partner is no longer of any benefit to the psychopath within the workplace. The psychopath may already be seducing a further victim by this point. There is no genuine emotional connection from the psychopath and so partners are disposable and are left feeling emotionally bereft, victimized, sexually exploited, and betrayed (Freeman, 2017). This type of serial seduction behavior has been discussed in an early book (Clarke, 2005) on workplace psychopaths and is sometimes hinted at in the qualitative research that one of the current authors has been involved in conducting.

In terms of other behavior, employees report that when working under corporate psychopaths they are less likely to feel that they are given due recognition for performing well, that their work is appreciated by their superiors, or that they were as rewarded for their good work as much as they deserved (Boddy et al., 2010).

These must be emotionally damaging to employees and result in a feeling of being unloved and unappreciated. This was examined by the current authors to explore how the lack of love or care in psychopathic managers influences employees. We theorized that the lack of emotions in corporate psychopaths would have an influence on the emotional reactions from those employees who report to them. Further, the inability of the psychopath to correctly read emotions, to identify the meaning of affective situations, and to link cause and effect in emotional situations (Gawda, 2015) may impair their ability to lead effectively, even if they wanted to. Additionally, psychopaths may seek to destroy emotional bonding in others because they are envious of it, being incapable of establishing such close affective bonds themselves (Howell, 2018). We examined this within the transcripts of people interviewed after working alongside corporate psychopaths. This investigation was undertaken through the lens of affective events theory (AET) as outlined below.

AET was put forward by Weiss and Cropanzano in 1996 and it places significance on follower emotional reactions resulting from workplace events (Weiss & Cropanzano, 1996). In line with AET, workplace events have the ability to trigger negative and positive discrete emotions in followers including anger, fear, joy, love, and sadness. In turn, positive and negative emotions form and impact follower workplace attitudes (e.g., job satisfaction) and behavior (e.g., turnover intention). AET is conceptualized as an emotional elicitation process. First, emanating from the workplace environment, a workplace event occurs, and this is subject to an initial appraisal by the follower – typically constructed along the lines of "what does this mean for me in view of the goals I want to attain?" This leads to positive or negative affect, with more discrete emotions emanating when a more contextual consideration is given to the event including the "degree of personal control, coping potential, consequences of the event and future expectations about this situation" (Gaddis, Connelly, & Mumford, 2004).

Following Haidt we define moral emotions as those emotions which respond to moral violations and/or motivate moral behavior and are therefore linked to the welfare of wider society. Haidt suggests that only a psychopath would make entirely rational (nonemotional) decisions (Glenn, Iyer, Graham, Koleva, & Haidt, 2009; Haidt, 2003). However, this section of the chapter is focused on followers' responses to the nonemotional psychopath, rather than the emotionality of the actual psychopath. Haidt structures moral emotions into categories relating to their focus of attention. "Other-condemning" emotions (that condemn other people) may include anger, contempt, disgust, and related emotions. "Other-praising" emotions may include admiration, elation, gratitude, and respect. "Self-conscious" emotions could be guilt, shame, embarrassment, and related emotions like pride. Pity and sympathy are "other suffering" emotions, those aroused through seeing the travails of others. We speculated that the psychopath leader's behavior generates significant workplace events that trigger negative follower emotional responses (Boulter & Boddy, 2020).

An affective workplace event has been defined by Basch and Fisher (1998) as "an incident that stimulates appraisal of and emotional reaction to a transitory or on-going job-related agent, object or event." At the same time, a negative event is defined in terms of either "potentially or actually having the ability to create harmful outcomes for an individual" (Lazarus & Folkman, 1984). We can also ascertain a flavor of what constitutes a negative affective workplace event from past studies. Thus, leader feedback failure (Gaddis et al., 2004), interpersonally unfair treatment (Judge, Scott, & Ilies, 2006), breach of the psychological contract (Zhao, Wayne, Glibkowski, & Bravo, 2007), and bullying (Glaso, Vie, Holmdal, & Einarsen, 2011) have all been put forward as negative affective workplace events.

Various taxonomies of emotions have been put forward in the literature. For the purposes of this chapter, we are especially interested in moral emotions that might be triggered in followers as a result of interaction with the psychopath leader. Given the abusive characteristics of corporate psychopaths we were especially interested in negative moral emotions, for example, anger rather than admiration, because these would be expected among followers (Boulter and Boddy, 2020).

Also given the understanding provided by Peeters' ideas on the asymmetrical effects of negative emotions, negative emotional responses may be expected to be impactful vis-à-vis the wider society (i.e., the organization) in which the negative emotions are generated.

Based on Weiss and Cropanzano's (1996) work, plus the comprehensive account put forward by Lazarus and Cohen-Charash (2001), negative emotions that have been identified in prior studies include anger and fear (Ekman, 1992; Izard, 1977; Shaver, Schwartz, Kirson, & O'connor, 1987), sadness (Ekman, 1992; Lazarus, Cohen-Charash, Payne, &

Cooper, 2001; Shaver et al., 1987), disgust (Ekman, 1992; Izard, 1977), and shame (Izard, 1977; Lazarus et al., 2001).

Negative emotions that are triggered by a workplace event are identified as follows: "becoming frustrated, ashamed, afraid, angry and stressed." Dasborough's (2006) study, which also calls on evidence from prior studies (Keenan & Newton, 1985; Narayanan, Menon, & Spector, 1999), identifies the most prevalent negative emotions discussed by followers as being anger and annoyance, frustration, and loathing, with specifically anger being triggered when followers were rudely spoken to (Boulter and Boddy, 2020).

According to Judge, Scott, and Ilies (2006), unfair treatment triggers anger and hostility; they support Watson's view (2000) that "when we are treated unfairly by another person we feel anger and annoyance, not guilt or nervousness." Similarly, destructive criticism triggers anger and disgust (Gaddis et al., 2004), while anger, anxiety, fear, helplessness, distress, and a high prevalence of shame are triggered by bullying (Glaso et al., 2011). Negative events are associated with higher emotional intensity (Taylor, 1991) with anxiety and especially fear being flagged as pivotal resulting in extreme physical symptoms (Clark & Watson, 1991). Emotional intensity is also "heightened" by unexpectedness (Clore, Schwarz, & Conway, 1994) and by working in an unhealthy work place environment "for a long time" (Dasborough, 2006).

An important dimension of AET is the impact of affective workplace events upon workplace attitudes (such as job satisfaction and organizational commitment), affect-driven behavior (such as lateness), and judgment-driven behavior (such as intention to quit) (Boulter and Boddy, 2020).

Negative emotions are associated with follower job inhibitors in terms of decreasing job satisfaction and performance. A negative event cognitively distracts a follower from successful job performance (Basch & Fisher, 1998; Weiss & Cropanzano, 1996). Prior AET studies have also suggested evidence that negative affective workplace events are associated with decreases of work attitudes and increases of negative affect and judgment-driven behaviors. Identified consequences of leader follower negative interactions include reduced job satisfaction and intention to quit (Dasborough, 2006). Intention to quit is a common outcome in existing AET studies – specifically bullying (Glaso et al., 2011) and psychological breach of contract (Zhao et al., 2007). Other AET studies have found that negative affective workplace events can result in workplace deviance, although specific examples of workplace deviance are not put forward (Judge et al., 2006).

While writing this chapter, one of the few studies that the authors found and that considers follower emotions and corporate psychopaths was that of Nelson and Tonks (2011). In their qualitative study of Australian employees who had worked with psychopathic managers, using semi-structured, in-depth interviews, they found an indifferent lack of empathy and emotions among psychopath managers.

In terms of the emotional impact of the psychopathic behavior, Australian employees were reported to have experienced a range of negative emotions and feelings, including despair, frustration, anger, depression, disempowerment, and stress. As was found in UK research, some of those Australian workers who had worked with psychopathic managers reported extreme levels of emotional disturbance, and these are self-conscious moral emotions under Haidt's typology, including a persistent sense of terror (Nelson & Tonks, 2011).

This is exemplified in the quote from one research participant below.

> If he walked into this room today I would be terrified and scream; I have taken counselling but could not go anywhere near that building again.
>
> (Nelson and Tonks' Australian research participant)

Corporate psychopaths charm those above them into thinking that they are exemplary employees and managers while being callously and unemotionally destructive to those beneath them (Boulter and Boddy, 2020). Not surprisingly turnover and withdrawal were reported to be among the main consequences of the presence of psychopathic managers in the Australian study, together with a reduction in organizational performance (Nelson & Tonks, 2011) and this corresponds closely with the findings from the qualitative UK research reported in this chapter.

In view of the findings from Australia (above) and prior AET studies, we expected that the psychopath leader would be a source of negative affective workplace events. Further, that exposure to the psychopathic leader's behavior can result in extreme negative follower moral emotions, which result in reduced job satisfaction, increased negative workplace attitudes and behaviors, and reduced performance.

We re-examined ten in-depth interviews which had been conducted from 2013 to 2014 with nine research participants (one interviewed twice). All participants identified a leader they had worked with or were still working with as being highly toxic. Further investigation revealed that the leaders they each referred to scored sufficiently highly on a psychopathy measure to be identified as corporate psychopaths. This measure is called the Psychopathy Measure Management Research Version 2 (PM-MRV2). It is a measure of corporate psychopathy which has shown itself to have good face validity, predictive validity, and reliability in use (C R Boddy, Miles, Sanyal, & Hartog 2014). The study participants comprised five females and four males. All were senior managers from a cross section of mainly private sector organizations, with two organizations being in the not-for-profit sector. Interviews lasted for approximately 50–60 minutes and, with the permission of the research participants, were taped and later transcribed.

Emotionless Psychopath Leaders and Orchestration of Affective Workplace Events

With regard to the current investigation it was found that psychopathic leaders are a source of negative affective workplace events – with exposure to a psychopathic leader's behavior triggering negative emotions in followers. We report on our findings below as they relate to the fearful and loveless workplace environment created by the presence of corporate psychopaths.

Lack of Empathy – The Emotionless Psychopath Leader

In line with the information on the emotional poverty and lack of love in psychopaths, our data supports the idea that psychopathic leaders are largely emotionless and unloving (Boulter and Boddy, 2020). This is a strong and recurrent theme throughout and flavors the emotional episodes recounted to us by followers. Specific incidents include a psychopathic leader who was described by a follower as being poor at negotiating with clients because of their inability to understand clients' emotional responses. The psychopathic manager was seen as being able to understand spreadsheets but not the emotional connection between the customer and the brand (Boddy & Croft, 2016). The research participant reported that because of this lack of understanding, and of declining ethics, clients started to leave the company. Lack of emotional empathy is also apparent in this psychopath leader's dealing with followers. When one employee asked to be given a redundancy package so that she could leave the abusive workplace, the psychopath leader laughed at her and did not otherwise respond to her request.

The following also supports the idea that the psychopath leader lacks empathic emotion. The corporate psychopaths examined here were reportedly indifferent to the fate of other employees. They did not care if they were disliked or not and so were prepared to use bullying and rudeness to control employees (Boulter and Boddy, 2020). A narcissistic manager differs in this respect because they want to be liked and admired (Ashton-James & Levordashka, 2013). This abusive behavior in the corporate psychopath resulted in self-conscious moral emotional responses such as a feeling of humiliation (C. Boddy, Miles, Sanyal, & Hartog, 2015).

> It was unpleasant. You were undermined quite regularly… . just shouting very loudly and telling people to come into an office without any niceties, any basic pleasantries, it was hostile… . I saw the behaviors of being screamed at and shouted at and what felt like humiliation quite a lot.
>
> (HR Director, Interview 4)

The fact that corporate psychopaths demonstrate unemotional behavior is illustrated by the following comment.

> I think he would probably have seen it (that he was very disliked) as a badge of honor for being a tough, hard manager. That is a good thing to be so disliked.
>
> (HR Director, Interview 2)

This participant also described the emotionless state of the psychopath leader using phrases that one might associate with criminal psychopaths:

> This individual could actually do things without batting an eyelid.
>
> (HR Director, Interview 4)

Another participant went into more detail – again, illustrating an emotionality in corporate psychopaths which does not correspond to usual behavior.

> He didn't really respond to trust or kindness in a normal manner. In fact, if anything he got people in to positions where there was a degree, they thought, of mutual trust and understanding and he then manipulated them to take advantage.
>
> (HR Director, Interview 1)

Our data also indicate that the psychopath leader's behavior is unethical, and employees are asked to undertake unprofessional and immoral activities with no moral compass being evident in decision-making and managerial lying being evident.

> The outcome for the organization was not really apparent as he was good at presenting himself to his managers; claimed success for the work done by the team, he lied to make himself look good.
>
> (Manager, Interview 10)

Follower Negative Emotions Triggered by the Emotionless Psychopath Leader

In general, the workplace atmosphere that is generated by a psychopath leader can be summarized as emotionally extreme (C. Boddy et al., 2015). A number of participants used the following words to describe the workplace atmosphere: "nasty," "vicious," "ruthless," "hostile," "unpleasant," "lack of trust," and "terrified." Further comments are categorized in terms of Haidt's typology of moral emotions as below.

Other-Condemning Moral Emotions

For many participants a commonly reported emotional response triggered by the behavior of the psychopath leader is fear. We characterize this as an "other-condemning" moral emotion because of its links with generating anger and resentment toward the one feared, that is, the corporate psychopath. As one participated stated, there was fear and a loss of morale associated with dealing with corporate psychopaths.

> The team morale was just going downhill.
>
> (Financial Services Manager, Interview 10)

One participant likened the workplace environment generated by the psychopath leader to being in the reign of terror created by the frequent use of the guillotine in the French revolution:

> He (a subordinate of the psychopathic leader) was genuinely terrified of what this man was going to do if he found out he was talking (to HR) about him.....He was convinced he (the psychopathic leader) was going to come and kill him... It was through intimidation and fear downwards.... (There was)...psychological and physical intimidation.
>
> (HR Director, Interview 1)

In this case, the police were eventually brought in to help regulate the psychopath leader who was then convicted of fraud and imprisoned. Further, many subordinates were reported to "hate" (another "other-condemning" emotion, which is also the opposite of love) him because of his intimidating and bullying manner. Corporate psychopaths are theorized to create chaos and emotional disturbances around them so that they can pursue their self-seeking agenda undisturbed by a staff that are too occupied with their own emotional work environment to notice that the corporate psychopath is not working toward the best interests of the organization.

Theoretically the emotional chaos that is created by the corporate psychopath has the effect of making them appear to be the only person involved who is rational and sensible. This was the case in the interview quoted from below. The "other-condemning" moral emotions of anger and even rage, as well as resentment, were generated by the corporate psychopath leader in this follower.

> I was suspended from my job (and then dismissed) for alleged gross misconduct. I raised my voice to my line manager on 2 occasions. My defense was that I had felt subtly bullied and harassed by my line manager for the past year building up to the incidents in (date deleted) where I was provoked to react so that my behavior could be complained about.
>
> (UK Female clerical officer, Interview 9)

This type of verbal reaction can be viewed as "going too far" by other employees (Geddes & Stickney, 2011) who are perhaps unaware of the provocation behind it. The strong emotional reaction, including the "other-condemning" emotions of anger and indignation created by the cold and manipulative behavior of the corporate psychopath, is evident in the following quote:

> When I reacted to her bullying and raised my voice to her, the Director of our company came out of his office to find me standing there stressed out, red faced, shaking and tearful and my line manager standing there cold and emotionless and gesturing towards me shaking her head. I was the victim and I lost my job and my line manager was/is the bully and she remains at work! I couldn't understand why no one else could see it.
>
> (UK Female clerical officer, Interview 9)

Self-Conscious Moral Emotions

The behavior of a senior psychopath leader (a board director) is described by an HR director as making the HR director feel "vulnerable" and "unsure" about the future of their own job as well as making followers in general "afraid":

> You are not quite sure how to predict somebody's behavior. ...there was a fear factor.
>
> (HR Director, Interview 4)

Corporate psychopaths display an appearance or façade of normality, especially in front of their superiors and this was the case for the employee interviewed below. She was bullied in and abused in private but treated normally and in an apparently friendly manner in public. This left her unable to convince her superiors that she had been bullied at all. The emotional impact of the bullying was evident in terms of the feelings of the self-conscious emotions evoked as well as the low self-confidence and self-esteem that the participant reported.

> I was micro managed, ignored and undermined. My self-confidence and self-esteem were slowly bashed. None of my accusations were believed because I had no proof. My line manager was very clever in that she would show two different sides to her character. When I was alone with my line manager, she was cold, abrasive, ignorant and demanding, but whenever there were witnesses, she would start talking to me and smiling and saying how good my work was, etc. Everyone thought she was a nice person because she always seemed to be praising me, but this was a façade.
>
> (UK Female clerical officer, Interview 9)

In another case, a psychopath leader who had been extensively briefed on a major new internal project for the organization that he worked for claimed at the last minute to know nothing about this project, causing it to be halted on the day that implementation was supposed to start (Boddy & Croft, 2016). This created a highly emotional reaction to the psychopath leader with boardroom expressions of anger, trauma, resentment, and crying, as followers struggled to understand and cope with this unexpected abjuration. Another common theme reported by participants was that the workplace environment was marked by a lack of trust in the psychopathic leader:

> I think if I think about the other people that I met he was simply distrusted by anybody else in the organization….. no-one would or very few people would give any confidences to him because the view would be that that would be used against you.
>
> (HR Director, Interview 2)

The following quote perhaps expresses resentment at the management style of the corporate psychopath:

> The well-being of the workforce was subservient to his whims and fancies. Anyone and everyone was expendable.
>
> (HR Director, Interview 4)

Followers' mistrust, we propose, was triggered by the psychopath leaders' behavior, including lying, being unpredictable, undermining, and "Machiavellian," as well as embarrassing and humiliating people:

> They could really undermine somebody by completely belittling them in front of others and knowing that they are doing it.
>
> (HR Director, Interview 6)

Such belittling of other people is evidence of the corporate psychopath generating self conscious moral emotions in followers.

Other-Praising Moral Emotions

Corporate psychopaths are theorized to be good at upward impression management and this has been found in recent UK research where the reputation and image of the corporate psychopath among those below them was diametrically opposed to that of those above them (C R Boddy et al., 2014). Corporate psychopaths were contemptuously "hated" (an "other-condemning" moral emotion) by those working under them, who reported that they were liars, untrustworthy, and destructive to the organization. However, senior management reportedly thought of the same corporate psychopaths as being highly trustworthy, admirable, and successful managers ("other-praising" moral emotions).

> Absolutely intelligent, like I said. Could be really charming, especially upwards management, especially from afar, definitely very confident.
>
> (HR Director, Interview 6)

Consequences of the Emotionless Psychopath Leader–Follower Negative Affective Workplace Attitude and Behavior

A consequence of negative workplace emotions is a reduction in job satisfaction, and organizational commitment. Evidence of this can be found in participants reported affective-driven behavior. A common theme is that followers took active measures to withdraw from exposure to the psychopath leader. This included taking longer coffee breaks, absenteeism due to "sickness," taking longer lunch breaks, and evading the psychopath leader by moving to different parts of the office.

In one organization that had a psychopath CEO leader, absenteeism due to illness was reported to have gone from a rare occurrence to a daily event involving up to 10% of employees. As one participant stated:

> I used to take my holidays when I knew he wasn't on holiday so I could build up a maximum amount of time as I could so that I wasn't in the office at the same time. It was all techniques either to just keep my head down or get myself out of the way so I didn't have to go through what felt like somebody's game of power.
>
> (HR Director, Interview 4)

While another participant stated that employees lost their direction, sense of purpose, self-motivation, and pride in their work when working under a psychopath leader.

> So people have lost… respect, lost direction and there is no control.
>
> (Senior Manager, Interview 7)

Another common theme in the literature in terms of judgment-driven behavior is intention to quit and we found support for this. Moreover, when followers were directly reporting to a psychopathic leader, the intention to quit became a reality. Followers would actually quit their job even with no other job to go to:

> Team morale went down. I resigned and then another, 3rd person resigned this year and the 4th and last person in the team is due to resign soon.
>
> (Financial Services Manager, Interview 10)

The generation of "self-conscious" moral emotions, such as that of embarrassment, was a factor in staff turnover decisions as the following quotes demonstrate:

There was a lady called (name removed) who was one of the payroll people and not long before I'd left there she'd been called in for her usual shouting at and she got up and walked out and never went back again.

(HR Director, Interview 4)

The HR director speaking, as quoted below, met people who had just been fired, on his first day at a new job with a corporate psychopath as a leader. This generated various moral emotions in the HR director, including the "other-suffering" moral emotion of pity as well as the "other-condemning" moral emotions of anger and fear. This made this HR director decide to leave that position and from his first day there he started to plan his exit. Another research participant reported that the position under the corporate psychopath would not even be attractive if twice as much financial reward was offered for it.

In terms of individual follower health, there is some evidence that followers were getting "damaged" through exposure to psychopathic leader behavior, including bullying and harassment:

I would spend a lot of time with other individuals counselling them and talking to them about their experiences because you would see the debris scattered across (the organization).

(HR Director, Interview 1)

Some "self-conscious" moral emotions were alluded to like shame and regret for being the vehicle whereby unfair workplace decisions were delivered, as in the quote below, with a research participant who felt undermined in his integrity. Other research participants expressed "other suffering" moral emotions like sympathy for unlawfully dismissing a senior employee (at the orders of a corporate psychopath). In this case the employee (as expected by the research participant) won a case for unfair dismissal against the company concerned.

I felt much stress in my role. I felt my professional integrity was undermined. I felt there was nowhere to turn given the nature of the management team leading the business.

(HR Director, Interview 4)

Other-Suffering Moral Emotions

In terms of other-suffering moral emotions, some sympathy for employees who were perceived as being "damaged" by the experience of working with a corporate psychopath was also evident as detailed in the following quote:

Well I think there were lots of issues. If you mean by HR issues, grievances, people off sick, people having to move on to new roles very, very quickly, people getting damaged along the way, performance not being great, not positive behaviors permeating down the organization, lack of willingness to tackle what was becoming quite evident.

(HR Director, Interview 6)

Findings, Implications, and Limitations

Our findings provide preliminary evidence that the psychopath leader is a source of almost entirely negative and "other-condemning" workplace moral emotions and an impetus to hatred rather than love (Boulter and Boddy, 2020). Also, exposure to a psychopath leader's behavior triggers extreme negative moral emotions in followers, with the predominant emotion in participants being one of fear (Boulter and Boddy, 2020).

There was also less-tangible evidence of self-conscious emotions in research participants. They were still somewhat embarrassed to discuss working with a corporate psychopath, even many years after the event. Nightmares up to ten years afterward were reported by one research participant (he initially reported these as "dreams" but when the researcher probed him on this ("do you mean nightmares?"), he agreed that "nightmares" was a more appropriate term to use.

This reluctance may be seen as evidence of embarrassment. The less-tangible evidence included the body language of the research participants in this research, and the research participants were clearly self-conscious about the moral trauma they had been through.

There is also evidence to suggest that exposure to the psychopath leader impacts implicitly upon job performance in terms of reducing job satisfaction and organizational commitment. In line with AET, this increases negative affective workplace behavior. This is reported by our follower participants in terms of workplace avoidance tactics that ultimately, for many of our participants, result in terminating contracts of employment (Boulter and Boddy, 2020).

This investigation contributes to an understanding of the impact that the largely emotionless state of the psychopath leader has upon follower moral emotions and workplace behavior, which, to date, is an underexplored area. The evidence from participant responses and existing literature supports the commonly accepted view that psychopath leaders are largely emotionless and loveless, without an emotional understanding of their actions or indeed of the feelings of others. In particular, we find that they are without empathic emotion and can be particularly cold, cruel, ruthless, and bullying to followers (Boulter and Boddy, 2020).

Overall, evidence from our investigation supports the idea that a workplace environment characterized by fear, mistrust, and unfriendliness is generated by psychopath leaders. A reason for negative emotions, and in turn decreasing work performance, has been attributed to lack of follower-leader trust (Zhao et al., 2007). Trust is identified as constituting a significant factor for interpersonal workplace leader–follower relations (Young & Daniel, 2003). According to Young and Daniel's (2003) study, effectual trust is a combination of an emotional and cognitive assessment of risk. Support for lack of trust or "mistrust" being an emotional response can be found in McAllister's work (McAllister, 1995). Negative critical workplace incidents that are linked to mistrust include lack of management "back-up," power that is either unequal or exercised unjustly, and unacceptable levels of uncertainty (Zhao et al., 2007).

Based on our participants' accounts of these types of behavior, including bullying, lying, and uncertainty created through unexpectedness, we posit that mistrust was created among followers in our investigation by the psychopath leader's behavior. This mistrust impacts negatively followers' job performance. Moreover and worthy of note is that the prevalent negative emotion triggered by exposure to the psychopath leader in our investigation is fear, an emotion that we posit was further heightened through "unexpectedness" (Clore et al., 1994) in view of the psychopath leader's behavior.

With regard to the current investigation, we recognize that our sample size is small and due to the sensitive nature of this study we could not access the psychopath leaders directly. Finding corporate psychopaths to study is difficult because of their rarity (circa 1% incidence), a point that is made in the existing literature where there are acknowledged to be difficulties involved in obtaining suitable subjects (Mullins-Sweatt, Glover, Derefinko, Miller, & Widiger, 2010; Widom, 1977). Nonetheless, corporate influence those around them at work and reports indicate that 5.75–13.9% of employees may be working with a corporate psychopath at any one point in time.

While the importance of qualitative approaches to leadership research has been acknowledged (Alvesson, 1997; Conger, 1998; Dasborough, 2006), we recognize that future work could include quantitative studies that allow for more objective testing of data (Boulter and Boddy, 2020). Also in relation to participants' recollections of emotions, people can be deficient (Fenton-O'Creevy, Soane, Nicholson, & Willman, 2011) although impactful events, such as those triggered by exposure to psychopath managers, can be remembered many years afterward, as we have seen in the investigation reported in this chapter.

A purpose of this investigation was to add to the emergent literature on corporate psychopaths by looking at their influence on moral emotions such as love and hatred, and the emotional responses of those employees who work under them. Workplaces are full of emotions (Gabriel & Griffiths, 2002) and it is therefore important to understand where they come from and what they lead to. In the investigation reported in this chapter, which was later reported in more detail in a full paper on emotions (Boulter and Boddy, 2020) we expand our understanding of the emotional link between the adverse affective impact of psychopath leaders and followers.

Neuroscience consistently shows common brain connectivity and chemistry issues with psychopaths in the areas of the brain that are linked to emotional processing. In summary, psychopaths process emotional stimuli intellectually rather than affectively and they are concomitantly cold and indifferent to the fate of their followers. Followers react to this with a limited range of negative moral emotions that are mainly focused on "other-condemning" emotions. Little evidence of the generation of any "other-praising" moral emotions (e.g., admiration and respect) was found in this research among followers. However, the corporate psychopaths reported on here were all well known to research participants.

Writers on toxic leaders such as Lipman-Blumen report that initially these leaders may evoke what Haidt would classify as "other-praising" emotions like admiration but that once they are better known and their intentions are more clearly elaborated, these initial praising estimations subside. In other words, a curvilinear effect is hypothetically expected, involving initial praise which declines over time and acquaintance. One or two of our research participants (in the cases where our research participants were in place before the corporate psychopath arrived) did report that their corporate psychopath initially presented as admirable. However, this was a short-lived experience for those who worked along-side the corporate psychopath.

On the other hand, "other-praising" moral emotions of admiration and respect were reportedly evident from those above the corporate psychopath (Boulter and Boddy, 2020). For example, one of the corporate psychopaths who was subsequently found to have defrauded the company of large amounts of money and had made death threats to employees and had claimed to hold a prestigious academic business qualification that he did not really possess was reported as being considered a "star" senior manager up to that point. The main board of directors considered him so admirable that when the initial accusations were brought forward by the HR Director involved, they were dismissed as being driven by professional jealousy (an "other-condemning emotion" in Haidt's typology).

Corresponding with theoretical expectations, corporate psychopaths appear to generate inappropriate (factually unfounded) "other-praising" moral emotions in those above them and mainly appropriate "other-condemning" moral emotions in those below them.

The investigation presented in this section of the chapter is the first to qualitatively investigate the emotions involved in the lived experience of working with corporate psychopaths. In line with AET, our investigation finds that the psychopath leader's emotional poverty and loveless character is a source of negative moral emotions at work, mainly of the "other-condemning" variety (Boulter and Boddy, 2020). In other words, corporate psychopaths are not just "ineffective" (Lindebaum, 2013), they are also unethical and destructive. The negative events they are perceived to cause lead to negative moral emotions and negative emotional outcomes for followers. This in turn impacts the drivers of performance such as commitment, job satisfaction, withdrawal, and turnover. These findings, we propose, have important implications for individual followers given that fear, for example, is an emotion that is associated with severe symptoms (Clark & Watson, 1991).

Further, there are implications for employee well-being and organizational performance in view of followers resorting to behaviors that reduce organizational goal attainment. When corporate psychopaths are in leadership positions, conflict escalates and employees are likely to feel angry, hurt, unappreciated, unloved, depressed, discouraged, aimless, and leaderless (Boulter and Boddy, 2020). Corresponding with the idea that negative events have a disproportionate negative impact on followers, we find that some employees even feel terrified about the events concerning the corporate psychopath.

This investigation indicates that at least some of the dark side of leadership can be explained by the emotional coldness and ruthless indifference of the corporate psychopathic. Some employees react by emotionally or physically fleeing from the organizational environment concerned. Callous and unemotional leadership is therefore the catalyst for relatively large emotional responses in employees and this exploratory investigation provides initial evidence of this.

Conclusions

The literature review and investigation of transcripts discussed in this chapter support the view that psychopaths not only engender decay via their lack of love and empathy but that they also seek to actively destroy what they see as good and loving in others. This makes for a cold and heartless workplace. Psychopaths in organizations and organizations which are systemically psychopath have no love for employees, the organization, or the future. This manifests in a lack of care and a loveless workplace environment characterized by negative emotions. Employees respond with emotional distress and with some attempts at redress, but otherwise with hurt, hatred, withdrawal, and finally abandonment, as they seek a more loving and emotionally rewarding workplace elsewhere.

References

Ali, F., & Chamorro-Premuzic, T. (2010). The dark side of love and life satisfaction: Associations with intimate relationships, psychopathy and Machiavellianism. *Personality and Individual Differences, 48*(2), 228–233.

Alvesson, M. (1997). Leadership studies: From procedure and abstraction to reflexivity and situation. *The Leadership Quarterly, 7*(4), 455–485.

Anderson, N. E., & Kiehl, K. A. (2012). The psychopath magnetized: Insights from brain imaging. *Trends in Cognitive Sciences, 16*, 52–60.

Ashton-James, C. E., & Levordashka, A. (2013). When the wolf wears sheep's clothing: Individual differences in the desire to be liked influence nonconscious behavioral mimicry. *Social Psychological and Personality Science*, Online first. Retrieved from http://spp.sagepub.com/content/early/2013/04/03/194855061 3476097.abstract.

Babiak, P. (1995). When psychopaths go to work: A case study of an industrial psychopath. *Applied Psychology: An International Review*, 44(2), 171–188.

Babiak, P., & Hare, R. D. (2006). *Snakes in suits when psychopaths go to work* (1st ed.). New York, NY: HarperCollins.

Bakan, J. (2004). *The corporation: The pathological pursuit of profit and power* (vol. 2006). New York, NY: New York Free Press.

Basch, J., & Fisher, C. D. (1998). Affective events-emotions matrix: A classification of work events and associated emotions. *School of Business Discussion Papers*, 1–22.

Benning, S. D., Patrick, C. J., & Iacono, W. G. (2005). Psychopathy, startle blink modulation, and electrodermal reactivity in twin men. *Psychophysiology*, 42, 753–762.

Blair, J., Mitchell, D., & Blair, K. (2005). *The psychopath: Emotion and the brain*. Hoboken, NJ: Blackwell Publishing.

Blair, R. (2008). The amygdala and ventromedial prefrontal cortex: Functional contributions and dysfunction in psychopathy. *Philosophical Transactions of the Royal Society B: Biological Sciences*, 363(1503), 2557–2565.

Blair, R. J. R. (2001). Neurocognitive models of aggression, the antisocial personality disorders, and psychopathy. *Journal of Neurology, Neurosurgery and Psychiatry*, 71(6), 727–731.

Blair, R. J. R., & Cipolotti, L. (2000). Impaired social response reversal. A case of acquired sociopathy. *Brain*, 123(6), 1122–1141.

Boddy, C. (2019, September 2–5). *The development and validity of the Psychopathy Measure–Management Research Versions 1 & 2*. Paper presented at the British Academy of Management Annual Conference, Aston University.

Boddy, C., Miles, D., Sanyal, C., & Hartog, M. (2015). Extreme managers, extreme workplaces: Capitalism, organizations and corporate psychopaths. *Organization*, 22(4), 530–551.

Boddy, C. R. (2010a). *Corporate psychopaths and organisational constraints*. Paper presented at the British Academy of Management Annual Conference, Sheffield.

Boddy, C. R. (2010b). Corporate psychopaths and productivity. *Management Services, Spring*, 26–30.

Boddy, C. R. (2011a). The corporate psychopaths theory of the global financial crisis. In *Journal of Business Ethics* (vol. 102, pp. 255–259). Springer Netherlands.

Boddy, C. R. (2011b). *Corporate psychopaths: Organisational destroyers*. Basingstoke: Palgrave Macmillan.

Boddy, C. R. (2013). Corporate psychopaths: Uncaring citizens, irresponsible leaders. *Journal of Corporate Citizenship: (Special Issue) Creating Global Citizens and Responsible Leadership*, 49, 8–16.

Boddy, C. R. (2016). Psychopathy screening for public leadership. *International Journal of Public Leadership*, 12(4), 254–274.

Boddy, C. R. (ed.) (2017). *A climate of fear: Stone cold psychopaths at work*.

Boddy, C. R. (2019). Corporate psychopathy. In D. C. Poff & A. C. Michalos (Eds.), *Encyclopedia of business and professional ethics* (pp. 1–3). Cham: Springer International Publishing.

Boddy, C. R., & Croft, R. (2016). Marketing in a time of toxic leadership. *Qualitative Market Research: An International Journal*, 19(1), 44–64.

Boddy, C. R., Ladyshewsky, R., & Galvin, P. G. (2010). The influence of corporate psychopaths on corporate social responsibility and organizational commitment to employees. *Journal of Business Ethics*, 97(1), 1–19.

Boddy, C. R., Miles, D., Sanyal, C., & Hartog, M. (2015). Extreme managers, extreme workplaces: HR directors, organisational managers and corporate psychopaths. *Organization* 22, 530–551.

Boulter, L., & Boddy, C. R. (2020). Subclinical psychopathy, interpersonal workplace exchanges and moral emotions through the lens of affective events theory. *Journal of Organizational Effectiveness: People and Performance*, 8, 44–58.

Brook, M., & Kosson, D. S. (2013). Impaired cognitive empathy in criminal psychopathy: Evidence from a laboratory measure of empathic accuracy. *Journal of Abnormal Psychology*, 122(1), 156.

Clark, L. A., & Watson, D. (1991). Tripartite model of anxiety and depression: Psychometric evidence and taxonomic implications. *Journal of Abnormal Psychology*, 100(3), 316.

Clarke, J. (2005). *Working with monsters. How to identify and protect yourself from the workplace psychopath*. Sydney: Random House.

Cleckley, H. (1941/1988). *The mask of sanity* (5th ed.). Augusta Georgia: Private Printing for Educational Use by Emily Cleckley (Formerly first published by C.V. Mosley Co. in 1941).

Clore, G. L., Schwarz, N., & Conway, M. (1994). Affective causes and consequences of social information processing. In R. S. Wyer & T. K. Srull (Eds.), *Handbook of social cognition* (vol. 1, pp. 323–417). Hillside, NJ: Erlbaum.

Cohan, M. (2012). Did psychopaths take over Wall Street asylum? Bloomberg, January 2.

Conger, J. A. (1998). Qualitative research as the cornerstone methodology for understanding leadership. *The Leadership Quarterly*, 9(1), 107–121.

Cowan, L. (2014). The psychopath: What's love got to do with it? *Psychological Perspectives*, 57(3), 291–311.

Daneke, G. A. (1985). Regulation and the sociopathic firm. *Academy of Management Review*, 10(1), 15–20.

Dasborough, M. T. (2006). Cognitive asymmetry in employee emotional reactions to leadership behaviors. *The Leadership Quarterly*, 17(2), 163–178.

Ekman, P. (1992). An argument for basic emotions. *Cognition & Emotion*, 6(3–4), 169–200.

Fenton-O'Creevy, M., Soane, E., Nicholson, N., & Willman, P. (2011). Thinking, feeling and deciding: The influence of emotions on the decision making and performance of traders. *Journal of Organizational Behavior*, 32(8), 1044–1061. Retrieved from http://dx.doi.org/10.1002/job.720 DO - 10.1002/job.720

Freeman, R. (2017). Why does it feel like two different relationships when one unwittingly falls for a psychopath? Retrieved from https://neuroinstincts.com/feel-like-two-different-relationships-one-unwittingly-falls-psychopath/

Gabriel, Y., & Griffiths, D. S. (2002). Emotion, learning and organizing. *The Learning Organization*, 9(5), 214–221.

Gaddis, B., Connelly, S., & Mumford, M. D. (2004). Failure feedback as an affective event: Influences of leader affect on subordinate attitudes and performance. *The Leadership Quarterly*, 15(5), 663–686.

Gawda, B. (2015). Model of love, hate, and anxiety scripts in psychopathic individuals. *Frontiers in Psychology*, 6, 1722.

Geddes, D., & Stickney, L. T. (2011). The trouble with sanctions: Organizational responses to deviant anger displays at work. *Human Relations, 64*(2), 201–230. Retrieved from http://hum.sagepub.com/cgi/content/abstract/64/2/201

Glaso, L., Vie, T. L., Holmdal, G. R., & Einarsen, S. (2011). An application of affective events theory to workplace bullying. *European Psychologist, 16*(3), 198–208. Retrieved from http://dx.doi.org/10.1027/1016-9040/a000026 DO - 10.1027/1016-9040/a000026

Glenn, A. L., Iyer, R., Graham, J., Koleva, S., & Haidt, J. (2009). Are all types of morality compromised in psychopathy? *Journal of Personality Disorders, 23*(4), 384–398.

Glenn, A. L., Raine, A., & Schug, R. (2009). The neural correlates of moral decision-making in psychopathy. *Molecular Psychiatry, 14*, 5–6.

Haidt, J. (2003). The moral emotions. *Handbook of affective sciences* (vol. 11, pp. 852–870). Oxford: Oxford University Press

Hancock, J. T., Woodworth, M. T., & Porter, S. (2011). Hungry like the wolf: A word-pattern analysis of the language of psychopaths. *Legal and Criminological Psychology*. Retrieved from http://dx.doi.org/10.1111/j.2044-8333.2011.02025.x DO - 10.1111/j.2044-8333.2011.02025.x

Hare, R. (1999). *Without conscience: The disturbing word of the psychopaths among us*. New York, NY: Guildford Press.

Harenski, C., Kim, S., & Hamann, S. (2009). Neuroticism and psychopathy predict brain activation during moral and nonmoral emotion regulation. *Cognitive, Affective and Behavioral Neuroscience, 9*(1), 1–15. Retrieved from http://proquest.umi.com.dbgw.lis.curtin.edu.au/pqdweb?did=1683539551&Fmt=7&clientId=22212&RQT=309&VName=PQD

Harris, G. T., Rice, M. E., Hilton, Z., Lalumiere, M. L., & Quinsey, V. L. (2007). Coercive and precocious sexuality as a fundamental aspect of psychopathy. *Journal of Personality Disorders, 21*(1), 1–27.

Hoff, H. A., Rypdal, K., Mykletun, A., & Cooke, D. J. (2012). A prototypicality validation of the Comprehensive Assessment of Psychopathic Personality model (CAPP). *Journal of Personality Disorders, 26*(3), 414–427.

Holtzman, N. S., & Strube, M. J. (2013). People with dark personalities tend to create a physically attractive veneer. *Social Psychological and Personality Science, 4*(4), 461–467. Retrieved from http://spp.sagepub.com/content/4/4/461.abstract

Howell, E. F. (2018). Outsiders to love: The psychopathic character and dilemma. *Contemporary Psychoanalysis, 54*(1), 17–39.

Intrator, J., Hare, R. D., Stritzke, P., Brichtswein, K., Dorfman, D., Harpur, t., . . . Machac, J. (1997). A brain imaging (single photon emission computerized tomography) study of semantic and affective processing in psychopaths. *Biological Psychiatry, 42*, 96–103.

Iria, C., & Barbosa, F. (2009). Perception of facial expressions of fear: Comparative research with criminal and non-criminal psychopaths. *The Journal of Forensic Psychiatry & Psychology, 20*(1), 66–73.

Ishikawa, S. S., Raine, A., Lencz, T., Bihrle, S., & Lacasse, L. (2001). Autonomic stress reactivity and executive functions in successful and unsuccessful criminal psychopaths from the community. *Journal of Abnormal Psychology, 110*(3), 423.

Izard, C. E. (1977). *Human emotions*. Boom Koninklijke Uitgevers.

Jonason, P. K., Valentine, K. A., Li, N. P., & Harbeson, C. L. (2011). Mate-selection and the Dark Triad: Facilitating a short-term mating strategy and creating a volatile environment. *Personality and Individual Differences, 51*(6), 759–763. doi:10.1016/j.paid.2011.06.025

Judge, T. A., Scott, B. A., & Ilies, R. (2006). Hostility, job attitudes, and workplace deviance: Test of a multilevel model. *Journal of Applied Psychology, 91*(1), 126–138.

Keenan, A., & Newton, T. J. (1985). Stressful events, stressors and psychological strains in young professional engineers. *Journal of Organizational Behavior, 6*(2), 151–156.

Khan, R., Brewer, G., Kim, S., & Centifanti, L. C. M. (2017). Students, sex, and psychopathy: Borderline and psychopathy personality traits are differently related to women and men's use of sexual coercion, partner poaching, and promiscuity. *Personality and Individual Differences, 107*, 72–77.

Kiehl, K. A., Laurens, K., R, Bates, A. T., Hare, R. D., & Liddle, P. F. (2006). Brain potentials implicate temporal lobe abnormalities in criminal psychopaths. *Journal of Abnormal Psychology, 115*(3), 443–453.

Kiire, S. (2017). Psychopathy rather than Machiavellianism or narcissism facilitates intimate partner violence via fast life strategy. *Personality and Individual Differences, 104*, 401–406.

Kreis, M. K., & Cooke, D. J. (2011). Capturing the psychopathic female: A prototypicality analysis of the Comprehensive Assessment of Psychopathic Personality (CAPP) across gender. *Behavioral Sciences & the Law, 29*(5), 634–648.

Kreis, M. K., Cooke, D. J., Michie, C., Hoff, H. A., & Logan, C. (2012). The Comprehensive Assessment of Psychopathic Personality (CAPP): Content validation using prototypical analysis. *Journal of Personality Disorders, 26*(3), 402–413.

Laurell, J., & Dåderman, A. M. (2005). Recidivism is related to psychopathy (PCL-R) in a group of men convicted of homicide. *International Journal of Law and Psychiatry, 28*(3), 255–268.

Lawrence, P. R., & Pirson, M. (2015). Economistic and humanistic narratives of leadership in the age of globality: Toward a renewed Darwinian theory of leadership. *Journal of Business Ethics, 128*(2), 383–394.

Lazarus, R. S., Cohen-Charash, Y., Payne, R., & Cooper, C. (2001). Discrete emotions in organizational life. In R. L. Payne & C. L. Cooper (Eds.), *Emotions at work: Theory, research and applications for management* (pp. 45–81). Chichester: John Wiley & Sons.

Lazarus, R. S., & Folkman, S. (1984). *Psychological stress and the coping process.* New York, NY: Springer.

Levenson, M. R. (1992). Rethinking psychopathy. *Theory & Psychology, 2*(1), 51–71.

Levenson, M. R. (1993). Psychopaths are not necessarily impulsive, etc. A reply to feelgood and Rantzen. *Theory & Psychology, 3*(2), 229–234.

Levenson, M. R., Kiehl, K. A., & Fitzpatrick, C. M. (1995). Assessing psychopathic attributes in a noninstitutionalized population. *Journal of Personality and Social Psychology, 68*(1), 151–158.

Lindebaum, D. (2013). Pathologizing the healthy but ineffective: Some ethical reflections on using neuroscience in leadership research. *Journal of Management Inquiry, 22*(3), 295–305. Retrieved from http://jmi.sagepub.com/content/early/2012/11/21/1056492612462766.abstract

Louth, S. M., Wiliamson, S., Alpert, M., Pouget, E. R., & Hare, R. D. (1998). Acoustic distinctions in the speech of male psychopaths. *Journal of Psycholinguistic Research, 27*(3), 375–384.

Lowney, C. (2003). *Heroic leadership: Best practices from a 450-year-old company that changed the world.* Chicago: Loyola Press.

Maak, T. (2007). Responsible leadership, stakeholder engagement, and the emergence of social capital. *Journal of Business Ethics, 74*(4), 329–343. Retrieved from http://dx.doi.org/10.1007/s10551-007-9510-5

Maak, T., & Pless, N. M. (2009). Business leaders as citizens of the world. Advancing humanism on a global scale. *Journal of Business Ethics, 88*(3), 537–550.

Maak, T., & Stoetter, N. (2012). Social entrepreneurs as responsible leaders: Fundación Paraguaya and the case of Martin Burt. *Journal of Business Ethics, 111*(3), 413–430.

Marshall, A. J., Ashleigh, M. J., Baden, D., Ojiako, U., & Guidi, M. G. (2014). Corporate psychopathy: Can "search and destroy" and "hearts and minds" military metaphors inspire HRM solutions? *Journal of Business Ethics, 128* (3), 495–504.

McAllister, D. J. (1995). Affect-and cognition-based trust as foundations for interpersonal cooperation in organizations. *Academy of Management Journal, 38*(1), 24–59.

Motzkin, J. C., Newman, J. P., Kiehl, K. A., & Koenigs, M. (2011). Reduced prefrontal connectivity in psychopathy. *The Journal of Neuroscience, 31*(48), 17348–17357.

Mulhern, G. (2010). President's column. *The Psychologist (The Magazine of the British Psychological Society), 23*(8), 1–2.

Mullins-Sweatt, S. N., Glover, N. G., Derefinko, K. J., Miller, J. D., & Widiger, T. A. (2010). The search for the successful psychopath. *Journal of Research in Personality, 44*(4), 554–558. doi:10.1016/j.jrp.2010.05.010

Muñoz, L. C., Khan, R., & Cordwell, L. (2011). Sexually coercive tactics used by university students: A clear role for primary psychopathy. *Journal of Personality Disorders, 25*(1), 28–40.

Murphy, C., & Vess, J. (2003). Subtypes of psychopathy: Proposed differences between narcissistic, borderline, sadistic and antisocial psychopaths. *Psychiatric Quarterly, 74*(1), 11–29.

Nadis, S. (1995). Utter amorality: Can psychopaths feel emotions? *Omni, 17*(9), 12.

Narayanan, L., Menon, S., & Spector, P. E. (1999). Stress in the workplace: A comparison of gender and occupations. *Journal of Organizational Behavior, 20*(1), 63–73.

Nelson, L., & Tonks, G. (2011, 13–15th September). *Management inertia and psychopathic behaviour.* Paper presented at the British Academy of Management Annual Conference, Aston University, Birmingham, UK.

Nickerson, S. D. (2014). Brain abnormalities in psychopaths: A meta-analysis. *North American Journal of Psychology, 16*(1), 63.

Osumi, T., Nakao, T., Kasuya, Y., Shinoda, J., Yamada, J., & Ohira, H. (2012). Amygdala dysfunction attenuates frustration-induced aggression in psychopathic individuals in a non-criminal population. *Journal of Affective Disorders, 142*(1–3), 331–338.

Patrick, C.J. (1994). Emotion and psychopathy: Startling new insights. *Psychophysiology, 31*(4), 319–330.

Pavlić, I., & Međedović, J. (2019). Psychopathy facilitates workplace success. *Psihološka istraživanja, 22*(1), 69–87.

Porter, S. (1996). Without conscience or without active conscience? The etiology of psychopathy revisited. *Aggression and Violent Behavior, 1*(2), 179–189.

Ray, J. V., & Jones, S. (2011). Self-reported psychopathic traits and their relation to intentions to engage in environmental offending. *International Journal of Offender Therapy and Comparative Criminology, 55*(3), 370–391. Retrieved from http://ijo.sagepub.com/content/55/3/370.abstract

Robertson, D. C., & Ross Jr, W. T. (1995). Decision-making processes on ethical issues: The impact of a social contract perspective. *Business Ethics Quarterly, 5*(2), 213–240.

Ross, S. R., Benning, S. D., Patrick, C. J., Thompson, A., & Thurston, A. (2009). Factors of the psychopathic personality inventory: Criterion-related validity and relationship to the BIS/BAS and five-factor models of personality. *Assessment, 16*(1), 71–87.

Seara-Cardoso, A., Neumann, C., Roiser, J., McCrory, E., & Viding, E. (2012). Investigating associations between empathy, morality and psychopathic personality traits in the general population. *Personality and Individual Differences, 52*(1), 67–71.

Shaver, P., Schwartz, J., Kirson, D., & O'connor, C. (1987). Emotion knowledge: Further exploration of a prototype approach. *Journal of Personality and Social Psychology, 52*(6), 1061–1086.

Shaw, J., & Porter, S. (2012). Forever a psychopath? Psychopathy and the criminal career trajectory. In H. Häkkänen-Nyholm & J. Nyholm (Eds.), *Psychopathy and law* (pp. 201–221). San Francisco, CA: John Wiley & Sons, Ltd.

Spencer, G. L., & Wargo, D. T. (2010). Malevolent employees and their effect on the ethical culture of business organizations. Retrieved from http://forumonp ublicpolicy.com/spring2010.vol2010/spring2010archive/wargo.pdf.

Steuerwald, B. L., & Kosson, D. S. (2000). Emotional experiences of the psychopath. In C. B. Gacono (Ed.), *The clinical and forensic assessment of psychopathy: A practitioner's guide* (pp. 111–135). Mahwah, NJ: Lawrence Erlbaum Associates Publishers.

Stout, M. (2005). The ice people: Living among us are people with no conscience, no emotions and no conception of love: Welcome to the chilling world of the sociopath. *Psychology Today, January/February 2005,* 72–76.

Taylor, S. E. (1991). Asymmetrical effects of positive and negative events: The mobilization-minimization hypothesis. *Psychological Bulletin, 110*(1), 67–85.

Unrau, A. M., & Morry, M. M. (2019). The subclinical psychopath in love: Mediating effects of attachment styles. *Journal of Social and Personal Relationships, 36*(2), 421–449.

Voegtlin, C. (2012). Development of a scale measuring discursive responsible leadership. *Journal of Business Ethics, 98,* 57–73.

Voegtlin, C., Patzer, M., & Scherer, A. (2010). Responsible leadership in global business: A contingency approach. *Journal of Business Ethics, 105*(1) (January 2012), 1–16.

Voegtlin, C., Patzer, M., & Scherer, A. (2012). Responsible leadership in global business: A new approach to leadership and its multi-level outcomes. *Journal of Business Ethics, 105*(1), 1–16.

Watson, D. (2000). *Mood and temperament.* New York: Guilford Press.

Weber, S., Habel, U., Amunts, K., & Schneider, F. (2008). Structural brain abnormalities in psychopaths a review. *Behavioral Sciences & the Law, 26*(1), 7–28. Retrieved from http://dx.doi.org/10.1002/bsl.802 DO - 10.1002/bsl.802

Weiss, H. M., & Cropanzano, R. (1996). Affective events theory: A theoretical discussion of the structure, causes and consequences of affective experiences at work. In B. M. Staw & L. L. Cummings (Eds.), *Research in Organizational Behavior: An Annual Series of Analytical Essays and Critical Reviews* (Vol. 18, pp. 1–74). Elsevier Science/JAI Press.

Widom, C. S. (1977). A methodology for studying noninstitutionalized psychopaths. *Journal of Consulting and Clinical Psychology, 45*(4), 674–683.

Young, L., & Daniel, K. (2003). Affectual trust in the workplace. *The International Journal of Human Resource Management, 14*(1), 139–155. Retrieved from http://dx.doi.org/10.1080/09585190210158565

Zhao, H., Wayne, S. J., Glibkowski, B. C., & Bravo, J. (2007). The impact of psychological contract breach on work-related outcomes: A meta-analysis. *Personnel Psychology, 60*(3), 647–680.

Index

Taylor & Francis eBooks

www.taylorfrancis.com

A single destination for eBooks from Taylor & Francis
with increased functionality and an improved user
experience to meet the needs of our customers.

90,000+ eBooks of award-winning academic content in
Humanities, Social Science, Science, Technology, Engineering,
and Medical written by a global network of editors and authors.

TAYLOR & FRANCIS EBOOKS OFFERS:

A streamlined
experience for
our library
customers

A single point
of discovery
for all of our
eBook content

Improved
search and
discovery of
content at both
book and
chapter level

REQUEST A FREE TRIAL
support@taylorfrancis.com

Made in United States
North Haven, CT
21 February 2024

48912301R10193